Masculinity in British Cinema, 1990–2010

Masculinity in British Cinema, 1990–2010

Sarah Godfrey

EDINBURGH
University Press

Edinburgh University Press is one of the leading university presses in the UK.
We publish academic books and journals in our selected subject areas across the
humanities and social sciences, combining cutting-edge scholarship with high editorial
and production values to produce academic works of lasting importance. For more
information visit our website: edinburghuniversitypress.com

Edinburgh University Press Ltd
The Tun – Holyrood Road
12(2f) Jackson's Entry
Edinburgh EH8 8PJ

First published in hardback by Edinburgh University Press 2022

Typeset in Monotype Ehrhardt by
Cheshire Typesetting Ltd, Cuddington, Cheshire,
printed and bound by CPI Group (UK) Ltd,
Croydon, CR0 4YY

A CIP record for this book is available from the British Library

ISBN 978 1 4744 1414 2 (hardback)
ISBN 978 1 3995 2779 8 (paperback)
ISBN 978 1 4744 1415 9 (webready PDF)
ISBN 978 1 4744 1416 6 (epub)

Contents

Figures

Acknowledgements

This book began its genesis as an AHRC-funded PhD at the University of East Anglia where I was fortunate to be supervised by Professor Yvonne Tasker and Professor Su Holmes; their ongoing friendship and mentoring during the intervening years has been and continues to be invaluable, I could not have asked for more. I have been incredibly lucky to have had the support, friendship and encouragement of many of my colleagues in the Department of Film and Television at the University of East Anglia. Stephanie Clayton, Claire Hines, Su Holmes and Melanie Williams have been constant in their patience and dedication to helping me to bring this book to fruition and endured hours of reading drafts of chapters, coffee drinking and cake eating in this endeavour. Keith Johnston and Emma Pett have also been the best kinds of colleagues, offering wisdom, feedback and support.

A special note of thanks must go to Elizabeth Short for her support, enthusiasm and dedication to reading the transcript and for her keen editorial judgement at the end of the project. I look forward to repaying your kindness. It goes without saying that any errors or oversights that remain in the book are my own.

I owe a great debt of thanks to Gillian Leslie and Fiona Conn at Edinburgh University Press for their ongoing patience and encouragement for this project, and to Geraldine Lyons for her meticulous copy-editorial work.

The journey to complete this book was made lighter by the support and love of Hannah Bushell-Walsh and Lucy Toseland-Bolton, who were always kind enough to indulge in wine and pontification or cajoling and encouragement as needed. The biggest thanks must go to my family who have been beside me for the entire journey. Darren, Ori, Zak and Jemima have been my biggest cheerleaders and provided much needed moments of relief, distraction and laughter; I love you, thank you for making my life more fun.

There are three people to whom this book is dedicated but who are not here to see the final result: my father, Ray, my brother, Ian, and my sister, Judy, all of whom are greatly missed and dearly loved.

Masculinity in British Cinema, 1990–2010: Postfeminist Manifestations

This book uses the analysis of cinematic representation as the lens through which to examine and make sense of what I argue is a specifically British version of postfeminist cis-gendered masculinity that emerged and developed during the 1990s and 2000s. This era is of particular interest for several reasons. In terms of British cinema this was a phase of renaissance and rejuvenation following the rather less prolific or profitable period during the 1980s. This was the period in which the British film industry benefited from a series of political and economic interventions that afforded levels of inward investment via initiatives including National Lottery funding. This twenty-year-long span was also one of significant social, cultural, economic and political shifts, many of which were perceived as impacting particularly powerfully on both cultural discourses of masculinity and men's lived experiences as gendered subjects.[1] Film became an important site for producing an impressive array of narratives and representations of masculinity over the two decades. From microbudget films such as *TwentyFourSeven* (Shane Meadows, 1997) through to the resurgent Bond franchise, British cinema during this period provided a consistent but expansive repertoire of masculinities and this book seeks to mine this recent and rich historical material in order to analyse the ways in which British film constructed narratives of masculinity and how these can be seen as constituting a culturally inflected iteration of postfeminist masculinity.

The central argument presented in *Masculinity in British Cinema, 1990–2010* is that this proliferation of cinematic narratives of masculinity demands more detailed and thoroughgoing scholarly analysis in order to better understand the discursive function of these representations within the specific context of British postfeminist culture. Drawing on case studies taken from a wide range of genres and settings, I argue that analysing key paradigms from across the representational palette of masculinities that were circulating during the period provides an opportunity to better understand the ways in which the convergent cultural phenomena of postfeminism and neoliberalism function to create culturally inflected idioms of cinematic masculinity. In this way, *Masculinity in British Cinema, 1990–2010* offers a significant and timely intervention into both British film and gender studies, mobilising a range of conceptual and methodological frameworks from feminist film history, gender and masculinity studies and cultural historical studies in order to create the first sustained scholarly account of these cinematic representations and their discursive function within the broader cultural landscape of postfeminist, neoliberal Britain.

This book emerges out of an established history of feminist approaches to the representation of gender in British film and, in common with this work, I emphasise the importance of locating the analysis of gender politics within the socio-cultural context in which they emerge. In turning critical attention to the historical period 1990–2010 I locate the analysis of the various case studies within the specific socio-economic context of British culture in order to establish the ways in which British cinematic representations of masculinity throughout the period can be seen to constitute culturally inflected paradigms of postfeminist masculinity. While postfeminism has, for some time now, been the dominant approach to understanding the gender politics of much Anglo-American media culture, there is, I argue, an important and often overlooked specificity of postfeminism within a British context, something that Justine Ashby picks up on in her 2006 article 'Postfeminism in the British Frame' where she makes the case that 'there can be no "one size fits all" framework for thinking through its political and cultural currency'.[2] My work proceeds from a similar perspective which is to examine the ways in which an homogenous notion of postfeminism is culturally deterministic and as such has the potential to elide complex issues of cultural, historical and political specificity.

In the time that has elapsed since Ashby's observations a range of scholarship has emerged which has sought to explore aspects of British postfeminist culture; my work here contributes to this growing corpus.[3] There has also been scholarship which focuses on the ways in which British cinematic representations of femininity are mediated via the cultural mores of postfeminism, most notably recent work by Sarah Hill which notes the ways in which 'articulations of postfeminism differ according to national context'.[4] Further, there was a burst of scholarly activity focused on analysing the representation of masculinity in the British men's magazine markets during the latter end of the 1990s and early part of the 2000s, much of which was predominantly concerned with the seemingly inexorable rise of 'new' lad culture.[5] Rather more scholarship exists in terms of American cinema and postfeminist masculinities, such as that by Hannah Hamad, Elizabeth Abele and John Gronbeck-Tedesco, and Stephanie Genz and Benjamin Brabon.[6] However, there has been very little work which brings these various threads and themes into dialogue with one another in order to discuss the cinematic representation of British postfeminist masculinity, and it is in this specific lacunae that this work intervenes.

Turning scholarly attention to the representational palette of cinematic masculinities produced across a twenty-year period is not an attempt at narrowing down or offering a singular definition of British postfeminist masculinity – indeed, as Andrew Spicer surmises, the representation of masculinity in British cinema of the 1990s and 2000s is a productive and fascinating site for analysis precisely because of the complexities, points of tension, contradiction and conflict that are being continually presented, re-presented and negotiated.[7] Following a similar line of thinking to that put forward by Stephanie Genz and Benjamin Brabon, I approach the idea of postfeminist masculinity as inherently multiple and malleable; occupying a 'compound and conflicted subject position that had developed out of a series of competing social and economic hybrid scripts' of masculinity that are inextricable from their cultural context of production and circulation.[8]

My aim here is not to offer an historiography of cinematic masculinity for the entirety of the twenty-year period in question, rather it is to provide a carefully contextualised history of certain key cinematic tropes of masculinity and to locate them within their specific cultural context. My aim is to explore the ways in which these representations function within the shifting terrain of British gender politics and media culture in a period that saw considerable social, economic and political shifts, as the nation negotiated the transition from an industrial economy into a post-industrial one operating within an increasingly technologised global marketplace. Considering the complex and at times contradictory interplay between cinematic representations and the variously shifting social, economic and political landscapes within which they circulate, my aim is to explore a range of particularly popular or pertinent paradigms of masculinity in order to elaborate a better understanding of the ways in which postfeminism, neoliberalism and British cinema intersect and the various iterations of masculinity that are produced as a result.

The remainder of this introduction elaborates on the specific frames of reference from which the more focused case studies proceed. I begin by outlining my conceptualisation of masculinity and situating this in relation to critical masculinity studies' central approaches to the broader study of masculinity, developing some of the key ideas that underpin the focus and approach of this book. The next section elaborates on the conceptualisation of a culturally inflected iteration of British postfeminist masculinity and its mobilisation in British cinema during the period. Following this is a section in which I elaborate on the complex and convoluted intersections between postfeminism and neoliberalism and the ways in which their symbiotic relationship is fundamental in shaping the cultural context within which British cinema and its representations of masculinity must be understood. Having outlined this, I move on to provide a contextual overview of British film during the period in order to elaborate upon the cinematic context for the case study chapters before going on to draw these various threads together to identify what I see as foremost amongst the issues, themes and trends in the representations of masculinity in British films of the era.

Critical Masculinity Studies

While the focus of this book is British cinema studies, it is also concerned with the analysis of gendered media cultures and in particular the field of critical masculinity studies. From its inception in the early 1980s, where it emerged in response to second wave feminism, critical masculinity studies has developed into an interdisciplinary field of analysis. Within the broader field of masculinity studies there has long been an ideological tension between that work which, like my own, aligns with feminist ideologies and that which is more masculinist in its political framework.[9]

My approach to masculinity as an object of enquiry proceeds from the position of understanding it as a performative material discourse that must be understood within specific historical and cultural contexts. In this regard, masculinity is simultaneously individual and cultural. It is both concept and practice, and it is, therefore, inherently political and inextricable from the structures of power and discourse that shape the cultural landscape. In theorising masculinities as intersectional, malleable and contingent, and by pursuing a line of enquiry that takes into account the relations between transnational discourses and their localised manifestations, my work forges new understandings about the specific representational strategies of British masculinities. To this end, my approach to masculinity brings together a number of theoretical frameworks in order to explore the complexities, nuances and contradictions that are at play within the texts under discussion. While I approach masculinity as intersectional and contingent, it is important to note that the case studies featured in the course of this book are all cis-gendered, something which has been largely determined by the absence of transgender men in the more mainstream forms of British cinema during this period.

My approach to masculinity as a performative material discourse draws on the work of Judith Butler and Michel Foucault in particular; I augment these approaches, along with those taken from feminist media and cultural studies, with the influential approach to masculinity developed by R. W. Connell.[10] By employing the notion of hegemony as a mechanism for understanding the political machinations of masculinity, Connell's work has proven to be particularly productive for facilitating a better understanding of 'the dominance within society of certain forms and practices of masculinity', and I extend this theoretical framework in the next chapter.[11] While Michael Moller critiques the concept of hegemonic masculinity as being overly deterministic and 'refuse[ing] an engagement with post-structural feminist critiques of the ways in which gendered subjectivities have been theorised as coherent, unified, whole',[12] my own application not only acknowledges the multiplicity and intersectionality of masculine identities and their cinematic representations, but also emphasises the contingent and dynamic nature of gender as simultaneously embodied and enacted through social practice and as discursively and conceptually constituted.[13] Furthermore, the focal point of this book is to examine the complexities, tensions and vicissitudes at play in the cinematic representation of masculinities, and as such hegemony provides a productive theoretical framework through which to approach the gendered politics of masculinity within culture.

Masculinity and the cinematic representations thereof are necessarily embedded within and inextricable from culture. The period covered by this book was one of considerable cultural change and these developments invariably impacted upon masculinity as both a lived reality and as a cultural discourse. For Connell, hegemony offers a useful framework through which to make sense of this; she suggests that the period is one in which hegemonies of masculinity were in transition and shifting, in order to 'embody the current accepted answer to the problem of the legitimacy of patriarchy'.[14] It would seem that the socio-economic shifts of the 1980s, and the subsequent rise of postmodernism and poststructuralism which facilitated more complex conceptualisations of identities, brought about a troublesome period of transition in established hegemonic forms of masculinity. As gender scholar, Maggie Carey pointed out in the mid-1990s, the 'belief that traditional definitions of masculinity no longer work, that the models of masculinity that today's men inherited are no longer desirable or appropriate and that they need to be challenged and re-worked' had developed as a central theme in both popular and academic accounts of masculinity.[15] This included the cinema of the period. An overview of British films from 1990 to 2010 attests that these themes remained predominant throughout the period and across a range of genres. It exemplified the broader discursive turn towards attempting to theorise masculinity; to render it a visible, historically and geographically contingent ontological category operating within a complex matrix of power relations and hierarchies. To date, there has been scant work on the representation of masculinities in British film in this period, particularly given the volume of films that are explicitly engaged in constructing narratives of masculine identities. This book therefore fills an important gap, making visible the machinations of masculinity as a discursive entity and understanding the cultural and political function of its representation within a defined national context.

Conceptualising British Postfeminist Masculinity

One of this book's key interventions is to produce a thoroughgoing theorisation and analysis of postfeminist masculinity in British cinema. In proposing a nationally specific conceptualisation of postfeminism which corresponds with the distinctive socio-political and cultural landscape, my aim is not to disregard the significance of the transnational interchanges between British and US popular culture, nor to dismiss the important scholarly work that has proliferated around contemporary media and gender politics in this regard. Neither is it to underplay the important role played by US media forms and figures within British culture.[16] Rather, it is about recognising the utility of postfeminism as an influential component – or sensibility, as Rosalind Gill terms it – of British culture during the period, in order to explore the ways in which it evolved and functioned within the particular context of British culture and cinema in the period.[17]

In developing a notion of British postfeminist culture, I draw on the foundational work by scholars such as Angela McRobbie, Yvonne Tasker, Diane Negra and Rosalind Gill, all of whom have been influential in advancing the conceptualisation of the term.[18] Despite the array of extant work dedicated to explaining, debating and analysing postfeminism and how best it might be defined and deployed in attempts to make sense of popular culture, it remains a contested and complex term that can be variously adapted and applied. Despite the divergent ideas and uses to which the concept is devoted, there seems to be a broad consensus regarding the idea that postfeminism is fundamentally shaped by a series of complex and often contradictory interplays between progressive and reactionary cultural politics.[19] While the implications of this have been more fully theorised in relation to the representation of women and discourses of postfeminist femininity across a range of cultural platforms and media circulating in both the British and North American context, the ways in which postfeminism functions with regards to masculinity, and cinematic representations of masculinity within the national context of British culture in particular, have been less thoroughly mined.[20] The case study chapters in this book demonstrate the complexities of the cinematic representation of British postfeminist masculinities and provide an analysis of the ways in which they are shaped by inevitable tensions between progressive, liberal discourses of masculinity on the one hand, and of unreconstructed conservative discourses on the other.

Given that the theorisation of postfeminism emerges out of feminist media and cultural studies, it is perhaps inevitable that the majority of scholarship pertaining to postfeminism and media representations of gender has focused on questions of women and representations of femininity thus far. However, as Christine Griffin and Joyce Canaan cautioned at the time when masculinity studies was first emerging, maintaining critical feminist interventions into questions of masculinity is imperative.[21] Their point is borne out in Tania Modleski's foundational discussion of the ways in which the discourses of a crisis in masculinity and their subsequent resolution are intrinsically postfeminist for the ways in which they efface or, as she prefers, de-realise female characters and narratives of femininity from popular culture; simultaneously functioning to consolidate male power and the structural mechanisms of patriarchal culture via the performative appropriation of disempowerment.[22] Building on Modleski's argument that it is vital to understand the political imperatives giving rise to these performative discourses of crisis, Yvonne Tasker and Diane Negra argue that textual and cultural politics are rarely straightforward and that it can be difficult to discern exact 'distinctions between progressive and regressive texts' within postfeminist media culture more broadly. Instead, scholars who are undertaking analysis of gender and media need to look more closely at the minutiae of the text and the specific moments in which discursive tensions and contradictions become manifest.[23] I would contend that no film can be uncontentiously categorised along a progressive/regressive dichotomy, and that the films featured in the case study chapters have been selected for the ways in which they engage with and negotiate the specific vicissitudes of British postfeminist culture.

Postfeminist gender politics seems to be characterised by a discursive malleability, which can, at times, appear to function in order to deliberately create contradiction and confound a sense of certainty. Throughout the case studies in this book, there are several examples of this slippage being mobilised in order to produce a range of discursive trends and tropes, many of which appear to be deliberate in their contradiction and ambiguity in terms of positionality. Tom Hardy's portrayal of British 'hard man' Charles Bronson in the eponymous biopic (Nicolas Winding Refn, 2008), for example, veers from warmth, charm, wit and sincerity to violent frenzy with impressive alacrity, while films such as *Nil By Mouth* (Gary Oldman, 1997) appear to mobilise a rather more problematic paradox in which the violence of the male characters is presented as inextricable from their own victimised subject positions. Occupying a position somewhere between this are films such as *Brassed Off* (Mark Herman, 1996), *The Full Monty* (Peter Cattaneo, 1997) and *TwentyFourSeven*, which vary from oblique to explicit in terms of identifying female (over) empowerment as being foremost amongst the various factors that have led to the disempowered status of their various male characters.

Indeed, the thematic focus on male disempowerment can be seen as one of the most defining characteristics of representations of masculinity in British films during this time and can be seen to connect examples as diverse as *The Full Monty*, *Twin Town* (Kevin Allen, 1997), *All or Nothing* (Mike Leigh, 2002), and *Eden Lake* (James Watkins, 2008). Alongside these titles and the cycle of early 2000s films described by Mark Featherstone as 'hoodie horror' there is a specific preoccupation with the deleterious effects of neoliberalism upon erstwhile working–class men whose identities have been rendered untenable and obsolete within the new socio–economic order.[24] The triangulation between masculinity, postfeminism and neoliberalism is fraught with complexity and tension. Having outlined the way in which I conceptualise the idea of a British cinematic version of postfeminist masculinity, the next section develops this to take into account the ways in which neoliberalism is inextricable from the discussion.

Postfeminist Masculinities and Cultural Neoliberalism

Much like the concept of postfeminism, neoliberalism seems to have become almost ubiquitous as a frame of reference for any academic discussion of gender, social politics and media culture within Anglo-American culture in the late twentieth and early twenty-first centuries. Used separately and in conjunction with one another postfeminism and neoliberalism have become frequently deployed across a myriad of social, economic, cultural, political, ideological, discursive and material elements. Despite their proliferation within scholarly discourse, postfeminism and neoliberalism remain individually contentious and multivalent; their malleability means that both terms share considerable common discursive ground despite their very different origins.[25]

In this section I elaborate on what I see as the various salient points of intersection between postfeminism and neoliberalism in the specific context of this study and outline their application within this project. Much like postfeminism, neoliberalism is what Justine Ashby might consider a 'globalised term' which appears to presume a North American perspective in order to seemingly 'cut across and . . . blur national specificities'.[26] In this regard, I take a similar perspective to the one outlined above in relation to postfeminism and argue that while there are clearly transcultural connections inherent in the very structure of neoliberalism as it originated in an economic context, there are also important cultural nuances and nationally inflected points of specificity which must be taken into account when mobilising the concept outside of a North American cultural context.

As concepts, postfeminism and neoliberalism share an emphasis on individual subjectivity (over mutuality and collectivity) and the construction and performance of the self which is undertaken and maintained via specific modes of consumption that are determined along hegemonically heteronormative and gendered dichotomies. Much has been written about the ways in which the convergence of postfeminism and neoliberalism has functioned in relation to women's bodies as a Foucauldian system of self-governance maintained via discourses of choice, empowerment, self-improvement and the internalised mechanics of self-surveillance. Stephanie Genz and Benjamin Brabon argue that the discursive construction of masculinity from the 1990s onwards was 'derived in part from the commercialisation of masculinity . . . as new masculinities [such as postfeminist masculinities] have become part of selling lifestyle choices to men'.[27] The construction of the subject and the self via consumerism which is so central to postfeminist discourse appears to find a natural fit with the ideologies of neoliberalism described by Gill and Scharff as a 'technology for governing subjects who are constituted as self-managing, autonomous and enterprising'.[28] In this regard, the correlation between postfeminism and neoliberalism and their correspondence with gendered discourses becomes clear, as the increasing commodification of masculinities from the 'new' man to the metrosexual that took place during this period attests.

Neoliberalism is a concept that emerged out of political economics. It is an economic ideology that 'imagines the free-play of market forces – the ineluctable laws of supply and demand that operate unencumbered . . . is the magical elixir for prosperity'.[29] It has, however, developed to become much more than this. The economic anthropologist, David Harvey, suggests that while neoliberalism originated as an economic ideology it has become *the* hegemonic mode of discourse of Western culture.[30] Whilst the seemingly indomitable hold of neoliberalism as the defining principle of Western culture may be true, the cultural theorist Stuart Hall puts forward a more fluid and malleable account of the term that recognises the multiplicity of points of distinction, nuance and cultural forms of neoliberalism, suggesting that 'there are critical differences between American and British variants'.[31] While recognising that in both the UK and the US a key component of the neoliberal project has been to dismantle any semblance of welfare state provision in favour of an increasing reliance on 'dynamic capitalist growth to create wealth to distribute', Hall argues that the specific contexts within which the disestablishment of the welfare state was taking place meant that there would be inevitable political and material distinctions at play. These distinctions largely occupy the ideological impetus, the actual processes of dismantling the structures and machinery of the welfare state, and the material consequences of the process.[32] For Hall this is epitomised in the British context by the raft of Public Finance Initiatives instituted by Tony Blair's Labour government in the late 1990s which essentially minimised the boundaries between the publicly owned state sector and the privately owned market sector. This not only 'opened up the state to capital' but also affected a significant cultural shift whereby 'the habits and assumptions of the private sector became embedded in the state'.[33] In this regard we can also observe the intersections between neoliberalism and post-industrialisation which are aptly summarised by the historian Christopher Lawson.[34]

While Lawson's article offers a productive analysis of the linkages between neoliberalism and the seemingly inexorable decline of an industrial economy, Stuart Hall cautions against deterministic approaches, arguing that neoliberalism, much like postfeminism, cannot be reduced to any singular issue, form or moment, and it can no longer be understood purely in terms of the economic ideological practice and fiscal governmentality from which it emerged. Reflecting upon this complexity, sociologists Vaughn Higgins and Wendy Larner argue that neoliberalism is more appropriately described as an assemblage of 'diverse, complex and ambiguous . . . spaces, sites and subjects' which necessarily intersects with and informs ideologies, discourses and practices of gender.[35] In this way I am interested in what Patricia Ventura describes as 'cultural neoliberalism' in recognition of the ways in which the term expanded beyond its economic origins, gradually encroaching into and taking over the cultural realm and becoming the defining feature of contemporary culture in both the UK and the US.[36] Developing a cultural studies approach to understanding neoliberalism is a vital step in order to make sense of how 'the massive infrastructures that create the environment in which these quotidian routines and habits are lived out'.[37] Moreover, this approach assists in understanding how these macro-level systems intersect with median-level structures and micro-level experiences; gaining clarity on the ways in which they necessarily impact upon masculinity as discourse, representation and lived experience.[38]

I follow a similar line of enquiry in my own approach to neoliberalism, seeking to better understand the ways in which it, as a form of economics, has a simultaneous and irrevocable cultural manifestation as the fundamental structuring mechanism in this period of British history. More specifically, I am interested in the means by which cultural neoliberalism becomes inherently integrated with postfeminism and thus functions with regard to both discourses and social practices of masculinity within this British context. Such an approach is productive because of the ways in which the cultural project of neoliberalism is fundamentally connected to the shifting modalities of masculinity under discussion in this book. For working-class men, the privatisation of national industries and services led to significant swathes of unemployment and economic obsolescence while the discourses of creativity, enterprise and entrepreneurialism reconstructed the traditional notions and patterns of middle-class masculinity as 'acquisitive, individualized and "flexible" subjects of value'.[39]

My approach as a feminist film scholar is to understand the ways in which cinematic representations of masculinity function as a key site through which the cultural politics of gender are constructed and negotiated. To this end, the representations of masculinity that I am concerned with in this book are intrinsically connected to neoliberalism in its fullest forms and with specific regard to the modalities of British postfeminist culture, and the representations of cinematic masculinities within this context. As such, my aim here is not to advance a cultural model of British neoliberalism rather than to draw attention to the ways in which it appears conjoined with the culturally specific idioms of postfeminist masculinity with which I am concerned. In so doing I conceptualise postfeminism and neoliberalism as synergistic ideologies whose symbiotic relationship was perhaps foremost among the defining forces that shaped the political, social and cultural milieu of Britain during the 1990s and 2000s. I argue that both of these idioms had very clear ramifications on the shape of the British film industry during this time, and upon the ways in which representations of masculinity were constructed within the films produced.

British Film and Postfeminist Culture in Context

As I outline in more detail in the next chapter, the twenty-year period from 1990 to 2010 was one of change on many levels, encompassing substantive developments in terms of social and economic structures, cultural practices, and national and regional identities. There were considerable shifts in terms of gender politics, with the emergence of a culture defined by the connected ideological processes of neoliberalism and postfeminism, both of which emphasise individualism over collectivity, foregrounding consumption and active self-maintenance as essential components in the construction and performance of selfhood.[40] Within these contexts, masculinity (as an identity, a discourse and a lived subjectivity) became the focus of questions and concerns emerging as an increasingly important discursive site, through which a range of issues were negotiated and explored. From the declining tenability of masculine identities defined by occupational roles and the associated status of breadwinners to the problem of male violence against self and others, there was an increasing incitement to debate and frame masculinity and men's social and cultural practices as problematic.[41]

One of the most significant developments to come out of scholarly endeavours aimed at theorising and understanding men and masculinity was the understanding of male identities as plural and multifaceted, as opposed to universal, timeless and homogenous. It was increasingly acknowledged that masculinity operated as both at the abstract and macro level of discourse and ideology, as well as at the micro and material levels of social practice and individual lived experience. Another theme which emerged out of the wealth of academic and popular debates that emerged from the end of the 1980s through to the current moment was that both 'masculinity' as a concept and 'men' as a social group of individuals were 'in crisis' as a result of the convergence of manifold social, economic and cultural changes.[42]

The twenty-year period from 1990–2010 also saw notable growth and innovation in the British film industry, partly due to increased economic support through an array of public funding initiatives and tax incentives. In the output that emerged from this British film renaissance, both masculinity and masculine crisis became the basis of key narrative tropes across a generic spectrum. Through recurrent narrative trajectories and representational strategies, many films from this era actively engaged in the discursive constitution of masculinity and crisis, reiterating the notion that contemporary social and gender politics (particularly the impact of second wave feminism) had been unremittingly negative for men. Across a range of genres, points of connection emerged, creating what might be described as a national narrative of male malaise. Differentiated by class, race, sexuality, region, age and multiple other markers of identity, representations of masculinity in British films of the period were, as Andrew Spicer notes in *Typical Men: The Representation of Masculinity in Popular British Cinema*, far from homogenous.[43] What proliferated instead was a cinematic corpus which engaged with and represented masculinity in diverse forms characterised by plurality and contradiction.[44] In presenting a feminist critical analysis of these cinematic representations, I place them within the key contexts of both postfeminism and neoliberalism while remaining attentive to each one's generic and cultural specificities, providing a productive means of framing and understanding the various tensions and intersections at play within them.

British Cinema and Masculinity

This book builds on an established body of scholarship on British cinema and, in particular, work foregrounding masculinity and gender politics as a key site for cultural analysis. Taking Spicer's work in *Typical Men* as a point of departure, I use this book as a means of extending and deepening the academic analysis of masculinity in British cinema within a more recent historical period and to bring to bear the specific perspectives provided by critical feminist film and cultural studies in order to do this.[45] The case study chapters which provide the structure for my analysis have been chosen in order to take into account some of the trends and formulations of cinematic masculinity during this period and to map key points of connection and disparity across their different manifestations.

The 2000 anthology *British Cinema in the 90s*, edited by Robert Murphy, provides another touchstone in terms of historicising recent British cinema history.[46] Its useful overview of key debates and issues of the time includes Claire Monk's chapter on masculinity in 1990s British film, which is one of the first pieces of feminist film scholarship to draw attention to the modes of representation emerging at the time. Her article is foundational for identifying the need for deeper and more thoroughgoing analysis of masculinity in 1990s British films.[47] Karen Alexander's chapter in the same anthology is insightful for the ways in which it addresses the pervasive whiteness of British cinema, ruminating on the enduring structural and cultural barriers to filmmakers of colour and debating how these must be addressed both in terms of representation and production cultures.[48] Other chapters in the anthology, including those by Moya Luckett, John Hill and Stella Bruzzi, provide valuable perspectives on questions of image and nation, class representation and sexual plurality in cinema respectively.[49] In addition to the holistic approach afforded in Murphy's anthology there are also articles by Sarita Malik that explore issues of race and representation in the 1990s, as well as book-length studies on class and genre: *Visions of England* by Paul Dave and *Tears of Laughter* by Nigel Mather respectively.[50] This book is necessarily informed by that which has come before, but also carves out a new and as yet under-mined direction by adopting a critical cultural feminist approach to the specific issue of representations of masculinity during the 1990s and the following decade.

My approach to British film studies has also benefited from recent developments in feminist media and cultural studies more broadly, particularly with regards to the theorisation of postfeminism, the cultural implications of neoliberalism and their implications for the representation of masculinity in British cinema.[51] While my focus is on masculinity in particular, my approach to this as a feminist project takes a conceptual lead from the American scholar Kimberlé Crenshaw and her vital work around intersectionality, a concept that was originally used in order to draw attention to the complex ways in which race and gender operate at multiple sites and in compound ways.[52] While intersectionality has become a dominant theoretical paradigm in feminist cultural theory generally, Crenshaw's framework is particularly productive for taking into account the multidimensional nature of media representations as performative constructions of identity that are inextricable from the complex cultural matrix of intersecting sites of power. No analysis of the discursive politics of media representations of gender can avoid the ways in which issues of class, race, sexuality, age, ability, and so forth are enmeshed within them, functioning as simultaneously individual and structural.

Scholarship of millennial British cinema has begun to emerge more recently. The third edition of *The British Cinema Book*, edited by Robert Murphy, and James Leggott's *Contemporary British Cinema* represent definitive steps in beginning this process.[53] In addition to this, the *Journal of British Cinema and Television* has produced a number of special issues such as 'Film in Britain in the New Millennium' and 'Post-Millennial British Art Cinema' and has included features on directors Shane Meadows and Andrea Arnold.[54] Further auteur style studies have also proliferated around Joanna Hogg, Clio Barnard and Nicholas Winding Refn.[55] Jack Newsinger and James Caterer both engage with film policy in the period and *The Rise and Fall of the Film Council* provides a book-length study of the UK Film Council.[56] In addition, there are nascent clusters of work around key genres and film cycles, with Johnny Walker's work on horror and David Forrest's research on social realism being foremost in this regard.[57] Clive James Nwonka and Sarita Malik have written independently and in collaboration to develop scholarship that examines representations of race in British film culture.[58] Imelda Whelehan, Andrew Pope and Dario Llinares have written articles pertaining to gender and post-millennial British cinema, a topic also addressed in my own previous work.[59]

Questions of national cinema remain integral to British cinema studies and scholars including Andrew Higson, Duncan Petrie, Sarah Street, Ian Christie and Debbie Ging consider questions of national cinema in terms of the constituent nations of the UK, rightly critiquing the ways in which Britishness is invariably conflated with Englishness in ways that efface important national specificities of Scotland, Wales and Northern Ireland, questions that become particularly pressing within an era of devolution.[60] In writing a book-length study of British cinema, I am necessarily involved in contributing to the discursive constitution of a form of national cinema as an object of study. However, while I suggest that there is value in retaining British cinema as a heuristic category for the ways in which it facilitates an engagement with cultural specificity within an increasingly transnational context, the notion of British cinema is, as Ian Christie suggests, neither a neutral nor self-evident entity, and my interrogation of the specific manifestations of postfeminism and masculinity within this context take heed of Christie's point.[61]

British Film Production, 1990–2010

The landscape of British film production during this time became increasingly diverse, in part at least due to government policies that provided financial incentives to production companies; such initiatives were crucial in attracting large-budget feature films exemplified by the *Harry Potter* (various, 2001–2011) franchise and *Bridget Jones's Diary* (Sharon Maguire, 2001), through to micro-budget, locally based and produced films such as *TwentyFourSeven* (Shane Meadows, 1997) or *Bullet Boy* (Saul Dibb, 2004). Whereas the latter drew their cast (and in the case of *TwentyFourSeven*, their crew) from local workshops and community initiatives, the former were financed by American media conglomerates calling on an international roster of stars and crew. Following this logic, I mobilise deliberately select case studies as a means of drawing attention to matters of national and regional specificity as part of a wider conceptual engagement with representations of British postfeminist masculinity. In making choices about the corpus of films included as case studies, I have sought to include films that are illustrative of the diversity of British cinema in terms of regional, national and geographical location, as well as reflecting major genres and cycles. As such, this book suggests that the films of the period are particularly interesting in terms of the function of Britishness as an articulation of national identity within the broader contexts of Europe and transnational film culture.

British cinema, like Britain as a nation state is not a singular entity but an amalgam of constituent regions and nations. The balance of power within this structure is not equitable; even within a period of devolution, England retains economic and cultural dominance over the nations of Scotland, Wales and Northern Ireland. Even within England, it is London and the south-east that appear to dominate the imaginary of national identity. This situation is reflected in the output of British cinema in which the label of 'British' invariably perpetuates a 'correlation of Englishness and Britishness'.[62] While the majority of case studies are of English films, this is neither an oversight nor an attempt to reinforce the privilege and dominance of England either symbolically or literally, nor is it to deny the role of Scottish, Welsh and Irish films in the negotiation of contemporary masculinity. The films selected for detailed analysis have been chosen to demonstrate the thematic and generic diversity of British film culture throughout this period and attempt to strike a balance between well-known and less well-known films and directors. They facilitate the exploration of how different paradigms of masculinity are mobilised across a range of films in order to investigate the intersections between film, gender and culture within this historical and geographical context.

The focus of this study is on narrative films and to this end it does not include documentary films such as *Blue Blood* (Steven Reilly, 2006), *Crossing the Line* (Daniel Gordon and Nicholas Bonner, 2006) or *The Battle of Orgreave* (Jeremy Deller, 2001), nor does it include abstract or avant-garde films such as *Faceless* (Manu Luksch, 2007), *Body Song* (Janine Marmot, 2003) or *Rubber Johnny* (Chris Cunningham, 2005). This is not to suggest that these films do not engage with questions of masculinity nor that they are somehow removed from the discursive construction of British postfeminist masculinity; indeed, Deller's film, for example, focuses on a re-enactment of one of the particularly violent clashes between police and Yorkshire miners during the 1984 miner's strike, offering a clear example of a cinematic engagement with masculinity. Similarly, I do not include any examples of heritage films within my case studies; again this is not because they are not germane to an understanding of the representations of masculinity in British cinema of the period – indeed, heritage films were particularly popular during this period, featuring a range of male characters that were actively engaged in the discursive construction of forms of British masculinity. Heritage films ought not to be dismissed as irrelevant to studies of contemporary society. Films such as *Elizabeth* (Shekar Kapur, 1998), *Shakespeare in Love* (John Madden, 1998) and *Atonement* (Joe Wright, 2007) all mobilise nostalgia and an historical setting as a mechanism through which to articulate, negotiate and reify certain forms and practices of masculinity. Further, as Antje Ascheid suggests, the representations of gender within heritage films are inextricable from the postfeminist context in which they circulate.[63] She argues that many heritage films appear to reconcile 'often contradictory narrative trajectories within a pre-feminist historical setting to create postfeminist fantasies of romantic emancipation'.[64] The historical setting of these films necessarily augments the symbolic and narrative engagement with postfeminist culture, creating its own specific inflection of Britishness and postfeminism. These films are, perhaps, less productive for understanding the very contemporary and contextually located discourses of post-industrial, postfeminist masculinity that I focus on in this book; in this regard, I position these films as part of the broader cultural context but do not directly draw on them for the case studies.

Structure

This book is organised around some of the most prominent tropes found in British cinema during the 1990s and 2000s in order to explore the tensions and contradictions as well as the continuities that are central to constructions of British postfeminist masculinity in British film. The first chapter provides contextual framing and conceptual elaboration, outlining some of the key social, economic and political touchpoints of the period and examining the ways in which they connect with gender politics and the cinematic representations of masculinity. Through an investigation into the connections between culture and gender politics, I use this chapter to develop what I term British postfeminist masculinity.

The case study chapters provide a closer examination of some of the key paradigms of cinematic masculinity from the period in question and offer an analysis of these from the theoretical perspective of critical feminist studies. Each case study chapter features close analysis of four films, two from the 1990s and two from the 2000s. Chapter 2, the first of the case study chapters, focuses on the broader paradigm of masculinity as beleaguered and in crisis and interrogates the political function of crisis discourses. Chapter 3 examines the emergence of new lad culture within British cinema and explores the ways in which its legacy is evident in the cycle of football hooligan films that emerged in the first decade of the

2000s. Chapter 4 is explicitly concerned with intersectional questions of class, race and age, examining the representation of younger, unemployed men and how British cinema negotiated and articulated the shifting politics of masculinity during the period. These chapters are all organised chronologically with the aim of understanding the historical trajectories of these discourses. Chapter 5 is an exception to this rule, with the analysis in this chapter organised thematically in order to better interrogate the intersections between class and race and the representation of fatherhood in British cinema of the time. Chapter 6, the final case study chapter, examines what I term excessive masculinities. These brutally violent and unreconstructed representations of masculinity are seen in some of the most contentious, confrontational and controversial British films from the period. I suggest that the representations of masculinity within these films are historically significant and they are usefully understood as historical precursors to the current resurgence of misogyny and the associated discourses of 'toxic' masculinity.

This structure enables me to provide a critical snapshot of an especially dynamic and exciting moment in British film culture and British culture more broadly. This book will, I hope, produce new knowledge about our recent cultural and cinematic history. More specifically, in elaborating on the intricacies of British idioms of postfeminist masculinity and its role within British film culture, I bring new approaches to the ways in which we might understand, theorise and analyse this recent history.

Notes

1 Edwards, Tim, 2006, *Cultures of Masculinity*, Routledge, London.
2 Ashby, Justine, 2005, 'Postfeminism in the British Frame' in *Cinema Journal*, Vol. 44, No. 2, pp. 127, 128, 132.
3 See for example McRobbie, Angela, 2009, *The Aftermath of Feminism: Gender, Culture and Social Change*, Routledge, London; and Whelehan, Imelda, 2000, *Overloaded: Popular Culture and the Future of Feminism*, The Women's Press, London.
4 Hill, Sarah, 2020, *Young Women, Girls and Postfeminism in Contemporary British Film*, Bloomsbury Press, London, p. 1.
6 Jackson, Peter, Stevenson, Nick and Brooks, Kate (eds), 2001, *Making Sense of Men's* Magazines, Polity Press, Cambridge. Benwell, Bethan (ed.), 2003, *Masculinity and Men's Lifestyle Magazines*, Blackwell Publishing, London. Crewe, Ben, 2003, *Representing Men: Cultural Production and Producers in the Men's Magazine Market*, Berg, Oxford.
6 Hamad, Hannah, 2013, *Postfeminism and Paternity in Contemporary US Film*, Routledge, London. Abele, Elizabeth and Gronbeck-Tredesco, John A. (eds),

2016, *Screening Images of American Masculinity in the Age of Postfeminism*, Lexington Books, London. Genz, Stephanie and Brabon, Benjamin 2018, *Postfeminism: Cultural Texts and Theories*, Edinburgh University Press, Edinburgh, pp. 198–199.

7 Spicer, Andrew, 2003, *Typical Men: Representations of Masculinity in British Cinema*, I. B. Tauris, London.

8 Genz, Stephanie and Brabon, Benjamin, 2018, *Postfeminism: Cultural Texts and Theories*, Edinburgh University Press, Edinburgh, pp. 198–199.

9 See Bly, Robert, 1990, *Iron John: A Book About Men*, Addison-Wesley, Boston. Farrell, Warren, 1993, *The Myth of Male Power*, Berkeley Trade, New York.

10 Connell, R. W., 1995, *Masculinities*, Polity Press, Cambridge, p. 84. Butler, Judith, 1990, *Gender Trouble: Feminism and the Subversion of Identity*, Routledge, London. Foucault, Michel, 1978, *The History of Sexuality* (Vol. 1), Penguin, London.

11 Hearn, Jeff and Morgan, David (eds), 1990, *Men, Masculinities and Social Theory*, Unwin Hyman, London, p. 11.

12 Moller, Michael, 2007, 'Exploiting Patterns: A Critique of Hegemonic Masculinity' in *Journal of Gender Studies*, Vol. 16, No. 3, pp. 263–276. https://doi.org/10.1080/09589230701562970

13 Butler, Judith, 1990, *Gender Trouble: Feminism and the Subversion of Identity*, Routledge, London.

14 Connell, R. W., 1995, *Masculinities*, Polity Press, Cambridge, p. 76.

15 Carey, Maggie, 1996, 'Perspectives on the Men's Movement' in McLean, Christopher, Carey, Maggie and White, Cheryl (eds), *Men's Ways of Being*, Westview Press, Oxford, p. 153.

16 Ashby, Justine, 2005, 'Postfeminism in the British Frame' in *Cinema Journal*, Vol. 44, No. 2, p. 128.

17 Gill, Rosalind, 2007, 'Postfeminist Media Culture: Elements of a Sensibility' in *European Journal of Cultural Studies*, Vol. 10, No. 2, pp. 147–166.

18 McRobbie, Angela, 2004, 'Postfeminism and Popular Culture' in *Feminist Media Studies*, Vol. 4, No. 3, pp. 255–267. McRobbie, Angela, 2007, 'Postfeminism and Popular Culture: Bridget Jones and the New Gender Regime' in Tasker, Yvonne and Negra, Diane (eds), *Interrogating Postfeminism: Gender and the Politics of Popular Culture*, Duke University Press, New York. Gill, Rosalind, 2006, *Gender and the Media*, Polity Press, Cambridge. ill, Rosalind. 2007. 'Postfeminist Media Culture: Elements of a Sensibility' in *European Journal of Cultural Studies*. Vol.10. No. 2. pp.147–166. Rosalind, 2008, 'Culture and Subjectivity in Neoliberal and Postfeminist Times' in *Subjectivity*, Vol. 25, pp. 432–445. Gill, Rosalind, 2011, 'Sexism Reloaded. Or It's Time to get Angry Again' in *Feminist Media Studies*, Vol. 11, No. 1, pp. 61–71. Gill, Rosalind, 2016, 'Post-postfeminism?: New Feminist Visibilities in Postfeminist Times', in *Feminist Media Studies*, Vol. 16, No. 4, pp. 610–630.

19 McRobbie, Angela, 2004, 'Postfeminism and Popular Culture' in *Feminist Media Studies*, Vol. 4, No. 3, pp. 255–267.

20 Hill, Sarah, 2020, *Young Women, Girls and Postfeminism in Contemporary British Film*, Bloomsbury Press, London. Hamad, Hannah, 2013, *Postfeminism and Paternity in Contemporary US Film*, Routledge, London.

21 Canaan, Joyce and Griffin, Christine, 1990, 'The New Men's Studies: Part of the Problem or Part of the Solution' in Hearn, Jeff and Morgan, David (eds), *Men, Masculinities and Social Theory*, Unwin Hyman, London, p. 207.

22 Modleski, Tania, 2014, *Feminism Without Women: Culture and Critique in a Postfeminist Age*, Routledge, London, p. 7.

23 Tasker, Yvonne and Negra, Diane (eds), *Interrogating Postfeminism: Gender and the Politics of Popular Culture*, Duke University Press, New York, p. 22.

24 Featherstone, Mark, 2013, '"Hoodie Horror": The Capitalist Other in Postmodern Society' in *The Review of Education, Pedagogy and Cultural Studies*, Vol. 35, No. 3, pp. 178–196.

25 Gill, Rosalind and Scharff, Christina (eds), 2011, *New Femininities: Postfeminism, Neoliberalism and Subjectivity*, Palgrave Macmillan, London. Kennedy, Melanie, 2017, '"Come on, [. . .] let's go find your inner princess": (Post-)Feminist Generationalism in Tween Fairy Tales' in *Feminist Media Studies*, Vol. 18, No. 3, pp. 424–439.

26 Ashby, Justine, 2005, 'Postfeminism in the British Frame' in *Cinema Journal*, Vol. 44, No. 2, p. 127.

27 Genz, Stephanie and Brabon, Benjamin, 2018, *Postfeminism: Cultural Texts and Theories*, Edinburgh University Press, Edinburgh, pp. 198–199.

28 Gill, Rosalind and Scharff, Christina (eds), (2011), *New Femininities: Postfeminism, Neoliberalism and Subjectivity*, Palgrave Macmillan, London, p. 5.

29 McGuigan, Jim, 2014, 'The Neoliberal Self' in *Culture Unbound*, Vol. 6, p. 224.

30 Harvey, David, 2005, *A Brief History of Neoliberalism*, Oxford University Press, Oxford, p. 3.

31 Hall, Stuart, 2011, 'The Neoliberal Revolution' in *Cultural Studies*, Vol. 25, No. 6, pp. 708.

32 Ibid.

33 Ibid., p. 715.

34 Lawson, Christopher, 2020, 'Making Sense of the Ruins: The Historiography of Deindustrialisation and its Continued Relevance in Neoliberal Times' in *Historical Compass*, Vol. 18, No. 8. doi.10.1111/hic3.12619

35 Higgins, V. and Larner, W., 2017, 'Introduction' in Higgins, Vaughn and Larner, Wendy (eds), *Assembling Neoliberalism*, Palgrave Macmillan, London, p. 3.

36 Ventura, Patricia, 2017, *Living With American Neoliberalisms*, Palgrave Macmillan, London.

37 Ibid.

38 Ibid.
39 Tyler, Imogen, 'Classification Struggles: Class, Culture and Inequality in Neoliberal Times' in *Sociological Review*, Vol. 63, No. 2, pp. 493–511, 500.
40 Larner, Wendy, 2000, 'Neoliberalism, Policy, Ideology, Governmentality' in *Studies in Political Economy*, Vol. 63, No. 1, pp. 5–25. Gill, Rosalind, 2008, 'Culture & Subjectivity in Neoliberal and Postfeminist Times' in *Subjectivity*, Vol. 25, No. 1, pp. 432–445. McGuigan, Jim, 2014, 'The Neoliberal Self' in *Culture Unbound*, Vol. 6, pp. 223–240. Rottenberg, Catherine, 2014, *The Rise of Neoliberal Feminism*, Oxford University Press, Oxford.
41 Kimmel, Michael, 1987, 'Rethinking Masculinity' in Kimmel, Michael (ed.), *New Directions in Research on Men and Masculinity*, Sage, London. Easthope, Anthony, 1990, *What A Man's Gotta Do: The Masculine Myth in Popular Culture*, Routledge, London. Connell, R. W., 1995, *Masculinities*, Polity Press, Cambridge. Faludi, Susan, 1999, *Stiffed: The Betrayal of the Modern Man*, Chatto & Windus, London. Edwards, Tim, 2006, *Cultures of Masculinity*, Routledge, London.
42 Horrocks, Roger, 1994, *Male Myths and Icons: Masculinity in Popular Culture*, Macmillan, Basingstoke. Clare, Anthony, 2000, *On Men: Masculinity in Crisis*, Arrow Books, London. Walsh, Fintan, 2010, *Male Trouble: Masculinity and the Performance of Crisis*, Palgrave, London. Brooks, Gary, 2010, *Beyond the Crisis of Masculinity: A Theoretical Model for Male Friendly Therapy*, American Psychological Association, New York.
43 Spicer, Andrew, 2003, *Typical Men: Representations of Masculinity in Popular British Cinema*, I. B. Tauris, London.
44 Monk, Claire, 2000, 'Men in the 90s' in Murphy, Robert (ed.), *British Cinema of the 90s*, BFI Publishing, London, p. 157.
45 Spicer, Andrew, 2003, *Typical Men: Representations of Masculinity in Popular Culture*, I. B. Tauris, London.
46 Murphy, Robert (ed.), *British Cinema of the 90s*, BFI Publishing, London.
47 Monk, Claire, 2000, 'Men in the 90s' in Murphy, Robert (ed.), *British Cinema of the 90s*, BFI Publishing, London.
48 Alexander, Karen, 2000, 'Black British Cinema in the 90s: Going, Going, Gone' in Murphy, Robert (ed.), *British Cinema of the 90s*, BFI Publishing, London.
49 Luckett, Moya, 2000, 'Image and Nation in 1990s British Cinema' in Murphy, Robert (ed.), *British Cinema of the 90s*, BFI Publishing, London. Hill, John, 2000, 'Failure and Utopianism: Representations of the Working Class in Britain' in Murphy, Robert (ed.), *British Cinema of the 90s*, BFI Publishing, London. Bruzzi, Stella, 2000, 'Two Sisters, the Fogey, the Priest and his Lover: Sexual Plurality in 1990s British Cinema' in Murphy, Robert (ed.), *British Cinema of the 90s*, BFI Publishing, London.
50 Dave, Paul, 2006, *Visions of England: Class and Culture in Contemporary Cinema*, Berg, London. Mather, Nigel, 2006, *Tears of Laughter: Comedy-Drama in 1990s British Cinema*, Manchester University Press, Manchester.

Malik, Sarita, 1996, 'Beyond the "Cinema of duty?" – The Pleasures of Hybridity: Black British Film of the 1980s and 1990s' in Higson, Andrew (ed.), *Dissolving Views: Key Writings on British Cinema*, Cassell, London. Malik, Sarita, 2009, 'Race and Ethnicity' in Albertazzi, Daniele and Cobley, Paul (eds), *The Media: An Introduction*, Pearson, London.

51   McRobbie, Angela, 2004, 'Postfeminism and Popular Culture' in *Feminist Media Studies*, Vol. 4, No. 3, pp. 255–267. McRobbie, Angela, 2007, 'Postfeminism and Popular Culture: Bridget Jones and the New Gender Regime' in Tasker, Yvonne and Negra, Diane (ed.), *Interrogating Postfeminism: Gender and the Politics of Popular Culture*, Duke University Press, New York. Gill, Rosalind, 2006, *Gender and the Media*, Polity Press, Cambridge. Gill, Rosalind, 2007, 'Postfeminist Media Culture: Elements of a Sensibility' in *European Journal of Cultural Studies*, Vol. 10, No. 2, pp. 147–166. Gill, Rosalind, 2008, 'Culture and Subjectivity in Neoliberal and Postfeminist Times' in *Subjectivity*, Vol. 25, pp. 432–445. Gill, Rosalind, 2011, 'Sexism Reloaded. Or It's Time to get Angry Again' in *Feminist Media Studies*, Vol. 11, No.1, pp. 61–71. Gill, Rosalind and Scharff, Christina (eds), (2011), *New Femininities: Postfeminism, Neoliberalism and Subjectivity*, Palgrave Macmillan, London. Gill, Rosalind, 2016, 'Post-postfeminism?: New Feminist Visibilities in Postfeminist Times', *Feminist Media Studies*, Vol. 16, No. 4, pp. 610–630. García-Favaro, Laura and Gill, Rosalind, 2016, '"Emasculation nation has arrived": Sexism Rearticulated in Online Responses to Lose the Lads' Mags campaign' in *Feminist Media Studies*, Vol. 16, No. 3, pp. 379–397. McGuigan, Jim, 2014, 'The Neoliberal Self' in *Culture Unbound*, Vol. 6, pp. 223–240. Hall, Stuart, 2011, 'The Neoliberal Revolution' in *Cultural Studies*, Vol. 25, No. 6, pp. 705–728. Larner, Wendy, 2000, 'Neoliberalism, Policy, Ideology, Governmentality' in *Studies in Political Economy*, Vol. 63, No. 1, pp. 5–25. Harvey, David, 2005, *A Brief History of Neoliberalism*, Oxford University Press, Oxford. Mudge, Stephanie, 2008, 'What is Neoliberalism?' in *Socio-economic Review*, Vol. 6, No. 4, pp. 703–731. Peck, Jamie, 2010, 'Zombie Neoliberalism and the Ambidextrous State' in *Theoretical Criminology*, Vol. 14, No. 1, pp. 104–110.

52   Crenshaw, Kimberlé, 1989, 'Demarginalizing the Intersection of Race and Sex: A Black Feminist Critique of Antidiscrimination Doctrine, Feminist Theory and Antiracist Politics', University of Chicago Legal Forum, pp. 138–167.

53   Murphy, Robert (ed.), 2009, *The British Cinema Book*, Palgrave Macmillan, London. Leggott, James, 2008, *Contemporary British Cinema: From Heritage to Horror*, Wallflower Press, London.

54   *Journal of British Cinema and Television* special issues: 2012, 'Film in Britain in the New Millennium', Vol. 9, No. 3; 2013, 'Shane Meadows', Vol. 10, No. 4; 2016, 'Andrea Arnold', Vol. 13. No. 1; 2016, 'Post-Millennial British Art Cinema', Vol. 13, No. 2.

55   Forrest, David, 2018, 'The Films of Joanna Hogg: New British Realism and

Class' in *Studies in European Cinema*, Vol. 11, No. 1, pp. 64–75. Barrett, Ciara, 2015, 'The Feminist Cinema of Joanna Hogg: Melodrama, Female Space and the Subversion of Phallogocentric Narrative' in *Alphaville*, Issue 10. Johnson, Beth, 2016, 'Art Cinema and *The Arbour*: Tape Recorded Testimony, Film Art & Feminism' in *Journal of British Cinema and Television* Vol. 13, No. 2, pp. 278–291. Wood, Jason, 2014, *Last Words: Considering Contemporary Cinema*, Columbia University Press, New York.

56   Newsinger, Jack, 2009, 'The Cultural Burden: Regional Film Policy and Practice in England' in *Journal of Media Practice*, Vol. 10, No. 1, pp. 39–55. Newsinger, Jack, 2012, 'The Politics of Regional Audio-Visual Policy in England: Or, How We Learnt to Stop Worrying and Get "Creative"' in *International Journal of Cultural Policy*, Vol. 18, No. 1, pp. 111–125. Newsinger, Jack, 2012, 'British Film Policy in an Age of Austerity' in *Journal of British Cinema and Television*, Vol. 9, No. 1, pp. 133–142. Newsinger, Jack, 2015, 'A Cultural Shock Doctrine? Austerity, the Neoliberal State and the Creative Industries Discourse' in *Media, Culture and Society*, Vol. 37, No. 2, pp. 302–313. Caterer, James, 2008, 'Carrying a Cultural Burden: British Film Policy and its Products' in *Journal of British Cinema and Television*, Vol. 5, No. 1, pp. 146–156. Caterer, James, 2011, 'Reinventing the British Film Industry: The Group Production Plan and the National Lottery Franchise Scheme' in *International Journal of Cultural Policy*, Vol. 17, No. 1, pp. 94–105. Caterer, James, 2011, *The People's Pictures: National Lottery Funding and British Cinema*, Cambridge Scholar's Press, Cambridge. Doyle, Gillian, Schlesinger, Philip, Boyle, Raymond and Kelly, Lisa W., 2015, *The Rise and Fall of the Film Council*, Edinburgh University Press, Edinburgh.

57   Walker, Johnny, 2011, 'Nasty Visions: Violent Spectacle in Contemporary British Horror Cinema' in *Horror Studies*, Vol. 2, No. 1, pp. 115–130. Walker, Johnny, 'A Wilderness of Horrors? British Horror in the New Millennium' in *Journal of British Cinema and Television*, Vol. 9, No. 3, pp. 436–456. Walker, Johnny, 2105, *Contemporary British Horror Cinema: Industry, Genre and Society*, Edinburgh University Press, Edinburgh. Forrest, David, 2010, '*Better Things* (Duane Hopkins, 2008) and New British Realism' in *New Cinemas: Journal of Contemporary Film*, Vol. 8, No. 1, pp. 31–43. Forrest, David, 2013, *Social Realism: Art, Nationhood, Politics*, Cambridge Scholar's Press, Cambridge. Forrest, David, 2014, 'The Films of Joanna Hogg: The New British Realism and Class' in *Studies in European Cinema*, Vol. 11, No. 1, pp. 64–75.

58   Nwonka, Clive James, 2014, '"You're What's Wrong with Me!" *Fish Tank*, *The Selfish Giant* and the Language of Contemporary Social Realism' in *New Cinemas: Journal of Contemporary Film*, Vol. 12, No. 3, pp. 205–223. Nwonka, Clive James, 2015, 'Diversity Pie: Rethinking Social Exclusion and Diversity Policy in the British Film Industry' in *Journal of Media Practice*, Vol. 16, No. 1, pp. 73–90. Nwonka, Clive James, 2016, '*Hunger* as Political Epistemology' in *Studies in European Cinema*, Vol. 13, No. 2, pp. 138–148. Nwonka, Clive

James, 2017, 'Estate of the Nation: Social Housing as Cultural Verisimilitude in British Social Realism' in Forrest, David, Harper, Graham and Rayner, Jonathan (eds), *Filmurbia: Cinema and the Suburbs*, Palgrave Macmillan, London.

59 Whelehan, Imelda, 2009, 'Not to be Looked At: Older Women in Recent British Cinema' in Bell, Melanie and Williams, Melanie (eds), *British Women's Cinema*, Routledge, London. Pope, Andrew, 2015, 'Thatcher's Sons? 1980s Boyhood in Britain 2005–2010' in *Journal of Boyhood Studies*, Vol. 12, No. 1, pp. 22–39. Llinares, Dario, 2015, 'Punishing Bodies: British Prison Films and the Spectacle of Masculinity' in *Journal of British Cinema and Television*, Vol. 12, No. 2, pp. 207–228. Godfrey, Sarah and Hamad, Hannah, 2011, 'Save the Cheerleader, Save the Males: Resurgent Protective Paternalism' in Ross, Karen (ed.), *The Handbook of Gender Sex and Media*, Wiley-Blackwell, London. Godfrey, Sarah, 2012, 'The Hero of my Dreams: Framing Fatherhood in Mamma Mia!' in Williams, Melanie and FitzGerald, Louise (eds), *Mamma Mia! Exploring a Cultural Phenomenon*, I. B. Tauris, London. Godfrey, Sarah, 2013, '"I'm a casualty, but it's cool": Masculinity in *TwentyFourSeven*' in *Journal of British Cinema and Television*, Vol. 10, pp. 846–862. Godfrey, Sarah, 2013, 'Taking the Temperature: Masculinities and Male Identities from *Bleak Moments* To *Happy-Go-Lucky*' in Cardinale-Powell, Bryan and DiPaulo, Marc (eds), *Devised and Directed by Mike Leigh*, Bloomsbury, London. Fitzgerald, Louise and Godfrey, Sarah, 2013, '"Them over there": Motherhood and Marginality in Shane Meadows' Films' in Fradley, Martin, Godfrey, Sarah and Williams, Melanie (eds), *Shane Meadows: Critical Essays*, Edinburgh University Press, Edinburgh. Fradley, Martin, Godfrey, Sarah and Williams, Melanie (eds), 2013, *Shane Meadows: Critical Essays*, Edinburgh University Press, Edinburgh. Godfrey, Sarah and Walker, Johnny, 2015, 'From Pinter to Pimp: Danny Dyer, Class, Cultism and the Critics' in *Journal of British Cinema and Television*, Vol. 12, pp. 101–120.

60 Higson, Andrew, 1989, 'The Concept of National Cinema' in *Screen*, Vol. 30, No. 4. Higson, Andrew, 1996, *Dissolving Views: Key Writing on British Cinema*, Cassell, London. Higson, Andrew, 1997, *Waving the Flag: Constructing a National Cinema in Britain*, Oxford University Press, Oxford. Higson, Andrew, 2003, *English Heritage, English Cinema: Costume Drama since the 1980s*, Oxford University Press, Oxford. Higson, Andrew, 2010, *Film England: Culturally English Film Making Since the 1990s*, I. B. Tauris, London. Petrie, Duncan, 1991, *Creativity and Constraint in the British Film Industry*, Palgrave Macmillan, London. Petrie, Duncan, 2000, *Screening Scotland*, BFI Publishing, London. Petrie, Duncan, 2000, 'The New Scottish Cinema' in Horte, Mette and MacKenzie, Scott (eds), *Cinema and Nation*, Routledge, London. Street, Sarah, 2009, *British National Cinema*, Taylor & Francis, London. Street, Sarah, 2016, *British National Cinema in Documents*, Taylor & Francis, London. Christie, Ian, 2013, 'Where is National Cinema

Today? (And Do We Still Need It?)' in *Film History: An International Journal*, Vol. 25, No. 1, pp. 19–30. Ging, Debbie, 2012, *Men and Masculinities in Irish Cinema*, Palgrave, London.

61 Christie, Ian, 2013, 'Where is National Cinema Today? (And Do We Still Need It?)' in *Film History: An International Journal*, Vol. 25, No. 1, p. 26.

62 Williams, Melanie, 2017, *Female Stars of British Cinema: The Woman Question*, Edinburgh University Press, Edinburgh, p. 14.

63 Ascheid, Antje, 2006, 'Safe Rebellions: Romantic Emancipation in the Woman's Heritage Film' in *Scope: An Online Journal of Film Studies*.

64 Ibid.

CHAPTER 1

Changing Britain, Changing Men: From 'New' Man to the New Millennium

The twenty years from 1990 to 2010 were years of change on many levels, encompassing substantive developments in terms of social and economic structures, cultural practices, and national and regional identities. Politically, the period is rather conveniently bookended by the end of the Thatcher era (if not the Conservative government) in November 1990 at one end, and the election of David Cameron in May 2010 at the other. During this time the shift from a manufacturing-based industrial economy to a technology-led, service-orientated post-industrial economy was consolidated. This brought about changes in both cultural discourses of masculinity and the lived social experiences of men. In this chapter I argue that these developments occurred partially in tandem with, and partially as a result of, the interconnected economic and cultural processes of neoliberalism and postfeminism respectively.[1] Within this broader context masculinity, as an identity, a discourse, a lived subjectivity and a mode of representation, became a focal point of discussion and debate in academic and popular culture alike: to borrow from Michel Foucault one might term this an 'incitement to discourse' around the subject of masculinity.[2] Foremost amongst the cultural discourses was the idea of a perceived decline in men's social and economic power which was invariably posited as a causal factor for a range of attendant issues including male violence, men's mental health, and changing familial and domestic roles. Masculinity and the attendant social and cultural practices of men alike were thus framed as inherently problematic.[3]

British films of the period were quick to engage with the themes and tropes of troubled male characters; to use Claire Monk's phrasing, British films of the 1990s in particular were 'almost unprecedented' in their preoccupation with men and narratives of masculinity in crisis.[4] For this reason I suggest that the analysis of key films can be illuminative in attempting to better understand the cultural formation and mediation of masculinity at the time.

The purpose of this chapter is to establish the broader socio-cultural context of the 1990s and 2000s and to examine the emergence of British postfeminist masculinity and its connection with British neoliberalism within this. In so doing, I follow an established methodological approach to feminist work in British film and cultural studies which is concerned with exploring and understanding the cultural politics involved in the representation and mediation of gendered subjectivities within national cinema. This chapter is not an attempt to produce a definitive account of this period of British history, rather it is to set up the broader social, cultural and political context within which the case study films and their representations of masculinity must be located and understood.

I begin by presenting the idea of British postfeminist masculinity, examining its emergence in the early part of the 1990s and its subsequent development. The following section examines in more detail the connections between postfeminism, post-industrialisation, neoliberalism and their relationship to masculinity within the context of British culture. The third section connects these debates to the ongoing discussions about British national identity and the socio-political shifts that gave way to the 'Cool Britannia' phenomenon at the end of the 1990s, focusing specifically on the emergence of new lad culture within this moment. From here I move on to explore the ways in which the 9/11 terror attacks impacted upon gender and cultural politics in the UK and how this appeared to reignite a particularly reactionary rhetoric around race, class and gender. The final section provides an overview of the industrial and institutional history of the British film industry over the period, in order to locate the case study films within these contexts.

This chapter necessarily covers considerable conceptual and historical ground in order to explore the various points of connection, and to explain how the array of social, cultural and political threads must be viewed holistically and historically with regards to understanding the complexities of gender discourse and their cinematic mediations. In drawing on a raft of social, cultural and political histories, this chapter functions to establish the contours of British postfeminist masculinity and its connections with British neoliberal culture during a particularly rich era for British cinema.

A Perpetual State of Crisis? Conceptualising Discourses of British Postfeminist Masculinity 1990–2010

Susan Jeffords identified what she saw as a significant 'switch' in the ways in which masculinity was being presented in a number of Hollywood films towards the end of the 1980s, as the 'hard bodied' action heroes were replaced by male characters who, she argued, offered a 'kinder and gentler' iteration of masculinity than their forebears.[5] While the so-called 'new man' proliferated across a number of media platforms such as magazines and advertising, his manifestation in British cinema was rather muted. Claire Monk notes that where cinematic iterations of the British new man occurred, they tended to be the more affluent characters found in romance and costume dramas; genres, she observes, that have 'a known appeal to female filmgoers'.[6] Outside of these genres the figure of the disempowered, downtrodden and often disconsolate versions of British masculinity were far more commonly found. Although specific in their exact and narrative trajectories, films ranging from social realism to comedy frequently drew on an increasingly prevalent trope of male characters as enduring some form of gender-based crisis.

Outside of cinema the notion of 'crisis' became one of the defining characteristics of academic and popular discourses of masculinity during this time. Indeed, the idea of masculinity in crisis was already well-established by the end of the 1980s when Michael Kimmel proclaimed that 'men are today confused about what it means to be a "real man"' and claimed that the notion of masculinity in crisis has become 'a cultural commonplace'.[7] While in 2020 Calum Neil describes a 'contemporary suspicion' of crisis claims, cultural tropes of dislocated and disempowered masculinities remain prevalent across the media landscape.[8] In this section I examine the ways in which discourses of crisis are connected with the broader socio-economic environment and are inextricable from the British neoliberal post-industrial economy and the emergent cultural sensibility that would come to be understood as postfeminism.

The early part of the 1990s saw a convergence of circumstances that were key in creating a cultural environment in which forms of British postfeminist masculinity could emerge. That academic interest in masculinity should also re-emerge during this moment is, I suggest, significant. The institutional regard is connected both with the economic shifts that were occurring at the time and their impact upon men's lives alongside the proliferation of neoliberal consumer culture, and the increasing commodification of masculinity within it.[9] Much of the work from this time adopted a poststructuralist perspective which sought to question what is saw as the hitherto 'unmarked norm' of masculinity and its ideological position in terms of the maintenance of patriarchal cultures. The aim was to challenge what Anthony Easthope described as the 'masculine myth' and to analyse it in order to challenge the ways in which patriarchy relied upon a particular notion of masculinity as the 'universal norm' against which all else was measured.[10] Thus the scholarship emerging during the early 1990s was instrumental in opening up questions about masculinity as an identity and interrogating the ways in which connections between discourse and lived experience functioned. Rejecting socio-biological accounts of 'natural masculinity' as 'almost entirely fictional', scholars such as Easthope, Stearns, Connell and Seidler argued instead for a conceptual approach that located masculinity and male-gendered identities as 'a subject position in discourse, the place from which one speaks'.[11] This perspective produced a theorisation of masculinities and male identities as plural, mobile and multifaceted, in turn facilitating an acknowledgement of the complex intersectionality of gendered subjectivities. This work was crucial in establishing a conceptualisation of masculinity which is understood as existing at both the macro, abstracted level of discourse and ideology as well as the micro level of materiality, lived experience and social practices, and at various intermediate levels simultaneously.

One of the most influential theorisations of masculinity to emerge out of this flurry of scholarship was R. W. Connell's model of hegemonic masculinity.[12] Hegemonic masculinity has proven to be a particularly useful theoretical model for understanding the ways in which masculinity operates within the material/discursive matrix and the multiple ways in which it is subsequently embedded and performed within a wider more complex system of power relations.[13] Connell's approach enables an understanding of masculinity as historically and geographically contingent; in this model masculinity is mobile, dynamic, intersectional and subject to shifts and changes over time, while also maintaining dominance as a normative discourse. In Connell's conceptualisation, masculinity is inevitably multifaceted, comprising a range of cultural, social and economic aspects that have developed over time; these are continually evolving, giving rise to multiple types, styles or forms of masculinity circulating in culture at any given time. The concept of hegemonic masculinity offers a means of understanding the complexities of masculinity as intersectional, identifying those aspects of masculinity that are valourised (cis-gendered, heterosexual, white, affluent) and, thus, those that are subordinate, oppressed or denigrated (transgendered, queer, Black, Brown, poor) at any point in time. While scholars such as Connell, Hearn and Morgan all agree that hegemonic masculinity is a dynamic construction that is continually in flux, there is, according to Kimmel, one fundamental aspect that remains constant: 'a man, it would appear, can hold any attitude about women he likes, but his masculinity is still bound up with behaving differently from them'.[14] Hegemonic masculinity will therefore always be embedded within and informed by heteronormative patriarchal hegemonies of sexuality and thus it will inevitably function to maintain heterosexuality as the normative form of sexual identity. This points to the complex interstices between bodies, gender and sexuality and the organisation of these within a heteronormative, patriarchal, capitalist culture.

The proliferation of academic interest in masculinity created what might be understood in Foucauldian terms as an incitement to discourse which quickly spread into popular culture. The idea that 'we live in an era of transition in the definition of masculinity' readily took hold as the starting point for a raft of books ranging from pop-psychology and self-help manuals to tomes such as *Stiffed*, Susan Faludi's influential treatise on the problems facing men at the end of the twentieth century.[15] Over the course of the 1990s, the idea that masculinity was 'in crisis' became deployed with increasing frequency to refer to a whole gamut of issues all of which hinged on the notion that men were suffering from an erosion of social and economic power and that this was having a negative impact upon them. Implicit within these discussions was the idea that female empowerment had been accomplished at the expense of men – a claim that is explicitly made in films such as *Brassed Off* and *The Full Monty*. In this regard, the proclamations of a crisis in masculinity both rely upon and perpetuate a specifically postfeminist rhetoric which argues that feminist politics are no longer needed because women are now empowered. Male disempowerment becomes mobilised as evidence of feminism's success, functioning to confirm that feminist politics are not only no longer needed but that pursuing them any further is, in fact, damaging. When framed in this way the narratives of male crisis that pervaded the 1990s and 2000s are intrinsically postfeminist in their manifestation. The following section explores this within the specific cultural and economic context of the early 1990s, examining the connections between postfeminism, post-industrialisation, neoliberalism and masculinity in more detail.

Post-industrialisation and the Crisis of '90s Masculinity

As Britain entered the final decade of the twentieth century the political, cultural and economic outlook appeared rather unsettled as the economic boom of the late 1980s gave way to a period of recession brought about by a combination of high interest rates and a housing market that had collapsed under the weight of over-inflation. During this period, the programme of privatisation that had been central to the Thatcher government's neoliberal agenda continued. A raft of once publicly owned industries including British Airways, British Coal, British Rail, as well as gas, water and electricity boards, were sold into private ownership, opening them up to the competitive forces of the market economy. This process of privatising once public industries which had previously been the mainstays of working-class (and largely) male employment in central and northern England led to the entrenchment of pockets of deprivation and unemployment that still persist today.[16]

The deliberate disassembly of the industrial economy brought about a collapse in the economic power of working-class men in particular but also held ramifications within the social and domestic realms, destabilising the established hegemonic organisation of the nuclear family unit comprised of a male breadwinner and economically dependent wife and children. As Tim Edwards explains, unemployment invalidated one of the cornerstones of Western masculinity, creating a situation in which occupation could no longer function as 'the most fundamental foundation of masculine identity'.[17] This in turn disrupted the once unassailable and proprietorial privileges of domestic authority: economic dominance held by a patriarchal breadwinner.

The impact of the disestablishment of the industrial economy was further exacerbated, largely due to the majority of the men who were made redundant being without the requisite skills demanded in the emergent technologised economy. Sociologist, Beverley Skeggs notes the extent of the problem, arguing that masculine physicality had 'little worth' in the post-industrial landscape, and thus little economic value. The attendant cultural power of working-class masculinity was severely impacted.[18] Skeggs's argument is further borne out in Linda McDowell's study of the impact of post-industrialisation on the employment prospects of working-class boys who were leaving compulsory schooling in 1999.[19] McDowell describes how this generation of school leavers experienced a very different transition from adolescence to adulthood than their fathers before them: the industries that had once employed successive generations of men had been dismantled and replaced by a service sector dominated by casualisation, insecurity and part-time working hours.[20] McDowell argues that the emergence of a neoliberal, post-industrial economy drastically changed the relationship between masculinity and employment, not least because the 'care, deference, and docility' demanded at the lowest end of the service economy were 'more commonly defined as feminine rather than masculine traits'.[21]

The collapse of the industrial economy forced a physical relocation of men from the (oftentimes male dominated) workplace to the domestic (and thus feminised) space of the home. But, more significantly it also enforced a subjective relocation from breadwinner to financial dependent, reliant on spouse, children or state for sustenance and support. In this regard, post-industrialisation challenged traditional forms of working-class patriarchal masculinity at a fundamental level by under-mining the connections that upheld occupationally defined models of male identity. This disrupted a long-established hegemonic model of a heteronormative nuclear family, comprised of breadwinning husband with financially dependent homemaker wife and children. Crucially, from the perspective of a feminist analysis, these developments were constructed as overwhelmingly negative, both in popular and academic literature, as the narrative that 'men have lost, or are losing, power or privilege relative to their prior status' became entrenched within broader discourses of masculinity in crisis.[22]

Although the recession of the early 1990s receded, giving way to an era of economic growth that lasted almost undented until the global financial crisis of 2008, the shift towards a post-industrial, neoliberal economy caused social mobility to stagnate and left behind significant pockets of impoverished and unemployed men.[23] The psychological implications of unemployment proved to be fertile ground for British filmmakers with a multitude of films over the 1990s in particular taking creative inspiration from narratives of disempowered, unemployed men in rundown towns. Films including *Brassed Off*, *The Full Monty* and *TwentyFourSeven* are notable examples of films that explicitly present an array of male characters as disempowered victims, suffering as a result of the economic and social changes wrought by the inexorable processes of neoliberal privatisation.

From Warm Beer to Cool Britannia: 'New' Lads, 'New' Labour and the End of the 1990s

In 1993 the Conservative Prime Minister John Major gave a speech in which he extolled what he saw as a 'timeless' vision of Britain. His descrip-tion of 'a country of long shadows on cricket grounds, warm beer, invin-cible green suburbs, dog lovers and pools fillers . . . of old maids bicycling to holy communion through the morning mist' evoked a bucolic nostalgia that was anachronistic to the point of being almost entirely unrecognis-able as a treatise on contemporary Britain.[24] The wistful sentimentality inherent in this speech underlines the extent to which the Prime Minister himself seemed to be outdated and out of touch with the realities of British culture of the 1990s. Moreover, the nostalgic yearning for a mythologised past, in which Britain remained a global superpower by virtue of its colo-nial conquests, points to what cultural studies scholar Paul Gilroy might describe as evidence of 'post-colonial melancholia'. This affectation can be seen as an enduring consequence of an imperial past; a rhetoric that deliberately effaces itself with a sanitised and sentimental revision of the historical narrative.[25] Indeed, the murder of the Black British teenager, Stephen Lawrence, which took place in South London just months before Major's speech, is indicative of the disparity between the prime minister's imaginary and the realities of enduring systems of structural racism and racialised inequalities that were endemic in the UK. The Macpherson report commissioned as a public inquiry into the police handling of the Stephen Lawrence murder, drew a rather different conclusion to Major's Arcadian idyll with its implicit assumptions of social cohesion and a singular national identity. Macpherson found collective failures across multiple institutions and organisations which provided compelling evidence of systemic and institutional racism.[26] Major, like Thatcher before him, articulated a sense of national identity that sought to redress the current decline in Britain's status by appropriating an imagined and nostalgic version of its past; however, by 1993, this rhetoric sounded increasingly hollow and anachronistic.

At the same time that the Macpherson inquiry was happening there were fierce debates taking place around questions of the various national identities that comprised the UK, as Scotland, Wales and Northern Ireland began taking steps towards devolution and independence from the English parliamentary system. Major's speech not only overlooked the complexities of the composite nature of the UK effacing the important national specificities of Scotland, Wales and Northern Ireland, it also reinforced the very political hierarchies that were being objected to in the calls for devolution by promulgating a vision of 'Britishness' that was essentially 'English', and implicitly white and middle class. In much the same way that social and cultural changes were deemed to have created a crisis for masculinity, they also contributed to debates about Britishness as a national identity. Much like gender identities, national identity is a complex and multifaceted entity which is interwoven through history, culture and language into our social realities. It is as Mike Storry and Peter Childs suggest, 'a matter of allegiance and cultural affiliation' and something that is continually negotiated and performed in various ways.[27] National identity matters, according to Phillip Dodd's Demos report, *The Battle Over Britain*, because 'it stretches far beyond the ceremonies of state into the very idioms of language, and even into the ways we hold our bodies'.[28] Dodd opened his report with a cri de coeur:

> Britishness is not simply the issue of the hour. No moratorium on thinking about who the British are will make everything well. The reasons for the present self-consciousness are many and they are simply not going to go away. They would probably include the fact that Britain no longer enjoys a status as world power, whatever explanations are proffered to make sense of its decline; that attempts to halt its

economic decline never quite seem to work; that post-war immigration has thrown into relief an imperial history that has been repressed, and shown the British to be not quite as tolerant as they have imagined themselves to be; that demands for more autonomy from Scotland and Wales, not to mention the war in Northern Ireland, have thrown into question the claim that a single Britishness is subscribed to in all these countries.[29]

The cultural atrophy described by Dodd was not quite as terminal as suggested, it transpired. In the middle years of the decade the wistful melancholy around national identity began to give way to a sense of cultural invigoration across the economy, arts, culture and technology. The cultural renaissance which became known as 'Cool Britannia' marked a key moment in Britain's renegotiation of its national identity at home and abroad. A wave of new authors, musicians, artists, models, actors and filmmakers emerged across British cultural industries leading to *Newsweek* proclaiming London as the 'Coolest city on Earth' in 1996.[30] Where John Major had aligned himself with what he saw as a 'timeless' if inherently problematic imaginary of Britishness, the new Labour leader Tony Blair was quick to seize the opportunity to associate himself with the sense of regeneration, optimism and vivacity of the cultural moment.

Tony Blair's rise to the helm of 'New' Labour and subsequent election as Prime Minister was precipitated by the unexpected death of previous Labour Party leader, John Smith in 1994. Over the three-year period prior to the 1997 election, Blair began his political project of reconstructing the Labour Party into the political force that would come to dominate the remainder of the period covered by this book. New Labour took its ideological lead from ideas developed by the sociologist Anthony Giddens in his book *The Third Way: The Renewal of Social Democracy*, which sought to create a form of politics that amalgamated a left-wing belief in inclusivity, solidarity and equality within a neoliberal, globalised context.[31] Blair's strategic reconfiguration of the Labour Party appeared to chime with the cultural moment described by Dodd in his report: the emphasis on renewal and revitalisation of politics and society after eighteen years of Conservative government dovetailed with many of Dodd's ideas.[32] The political scientist Jonah Levy describes the biggest challenge facing Blair was that of convincing the electorate that Labour was a credible political party that would provide competent government.[33] Levy explains that Blair and Brown accomplished this in part by 'projecting a unified message' which they achieved by 'controlling the rank and file' party members in order to maintain strict party discipline and discourse as well as by appropriating and reconfiguring central tenets of neoliberalism and re-casting them via recourse to ideas of social responsibility and fiscal prudence.[34]

The 1997 election was a significant cultural moment for a variety of reasons. Not only did Blair and then Brown preside over the longest Labour governments in British history, but the length of their joint tenure meant that the social, cultural and economic influence of New Labour ideas were able to develop to fruition, and this is crucial in forming the specific ways in which neoliberalism became consolidated within British culture. Political scholars Florence Faucher-King and Patrick Le Galès suggest that, in many ways, the first Blair government in particular followed an agenda that could be described as 'activist', undertaking significant social reforms in public services and welfare that were largely in keeping with traditional social democratic politics.[35] However, by introducing private sector finance into these initiatives, New Labour created a situation in which the public sector became increasingly reconstructed via the mores of neoliberalism. The first New Labour government did introduce a range of social reforms (including Sure Start Children's Centres and the minimum wage) which were offset by a raft of more populist policies. The introduction of tighter regulations for claiming some benefits and reducing the value of others were only two deliberately deployed strategies aimed at reassuring centre-right, erstwhile Conservative voters of the credibility of the New Labour party. These domestic policies, alongside schemes such as the Public Finance Initiative, in which private companies bid for service tenders in the public sector, created an ever-closer relationship between the state and the market, consolidating neoliberalism as the hegemonic socio-economic model of British culture and politics.

A few months after Blair's election victory in May 1997, the independent think-tank, Demos, released Mark Leonard's research, *Britain™: Renewing Our Identity*, a report designed to negotiate how best to reconfigure Britishness as a contemporary national identity.[36] Proceeding from the premise that 'Britain's identity is in flux', Leonard uses the report to reflect on what he sees as the cultural malaise that had been afflicting the nation since the end of the 1980s boom, arguing that the project of 'finding a better fit between our heritage and what we are becoming' was a central priority.[37] The report was notable for its acknowledgement of the malleable and discursive constitution of national identities, and for seeking to facilitate a reconstructed articulation of Britishness as a national identity within the contemporary global context. Outlining what he saw as the key problems besetting Britain's identity both at home and abroad, Leonard argued that Britain's image 'remains stuck in the past (. . .) a backward looking has-been, a theme park of royal pageantry', with a reputation for 'low-tech and bad value' products whose businesses are 'strike-ridden and hostile to free-trade' and whose image suffers from perceptions of 'bad weather, poor food and stand offish people'.[38]

Britain™ is, in many ways, exemplary as a neoliberal exercise in rebranding; to this end, the act of reconfiguring Britishness as a national identity was a process of constructing and curating a particular set of discourses and tropes that needed to be coherent but diverse and interesting and, above all else, marketable to a global tourist market. Leonard uses the report to set out why this work was so vital at that exact moment in time; he explains the role of reconstruction as 'the identity premium' – that is to say that he saw the rethinking of national identity as a rebranding exercise and that the British 'brand' needed to appeal to investors and tourists as much as it did the domestic population. Citing a number of countries including Spain, Chile and Argentina that had already successfully rebranded their national image, Leonard uses the report to make a persuasive case for the conscious rebranding of Britishness as a national identity achieved via the strategic development of ongoing 'brand management'.[39]

Just three months after Blair became prime minister, Diana, Princess of Wales, was killed in a car crash, an accident that sent cultural shockwaves through the nation. She was one of the most popular members of the royal family during a period of turbulence and change within the institution of the monarchy. The media canonised her as glamorous but troubled; her struggles with eating disorders and the unhappiness of her marriage to Prince Charles being extensively covered in the British tabloid press at the time. It was while attempting to evade the chasing paparazzi that her driver lost control of the car in which she was travelling; resulting in her death alongside that of the chauffeur and her lover, Dodi Fayed. What followed was unprecedented in British history: thousands of floral tributes were laid at St James's Palace by members of the public; the press criticism of both the Palace and the monarch's handling of her death; and the televised spectacle of her state funeral, including her two young sons accompanying the coffin from St James's Palace to Westminster Abbey. The funeral tribute performed by Elton John appeared to further underline the affective impact of her death. Indeed, in the edited collection *Mourning Diana: Nation, Culture and the Performance of Grief*, Adrian Kear and Deborah Lynn Steinberg argue that responses to Diana's death were evidence of the 'dramatic cultural changes' taking place at the time, suggesting how she became 'a projective touchstone for competing cultural values and political claims'.[40] Furthermore, her death came at a time when cultural emotions were already running high. Cultural studies scholar Valerie Hey confirms this, suggesting that Diana's death appeared to crystallise what she terms a range of 'political longings and social discontents' foremost amongst which she sees as the democratisation of society, or at least partial performance of this.[41] In this regard, Diana's death and the subsequent public grieving played an unexpected but key role in the 'reconstruction of cultural identities and political ideas'.[42] Indeed, Leonard interprets the public outpouring of grief at Diana's death similarly, suggesting that it was a 'symptom' of the transition of British national identity away from the traditional (masculine) 'stiff upper lip' into something more emotionally articulate.[43]

While the aftermath of Diana's death appeared to suggest an affective turn in British society, the modes of masculinity that were most dominant in media culture were quite the opposite. The emotionally articulate 'new man' of the early 1990s had all but disappeared from the cultural landscape, replaced by the defiantly unreconstructed 'new lad'. The 'new lad' arguably rose to become *the* defining mode of late 1990s British masculinity. Originating in the growing men's magazine market of the mid-1990s, *loaded* (first published in 1994) was the spiritual home of this emergent form of masculinity. Described by Imelda Whelehan as 'part soccer thug, part lager lout, part arrant sexist', whose frames of reference are 'very clearly demarcated – sport, pop, alcohol, soft drugs, heterosex and soft porn', the new lad can be seen as a clear riposte to his reconstructed predecessor.[44] The 'new lad' can be understood as the result of the convergence of postfeminism and neoliberalism within British culture; despite the claims that the 'new lad' resonated because of his 'authentic' masculinity, he was no more real or genuine than the 'new man' before him, a point astutely made by Monk who sees the success of the 'new lad' as driven by a realisation that 'it was amply possible to sell designer fashion and beauty products to men by appealing to their sexism rather than by exploiting the imagery of proto-feminist reconstruction'.[45] The 'new lad' was intrinsically postfeminist in his construction; lad culture was explicitly unabashed in its ambivalence towards feminism and gender politics, mobilising irony as a discursive mechanism to foreclose and dismiss ideological critique.

'New lad' culture quickly proliferated beyond its magazine origins, spreading to radio via the growth in zoo radio and personality DJs such as Chris Moyles and via television programmes such as *Men Behaving Badly* (ITV 1992–1993, BBC 1993–1998) and the replacement of Chris Evans with Johnny Vaughan on Channel 4's deliberately anarchic and brash *The Big Breakfast* (Channel 4, 1992–2002). Lad culture clearly influenced a number of films produced during the latter end of the 1990s, particularly the cycle of gangster films that proliferated in the years following the commercial success of Guy Ritchie's *Lock, Stock and Two Smoking Barrels* (1998). Contra to the 'post-political' rhetoric identified by Claire

Monk in films such as *Lock, Stock ...* and *Twin Town*, which deployed irony as a mechanism through which the social exclusion of young men was reconfigured 'not as a 'social problem' but as a subcultural 'lifestyle', were films such as *TwentyFourSeven*, *My Name is Joe* (Ken Loach, 1998), *Sweet Sixteen* (Ken Loach, 2002) and *Nil By Mouth*, all of which proffered images of dislocated young men, cast adrift in a post-industrial, neoliberal landscape that they were ill-prepared for. Films such as these can be understood within the historical narrative of realist British cinema and, as such, drew on a rather differently evoked notion of postfeminist male authenticity. These productions mobilised narratives of disempowerment and degeneration as a mechanism through which to present and explore the intersections of class, masculinity and male experiences within the postfeminist, neoliberal culture of the late 1990s.

While class might have remained a key narrative concern across a large part of British cinema during this time, whiteness remained intact and largely unquestioned as a dominant racial imagery – as the reconfiguration of *The Full Monty* from being a film about Black British men to featuring an overwhelmingly white cast demonstrates.[46] The Parekh Report, *The Future of Multi-Ethnic Britain*, which was published in 2000, aimed to 'analyse the current state of multi-ethnic Britain and to propose ways of countering racial discrimination and disadvantage and making Britain a confident and vibrant multicultural society at ease with its rich diversity'. Despite this political intention, the problems of racialised marginalistion and institutionalised racism persisted, particularly within the cultural and creative sectors. Indeed, the extent of white privilege within the cultural industries is evidenced by the mono-racial overtones in the much-vaunted renaissance of Cool Britannia. Key (but not necessarily voluntary) figureheads of this phenomenon included musicians (Blur, Oasis, Elastica, Menswear), fashion designers such as Alexander McQueen and models such as Kate Moss, novelists (Nick Hornby, Irivine Welsh) and artists (Damien Hirst and Tracey Emin), as well as filmmakers (Guy Ritchie, Dominic Anciano) and actors (Ray Burdis, Jude Law).

While on the one hand Cool Britannia might be understood as an integral part of the regeneration of Britishness both at home and abroad, it remained almost entirely dominated by white British people and their cultural products. The icons of Britpop, Brit-lit and Brit-art were at the vanguard of this process of cultural renewal and reinvigoration but the extent to which they were representative of a more modern, multicultural version of British national identity is less convincing. Films such as *The Full Monty*, *Trainspotting* and *Lock, Stock and Two Smoking Barrels* were produced and directed by white filmmakers and their narrative focus was overwhelmingly on the stories of white characters. If films such as these offer an intervention into shifting discourses of national identity they also reconstruct and rehearse a version of it in which whiteness remains the normative and unmarked symbol of Britishness. In this regard, and in specific relation to ideas about masculinity and the gender politics of post-feminism, the deleterious effects of cultural change on male characters are a matter for and about white working-class men. Post-industrialisation, neoliberalism and postfeminism become conflated to form a compelling challenge to British masculinity that is in turn mobilised as a nostalgic yearning for a past which is, by implication, white.

Despite the fact that the Labour government established considerable funding and training initiatives designed to diversify the British film industry, the impact on Black British filmmaking was, as Karen Alexander points out, negligible.[47] Nearly eight years later, Alexander's arguments continue to hold true and are evidenced once more in the 2007 report, *Barriers to Diversity in Film: A Research Review*, commissioned by the UK Film Council and written by Reema Bhavari.[48] The report covers industry and personnel as well as representation and includes both qualitative and quantitative evidence that leads to the unsurprising, if depressing, conclusion that despite the adoption of anti-discrimination legislation and a wealth of funded training initiatives aimed expressly at diversifying the industry, leadership roles remain dominated by white, middle-aged, able-bodied men.[49] Bhavari points to the ways in which the infrastructure of the film and media industries perpetuates a structural exclusivity via widespread casualisation and the ways in which social connections or, as it is termed in the report, 'who you know' function as pathways into the industry.[50]

Terror, Recession and the Early 2000s

As Britain entered the twenty-first century, upbeat rhetoric of Blair's 'New' Labour Party held firm, despite the government becoming embroiled in a very public debacle over the Millennium Dome, a project that political commentator Clive Gray suggests was fundamentally flawed from the outset and subsequently beset by issues of management, finance, structure and purpose.[51] The economy remained relatively buoyant and Britain also appeared to be enjoying a period of more settled and amicable relationships with its European partners despite remaining outside of the common currency. The *General Household Survey* by the National Office of Statistics bears testament to this apparently more settled and prosper-ous period, pointing to rising home ownership, increases in disposable income and an attendant boom in 'consumer durables'.[52] Technology was a particularly strong area, with high sales in home computers, mobile phones, games consoles and the like. Despite fears over the so-called millennium bug which, it was feared, would render all kinds of technology redundant as the clock switched from 1999 to 2000, this was the moment in which the internet began to move increasingly into popular culture.

This cultural and economic optimism was brutally shattered on 11 September 2001 when Al-Qaeda militants hijacked four commercial aeroplanes, crashing two of them into the World Trade Center in New York and one into the Pentagon in Washington.[53] Political scientist Stuart Croft described how the events of 9/11 created 'a fundamental shift in the nature of world politics' that was to have a substantial impact upon Britain, both domestically and internationally.[54] In the immediate aftermath of the terror attacks, Tony Blair pledged allegiance and unwavering support to the controversially elected US President George W. Bush, proclaiming that the two nations stood 'shoulder to shoulder' in the fight against terrorism. Further, Blair emphasised what he saw as the moral superiority of the UK/US alliance, surmising that 'this is not a battle between the United States of America and terrorism, but between the free and democratic world and terrorism'; in so doing, Blair cast this as an ideological, rather than territorial, war.[55]

To begin with, the majority of British MPs supported the prime minister's allegiance with the US, especially when the September dossier released in 2002 appeared to confirm that Iraq, thought to be sympathetic to Al-Qaeda's jihadism, not only had a range of chemical and biological weaponry at its disposal, but that the state was ready to deploy them within forty-five minutes of receiving a presidential order. The claims made in the September dossier were crucial in legitimising ongoing British military involvement in the Middle East, and shoring up both political and public support at home. However, some eight months later, public and political support was waning when rumours began to emerge about the veracity of the report's claims. Despite agreeing to the Hutton Inquiry in 2004, Blair's credibility and his once indefatigable popularity were fatally damaged, and the final years of his term of office were blighted by questions over his role in the Iraq War.

The fallout of 9/11 and the subsequent war on terror created cultural as well as political and economic aftermaths, particularly in terms of the politics of gender, race and multiculturalism. In American culture in particular there was widespread repudiation of feminist politics in the aftermath of the attack, with conservative commentators such as Kathleen Parker, Peggy Noonan and Patricia Leigh Brown proclaiming that feminist politics had led to the emasculation of the nation, making it vulnerable to attack. In this regard, 9/11 became appropriated as a rallying call to 'right the applecart of traditional gender roles'.[56] In Britain, one of the consequence of 9/11 and the subsequent war on terror was a rise in racially motivated crimes and islamophobia. Political scholar Lee Jarvis explains how the 'shifting demarcations of identities, peoples and nations were discursively manufactured' to provide further legitimacy to British military involvement in Iraq and Afghanistan.[57] Despite a political emphasis on Britain's position as 'a major target for terrorist attacks' in the immediate aftermath of 9/11, it was not until 2005 that a series of coordinated suicide bombings were staged across the London Transport network.[58] The attacks were carried out by four young men; the eldest, Mohammad Sidique Khan was aged 30, the other three men were aged 22, 19 and 18. One of them, Germaine Lindsay was Jamaican born but had moved to the UK aged just six months, the others were all British Pakistani and had been born in the UK. The coordinated attack struck a bus at Tavistock Square and tube trains at Aldgate, Edgeware Road and King's Cross during the morning rush hour on 7 July 2005, killing fifty-two people, including the four bombers. That all bar one of the terrorists were British born punctured the pervasive imagery of 'foreign' terrorists committed to a global programme of action. The imagery of the so-called 'enemy within' struck a profound chord in the populist press which was dominated by speculation regarding what could have 'gone wrong' to lead these young British men to become so dangerously radicalised.[59]

In his 2007 book *Urban Fears and Global Terrors: Citizenship, Multicultures and Belonging after 7/7*, Victor Seidler argues against what he sees as reductive and simplistic media and political commentary, stating that 'the questions they raise are complex and related to the complex dynamics related to issues of gender, sexuality and belonging as well as class and exclusion'.[60] He discusses the cultural politics mobilised in the press coverage which invariably sought to make sense of the attacks, and concurs with much of the media coverage that found connections between the 7/7 attacks and the wars in Iraq and Afghanistan. Seidler argues that the government's refusal to take public opinion about the war into account contributed to a set of circumstances in which young Muslim men, in particular, felt overwhelmingly dislocated and disconnected.[61] According to Seidler, this generation had a different relationship to the notion of 'home' than both their white, Anglo-Saxon peers and their parents; they are, he argues, 'uprooted from place, as if unable to identify with any space as their own'. Further, he claims that this disconnect makes belonging to a community via either religious or cultural identities significantly more appealing.[62] One of the central problems that this creates according to Seidler, is that it 'undermines' a sense of British identity and citizenship on account of the fact that identifying as British implies a level of complicity with military action against other Muslim communities.[63]

As the military action against Iraq was increasingly called into question, the British economy plunged into the deepest recession since the end of World War II. This came as a result of a global financial crisis sparked by the fallout from the collapse of the US investment bank, Lehman Brothers. With crises occurring around both the economy and self-determined foreign policy, the demise of New Labour seemed inevitable. Indeed, even its erstwhile champion Anthony Giddens admitted in 2010 that 'the era of Labour hegemony is over' and the 'New Labour project is dead'.[64] Nonetheless, when Gordon Brown called a general election in 2010, the outcome was far from certain. With no single party having enough parliamentary seats to form a government, several days of speculation ensued before a coalition government between the Conservatives and the Liberal Democrats was finally announced, with David Cameron taking on the premiership and Liberal Democrat leader Nick Clegg as his deputy.

Shortly after formation, the new coalition government instituted an austerity agenda of social and welfare cuts described by Yvonne Tasker and Diane Negra as 'consistently framed in terms of a language of toughness and austerity premised on supposedly masculine virtues'.[65] Contemporary cultural studies scholar Imogen Tyler is even more critical in her appraisal, arguing that the austerity project has not only exacerbated social and economic inequalities but has reignited a discourse of class politics that condemns unemployed and poor people for being a 'parasitical drain and threat to scarce national resources.[66] Tyler explains how, at the end of the period covered by this book, the 'chav' emerged as a new and particularly pernicious paradigm of social class. A consequence of increasing social inequalities, the 'chav' is unremittingly and consistently described in negative terms; while Tyler describes how the 'grotesque' imagery of the 'chav' mediates 'contemporary anxieties about sexuality, reproduction and fertility and "racial mixing"'.[67] Joe Bennett explains how the social vilification of the 'chav' utilises the choice rhetoric of neoliberalism as a mechanism for reinforcing the 'anti-poor rhetoric of politicians' and presents socio-economic inequality as a *consequence* of individual failure rather than as a systemic or structural issue.[68] In many ways, the election of David Cameron's Conservative government was the inevitable outcome of this moment. While 2010 provides a useful temporal marker, it is also a crucial political and cultural juncture in recent British history and one which was markedly removed from the buoyant and optimistic rhetoric that dominated culture and politics at the turn of the millennium.

British Cinema 1990–2010: From Crisis to Renaissance

In 1990 British cinema was in a dire state; just 60 films were produced and, despite occasional successes such as *Howards End* (James Ivory, 1992) or *Remains of the Day* (James Ivory, 1993), it was, Robert Murphy prophesied, 'a sickly plant unlikely to survive the millennium'.[69] While *Four Weddings and a Funeral* (Mike Newell, 1994) proved to be a surprise hit in both the domestic and international market in 1994, British film remained a rather niche corner of popular culture. Indeed, it was not until two years later with the release of *Trainspotting* and then *The Full Monty* that the renaissance in British cinema really got underway. In terms of volume, British cinema output has varied considerably over the twenty years from forty-seven domestic features in 1992 to 358 in 2010.[70] The types of production have evolved, too, with shifting ratios between domestically funded and produced films, those which are funded from outside of the UK but made in the UK, and those which are the outcome of co-funded co-production agreements with one or more partners. Therefore, while the number of domestic films fell between 1997 and 2004, there was a significant growth in co-productions shifting once more in the period from 2005–2008 due to policy changes that eroded the various tax-based initiatives around film production (BFI Yearbook, 2011).[71] The establishment of National Lottery funding for film production in 1995 was a key driver in enabling growth within an often-capricious environment. Although credited with facilitating a period of innovation and diversification in British film culture, the infrastructure through which the funding was allocated was regularly criticised for 'wasting' public money.[72] In 2000 the UK Film Council was established with a mandate to advocate for the industry, as Lisa Kelly suggests to 'professionalise' its processes so as to create a sustainable and durable business model.[73]

The largely favourable political environment of subsidies and tax incentives led to a productive era in British filmmaking from the middle of the 1990s onwards. The period was one of considerable diversity, with a number of genres and cycles such as horror, crime and gangster films becoming particularly abundant. Realist dramas continued to function as a generic mainstay, although they were, as David Forrest argues, shifting and evolving in terms of their form and style over the period and largely consumed within a limited domestic market.[74] At the other end of the spectrum, historical and heritage films remained commercially popular in both domestic and international markets, promulgating nostalgic and colonial-era images of Britain and Britishness. The majority of British films, however, were produced on significantly lower budgets and often, as Robert Murphy argues, suffered from a lack of distribution, exhibition and mainstream domestic audiences. In this regard, British cinema remains a niche genre, even within the domestic cinemagoing context.

The shifting patterns in British film production during this time raise questions that have been perennial to British film studies and its scholars about what exactly constitutes British film, to what extent this matters, and the role of British cinema in terms of producing and promulgating discursive constructions of British national identity in domestic and global contexts. Putting to one side the fact that the act of classifying and categorising films as 'British' is part of a broader discursive process through which ideas about national identity are enacted, there are a number of factors that are commonly used in order to ascertain whether a film is British. The 'criterion of selection' as Ian Christie argues, is far from being a neutral or self-evident entity, in so far as it is part of a longer historical process of identification.[75] Certainly, within this period, the relationship between national cinema and national identity is interesting for the ways in which British films 'draw on identities and representations already in circulation . . . but also produce new representations of the nation'.[76]

While this two-decade-long era is one in which British cinema became increasingly diverse, in terms of genre, style and economic composition, a narrative concern with masculinity was in evidence throughout. Film historian Andrew Spicer concludes that 'one of the most striking features of masculinity in contemporary British cinema is its heterogeneity and hybridity: the range of male types is much wider than before and the types themselves are more complex'.[77] One of the central questions which emerges over the course of the case study chapters is the extent to which this proliferation of masculinities is evidence of the kind of loosening of the performative and discursive codes of masculinity the likes of which Eric Anderson describes in his study on what he terms 'inclusive' masculinity.[78] In many ways, there is seemingly an increasing fluidity and mobility to discourses of masculinity towards the end of the period. In terms of cinematic representation, however, it would seem that these options are limited to specific moments and types of male characters and that, invariably, it is the more affluent and privileged characters who are able to exercise this right. For less socio-economically privileged male characters, masculinity remains tied to more traditional social practices and the homosocial, heteronormative hierarchies that they uphold.

The government interventions which had been crucial in revitalising the British film industry during the latter end of the 1990s and early 2000s were clearly successful and, as a result, tax incentives and government subsidies were gradually withdrawn. In 2004, for example, there was a 20 per cent reduction in funding for production and development, although a new fund aimed at providing professional training was established with the focus on maintaining the skills base for which the British film industry had become known. In addition to this, the scale and pace of change brought about by new digital technologies added a further layer of complexity to film policy during the 2000s, changing the economics of the industry and presenting significant challenges to policy makers according to the BFI report, *Film Policy in the UK 2000–2010*.[79] The global financial crash of 2008 consolidated the drive for efficiencies and a reduction in government grants for the film industry, and in 2009 the outgoing Labour government announced a plan to merge the BFI and the UK Film Council into one umbrella organisation. The then Culture Secretary Ed Vaizey revealed that the BFI would remain and subsume the work and role of the UK Film Council and it would seem that, at the end of the period covered by this book, the British film industry was once more facing a precarious and uncertain future.

Conclusion

Twenty-years is a considerable length of time, and to provide a comprehensive and holistic account would be beyond the scope of any singular project. My aim in this chapter has been to focus on some of the key social, political and cultural moments across the 1990s and 2000s, to explain the ways in which a specifically British idiom of postfeminist masculinity emerged during the time and to set up the case study chapters that follow. The locus of this introduction sets forward a foundational landscape upon which depictions of masculinity mirror the medial and wider cultural representations of the period; with the figure of the new man to the new lad in its inherent whiteness acting as an inheritor of post-imperial melancholia.

Notes

1 Larner, Wendy, 2000, 'Neoliberalism, Policy, Ideology, Governmentality' in *Studies in Political Economy*, Vol. 63, No. 1, pp. 5–25. Gill, Rosalind, 2008, 'Culture & Subjectivity in Neoliberal and Postfeminist Times' in *Subjectivity*, Vol. 25, No. 1, pp. 432–445. McGuigan, Jim, 2014, 'The Neoliberal Self' in *Culture Unbound*, Vol. 6, pp. 223–240. Rottenberg, Catherine, 2014, *The Rise of Neoliberal Feminism*, Oxford University Press, Oxford.

2   Foucault, Michel, 1978, *The History of Sexuality* (Vol. 1), Penguin, London, pp. 17–35.

3   Kimmel, Michael, 1987, 'Rethinking Masculinity' in Kimmel, Michael (ed.), *New Directions in Research on Men and Masculinity*, Sage, London. Easthope, Anthony, 1990, *What A Man's Gotta Do: The Masculine Myth in Popular Culture*, Routledge, London. Connell, R. W., 1995, *Masculinities*, Polity Press, Cambridge. Faludi, Susan, 1999. *Stiffed: The Betrayal of the Modern Man*, Chatto & Windus, London. Edwards, Tim, 2006, *Cultures of Masculinity*, Routledge, London.

4   Monk, Claire, 2000, 'Men in the 90s' in Murphy, Robert (ed.), *British Cinema of the 90s*, BFI Publishing, London, p 156.

5   Jeffords, Susan, 2012, 'The Big Switch: Hollywood Masculinity in the Nineties' in Collins, Jim, Preacher Collins, Ava and Radner, Hilary (eds), *Film Theory Goes to the Movies*, Routledge, London, p. 198.

6   See Claire Monk's 'Men in the 90s' for more information on genres and cycles.

7   Kimmel, Michael, 1987, 'Rethinking Masculinity' in Kimmel, Michael (ed.), *New Directions in Research on Men and Masculinity*, Sage, London, p. 121.

8   Neil, Calum, 2020, 'Masculinity in Crisis: Myth, Fantasy and the Power of the Raw' in *Psychoanalysis, Culture and Society*, Vol. 25, No. 1, pp. 4–17.

9   Connell, R. W., Hearn, Jeff and Kimmel, Michael, 2005, 'Introduction' in Connell, R. W., Hearn, Jeff and Kimmel, Michael (eds), *The Handbook of Studies on Men and Masculinity*, Sage, London.

10 Easthope, Anthony, 1992, *What A Man's Gotta Do! The Masculine Myth in Popular Culture*, Routledge, London, p. 1.

11 Connell, R. W., 1995, *Masculinities* (2nd edn), Polity Press, London, p. 47.

12 Ibid., p. 51.

13 Ibid.

14 Ibid., p. 15. Hearn, Jeff, and Morgan, Dave, 1990, 'Men, Masculinities and Social Theory' in Hearn, Jeff and Morgan, David (eds), *Men, Masculinities and Social Theory*, Unwin Hyman, London. Kimmel, Michael, 1987, 'Rethinking Masculinity' in Kimmel, Michael (ed.), *New Directions in Research on Men and Masculinity*, Sage, London.

15 Kimmel, Michael, 1987, 'Rethinking Masculinity' in Kimmel, Michael (ed.), *New Directions in Research on Men and Masculinity*, Sage, London, p. 9. Faludi, Susan, 1999, *Stiffed: The Betrayal of Modern Man*, Chatto and Windus, London. Clare, Anthony, 2000, *On Men: Masculinity in Crisis*, Arrow Books, London.

16 Nixon, Darren, 2006, 'I Just Like Working With My Hands: Employment, Aspirations and the Meaning of Work for Low-Skilled Unemployed Men in the British Service Economy' in *Journal of Education and Work*, Vol. 19, No. 2, pp. 201–217.

17 Edwards, Tim, 2006, *Cultures of Masculinity*, Routledge, London.

18 Skeggs, Beverley, 1997, *Formations of Class and Gender: Becoming Respectable*, London, Sage, p. 9.

19 McDowell, Linda, 2003, *Redundant Masculinities: Employment, Masculinities and White Working-Class Youth*, Blackwell, Oxford, p. 2.

20 Ibid., p. 3.

21 Ibid.

22 Edwards, Tim, 2006, *Cultures of Masculinity*, Routledge, London, p. 8. Similar claims had been made periodically. See Brittan, Arthur, 1989, *Masculinity and Power*, John Wiley & Sons, London, and also Tolson, Andrew, 1977, *The Limits of Masculinity*, Tavistock Publications, London.

23 Savage, Mike, 2011, *Moving On Up? Social Mobility in the 1990s and 2000s*, Resolution Foundation. https://www.resolutionfoundation.org/publications/moving-social-mobility-1990s-2000s/ (accessed 12 March 2019).

24 Major, John, 1993, Speech to Conservative Group for Europe, 22 April. http://www.johnmajorarchive.org.uk/1990-1997/mr-majors-speech-to-conservative-group-for-europe-22-april-1993/ (accessed 10 March 2020).

25 Gilroy, Paul, 2005, *Postcolonial Melancholia*, Columbia University Press, New York.

26 Macpherson, William, 1999, *The Stephen Lawrence Inquiry: Report of an Inquiry*. https://assets.publishing.service.gov.uk/government/uploads/system/uploads/attachment_data/file/277111/4262.pdf (accessed 20 October 2020).

27 Storry, Mike and Childs, Peter, 2016, *British Cultural Identities* (5th edn), Routledge, London, p. 1.

28 Dodd, Phillip, 1995, *The Battle Over Britain*, Demos, London, p. 3. http://www.demos.co.uk/files/thebattleoverbritain.pdf (accessed 20 October 2020).

29 Ibid.

30 'London Reigns' in *Newsweek*, 11 March 1996. https://www.newsweek.com/london-reigns-176148 (accessed 10 October 2020).

31 Giddens, Anthony, 1998, *The Third Way: A Renewal of Social Democracy*, Polity Press, Oxford.

32 Dodd, Philip, 1995, *The Battle Over Britain*, Demos, London. http://www.demos.co.uk/files/thebattleoverbritain.pdf

33 Levy, Jonah, 2010, 'Foreword' in Faucher-King, Florence and Le Galès, Patrick, *The New Labour Experiment: Change and Reform under Blair and Brown*, Stanford University Press, Stanford, CA.

34 Ibid.

35 Faucher-King, Florence and Le Galès, Patrick, 2010, *The New Labour Experiment: Change and Reform under Blair and Brown*, Stanford University Press, Stanford, CA.

36 Leonard, Mark, 1997, *Britain™*, Demos, London. https://www.demos.co.uk/files/britaintm.pdf (accessed 20 October 2020).

37 Ibid.

38 Ibid.

39 Ibid.

40 Kear, Adrian and Steinberg, Deborah Lynn (eds), 1999, *Mourning Diana: Nation, Culture and the Performance of Grief*, Routledge, London, p. 7.

41 Hey, Valerie, 1999, 'Be(long)ing: New Labour, New Britain and the "Dianaization" of Politics' in Kear, Adrian and Steinberg, Deborah Lynn (eds), 1999, *Mourning Diana: Nation, Culture and the Performance of Grief*, Routledge, London.

42 Ibid.

43 Leonard, Mark, 1997, *Britain*™, Demos, London.

44 Whelehan, Imelda, 2000, *Overloaded: Popular Culture and the Future of Feminism*, The Women's Press, London, p. 58.

45 Monk, Claire, 2000, 'Men in the 90s' in Murphy, Robert (ed.), *British Cinema of the 90s*, BFI Publishing, London, p. 158.

46 Alexander, Karen, 'Black British Cinema in the 90s: Going, Going, Gone' in Murphy, Robert (ed.), *British Cinema of the 90s*, BFI Publishing, London, p. 112.

47 Ibid.

48 Bhavnani, Reena, 2007, *Barriers to Diversity in Film: A Research Review*, UK Film Council. https://www2.bfi.org.uksites/bfi.org.uk/files/down loads/uk-film-council-barriers-to-diversity-in-film-2007-08-20.pdf (accessed 20 October 2020).

49 Ibid.

50 Ibid.

51 Gray, Clive, 2003, 'The Millennium Dome: Falling From Grace' in *Parliamentary Affairs*, Vol. 56, No. 3, pp. 441–455.

52 Walker, Alison et al., 2001, *Living in Britain: Results of the 2000/01 General Household Survey*, National Statistics Survey, HMSO, Norwich.

53 The fourth plane was en route to Washington but crashed in Pennsylvania after a number of passengers were able to overpower the hijackers and prevent the plane from reaching its intended destination.

54 Croft, Stuart, 'British Jihadis and the British War on Terror' in *Defence Studies*, Vol. 7, No. 3, p. 318.

55 White, Michael and Wintour, Patrick, 2001. 'Blair calls for World Fight Against Terror' in *The Guardian*, 12 September. https://www.theguardian.com/politics/2001/sep/12/uk.september11 (accessed 20 October 2020).

56 Noonan, Peggy, 2001, 'Welcome Back, Duke!: From the Ashes of 9/11 Rise the Manly Virtues' in *The Wall Street Journal*, 12 October. http://opin ionjournal.com/columnists/pnoonan/?id=95001309 (accessed 20 October 2020). See also: Brown, Patricia Leigh, 2001, 'Heavy Lifting Required: The Return of Manly Men' in *The New York Times*. http://www.nytimes.com/2001.10/28/weekinreview.ideas-trends-heavy-lifting-required-the-ret urn-of-the-manly-men.html (accessed 20 October 2020).

57 Jarvis, Lee, 2009, *Times of Terror: Discourse, Temporality and the War on Terror*, Palgrave Macmillan, London.

58 Croft, Stuart, 2007, 'British Jihadis and the British War on Terror' in *Defence Studies*, Vol. 7, No. 3.

59 Various front pages from the newspapers immediately after the attacks can be seen here: https://www.independent.co.uk/news/uk/home-news/77-bombings-how-the-papers-covered-the-news-following-the-attack-that-killed-52-10371523.html (accessed 20 October 2020).

60 Seidler, Victor, 2007, *Urban Fears and Global Terrors: Citizenship, Multiculturalism and Belongings After 7/7*, Taylor & Francis, London, p. 14.

61 Ibid.

62 Ibid.

63 Ibid.

64 Giddens, Anthony, 2010, 'The Rise and Fall of "New" Labour' in *New Perspectives Quarterly*, Vol. 27, No. 3, p. 32.

65 Negra, Diane and Tasker, Yvonne, 2014, 'Introduction: Gender and Recessionary Culture' in Negra, Diane and Tasker, Yvonne (eds), *Gendering the Recession: Media and Culture in an age of Austerity*, Duke University Press, London, p. ii.

66 Tyler, Imogen, 2013, *Revolting Subjects: Social Abjection and Resistance in Neoliberal Britain*, Zed Books, London, p. 8.

67 Tyler, Imogen, 2008, 'Chav Mum, Chav Scum: Class Disgust in Contemporary Britain' in *Feminist Media Studies*, Vol. 8, No. 1, pp. 17–34.

68 Bennett, Joe, 2013, '"*Chav-Spotting*" in Britain: The Representation of Social Class as Private Choice' in *Social Semiotics*, Vol. 23, No. 1, pp. 146–162.

69 Murphy, Robert, 2000, 'A Path Through the Moral Maze' in Murphy, Robert (ed.), *British Cinema of the 90s*, British Film Institute Publishing, London, p. 1.

70 https://stephenfollows.com/how-many-feature-films-are-shot-in-the-uk-each-year/ (accessed 20 October 2020).

71 http://www.bfi.org.uk/sites/bfi.org.uk/files/downloads/bfi-statistical-yearbook-2011.pdf (accessed 20 October 2020).

72 Caterer, James, 2011, *The People's Pictures: National Lottery Funding & British Cinema*, Cambridge Scholar's Press, Newcastle upon Tyne, p. 211.

73 Kelly, Lisa, 2016, 'Professionalising the British Film Industry: The UK Film Council and Public Support for Film Production' in *International Journal of Cultural Policy*, Vol. 22, No. 4, pp. 648–663.

74 Forrest, David, 2013, *Social Realism: Art, Nationhood and Politics*, Cambridge Scholars Press, Newcastle upon Tyne.

75 Christie, Ian, 2013, 'Where is National Cinema Today? (And Do We Still Need It?)' in *Film History*, Vol. 25, No. 1.

76 Higson, Andrew, 1995, *Waving the Flag: Constructing a National Cinema in Britain*, Clarendon Press, Oxford, p. 4.

77 Spicer, Andrew, 2000, *Typical Men: The Representation of Masculinity in Popular British Cinema*, I. B. Tauris, London, p. 184.

78 Anderson, Eric, 2009, *Inclusive Masculinity: The Changing Nature of Masculinities*, Routledge, London.
79 *Film Policy in the UK 2000–2010: An Overview*, UK Film Council. https://www2.bfi.org.uk/sites/bfi.org.uk/files/downloads/film-policy-in-the-uk-2000-2010-an-overview-2015-07.pdf (accessed 20 October 2020).

CHAPTER 2

Representations of Class, Crisis and White Masculinity in Postfeminist, Neoliberal Britain

Claims of a crisis in masculinity evolved to the point of being an almost ubiquitous feature of British culture throughout the 1990s and 2000s. Indeed, as sociologist and masculinity studies scholar Tim Edwards claims, the term became so commonplace within both academic and popular culture that it became frustratingly nebulous: 'the concept of crisis is used to incorporate a sense of panic or anxiety that on the one hand has already happened or on the other might happen, and it is applied equally to masculinity as a concept or to the experiences of men themselves'.[1] While concerns regarding a crisis of masculinity were particularly pronounced in the UK, America and Australia, I use this chapter to argue for the importance of understanding the cultural specificities of these discourses. The aim of this chapter is therefore to examine the ways in which discourses of crisis emerged and developed within the context of British culture in the 1990s and 2000s and the specific ways in which social class is used as a mediatory device for the representation cinematic narratives of crisis. This chapter is concerned with understanding the cultural, ideological and performative politics at play within a number of case studies and argues that what is significant about these images is not the question of whether there was a crisis of masculinity or not but rather the cultural and discursive work being done by these narrative claims being presented.

This chapter is not a debate about whether a crisis of masculinity existed or not; as Sally Robinson suggests, such an endeavour is rather a moot point – there is considerable evidence of the impact of cultural and economic change bought about by the combined forces of post-industrialisation and neoliberalism.[2] Rather, my interest is in understanding how and why crisis discourses should emerge at this particular moment in British history, and to examine the cultural politics mobilised in their cinematic representations. The secondary aim of this chapter is to investigate the idea of crisis as an intersectional phenomenon, drawing particular attention to the overwhelming cis-gendered whiteness of the representations of men in crisis in British cinema; to this end I use this chapter as a space in which to examine the ways in which class, race and age appear to augment cinematic tropes of crisis and their discursive function therein. Following literary scholar, Sally Robinson, I argue that white men have a specific relationship to the crisis phenomenon as a strategy through which they 'negotiate the widespread critique of their power and privilege' and that, as feminist film studies scholar Tania Modleski suggests, crisis narratives serve a patriarchal politics of consolidating the 'threat of female power by incorporating it'.[3] The case studies under discussion in this chapter demonstrate some of the ways in which class, age and whiteness are mobilised as mechanisms through which ideas of crisis are articulated, authenticated and then used in order to reassert the symbolic importance of traditional codes of masculinity.

I begin by developing a framework for understanding the crisis phenomenon as a material discourse, defining the characteristic and identifying the key issues in order to explore the ways in which crisis is mobilised as a cinematic device in the representation of masculinity. Having established the socio-political function of crisis discourses within the context of postfeminist, post-industrial, neoliberal Britain I move on to the textual analysis of four case study films, two from each of the 1990s and 2000s. Adopting a chronological structure for the close analysis of the four key texts enables a systematic appraisal of the ways in which cinematic representations of crisis manifested and developed over the period in response to the shifting cultural terrain in which they are both produced and consumed.

Focusing on *Brassed Off* (Mark Herman, 1996) and *The Full Monty* (Peter Cattaneo, 1997) from the 1990s, and *All or Nothing* (Mike Leigh, 2002) and *Archipelago* (Joanna Hogg, 2010) from the 2000s, I trace the evolution of crisis discourses over two decades. *Brassed Off* and *The Full Monty* are particularly useful for the way in which they connect with Cool Britannia, the other main cultural phenomenon of the 1990s – a period when British culture appeared to be on the precipice of substantial political and cultural change. I argue that *Brassed Off* presents something of a nostalgic eulogy for white, working-class masculinity that draws on cultural mythologies of embattled Northern mining communities to present its crisis narrative. The film is both explicit and sincere in evoking the spectre of the Thatcher government as being the progenitor of the crisis of working-class masculinity in particular. In this regards, and to borrow John Hill's terminology, I position *Brassed Off* as a 'delayed eighties film' in terms of form and style as well as in its discursive construction of masculinity and crisis. Focusing on the Grimley colliery band, the film offers a celebration of the traditions of white British, industrial, working-class male culture, mourning their demise and offering a nostalgic yearning for the deep fraternal bonds and the cultural community networks for the men in once vibrant industrial communities.

I position *The Full Monty* as a thematic counterpoint to *Brassed Off*. Despite similarities in terms of genre, theme, regional setting, and in the specific narratives of masculinity that both films rehearse, they are substantially different in the affective mobilisation of crisis. Where *Brassed Off* is characterised by a melancholic and melodramatic sentimentality, *The Full Monty* offers what Claire Monk terms an 'incongruous feelgood comedy' via a specifically postfeminist commodification of masculinity, arguing that comedy is mobilised in order to transform a crisis narrative into an endorsement of the entrepreneurial rhetoric of Blairite self-determination in which the male characters regain their agency, albeit temporarily, via the literal commodification of their bodies for the spectatorial consumption of the economically emancipated female audience.[4]

The pairing of *All or Nothing* and *Archipelago* is used to demonstrate the historical development of crisis discourses as a strategic mode of cinematic representation while also providing an opportunity to further explore the intersections of crisis, class and age. Much like *The Full Monty* and *Brassed Off*, *All or Nothing* and *Archipelago* broadly fit within or borrow from social realism. *All or Nothing* focuses on the day-to-day lives of a working-class family who live on a council estate in London. In many ways, *All or Nothing* is a typical Mike Leigh film; the narrative is episodic, the dialogue is often improvised and the cinematography offers the kind of cultural verisimilitude that has become his leitmotif. The male characters in *All or Nothing* are, in some ways, also typical of the kinds of masculinities found throughout Leigh's oeuvre: to varying degrees they are emotionally inept and drifting through life with relatively little direction or intent.

Archipelago is the second feature film by Joanna Hogg and it focuses on a very different demographic to the other case studies considered in this chapter. *Archipelago* is, like *All or Nothing*, a study of family dynamics, with a particular focus on the lived experiences and subjectivities of the male characters. The man in question in *Archipelago* is young and affluent, and his socio-economic privilege enacts a differently inflected idiom of crisis than the characters in the other films under discussion. Edward (Tom Hiddleston) is described by Hogg as in the midst of an existential 'quarter-life' crisis. Disenchanted by his well-paid career and looking for greater fulfilment, he quits his career working in 'the city' and plans to travel to Africa to undertake a period of voluntary work. The film focuses on the family as they spend a final holiday together before Edward's departure. As one of the few films outside of heritage drama to offer a sustained focus on upper middle-class masculinity, *Archipelago* is useful as a vehicle through which to explore the ways in which crises of masculinity intersect with and are mediated by both class and age.[5]

For their various points of distinction, these four films not only rehearse familiar narratives of masculinity as constituted by crisis but actively foreground the male characters and their problems as specific concern; each of them connects with a set of gender discourses that position men as disempowered, dislocated victims of postfeminist, neoliberal culture, while also bringing questions of tone, form and style to the fore. Characterised by a sustained and affective focus on male subjectivity and emotional interiority, these films actively engage in the discursive and cinematic construction of masculinity and crisis.

Conceptualising the Postfeminist Crisis of Masculinity

I conceptualise crisis as a material discourse that is adjacent to and informed by hegemonic masculinity.[6] I understand crisis discourses as having a performative function, employing Judith Butler's terminology to explain the ways in which the cultural phenomenon is brought into being by discursive systems of language and meaning.[7] In this respect, I follow a similar approach to Sally Robinson, who suggests that the process of 'naming a situation as a crisis puts into play a set of discursive connections and tropes that condition the meanings that [the] event will have'.[8] Foremost among the most significant discursive positions at play within the British postfeminist crisis of masculinity is that of the emancipated, empowered and independent woman, against whom the embattled, disempowered and dependent man is set. In this regard, crisis discourses dovetail with postfeminist culture, reproducing an implicit understanding that feminism has brought about a fundamental shift in the power structures of patriarchy in ways that have challenged white male power to the point of downfall.

Crisis discourses perpetuate a postfeminist narrative of second wave feminist goals as being accomplished, thus rendering contemporary feminist politics not simply redundant but actively damaging: feminism has been so successful that it is now men who are the disadvantaged victims of gender. That is not to say that crisis narratives necessarily proclaim a wholesale collapse of either patriarchy or the racialised power of whiteness, but that they mobilise a discourse that is emphatic in its insistence that male power has been irrevocably damaged. Writing in 1991, just as such claims of male disempowerment and crisis were becoming commonplace,

Tania Modleski argued that displays of male disempowerment were in fact a mechanism through which male power is actively consolidated.[9] Robinson takes this further suggesting that while discourses of crisis might appear to point to a 'trembling of the edifice of white male power . . . there is much symbolic power to be reaped from occupying the social and discursive position of subject in crisis'.[10] The textual analysis undertaken in this chapter aims to understand the ways in which cinematic narratives of crisis function to promulgate a postfeminist narrative of male victim-hood as a symbolic and recuperative strategy.

In a 2011 article for *The Public Intellectual*, feminist scholar Heather Tirado Gilligan argues that the phenomenon of masculinity in crisis has a historical lineage that can be traced back to at least the late nineteenth century and that there is a direct correlation between the emergence of crisis discourses and periods of economic instability.[11] While there were economic fluctuations in the period of 1990–2010 it is, I suggest, more productive to locate the crisis discourses of the era as emerging out of a specific culmination of cultural and social factors that are bound up with but more complex than being straightforwardly economically determined. In this way, the crisis of masculinity that dominated the 1990s and 2000s was a consequence of the broader cultural and ideological turbulence of gender politics and gender roles within the neoliberal, postfeminist and post-industrial context.

As already suggested, the crisis narratives of the 1990s and 2000s were predicated on the notion that there has been a fundamental subversion of patriarchal of power and politics and that this has been to the detriment of men. As gender scholar Stephen Whitehead points out, there is a prob-lematic disparity between crisis narratives and empirical evidence that suggest that inequalities of contemporary gender relations continue to endure and that affluent, white, cis-gendered, heterosexual men continue to retain, and in some instances expand, their already disproportionate cultural and economic power.[12] Whitehead's study illustrates the ways in which performative displays of crisis function to obfuscate the enduring existence of white patriarchal power relations via the appropriation of disempowerment and devaluation.

The traditional industries that had sustained generations of working-class communities were increasingly obsolete within the post-industrial service sector around which Britain's role in the global economy was constructed. Their decline and eventual collapse left significant swathes of male unemployment in the regions that had once sustained them. The collapse of the industrial economy and resulting unemployment of working-class men served to undermine the connections between work and masculinity that had endured since the Industrial Revolution. As the sociologist Arthur Brittan observed in 1989, a loss of power in the workplace equated to men having 'lost their sense of gender certainty, their sense of place in the world'.[13] The transition from a manufacturing, industrial economy to a knowledge/service economy was driven as much by the cultural economics of neoliberalism as it was by technological innovation. Crucially, these emergent industries did not simply replace their predecessors either in terms of the types of jobs offered or into the geographical areas left vacant by the industrial sector. Moreover, they changed the nature of work and employment at a fundamental level, demanding radically different skillsets from that of the industrial workplace, leaving the men who had expected to follow their fathers and grandfathers into industry with limited prospects and a lack of skills that were incompatible with the demands of the emergent service sector.

The seemingly indubitable consequences of post-industrialisation served to legitimate the discursive construction of white, working-class British masculinity as being irrefutably in crisis, a situation that emphasised a popular perception that the post-industrial workplace was inherently advantageous to women. Within the world of work at least it seemed that feminism was no longer needed; while many argued about the enduring gender pay gap and a lack of women in the most senior business and executive roles, the pervading populist stance (as articulated in *The Full Monty*, *My Name is Joe* and *Brassed Off* amongst others) was of female advance at the expense of men.[14] Perspectives such as these perpetuate a simplistic and flawed but pervasive populist narrative that overlooks the extent to which women's participation within the workplace has been predicated on part-time, menial, low-paid and insecure employment, and that fails to take into account the fact that men continue to hold the greater number of managerial positions and make up the majority of managing directors and company Chief Executive roles, and that fails to take into account the enduring pay gap.[15]

Despite its common use in the 1990s and 2000s, the term 'crisis of masculinity' remains unhelpfully amorphous and imprecise. This is in part because the crisis of masculinity is a complex and multifaceted phenomenon involving numerous components and intersections that are individually variable and always contextually contingent. Tim Edwards attempts to rationalise the complexities of crisis discourses by creating a taxonomy of seven key areas that he sees as central components in the crisis discourse – health, education, crime, sexuality, work, family and representation – which correspond with dominant clusters of empirical and statistical evidence from the era and are helpful in terms of identifying themes and connections across media and culture. Inevitably some of these themes are more prevalent than others in cinema: work, family, crime and sexuality are foregrounded in several films whereas debates about health and education are less commonly addressed within narrative cinema, although they still form part of the broader cultural context in which these cinematic representations are circulating, providing a useful guide to understanding the cultural context within which the representations circulate.

Like Edwards, masculinity scholars Anthony Easthope and Sean Nixon have posited connections between the crisis of masculinity that developed during the late twentieth century with the rise of neoliberal consumer culture;[16] all three discuss the ways in which neoliberalism functioned to commodify masculinity and the male body creating an increasingly diverse and consumer-driven representational palette of masculinity across a broad range of cultural forms from fashion and advertising to film and television.[17] This proliferation of more diverse configurations of masculinity inevitably created points of tension and contradiction, leading Michael Kimmel to conclude that contemporary men have the option to choose between 'ambitious breadwinner and compassionate father, between macho seducer and loving companion, between Rambo and Phil Donahue'.[18] Further, as Nixon noted, drawing on Steve Neale's foundational essay on the politics of male objectification, the use of visual codes of representation that had been traditionally associated with the sexualised objectification of femininity in representing masculinity foregrounded further instabilities.[19] By inverting the established patriarchal and heteronormative privilege of the gaze whereby men were positioned as the active viewer (as opposed to the passive object) the objectification of the male body not only afforded symbolic power to an assumedly heterosexual female viewer but also brought the homoerotic potential of the male body to the fore. According to Neale such representations compelled the foreclosure of the homoerotic potential on behalf of both the objectified male and the male viewer.[20]

The Full Monty is perhaps one of the clearest examples of this dynamic in action, whereby the men's (relative) willingness to subject themselves to objectification is motivated by the need to raise money to benefit Gaz's (Robert Carlyle's) access to his son; moreover, comedy is used to render the process of objectification as defiantly not homoerotic, a reason why, I suggest later on, the relationship between Guy (Hugo Speer) and Lomper (Steve Huison) had to be contained at the margins of the narrative rather than being privileged as a central storyline. In the case studies that follow, I explore the symbolic importance of crisis as the defining characteristic of masculinity in the period, examining the ways in which tropes of crisis develop over the twenty years with which this book is concerned and how they are enmeshed within the postfeminist, neoliberal and post-industrial context of the time. Further, these case studies enable a detailed analysis of the intersectionalities of crisis by drawing specific attention to the ways in which race (or whiteness, more specifically), class and age augment narratives of dispossession and disempowerment.

Cinema, Crisis, Melodrama and the White, Working-Class Man: *Brassed Off* and *The Full Monty*

Issues of social class have long been a thematic concern within British cinema; kitchen sink and social realist films focused predominantly on narratives of working-class characters while, at the other end of the spectrum, stories of the wealthy and aristocratic classes predominated in heritage cinema and costume drama. As such, it is unsurprising that class should remain a key site around which narratives of male crisis were negotiated.[21]

As a cinematic coupling, *Brassed Off* and *The Full Monty* are productive examples for examining the ways in which masculinity was mediated during one of the most significant cultural junctures of the 1990s. Released in 1996 and 1997 respectively, *Brassed Off* and *The Full* Monty straddled the years of Cool Britannia, the political shift from a Conservative to a New Labour government and the attendant debates about British national identity that were discussed in Chapter 1. Described by Paul Dave as a 'coda' to the long-running miner's strike of 1984, *Brassed Off* tells the story of the fictional Grimley colliery which, having been saved from closure in 1984, is once more under threat.[22] The film is sincere in its social critique and unambiguous politics, and explicit in its critique of Margaret Thatcher who is held personally responsible for the destruction of the once proud industry.[23] *Brassed Off* is invested in the affective and psychological traumas of its disempowered men and in this way it offers a form of eulogy for the white, working-class, industrial man and an imagined past in which his patriarchal and racial authority was unquestioned, absolute and intact. Where John Hill describes *The Full Monty* as a 'delayed 80s film' I suggest that it is a more appropriate description of *Brassed Off*.[24] Unlike Hill, I see *The Full Monty* as a product of its time, appearing to be more in keeping with the cultural optimism of Cool Britannia and the upbeat style and optimistic rhetoric of earliest years of Blairite Britain. Furthermore, *The Full Monty*'s comedic rendition of a tale of male unemployment not only eschews the affective sincerity of *Brassed Off* but does so through using irony, comedy and postmodern nostalgia, the last of which is used to particularly good effect via a soundtrack that relies on a seventies soundtrack provided by a number of prominent stars from the era.

Despite their distinctions, both films foreground the emotional interiority of male experience, mobilising the psychosocial malaise of their male characters as a vehicle through which to present and mourn a prefeminist past and the cultures and communities to which they belonged. While both films see the loss of male power as damaging, they mediate it differently. *The Full Monty* explicitly cites female (over) empowerment as a significant contributory factor in men's problems; further, it uses comedy as a device through which to negotiate any particular poignant or emotional moments in the film. For example, when Dave (Mark Addy) first sees Lomper in his broken-down car, he helps to get the engine running again; apparently unaware of the pipe that is at the top of the passenger window, he tells the younger man what he needs to buy to sort the problem out. Berating Lomper for his lack of gratitude, Dave ambles off back up the hill to join Gaz, then, realising his mistake, he turns and runs back to the car where he manhandles Lomper out of the gas-filled vehicle, only to throw him back in again momentarily when Lomper moans at his rescue.

A direct comparison can be made between *The Full Monty* and *Brassed Off* in their respective bailiff narratives. As I will demonstrate shortly, *Brassed Off* shows the devastation and humiliation of repossession, emphasised by Phil (Stephen Tompkinson), who is seen alone on the one remaining wooden chair in an otherwise empty house. This compares with *The Full Monty*, when the bailiffs turn up at Gerald's (Tom Wilkinson's) house; as he tries to reason with them, Gaz, Dave, Lomper, Horse (Paul Barber) and Guy burst in to the living room, naked but for their underpants, and the shocked debt collectors beat a hasty retreat, leaving the men laughing over their (temporary) victory. Although both films are described as comedies they are both clearly influenced by social realism and drama, and *Brassed Off* explicitly contextualises its drama within 'real-world' issues, politicising its narrative through the use of captions containing statistical information about the impact of the mine closure programme on working-class men. *The Full Monty* opens with a 1970s promotional film of Sheffield, which heralds the city's many attributes, boasting of the 90,000 men employed in producing the world's finest steel as evidence of 'a city on the move!' The critique is more implicit as the image from the film fades to black and a caption transports the viewer from the 1970s to the present day; the vibrant and energetic scenes of film are replaced by the silent, empty space of the derelict factory floor.

Foregrounding nostalgia so explicitly in the opening frames, both films clearly connect the decline in industry with the disempowerment of working-class men in post-industrial culture, although the means by which they mediate these are very different. The men in *The Full Monty* come to realise that they are the ones who have to adapt to the demands of the new economic order, even where this appears to compromise their masculine identities by requiring the literal commodification of their bodies as sexual objects for consumption by a financially independent female audience. In this respect, *The Full Monty* appears to draw on the dictates of neoliberal entrepreneurialism as a mechanism through which male pride, if not male power, can be regained; moreover, the film uses comedy to augment its tale of male disempowerment in order to make it more commercially appealing. Questions of male pride are equally foregrounded in *Brassed Off* – the colliery band represents the last source of pride for the men who are on the verge of both social and economic redundancy.

There are many reasons for classifying *Brassed Off* as a delayed '80s film, not least for the way in which it adopts the sincerity of cultural and political critique found in social realist films from the 1980s. Where *The Full Monty* uses comedy to augment its tale of male disempowerment in order to make it more commercially appealing, *Brassed Off* is unabashed in its political intent and the spectre of Margaret Thatcher looms large over the film.[25] At the heart of *Brassed Off* are the characters of Danny (Pete Postlethwaite), the proud conductor of the colliery band, and his son Phil. Phil is central to the film's political critique. He is presented as the character most severely impacted by the decade-long decline of the mining industry. As a husband and father of four young children he is keenly aware of the need to fulfil his role as a breadwinner, providing for and protecting his wife and their young children whilst also doing his best to make his father proud. However, the debts incurred during the 1980s strike remain punitive, and no matter how hard he tries Phil is unable to stabilise his financial situation, much to his wife Sandra's (Melanie Hill) frustration.

Our first glimpse of Phil is at the beginning of the film when we join the men as they come up out of the pit at the end of the working day, in a scene filled with smiles and the hubbub of friendly banter as they make their way from the lift shaft to the showers. The next time we see Phil, he is in his living room, trombone in one hand as he waits for his dad to collect him for band practice. Sandra is on the sofa, holding their youngest daughter and surrounded by the older children; she has her back to him as they talk about the looming closure of the pit. The combined drudgery of poverty and young children is etched onto Sandra's face, her exhaustion and frustration are evident in her demeanour as she tries to persuade Phil to vote against his principles and accept the redundancy deal offered by the mine's owners. Standing behind Sandra and the sofa, facing the camera, the same sense of embattled exhaustion is writ large across Phil's face. He shifts from side to side and either buries his hands in his pockets or fiddles with the fixings on his trombone and his wide blue eyes skip quickly and nervously around the room. Clearly uncomfortable with his wife's suggestion, he cautions her against voicing this opinion within the community, in which the memories of the decade-long fight for the survival of the mine were keenly felt. Phil is presented as naïve and well-meaning, lacking the kind of savvy or streetwise attitude that he needs in order to navigate the family's predicament. Phil's clothes further create this innocence, his oversized green coat and a red beanie giving the appearance of a child waiting to grow into his new clothes. His infantile position is further emphasised when he climbs aboard his father's push bike to go to band practice. Much in the manner of a child hitching a 'backie' from a friend, Phil wobbles precariously, trying to balance himself and his trombone as his father pedals up hills and streets to get to the practice hall.

With few options remaining, bailiffs knocking on his door, and the pit's fate looking increasingly doomed, Phil is running out of optimism. Similarly to the men in *The Full* Monty, he turns to an entrepreneurial, neoliberal sideline, resurrecting his alter ego, a clown named Mr Chuckles who performs at children's parties. The incongruity of the depressed and downbeat Phil dressed as a clown further emphasises his desperation and his compromised dignity. Clad in a brightly coloured, satin romper suit teamed with striped socks, a pink-spotted bow tie and ridiculously oversized red shoes that create a cumbersome and ungainly walk, he wears a curly, red, nylon wig with blue bowler hat and his face is traditionally, if clumsily, painted. The overall effect makes him look both ridiculous and pathetic. Much like Phil, Mr Chuckles is presented as incompetent and bungling; he messes up simple tricks and fluffs the lines in his jokes. Where Phil, however, is presented as foolish and naïve but well-meaning, Mr Chuckles enables a nascent malicious streak to find a voice.

Mr Chuckles only makes two appearances in the film, but both are significant in terms the constructing the melodrama of conflicting demands on the disempowered and entrapped character.

During his first appearance, Mr Chuckles is performing at a children's party. The young audience is seated on the floor, looking expectantly as their party entertainment makes his noisy arrival. Beginning his performance with enthusiasm, Phil is every bit the clown, his mannerisms are exaggerated and his voice loud and excited; however, the performance is quickly punctured when things start going wrong. He messes up his first card trick and just about rescues it by turning it into a joke, but when a young boy volunteers to be the assistant who smashes a watch with a hammer, Phil's inability to communicate and control the stage has disastrous consequences. The young boy fails to wait for the instructions and is overcome with enthusiasm, immediately smashing the cloth containing the watch with relish. Phil has to intervene. While trying to remain in persona as Mr Chuckles, Phil's despair and resignation are clear, voice flat he states, 'you were meant to wait!' The camera cuts to Phil bidding the host farewell at the end of the party; cash in hand he prepares to set off home. As he reaches the front door of the house, the client (Jacqueline Naylor) asks him 'so, what do you do for a day job?' He turns to her, lips tightly drawn and replies 'miner, love. You 'eard of them? Going extinct, like the dinosaurs!' There are several instances in *The Full Monty* where dinosaurs and extinction are alluded to, with Gaz proclaiming that within a few years men as a species will be 'extincto!' and will only exist in 'special zoos'.

Mr Chuckles's second appearance is rather more ominous, taking place shortly after Sandra and the children have left, the bailiffs have removed all of his belongings, and Danny is lying, seriously ill, in hospital. Taking to the stage at the local harvest festival, the performance goes wrong almost instantly; the children greet him with stony stares while Mr Chuckles proclaims to the children that he doesn't know much about harvest festivals, but he does have a story about God. A cut from Phil to the line of parents assembled at the back of the staged area creates an ominous atmosphere suggesting that something is about to go very wrong. Against the backdrop of the church filled with offerings from the children's harvest festival, Mr Chuckles delivers his vitriolic monologue and the camera switches from a wide shot to a closer one:

> So God was creating man. And his little assistant came up to him and he said: 'Hey, we've got all these bodies left, but we're right out of brains, we're right out of hearts and we're right out of vocal chords.' And God said: 'Fuck it! Sew 'em up anyway. Smack smiles on the faces and make them talk out of their arses.' And lo, God created the Tory Party.

The parents rush to the stage to retrieve their children who are seated, mouths open, aghast at the sacrilegious outburst. Having been removed from the stage and forced up the aisle of the church, Mr Chuckles/Phil finds himself standing next to an-almost-life-sized figure of Jesus Christ, smiling beatifically into the distance. Turning from the figurine back to the

Figure 2.1 *Brassed Off:* Phil's performance as Mr Chuckles
breaks down at the harvest festival

congregation, who are still reeling from shock, Mr Chuckles continues to give voice to Phil's insipient anger and frustration. He continues:

> What's He doin' eh? He can take John Lennon. He can take those three young lads down 't Ainsley Pit. He's even thinking of taking me old man. And Margaret bloody Thatcher lives! What's He sodding playing at, eh?

This outburst occurs as a result of the pressures facing Phil and the disparity between the requirements of his performance as Mr Chuckles and the increasingly desperate situation in his own life; further, this scene precipitates Phil's breakdown and the emotionally charged speech in front of the children in which his frustration and anger can no longer be contained. Claire Monk sees this outburst as an expression of 'problems of the post-industrial male in a "feminized" society'.[26] This speech implicitly positions Margaret Thatcher as emblematic of the feminised culture that Monk refers to; Thatcher's explicit refusal to claim the term feminist for herself is inconsequential to Phil in this moment. The fact that Margaret Thatcher was a female prime minister was in itself enough to make her an obvious target for those who were alienated by the political ideologies with which she was associated. Claiming the position of victim on behalf of all miners negates the misogynistic implications of the speech, evoking both gender and class politics in order to legitimate Phil's claim. Taking place within a context in which Phil's circumstances are understood by the viewer augments this scene with pathos; Phil's railings are not presented as symptomatic of his misogyny but as a result of the predicament in which his finds himself.

Having been pushed to the limit – losing his job and his family and discovering that his father has a terminal illness – Phil loses all hope. Harry (Jim Carter) calls the band members together for one last performance, a hospital vigil for Danny. Phil joins his colleagues as they congregate under Danny's window, each of the men dressed in their band uniform and adorned with their mining lanterns. The performance is punctuated by several close-up shots of Phil, tears rolling down his cheeks as he plays for his father, and doubtless grieves for Sandra and his children. When a nurse comes to advise the group that Danny has woken up, Phil makes his way inside to see his father. The scene is one that draws attention to the codes of emotional reticence that were central to traditional working-class masculinity; far more is left unsaid than is spoken but the emotion between the two is palpable, particularly as Phil stands in the doorway, bidding his father good night.

The scene cuts back to the darkness of the silent pit after Phil takes his leave. Two security guards are on patrol and the camera focuses on their confusion as they catch sight of something in the distance. As the men realise what it is they can see, the image cuts to a ground-level shot which looks up at the brightly coloured costume of Mr Chuckles before cutting again to a closer shot, showing Phil struggling as he attempts to hang himself. Although Phil is rescued, and the incident provides an opportunity for him to have a more open conversation with his father, Phil's suicide attempt is the culmination of his personal crisis, a response to the impossible demands of being a successful son and father within the postfeminist, neoliberal context. Phil's suicide attempt provides a mechanism for father and son to reunite at the hospital, where Phil breaks down. The two men share a warm scene of emotional honesty and openness which is distinguished for being one of the only moments of deep communication in the film. This scene is also crucial in allowing Danny to reconstruct himself as Phil's father and not *just* as his conductor.

As the conductor of the colliery band, Danny is not just Phil's father, he is also the symbolic patriarch of the community of Grimley; he is a timeless icon of respectable working-class masculinity with a stoic sense of duty. Danny is proud, fastidious, fierce, passionate and honourable; his pride in the traditions of working-class masculinity that are represented by the colliery band is evidenced by the care that he takes over his uniform – a symbol of the masculine heritage that is under threat. Danny is a familiar trope of northern working-class masculinity; his ailing health is an allegory for the decline of the traditions of industrial masculinity that, historically, had been passed on from father to son. The decline of the coal mine and the traditional communities of men that they supported are allegorically equated to Danny's own ailing health. The fate of the mine (and by implication that of the whole community of men that the mine supports) is metaphorically linked to Danny's illness; both the mine and the man are seemingly moribund. When the band return home after a victorious semi-final performance in a national brass band competition, their euphoria is cut short as they learn that the pit is being closed down with immediate effect. At this point, Danny is also overcome by his illness. The colossal frame of the once mighty bucket-wheel excavator dominates the skyline as Danny collapses to the ground in the shadows of the soon-to-be-obsolete pit. This sequence is typical of the pathos with which Herman treats the story of the disenfranchisement of working-class men. By linking the destiny of the male space of the coal mine with that of the local chief patriarch, the film's allusion to the death of certain forms of working-class masculinity is explicitly articulated.

Danny is taken to hospital where he begins to regain his strength even though the ultimate prognosis remains poor. He rallies when the men from the band take up their instruments on the pavement outside his hospital room, managing to abscond and catch up with the band at the Royal Albert Hall. In Danny's absence, Harry takes on the role of conductor; standing at the front of the stage, Harry gives a passionate performance as the band play the 'William Tell' Overture. Mid-way through, Danny appears at the rear of the stage and watches with pride as the music reaches its crescendo. The scene cuts from the stage to show the band, seated and awaiting the results. A number of be-suited white men line up on the stage for the announcement, which is delivered by a particularly well-spoken member of the group. The camera is positioned in amongst the band members as they are pronounced the champions, capturing the moment of joyous celebration as they jump up and hug one another. The next image shows the band members lined up with the judging panel, with the trophy posi-tioned to the left of the frame. Danny walks across the stage towards the trophy to rapturous applause. However, instead of accepting the trophy, Danny acknowledges the head judge before taking to the podium to deliver an impassioned and climactic speech of refusal. He explains that the act of declining the prize would be more newsworthy than winning it, and thus would ensure that his message was heard more widely than it would have been had they accepted the award. Moreover, this functions as an unequivocal rejection of neoliberal individualism; Danny's refusal to accept the trophy explicitly reframes the importance of the collective and the communal over the ambition and desire of the individual.

Danny goes on to address the audience, describing the devastation wrought by the political programme of post-industrialisation, explaining that 'over the last ten years this bloody government have systematically destroyed an entire industry. Our industry. And not just an industry, our communities, our homes and our lives.' Using one continuous close-up for this segment of the speech creates an intimacy of proximity; Danny delivers this speech directly to the viewer, holding their gaze and almost challenging them to look away. He goes on to tell the story of the Grimley miners who had also just been made redundant due to the closure of their pit. 'Most of these men', he explains, 'lost the will to win a while ago, a few of them even lost the will to fight . . . but, when it comes to losing the will to live, to breathe . . .', he pauses, overcome with emotion, looking over at Phil, his son who had tried to commit suicide in the face of mounting financial desperation. In using the victory speech to return the film to the explicitly political theme of the betrayal of working-class men, the film reiterates the position of white, working-class men as besieged, beleaguered and betrayed by 'progress'. Danny's speech reinforces the idea of white, working-class masculinity as culturally derogated, suggesting to the audience that had they been talking about whales or seals 'you'd all be up in arms, or sommat . . .'; he continues 'but they're not, they are just ordinary, common garden, decent, honest human beings, not one of them with an ounce of hope left . . .'. By explicitly locating the men as victims and as occupying a more lowly status than many animals, Danny's speech makes an impassioned plea for the recuperation and reaffirmation of the idealised image of a traditional form of masculinity that is white and working class as something worth protecting, Declining the title becomes a symbolic victory of the derogated working-class man over the authorities that are responsible for the death of male industries and the communities of men that they supported.

Having declined the prize, Danny and his band exit the grandeur of the Royal Albert Hall to a standing ovation and the image cuts to scenes of bittersweet celebration aboard their coach as they take in the sights of London. This final scene returns to a number of narrative threads, some of which are more readily concluded than others. Phil and Sandra are the first couple featured in this scene; even though Sandra is uncertain about any permanent reconciliation between herself and Phil, there is a renewed warmth to their relationship which provides a degree of optimism for their future, even if it does not offer full resolution. The camera tracks down the bus gangway, coming to rest on Gloria (Tara Fitzgerald) and Andy (Ewan McGregor); Gloria, the interloper, who found herself on working for the pit management before resigning her job and donating her salary to fund the trip to London, receives a squeeze on the shoulder from Harry as he makes his way along the bus. Delighted at her acceptance within the community her narrative is further consolidated when she shares a passionate kiss with Andy. While Andy's employment prospects might be in doubt, his romantic future appears to be secure.

As they travel through London, Danny commands the band to play Elgar's patriotic anthem, 'Land of Hope and Glory'. As they play, a caption appears in the centre of the frame, juxtaposing the patriotic connotations of the music with a stark reminder that since 1984, nearly a quarter of a million jobs have been lost due to the closure of 140 pits. These captions puncture what is otherwise a gently optimistic or 'feel-good' conclusion to the film, relocating it firmly within the realms of politically committed commentary on masculinity and male cultures at the end of the twentieth century. The credits begin to roll while the band continues to play, the camera pans around the bus, focusing on key individuals before settling in to a wider shot of the ensemble, with Danny at the centre back. The camera slowly zooms in to a closer shot of Danny, whose proud and defiant face stares back at us, slowly fading to black. Drawing the film to a close in this way provides Herman with the means of avoiding the inevitable and unpalatable aftermath of the competition which would see Grimley pit close, the men made redundant and Danny's inevitable death.

As I have shown, *Brassed Off* refuses to couch its melodramatic narrative of male malaise within postmodern or comedic terms. In this way, its explicit positioning as an anti-Thatcher film is one of the ways in which it harks back to an older tradition of social realism, being both sincere and serious. In this way, and certainly in comparison to *The Full Monty*, *Brassed Off* continues many of the themes and political concerns of its '80s counterpoints and frames them in a similar vein.

The changing economic and industrial infrastructure of nineties Britain had, as my discussion of Brassed *Off* has shown, extensive ramifications for working-class men, and these were unremittingly negative. Where these male characters are also fathers, the implications of unemployment and poverty were represented in films of the period as having even graver consequences than for single men. A central preoccupation of British cinema of the 1990s was the narrative negotiation of the impact of post-industrialisation upon men, and as such a recurrent thematic concern was the 'social problem' of unemployed men. However, where both *Brassed Off* and *The Full Monty* recount similar tales of post-industrial malaise and its implications for working-class men, the style and aesthetics of the films are very different, with *Brassed Off* offering a more backward-looking eulogy for the post-industrial white working-class man who remains pre-occupied with negotiating the ongoing spectre of Thatcher and the impact of her government's policies on the men.

Where *Brassed Off* is an explicitly politicised treatise on the crisis of white, working-class masculinity within the post-industrial, neoliberal culture, *The Full Monty* offers a rather different approach to similar issues. Although *The Full Monty* does draw on the heritage of social realist cinema in terms of setting, cinematography and an emphasis on natural-ism and cultural verisimilitude, its political agenda is not necessarily less explicit than *Brassed Off* but it is framed differently, and this is undoubt-edly a decision driven by commercial awareness.[27] *The Full Monty* is a film of and from a specific moment in British cultural history; released in August 1997 it capitalised on the wave of cultural optimism that was created by the election of Tony Blair's New Labour and it circulated in a culture where The Spice Girls were the embodiment of a specifically British form of postfeminist 'girl power'. The film is described by Claire Monk as a 'post-patriarchal' film that appears to come out of 'a strategy of commercial and political pragmatism intended to multiply and maximise audience appeal'.[28] Whereas *Brassed Off* offered a straightforward, nostal-gic eulogy for the white, working-class man, *The Full Monty* draws on the dictates of neoliberal entrepreneurialism as a mechanism through which male pride, if not power, can be regained. *The Full Monty*'s success came about partly because it chimed with dominant popular discourses around the state of contemporary British masculinity, but it was also able to adopt a fashionably ironic, irreverent and comedic approach to these narratives of male disempowerment. While the film draws on cinematic traditions of social realism – the focus on working-class, everyday experience, the use of regional locations, and so forth – it rejected the sentimentality and sincerity seen in *Brassed Off*, and in this way it is more in keeping with the cultural tone of the post-1996 Cool Britannia moment.

The detrimental effect of unemployment on industrial working-class men is the main narrative motivation for *The Full Monty*. The central narrative concerns a group of unemployed steelworkers, who, for a variety of reasons, end up forming a Chippendales-esque troupe. The comedy arises from the disparity between these 'normal' men and the sculpted and oiled bodies of the professional strippers; indeed, much of the comedy in the film comes from the hilarity of the respectively skinny, fat, saggy, hairy 'natural' masculinities on display. Where *Brassed Off* featured an ensemble of male characters but only fully developed the narratives of Danny, Phil and Andy in any detail, *The Full Monty* uses the broader character line-up to rehearse a number of different forms of male crisis.

From early on the film is preoccupied with the idea that the emergent postfeminist, post-industrial economy has proven so advantageous for women that it has led to a full-scale inversion of gender roles – an anxiety referred to via the implicit suggestion of role reversal that is central to the male stripper narrative. Having unsuccessfully attempted to steal a girder from the derelict steel factory, Gaz, Dave and Gaz's son, Nathan (William Snape), are making their way through the town when they pass the working men's club. They are met by a long and rowdy queue of women; a poster informs them that a male strip club is performing and that the working men's club is, for this evening at least, only open to women, an aberration on which the older men are quick to alight. When Gaz discovers that Dave's wife, Jean (Lesley Sharp), is going, he is indignant on his friend's behalf, even though Dave points out that Jean earns her own money so is able to do as she pleases. Gaz devises a plan to try and retrieve Jean from the show. He and Nathan break in to the club via a window in the men's cloakroom, a place he assumes will provide safety and sanctuary for their mission. We are placed alongside Gaz as he peers through a crack in the door to see the room full of raucous women, laughing, shouting and demanding that the men remove their clothes. Shuddering, Gaz is forced to hide in a cubicle when Jean and two of her friends make their way into the men's toilet. Once more Gaz spies on the women, this time through the broken lock of the cubicle door. Cutting from point-of-view shots to close-ups of Gaz, crouched down, peering through the hole, Gaz witnesses the whole scene which, much to his disgust, culminates in one of the women standing up to use the urinal. For Gaz this is an incursion too far; when the women return to the hall, Gaz emerges from the cubicle, shock written across his face, he stares after them, struggling to process all that he has seen and heard.

Reflecting on the incident at the job club the following day, Gaz gives voice to the film's central premise, explaining that 'when women start pissing like us, well, that's it, we're finished, Dave. Extincto!' The extent of such fears of women's ascendancy become apparent when one of the men puts forward a theory that these events are the result of 'genetic mutations' that are turning women into men. Holding court, Gaz spells out what he sees as being the future for men: 'A few years' time and men won't exist, except in a zoo or summat! I mean, we're not needed no more, are we? Obsolete . . . dinosaurs . . . yesterday's news!'

The assembled men look to each other and to their surroundings in the dreary governmental space of the job club, each of them struggling to find anything positive with which to counter Gaz's apocalyptic vision.

When Dave interjects that men were the reason that the women were in the club – 'You've got 1,000 women, each paying £10 to see them . . . that gives you, well, lots, very lots!' he observes, working out that there is the potential to earn a significant amount of money – they jokingly agree that it might be worth thinking about. While each of the men is unemployed they are all shown to be affected differently. As the main protagonist in putting the troupe together, it is Gaz's predicament that we are presented with first. From the botched attempt at stealing a steel girder to the arrest for indecent exposure, Gaz's failings as a father are continually referred to in the film, and critique comes from a variety of sources. For example, when Reg (Bruce Jones) auditions for a place in the troupe he declines the offer of a cup of tea because his children are waiting outside and it would be inappropriate to bring them in. Reg's comment inadvertently brings Gaz's judgement as a father into question because Nathan has been involved in the entire audition process. Gaz's inadequacies are further highlighted by the contrast between his and Mandy's (Emily Woof's) home. Mandy and Nathan live with her new partner, Barry (Paul Butterworth). Although he is not Nathan's biological father, Barry is clearly able to fulfil the financial and hegemonic demands of fatherhood and is thus presented as preferable to Gaz; he lives in a large, modern detached house with well-kept gardens and a car in the driveway. Even Nathan reluctantly he prefers his stepfather's clean and warm house over Gaz's, which is messy and cold.

Further aspersions are cast on Gaz's propriety as a father from a variety of formal institutions; children's services refuse to allow him to see his son after they discover that Nathan had been present at rehearsals, and the police also question Gaz's aptitude for fathering on the same basis. Mandy's application for sole custody of Nathan is successful on the basis that Gaz is no longer able to provide for their son when he has access and has also defaulted on his maintenance obligations. Despite moments in the film where Nathan is disappointed by his father's actions, the two of them remain close, they hug, walk arm in arm and share many warm moments. Their closeness is exemplified in the scene in which Nathan insists upon using his savings to pay the deposit for the hire of the working men's club for the performance. Nathan's desire to see his father succeed is doubly motivated: he wants his father to raise the money needed to be able to see him again, a demonstration of how important the father/son relationship is to him, but it also functions crucially as an expression of Nathan's belief in his father.

As Gaz's best friend, Dave is quickly recruited to the cause, despite significant misgivings. Dave's position in the film is established early on.

When Gaz discovers that Dave's wife Jean is attending the strip show, he is aghast. Dave reluctantly admits that his wife is the financial breadwinner in their relationship; his embarrassed explanation that 'it's her money innit? She can do what she likes' carries a resentful undertone, demonstrating the deleterious effects of economic gender inversion not only for Dave but for unemployed working-class men more generally. This, however, is not the main focus of Dave's anxieties; from the earliest moments in the film, attention is drawn to Dave's weight. First, he is unable to fit through the window to assist Gaz in his attempt to retrieve Jean and then Gerald scoffs at the thought of him (large) and Gaz (little) 'prancing about, widgers out!' Dave is acutely aware of his body, and when the men first strip to their underwear he begs his friends not to look and not to laugh at him. Dave's bodily insecurities provide a rare moment of gender reflexivity in the film. While he is perusing a magazine the other men start commenting on the figures of the women and joking about whether it is possible to ever have 'too big tits?' The fact that his friends seem to feel so free to make jokes and judgements about the women in the magazines strikes a chord with Dave who reminds them that they will soon be in a similarly vulnerable position and 'we'd better hope our audience is more forgiving!' The camera shows the shocked reactions of the men who, until that moment, appear not to have thought about the possibilities. Dave's bodily insecurities cast him as the character who is most sensitive or in touch with his emotions, but this is used as a mechanism through which to signify his emasculated status.

From early on in the film Dave is haunted by the idea that one of Jean's workmates fancies her and, without having asked his wife, Dave concludes that there can be no way in which she finds him attractive – a 'truth' that he holds on to despite the fact that she attempts to initiative sex and affection on a number of occasions. The film conflates Dave's lack of body confidence with his emasculation, emphasising the point non too subtly by making him sexually impotent and unable to sustain a sexual encounter with his wife. Shortly after this Dave leaves the flowery, feminine and romantic world of the shared bedroom and absconds to the garden shed – a symbolically masculine space. In the cramped confines he begins to wrap cling film around his girth in an attempt to lose weight, following a discussion with Gerald. Once happy that his body is appropriately contained, he rips open a Mars bar and begins to eat. The gendered codes in this sequence are particularly notable for being among the more nuanced and thoughtful within the film. Dave's fight to attain his ideal masculine body necessitates an engagement with 'feminine' spa-inspired practices, and thus locating this struggle within the manly domain of the garden shed

Dave attempts to limit the ways in which his masculinity is compromised. A similar strategy takes place when he opts for a Mars bar – a chunky chocolate bar that is invariably advertised as a 'manly' chocolate bar.[29] In this way, Dave reclaims his masculinity from the act of comfort eating, which is more commonly associated with women. The scene is both poignant and yet comedic; Dave's struggle to wrap the cling film around himself in the tight space of the shed and the subsequent image of him sitting in the dark, shiny plastic wrapped tightly around his torso in the futile hope that he will acquire the perfect body by the time of the show, is bittersweet. Where it is Nathan's belief in Gaz which facilitates his restoration and validation, it is Jean who fulfils this function for Dave. Having found the leather thong that the men wear in their performance, Jean assumes that Dave is having an affair. Devastated at this prospect, Jean confronts him just before the final show; incredulous at the thought, Dave is finally able to confess his anxieties. Jean reassures Dave, and her pride at seeing her husband on stage offers the final validation. She catches his shirt as he throws it into the audience, holding it to her face and performs an exaggerated swoon, emphasising her desire for her 'big man'.

While Gerald, Horse, Lomper and Guy are less prominent characters, each is used to articulate some aspect of male insecurity. Gerald has failed to tell his wife that he has lost his job, maintaining a pretence of going to work until such time as his house and belongings are repossessed. Having been a manager in the steel works, Gerald is initially presented as someone who is superior and snobby but who comes to learn that old hierarchies of masculinity do not convert to the post-industrial world of unemployment. The character of Horse is more marginal than Gerald and has a considerably less developed narrative. This is particularly interesting, given that the film was initially conceived of as having an entirely Black British line-up and is, I suggest, evidence of the ways in which crisis is appropriated as a mode of masculinity that is preserved for white men and mobilised as a performance of disempowerment in ways that further marginalise men of colour and consolidate white masculinity as the predominant cultural concern. Horse's anxieties only come to light towards the end of the film, just before the final performance, when it is revealed that Horse is concerned about the size of his penis. In this short scene the film alludes to enduring racist mythologies of the sexualized, Black, male body and the potential damage of such discourses on Black British men. A similar form of performed inclusivity is evident in the representation of Lomper and Guy, whose relationship is gestured to on two occasions in the film, once when they have escaped from the police raid of the warehouse and again when they are shown holding hands at Lomper's mother's funeral.

The development of their relationship, however, is relegated off-screen; in this regard, the film might be understood as offering little more than a performance of inclusivity which ensures that the heterosexual men who have closer connections to hegemonic masculinities (as Gaz does, being a father, as Dave does, being married, and as Gerald does, being married and having a more middle-class lifestyle) retain narrative dominance.

That the film is only able to offer limited narrative resolution (for Dave, via the reconciliation with Jean, and for Lomper and Guy, who have formed a successful relationship, as far as we are aware) is indicative of the way in which the precarity of post-industrial, postfeminist masculinity is conceived in the film. The final image of the film, the freeze-frame of the men's celebratory 'full monty' moment is typical of the ways in which the film negotiates the contradictory mores of postfeminist gender cultures. On the one hand, the men might be seen as having succumbed to a reconfigured sexual economy in which their male bodies are commodified and objectified. On the other hand, however, there is a suggestion that they have managed, temporarily at least, to reappropriate the gender subversion of postfeminism to their advantage and in so doing restored Gaz's position as the rightful postfeminist patriarch, securing a victory over both his ex-wife and her new, middle-class partner.

Both *Brassed Off* and *The Full Monty* perpetuate the performative politics of the postfeminist crisis of masculinity by conflating discourses of female empowerment with male disempowerment. The style and presentation of crisis narratives seen in the two films appear to correspond with broader cultural shifts; with the election of Tony Blair and the concurrent wave of Cool Britannia, it seemed that Britain had finally broken away from the established discourses of nation, politics and culture as the post-industrial cultures of neoliberalism consolidated. In this way, *Brassed Off* is, as I have shown, a film that is more retrospective than *The Full Monty*; it is a continuation of a strand of British cinema which is working through the consequences of Thatcherism on working-class men; its political sincerity is out of step with the kinds of ironic and playful double entanglement of postfeminist culture that is seen in *The Full Monty*.

Intersections of Class and Age:
All or Nothing and *Archipelago*

Like *Brassed Off* and *The Full Monty*, *All or Nothing* and *Archipelago* are familial dramas whose narratives are driven by male characters who are in crisis, in some way. In my analysis of *All or Nothing*, I suggest that the central character of Phil (Timothy Small) develops many of the themes seen in the previous section; while the men in *The Full Monty* and *Brassed Off* rail against what are seen as the injustices of post-industrial, post-feminist culture, Phil appears resigned to his marginality. In this regard, I suggest that *All or Nothing* is useful for understanding the ways in which narratives of the social and economic disempowerment of masculinity developed in the early years of the twenty-first century. *Archipelago* focuses on a different demographic group in its story of an affluent middle-class family coming together for a final holiday before the son, Edward (Tom Hiddleston), goes travelling to Africa. Edward's existential crisis, and his negotiation of it, are useful as a means of understanding the ways in which both age and class intersect with gender and race in the cinematic construction of masculinity in crisis.

Released in 2002, *All or Nothing* is, in many ways, a 'typical' Mike Leigh film, it uses an episodic narrative and focuses on the loosely interconnected lives of three families, living on a rundown estate in south-east London; it uses the familiar iconographical palette of concrete tower blocks, dingy corridors and passageways, and drab, scruffy interiors to construct the cultural habitus and living spaces of the lower working-class characters. The film features three families who live in the same tower block. Taxi driver Ron (Paul Jesson) lives with his unemployed, alcoholic wife and their daughter, Samantha (Sally Hawkins). Single mother Maureen (Ruth Sheen) works at a local supermarket and does other people's ironing to bring in extra money. Maureen is notable as the sole source of optimism within the film; even when she discovers that her daughter, Donna (Helen Cocker) is pregnant by her violent boyfriend (Daniel Mays) she remains upbeat, offering to accompany her to medical appointments and promising love and support instead of remonstration. It is, however, the Bassett family who are at the heart of the film and whose function is to create the narrative thread which connects the disparate families. Penny (Lesley Manville) works alongside Maureen at the supermarket while Phil, her partner, is a self-employed mini-cab driver, hiring radio space from the same company as Ron. They live with their children, both of whom are in their late teens and significantly overweight. Daughter Rachel (Alison Garland) works as a cleaner and at an old people's home; she is quiet, unobtrusive and unassuming. Rory (James Corden), her brother, is unemployed and seemingly content to spend his days on the sofa, watching television; Rory is aggressive and rude, and his standard response to questions and conversation is a snarled 'fuck off!' Phil is the character at the heart of the film; despite his apathy and inertia, it is his character who drives the narrative forward and it is his character who I will focus on in more depth, arguing that he is, in many ways, a character who emerges as a result of the cultural transformations that the men in *Brassed Off* and *The Full Monty* were fighting against. In this regard, I suggest that Phil can be thought of as the inevitable next step in the trajectory of post-industrial working-class masculinity.

Where the men in *The Full Monty* and *Brassed Off* were seen to be suffering as a result of the desecration of the industries that had supported generations of men, the men in *All or Nothing* are presented as existing within a hermetically sealed environment with neither history nor heritage and no obvious future to fight for. In addition to the main characters, *All or Nothing* features a number of more minor male characters who are also all, in some way, defined by being in crisis. Among these characters are Craig (Ben Crompton), who carves the letter 'S' over his heart as testament to his (unrequited) love for Samantha; Harold (Timothy Bateson), the care-home worker who expresses his interest in Rachel in clumsy and often inappropriate ways; and Ron, the heavy-drinking, accident-prone cab driver. The three main male characters of Rory, Jason and Phil are developed in more detail. The two younger men are both aggressive, quick to take offence and to retaliate verbally, and in Jason's case, physically. Jason sees himself as a dominant alpha male in the tower block, he wears designer labels like Nickelson and Lacoste teamed with gleaming white trainers as he swaggers around the area. He threatens anyone who dares to cross, question or even look at him, as the hapless Craig found out. Upon discovering that his girlfriend, Donna, is pregnant, Jason loses his temper, threatening and verbally abusing her as she is sitting on the stairs, naked but wrapped in a duvet. After walking out on Donna, Jason proceeds to pick up Samantha and the two of them end up en flagrante on the front seat of his car, the young girl naïvely unaware of what had taken place between him and Donna and dismissing his aggression as playful. Maureen cautions her daughter against Jason, trying to warn her of his violent and bullying behaviour. It is left to Maureen to literally push the larger man out of the door as he remonstrates with Donna; she succeeds, leaving him unable to do anything more than punch and kick the door while screaming profanities, but she also knows that the reprieve is almost inevitably temporary.

Rory, like Jason, is presented as physically and psychologically aggressive; he whines and wails when Penny enquires about his job hunting, yelling 'just fuck off! I'll get a job when I want one! Now, fuck off!' In this regard Rory shares much in common with other young men in Leigh's work; he is, as I have described elsewhere, 'quite literally a time bomb waiting to explode'.[30] As an older man and a father, Phil's character negotiates and articulates his personal sense of crisis very differently; where Jason and Craig might be described as explosive in their outbursts, Phil is

the opposite; characterised by a quiet, bewildered incongruity, Phil struggles to engage with other people. Despite his apparent inertia, Phil is the
pivotal character in the film; it is his experience that forms the basis of the
narrative, and it is through his character that viewers are encouraged to
understand the film and its central characters.

In many ways, the character of Phil might be seen as offering a natural
continuum of the hopeless alienation described in my analysis of *Brassed
Off* and *The Full Monty*, where various male characters are described as
having given up, having lost hope and having nothing left to fight for.
Whereas the men in *Brassed Off* and *The Full Monty* angrily remonstrate
against losing their breadwinning status, Phil and his unemployed son,
Rory, appear resigned to their dependant status, relying on Penny's supermarket wage as the family's main source of income. While *All or Nothing*
does not present an explicit causal link between male unemployment and
emotional or psychological crisis, and nor does it seek to position men as
victims of a feminist conspiracy and female advantage, the connections
are certainly implied. Phil's inability to get up in the morning, his lack of
engagement with other people and his surroundings, and his perpetually
semi-vacant, slack-jawed expression are all potential indicators of depression, which mask his inner reflexivity and frustration and are, undoubt-
edly, the result of his unemployed status.

In many ways, Phil's job as a taxi driver plays on his sense of transience
and alienation while his languid persona and the slowness of his movements are at odds with the perpetual motion of ferrying various passengers
around London. As a driver, Phil is continually at the periphery of his
client's lives, literally and metaphorically, a status that is emphasised in
shots where Phil is seen observing his clients via the rear-view mirror. In
mediating Phil's connection with his clients, the mirror also functions as
a physical manifestation of the emotional and psychological barriers that
pervade Phil's relationships with other people. Phil remains impassionate
and aloof as he watches a parade of passengers pass through his cab; from
a drunk man railing against his treatment by women, to a group of rowdy
schoolchildren, and a lone widower, en route to lay flowers on his wife's
grave. While Phil might appear detached throughout these interactions, his
continual desire to watch his clients through the mirror corresponds to the
Jungian idea of the mirror as a mechanism through which the viewer is able
to project onto the object of their interest, and thus give rise to empathy,
relation and understanding, something demonstrated when Phil allows one
of his fares to leave without paying because he feels sorry for him. Despite
this apparently latent empathic drive, Phil remains predominantly defined
by his apathetic, and almost apologetic, disengagement with his family.

The Bassett family are initially introduced individually, suggesting their disconnect from the beginning; we see both Rachel and Penny in their respective workplaces, Rory fighting with other unemployed lads from the estate, and Phil in his taxi, ferrying various clients around as they go about their lives. The first time that we see the family together is particularly interesting in terms of understanding Phil's character. Penny and Rachel are already home when Phil arrives, clutching three dozen long-life bread rolls that he has accepted from passenger in lieu of a tip. Penny and Rachel are in the cramped kitchen when Phil joins them; clutching the rolls carefully, Phil examines his haul as he explains their backstory to his wife and daughter. During this exchange Rory is in the living room, lying prone on the sofa, watching television. When Phil greets his son with a gentle ''ello son!' he is met with little more than a grunt in return, but when Penny begins to recount Rory's altercation to her husband she receives a barrage of abuse, culminating in him yelling at her to 'Fuck off! Just fuck off!' In a rare two-shot of the couple, Penny turns to her husband, her eyes pleading for support in dealing with their wayward son, but instead of backing up his wife Phil remains silent, before turning away to hang up his coat, leaving Penny staring after him, her frustration palpable. Phil's movement in this scene also sets up the character, he is slow and ponderous, and his shoulders are rounded and hunched as if they are weighted down. Having put his coat away he remains in the small hallway for several seconds, head bowed, almost leaning against his coat for support; he brushes his hair out of his face, staring at the floor as if contemplating his own impotence and inaction but unable to break the stasis.

The next shot shows the family seated together for their evening meal in the first of two supper-time sequences. The atmosphere is tense as the family sit eating, physically together but emotionally distant. Phil is the one to break the silence, making small talk about his day, commenting first on the cost of fuel and then recounting the story of an elderly passenger who only needed a lift for one street. When Phil explains that he charged the man a reduced rate, Penny is unimpressed, berating her husband and telling him that he should have done it for free. Throughout this sequence, Phil's eyes dart about and he brushes his hair back from his face, almost nervous of his wife. He listens intently as Penny asks their daughter to accompany her on a walk; when her request is gently rebuffed, Phil summons his courage and suggests that he could take his wife out for a drink. She is clearly unimpressed, her mouth drawn in a tight line, she barely conceals her resentment and irritation at the proposition and offers nothing more than a curt 'No!' by way of response.

Penny's hostility towards Phil might be understood as the result of resentment built up over years of having to carry both the emotional and financial burden for the family with little support, or even input, from her partner. Whether she desires it or not, Penny is the head of the Bassett family, not only by virtue of the fact that she earns a higher wage than her husband, but because she is, as she explains near the end of the film, the one who does all of the household chores, and the administration and organisation associated with them; from doing the food shopping and washing, to maintaining the family budget, the responsibility of emotional and domestic labour falls to Penny alone and this is seen as creating unhappiness and resentment for Penny as much as it is for Phil. Where Phil is rendered symbolically impotent via his emotional turmoil and introspective resignation, Penny is more obvious in her unhappiness, which is borne out of years of low-paid, hard work with little practical or emotional support from her husband. While Penny and Phil are very different people, the distinctions between them are literalised in the film; Phil's lumbering and overweight physique dwarfs that of the diminutive Penny, his dark, lank hair and unshaven face contrast with her fair complexion. Where Phil's movements are slow and cumbersome, Penny zips nimbly through the London traffic on her push bike. The couple's clothing is also used to illustrate their differences too; Phil's wardrobe is dominated by dark but muted colours, creased shirts and an old-looking, battered leatherette jacket, whereas Penny's is much lighter. In contrast with Phil's dishevelled, crumpled shirts, Penny's clothes are crisp and neat; where Phil is seated astride an armchair, legs and arms sprawled out, Penny is, once again, contained and confined. Unlike many of Leigh's episodic films, *All or Nothing* uses a clear three-part narrative structure to take us on Phil's narrative journey and ultimate restoration. The sequence begins when Phil picks up a French lady called Cécile (Kathryn Hunter), who needs to go from South London to the West End; laden down with a large piece of art work that she is collecting for a colleague, Cécile begins to question Phil about his life. Their conversation is intercut with images of Rory who, having played football with some of the other lads on the estate, collapses, struggling to breathe. Unaware of the events, Phil and Cécile continue their journey into the West End, sharing their insights on their relationships with their variously troubled sons. Having dropped Cécile in Bloomsbury, Phil turns off his radio and his mobile phone and heads to the open spaces of the Kent estuary in search of isolation and reflection. The peaceful ambience of the sequence is at odds with the variety of awkward and tense silences that have gone before it. Here the close-up shots of Phil's forlorn face are interspersed with much wider shots, which serve not to dilute the intensity of emotion but rather to emphasise the alienation and isolation of the character. Without an epiphany, or any sense of what his next steps will be, Phil turns back from the water and turns towards home. When he regains connectivity, Phil discovers what has transpired in his absence and rushes to the hospital where he finds Penny, Rachel and his sleeping son. His first glimpse of Rory is through the internal window; a nurse lets him in. As he walks round the bed, taking in the surroundings of the room, Penny watches him, her contempt barely disguised. Examining the machinery in the same slow way that he did the rolls at the beginning of the film, Phil begins to explain his delay, but he is quickly rebuffed and dismissed by Penny as 'pathetic'. Unimpressed at his disappearance and by his fatalistic explanation of events, Penny continues to scold Phil at their son's bedside; unable to meet her gaze, Phil hangs his head. Hearing the argument rouses Rory who opens his eyes briefly and pleads 'leave it out, mum, stop 'avin' a go at 'im!' Heartened by this, Phil goes to his son; standing over him at the bedside he starts chatting, then, much to Penny's dismay, he suggests that the family go away together: 'when 'e's better, the four of us. Disney World!' In this moment, Phil is redeemed to an extent, being positioned as a sympathetic and caring, if hapless dreamer while Penny, for all of her forebearance, is positioned as the relentlessly nagging and hard-to-please harridan.

While O'Sullivan describes the narrative events of Rory's heart attack and Phil's disappearance as 'arbitrary', I would suggest that it is a familiar dramatic device in which illness, accident or death function to bring disparate families together; in this way, Rory's hospitalisation, coming at the same time as Phil's moment of reflection, expedites the final stage of narrative resolution.[31] Leaving Rory in the hospital, Phil, Penny and Rachel make their way through the hospital; Phil places his hand on Penny's shoulder, only for her to shrug it off. Silence pervades the journey home. Mid-shots of each of the characters locate them in their individual and disconnected emotional bubbles. Once home, Phil opens a beer and sits on one of the chairs in the living room, while Penny stands in the doorway waiting for the kettle to boil, Phil and Rachel attempting to assuage her guilt at leaving Rory. Phil offers her a lift in the morning and proceeds to outline his renewed enthusiasm for work, describing how he plans to 'start early, finish late, weekends . . .'. Unable to tolerate the conversation Penny moves from the sitting room into the adjacent dining space, forcing space between the couple that emphasises the bad feeling and disconnect between them. Once more, his attempts to make amends fall on stony ground, as years of resentment come to the fore for Penny who can no longer hold it back. She berates Phil's sudden decision to 'be like [a] normal person' and get up early, dismissing his naïve plans to go to Florida, telling him 'it's about getting by, week in, week out, it ain't about 'olidays, it's about getting by, it ain't a game'. She then blames Phil's family for Rory's inherited heart condition and, when Phil tells Rachel to call him on his mobile, Penny unleashes another furious tirade, mocking him for not having it on during the day. Bemoaning her inability to switch off because she is the one responsible for everything, Penny pushes Phil to answer the question of where he had gone and why he had turned his phone off. He is, he replies, 'sick, sick of everything'. His answer hangs in the air as the image switches from him, to Penny, and back to him again. Finally, Phil is able to give voice to the issues that have been bothering him; breaking down, he asks Penny whether she loves him or not, in his longest exchange with her Phil proclaims 'you've not loved me in years, you don't like me, you don't respect me, you talk to me like I'm a piece of shit!' The tension in the scene is magnified by the framing used for the shots of Phil; in contrast to the lighter mid-shots of Penny, Phil is in the darkness of the sitting room; where she is upright, Phil is hunched over, unable to contain the emotion that he has been holding in for years.

In a reprieve from the intensity of the scene, Penny goes to find tissues for Phil and ends up having a conversation with Rachel who gently agrees with her dad; kissing her daughter on the head, Penny returns to Phil. Phil has now regained some composure and is upright in his chair, the two of them reconcile in an intense close-up, in which they reaffirm their love. Phil's renewed emotional honesty is seen as key in bringing about the family reunion because it forces Penny to acknowledge where she is at fault and, in turn, allows him to regain the respect he felt he had lost. The image cuts to the following morning when the reunited couple visit Rory in hospital, Phil is clean-shaven, his hair is washed and his clothes fresh; he regales the family with the tales of his early morning success at work. Confirming the new start for the family, Penny and Phil are seated side by side, making eye contact and joining in as the family laugh together. The final shot of Phil shows him looking adoringly at Penny, while she in turn gazes upon her children, a thoughtful but inscrutable expression on her face. The final shot of the film sees the family united, offering what seems to be a more optimistic and certain resolution than either *Brassed Off* or *The Full Monty* were able to offer.

Despite focusing on the very different lives of a middle-class family who have come together for a final holiday before Edward leaves for an eleven-month sojourn to Central Africa, *Archipelago* has a number of similarities to Leigh's portrayal of the Bassett family in *All or Nothing*. In this final section of the chapter, I will use *Archipelago* as a text through which to analyse the intersections between class and crisis, drawing attention to key connections and points of distinction between this film and *All or Nothing*. The sound of birdsong begins over the black screen of the opening credits, immediately signalling something other than the typical urban milieu of the social realist film; the opening image is of a large canvas covered in thick oil paint. The yellow, orange and brown tones suggest the beginning of a landscape that has yet to be realised. A large house and wooded copse frame the canvas, while the dusky pink skyline suggests that it is early evening. To the fore of the shot, the arm of the artist works, blending and mixing his image. The artist remains anonymous until the shot changes; cutting to a wider frame that lasts for several seconds, it reveals a male artist, his back to camera as he looks out at the coastal landscape. The next image is of the artist cycling down a narrow lane away from the camera, the painting tied to his back. The birdsong that, thus far, has been a continuous soundtrack is interrupted by the low thrum of an approaching Chinook helicopter; cyclist and aircraft travel towards one another and, as they meet, the shot cuts to show two women outside a small hangar, clearly waiting to meet someone. As the passengers disembark, Edward breaks away from the queue to greet the women.

The trio, it transpires, is revisiting family holidays on the idyllic island of Tresco in the Scilly Isles, a trip that David Forrest describes as using 'the holiday and its accompanying familial structure, to explore notions of rupture and alienation'.[32] The film features five main characters: Edward, his mother, Patricia (Kate Fahy), sister, Cynthia (Lydia Leonard), the young chef (Amy Lloyd) who they have hired to cater for them during the trip, and Christopher (Christopher Baker), a local artist who is teaching Patricia to paint. The primary focus on interpersonal dynamics within an upper middle-class family means that Christopher and Rose are less developed in comparison to the characters and interpersonal relationships between Edward, Cynthia and Patricia. While each of them brings their own problems to the film, it is Edward's so-called 'quarter-life crisis' that propels the narrative. Having resigned from his well-paid job in banking, Edward plans to travel to Africa and do voluntary work with young people, an experience that he believes will give his life the meaning and purpose that it currently lacks. While Patricia is clearly angry with and anxious about her husband's failure to materialise on the island, she negotiates the situation independently and with limited support from anyone else. Cynthia, on the other hand, is a more volatile character with a keenly defined sense of right and wrong and a firm perspective on social hierarchies and relationships. She cautions Edward on several occasions for being 'too friendly' towards Rose on account of the fact that she is being paid to do a job and 'it's probably quite nice, going away on paid holidays'. When Edward offers to help Rose in the kitchen Cynthia is scornful of what she sees as her brother's impropriety. Although the cause of Cynthia's emotional fragility is never revealed, Forrest suggests that it is the result of 'unspoken personal trauma that manifests itself in angry outbursts to both brother and mother'.[33]

The opening ten minutes of the film establish the family dynamic as affectionate and warm. In contrast to the profanity-strewn arguments of the younger characters in *All or Nothing*, the bickering between Cynthia and Edward is good-natured, with the former berating her brother for 'being so bloody nice all the time'. Despite the apparently amiable beginnings, as the relationship between Cynthia and Edward develops it becomes clear that it is fractured and, at times, fractious. In *Archipelago*, much like in *All or Nothing*, the dining table is a space of confrontation and tension. During the first meal that the family shares a discussion about Edward's intended Africa trip develops. Edward and Cynthia are seated next to each other and their mother is across the table, an empty seat offering a reminder of their father's absence. The setting of the table reinforces the middle-class status of the family, with red and white bottles of wine having replaced the cans of lager and glasses of cola that adorned the Bassett's table. Unlike in *All or Nothing*, there is no television in the room and, whereas the Bassetts sit largely in silence, eating their food while watching the television, ensconced in their private disconnect, the emphasis in *Archipelago* is on discussion and communication. The topic of discussion for this first mealtime sequence is Edward's decision to resign from his (assumedly) well-paid job in 'the city' in favour of travelling to Africa to undertake voluntary work. Edward speaks first in the scene; his tone is defensive as he attempts to pre-empt his sister's antipathy; cautioning her against calling it a gap year, Edwards's opening gambit establishes the timbre of the discussion. Responding with deliberate passive aggression, Cynthia tells her brother that what he is doing is 'wonderful, it's really great' but berates him for doing it at his age, suggesting 'of course, you could have done it a few years ago, and then you wouldn't be so out of step with your generation!' Cynthia delivers her opinion on her brother's lifestyle choice while looking straight ahead and continuing to eat her dinner. Edward on the other hand puts down his cutlery and stops eating, and fiddles with the stem on his wine glass, indicating his infuriation. Cynthia continues in her passive aggressive style to compliment her brother on his 'wonderful' and 'excellent' choice, and proclaims 'I am happy for you, you know, that you can be so cavalier about your future, it's a luxury and I think you are making and excellent choice!'

Figure 2.2 *Archipelago*: Edward discusses his future plans

Much like Penny in *All or Nothing*, Cynthia appears to be invested in the importance of work and financial security to a greater extent than her male relative is; she sees Edward's decision to leave the security of his career to head out into the unknown as indicative of immaturity. Although at this early stage of the narrative Edward remains certain about his plans and clear about his motivation, his reaction to Cynthia's admonishment is similar to Phil's reaction to Penny when she launches into one of her critical tirades. Like Phil, Edward stares down at the half-eaten food on his plate, unable to make eye contact or even engage with his sister, his lips pursed and jaw tense as he plays with his wine glass. It is Patricia who steps in to Edward's defence – she reproaches her daughter, reminding her that Edward actually does have a job and that his decision is 'not a luxury and is anything other than cavalier!' Cynthia remains defiant, staring straight ahead and refusing to meet her mother's gaze or to engage with her; Edward turns towards Cynthia, but remains tight-lipped and tense, playing with the stem of the wine glass while Patricia fixes a steely stare onto her daughter, the tension clear in her stiff shoulders and taut body language. With this, the scene draws to a close, as abruptly as it began, setting into motion the tension that will shape the remainder of the film.

The cinematography in this sequence becomes a familiar visual trope of the film; a long depth of field creates dual focal points in the shot, many of which are balanced between two rooms. In this instance, the dining table around which the family is gathered is in the foreground while the kitchen is at the rear of the shot, just in focus enough to see Rose flitting about as she prepares dinner. The effect of this technique during this particular scene seems to be to emphasise Cynthia's personality. In the scene immediately preceding the dinner-time argument, Cynthia admonishes Edward for being 'too friendly' with Rose; she pointedly reminds her brother, and viewers by association, that Rose is not a friend nor family member, but is staff, and therefore there is no need to offer help or to befriend her. Thus, the framing used during the argument scene functions to underscore the hierarchical difference between Rose and the family.

As Edward's relationship with Cynthia continues to deteriorate over the course of the film, he draws closer to Rose. Edward spends more scenes with Rose than with any other character; indeed, that Edward chooses one of the two upper 'servants'' rooms, and next door to Rose, suggests the potential affinity. The morning after the dinner-time argument, Edward is the first of the family to wake up, though we had seen Rose working long after the family had gone to bed and then rising and going to the shops before they awoke. Many of the scenes shared between Edward and Rose take place in the kitchen and, much like the conversations in *All or Nothing*, those between Edward and Rose are mundane, and punctuated as much with laughter as they are with silence. Rose explains to Edward the different ways of cooking lobster while he leans against the kitchen worktops, smiling and watching her work; his body language during this scene is markedly different from those in which he is engaging with his sister. Keen to learn more about the crustaceans and the methods used to cook them, Edward appears much more light-hearted in this scene than he did at the beach, his body language is open, and the pair seem at ease in each other's company.

The abrupt cut from this warm kitchen scene back to the dining room is matched by a sudden shift in Edward's mood and tone. The opening shot of the dining table suggests that we have entered the scene mid-way through a conversation. In a hushed voice, Edward suggests that they ask Rose to join them. Cynthia is typically scornful in her response, asking, 'Edward, don't you have your own friends? You don't have to make friends with the cook!' Despite Cynthia's dismissive and condescending attitude, she acquiesces but seizes the opportunity to have a final dig at her brother, turning to their mother and sniggering that 'I think Edward has a crush!' While Cynthia is cynical, Patricia reads Edward's request rather differently, suggestive of his empathic nature that has informed his decision to undertake voluntary work. The framing in this scene replicates that of the first dinner-time meal; Cynthia and Patricia are on one side of the table and Edward is opposite. The long depth of field keeps the kitchen in focus at the far end and, as before, this enables us to see Rose darting about in the kitchen and then to see, if not hear, the conversation between her and Edward regarding the plans for the following day. Cynthia and Patricia remain at the fore of the shot and it is their perspective on Edward's and Rose's relationship that we hear. The relaxed friendship that is developing between Edward and Rose contrasts with the restaurant scene. Having initially selected a table, the group, which also includes Cynthia, Patricia and Christopher, changes to an alternative at Patricia's request. Once settled they sit in awkward silence as their food is delivered. Cynthia soon finds fault with her guinea fowl, proclaiming it to be undercooked and 'dangerous'. This scene, perhaps more than any of the others in the film, shares much with Mike Leigh's approach. Shots are deliberately lengthy and static, and to emphasise the discomfort, the sound is limited; aside from Cynthia's complaining, the only other noise is of cutlery being used. When Patricia confirms that her own meal is fine, Cynthia becomes increasingly agitated, justifying her complaint to herself as much as to the others. Having spoken with the chef, Cynthia begrudgingly orders soup; the others remain silent and, for the most part, still, causing Cynthia to become even more indignant. Her outburst seems to have a particular effect on Edward who is motionless, staring at his sister, who then rounds on her brother. Unable to mollify, to pacify or to sympathise with her, Edward storms off, leaving Rose alone with his family in a moment that signals the beginning of his character's unravelling.

Edward stands in the gardens of the hotel, crying, as the drizzle falls harder. In the mini-sequence that ensues, we see Edward alone. He is distracted and unsettled, he looks to the ground, almost as if he is search-ing for something that he has lost; he looks up to the sky, as if looking for answers to unspoken questions. We next see him back at the cottage, in the kitchen with Rose; it is breakfast time and the two of them are alone in the kitchen. The tension and awkwardness has dissipated and the pair joke with one another as Edward demonstrates his spoon-playing skills. The following scenes belies his relaxed demeanour, hinting at an as-yet-unspoken anxiety or trauma. Seated on his mum's bed, Edward recounts a dream where he is late to see his father, who is annoyed by his tardiness, before going out, alone for a bike ride across the island. Using the now familiar long takes, the bike ride is intercut with a pheasant hunt, the yield from which becomes the family's final holiday dinner.

It is in this scene that Edward begins to reveal his anxieties. He begins by talking about the importance of respecting cultural practices when one is a white, Western aid worker. Much to Cynthia's surprise, it is revealed that Chloe, Edward's absent girlfriend, is unable to visit during the eleventh-month duration of his post. Cynthia begins questioning her younger brother, much to his irritation. She demands to know whether the couple will split up on account of not seeing one another, to which Edward responds with a curt, 'No, but I don't know what we are going to do.' Edward is finally able to protest his feelings. He bemoans the fact that the couple have just one more night together before his departure, and explains his irritation that Cynthia appeared to have vetoed Chloe's attendance on the island, on account that she is 'not a member of the family'. Cynthia stands her ground, reiterating her opinion that Chloe is not family and thus not entitled to be present, even if her brother is 'attached' to her, as he claims. She goes further, telling Edward that she doubts his commitment to Chloe and their relationship, and that his going away for eleven months seemed to suggest to her, if not to Chloe, that the relationship was 'not exactly a top priority'. Despite Edward's clear irritation that Cynthia has no qualms about judging him, Chloe, or their relationship, he admits that he has 'absolutely no idea' as to why he is going to Africa and that he is really no more qualified than anyone else to go and teach sex education to young people. In this single moment, Edward's crisis crystallises; his lack of confidence, despite privilege, and his lack of certainty and control belie his claims to the privileges of hegemonic masculinity in the early twenty-first century. That Cynthia is mobilised as a usurper in this sequence might be indicative of a feminist intervention into the patriarchal power dynamics of the white, middle-class man in crisis. By storming out, Cynthia recaptures the attention of the characters and the audience alike, and in so doing Hogg shuts down Edward's crisis, subverting the patriarchal power that is so evident in the other forms of crisis that I have explored in this chapter. As the film closes we are left none the wiser as to what the future might hold for any of the characters; in presenting an affluent, white, middle-class man in crisis, *Archipelago*, perhaps more than any of the other films in this chapter, offers a critique of contemporary hegemonic masculinity. In some ways, *Archipelago* follows the contradictory contours of postfeminist culture, serving to critique and consolidate this hegemonic configuration of white masculinity through moments of instability and rupture; for Edward, the position of alienation – of not belonging – is also his key to privilege.

Conclusion: Cycles of Crisis, Confusion and Consolidation

Looking at the four case study films in this chapter has shown how discourses of crisis have developed in line with broader cultural and socio-economic factors. The post-industrial crisis for Gaz, Dave, Danny and Phil in *The Full Monty* and *Brassed Off* respectively develop until, by the mid-point of the 2000s, the working-class male unemployment, or underemployment in the case of Phil Bassett, becomes taken for granted. Each of the films also draws on modes of social realism as a means of narrativising crisis masculinities, and this functions as a generic device through which the authenticity or validity of these claims is demonstrated and performed. Using *Archipelago* and *All or Nothing* to examine the ways in which the crisis discourses developed over the course of the 2000s provided an opportunity to examine the ways in which crisis was differentiated by class for the respective male characters. Each of these films can be understood as commenting, in some way, on the 'state of masculinity' in British culture and, as such, each of the films has something to offer in terms of the ways in which ideas about masculinity in crisis was articulated and mediated. Significantly, however, I would argue that each film uses its expression of crisis as a narrative device through which the masculinity of the characters is reinvigorated, celebrated or reasserted. *Brassed Off* and *The Full Monty* use their endings to provide a falsely 'feel-good' conclusion but one in which the variously beleaguered male characters are triumphant and successful. Relationships between father and son, husbands and wives, girlfriends and boyfriends are restated between several key characters in both films. The domestic relationships at the heart of *All or Nothing* are also resolved as Phil and Penny are reunited and reconnected with their children. The final scene, in which the family visit their son Rory in hospital, restates the primacy of a traditional family unit in such a way that it reinforces, rather than critiques, the gender politics within this. *Archipelago* clearly treads a different path to the other films under discussion here; with its focus on more a more privileged male character, the film does more to draw attention to the workings of patriarchal power dynamics that underpin the performative politics of crisis for Edward's character. Ultimately, it would seem that in each of these films crisis is deployed as a mechanism for framing the male characters, but it is in the resolution of their narratives that symbolic power is retained and restated.

Notes

1 Edwards, Tim, 2006, *Cultures of Masculinity*, Routledge, London, p. 7.
2 Robinson, Sally, 2000, *Marked Men: White Masculinity in Crisis*, Columbia University Press, New York, p. 11.
3 Ibid., p. 6. Modleski, Tania, 1990, *Feminism Without Women: Culture and Criticism in a Postfeminist Age*, Routledge, London, p. 7.
4 Monk, Claire, 2000, 'Men in the 90s' in Murphy, Robert (ed.), *British Film of the 90s*, BFI Publishing, London, p. 159.

5 Other examples include *Truly, Madly, Deeply* (Anthony Minghella, 1990), *Martha Meet Frank, Daniel, Laurence* (Nick Hamm, 1998), *Love Actually* (Richard Curtis, 2003), *Notting Hill* (Roger Michell, 1999), *Confetti* (Debbie Issit, 2006), *Bridget Jones's Diary* (Sharon Maguire, 2001).

6 Connell, R. W.. 1995, *Masculinities*, Routledge, London.

7 Butler, Judith, 1999, *Gender Trouble: Feminism and the Subversion of Identity*, Routledge, London, pp. 171–190.

8 Robinson, Sally, 2000, *Marked Men: White Masculinity in Crisis*, Columbia University Press, New York, p. 10.

9 Modleski, Tania, 1991, *Feminism Without Women: Culture and Criticism in a Postfeminist Age*, Routledge, London, p. 7.

10 Robinson, Sally, 2000, *Marked Men: White Masculinity in Crisis*, Columbia University Press, New York, p. 6.

11 Tirado Gilligan, Heather, 2011, 'It's the End of Men. Again' in *The Public Intellectual*, 27 June. http://thepublicintellectual.org/2011/06/27/its-the-end-of-men-again/ (accessed 20 October 2020).

12 Whitehead, Stephen, 2002, *Men and Masculinities: Key Themes and Directions*, Polity Press, London, p. 47.

13 Brittan, Arthur, 1989, *Masculinity and Power*, Basil Blackwell, Oxford, p. 23.

14 Of course, this also overlooked the fact that many of the jobs being done by women were menial, low paid and often circumscribed within a deliberately insecure and precarious framework.

15 As Kalwant Bhopal demonstrates in her book, *White Privilege*, this is not simply a question of gender privilege but is also one of racial politics; contra to the cinematic preoccupation with white men as the victims of the post-feminist, postindustrial economy, Bhopal shows that white men in particular continue to benefit on account of their gender and their race.

16 Easthope, Anthony, 1992, *What A Man's Gotta Do! The Masculine Myth in Popular Culture*, Routledge, London. Nixon, Sean, 1996, *Hard Looks: Masculinities, Spectatorship and Contemporary Consumption*, UCL Press, London. Edwards, Tim. 1997. *Men in the Mirror: Men's Fashion, Masculinity and Consumer Society*, London, Cassell Press.

17 Easthope, Anthony. 1992. *What A Man's Gotta Do! The Masculine Myth in Popular Culture*. London, Routledge. Nixon, Sean. 1996. *Hard Looks: Masculinities, Spectatorship and Contemporary Consumption*, UCL Press, London. Edwards, Tim, 1997, *Men in the Mirror: Men's Fashion, Masculinity and Consumer Society*, Cassell Press, London.

18 Kimmel, Michael, 1987, 'Rethinking "Masculinity" – New Directions in Research' in Kimmel, M. (ed.), *Changing Men: New Directions in Research on Masculinity*, Sage, London, p. 9.

19 Neale, Steve, 1983, 'Masculinity as Spectacle' in *Screen*, Vol. 24, No. 6, November–December, pp. 2–17. Nixon, Sean, 1996, *Hard Looks: Masculinities, Spectatorship and Contemporary Consumption*, UCL Press, London.

20 Neale, Steve, 1983, 'Masculinity as Spectacle' in *Screen*, Vol, 24, No. 6, pp. 2–17.

21 Examples of popular journalist pronouncements on the problem of lower-class masculinity include Cohen, D, 1996, 'It's a Guy Thing, Men are Depressed and That's Official' in *The Guardian*, 4 May. Coward, R., 1994, 'Whipping Boys Perspectives: Unemployed, Unmarriageable, Criminal and Above All, Male' in *The Guardian*, 3 September. Fukuyama, F., 1997, 'Who Killed the Family?' in *The Sunday Times*, 21 September. Also see 'Devalued Families' and 'Breakdown of a Breakup' both published in *The Guardian*, 2 April 1996.

22 Dave, Paul, 2006, *Visions of England: Class and Culture in Contemporary Cinema*, Berg Press, Oxford.

23 Ibid., p. 64.

24 Hill, John, 1999, *British Cinema in the 1980s*, Oxford, Oxford University Press.

25 Ibid., p. 29.

26 Monk, Claire, 2000, 'Men in the 90s' in Murphy, Robert (ed.), *British Film of the 90s*, BFI Publishing, London, p. 159.

27 Ibid.

28 Ibid.

29 https://www.genderfoodculture.com/tag/mars-bar/ (accessed 20 October 2020).

30 Godfrey, Sarah, 2013, '"Taking the Temperature": Masculinities and Male Identities from *Bleak Moments* to *Happy Go Lucky*' in Cardinale-Powell, Bryan and DiPaolo, Marc (eds), *Devised and Directed by Mike Leigh*, Bloomsbury Press, London, p. 147.

31 O'Sullivan, Sean, 2011, *Mike Leigh*, University of Illinois Press, Springfield, p. 115.

32 Forrest, David, 2014, 'The Films of Joanna Hogg: New British Realism and Class' in *Studies in European Cinema*, Vol. 11, No. 1, pp. 64–75.

33 Ibid., p. 69.

CHAPTER 3

From *Lock, Stock and Two Smoking Barrels* to *The Football Factory:* Lad Culture and its Legacy

One of the most significant tropes of masculinity to emerge in British culture during the 1990s was the so-called 'new' lad: a contentious and often deliberately provocative paradigm of masculinity that struck a chord in the ironic and playful postfeminist culture of the time. 'New lad' culture can be traced to the men's lifestyle magazines of the late 1980s and early 1990s but it developed into what Ian Penman described as 'the reigning cultural model' of nineties British male culture.[1] The new lad became one of the most pervasive paradigms of British masculinity during the mid- and late 1990s, and while the figure of the new lad may be less visible now than he was during his prime, his legacy remains present to this day across a range of media. Indeed, films such as the much-maligned *Sex Lives of the Potato Men* (Andy Humphries, 2004), the low budget, post-Guy Ritchie gangster films like *Love, Honour and Obey* (Dominic Anciano and Ray Burdis, 2000) and the football hooligan films that I examine at the end of this chapter are all indebted to him.

In this chapter, I focus on the ways in which new lad culture evolved in British cinema during the 1990s and examine its legacy in the early years of the 2000s. In the course of this analysis, I suggest that the new lad is an intrinsically postfeminist masculinity, exemplifying the 'double entanglement' that Angela McRobbie describes as enacted by simultaneous familiarity with and dismissal of feminism and progressive gender politics.[2] Using *Lock, Stock and Two Smoking Barrels* and *Trainspotting*, two of the most iconic films of the time, as primary case studies for the emergence of cinematic lad culture I examine how both films correspond with McRobbie's notion of the double entanglement, exploring the specific function of irony in creating deliberate points of contradiction and ideological ambiguity within laddish film texts, and I also argue that while lad culture is clearly a manifestation of shifting gender discourses, it is also bound up with a specific historical moment in which discourses and ideologies of Britishness were being dismantled and reconstructed. As such, it is around and through new lad culture that a set of interconnected debates and ideas – such as the gender politics of postfeminist masculinity, national identity, and attendant issues of race, class and sexuality – can be interrogated and understood. In the second part of the chapter I offer a close analysis of the Nick Love film *The Football Factory* (2003) as the basis from which to argue that the cycle of football hooligan films that emerged in the early 2000s is a cinematic legacy of lad culture and is illustrative of the postfeminist gender politics of the early 2000s.

The Origins of Lad Culture

Magazines such as *Arena* and *GQ* (Gentleman's Quarterly) were the progenitors of new lad culture. First published in 1986 and 1988 respectively, *Arena* and *GQ* were ground-breaking; until that time the men's magazine market had been made up of soft-porn titles such as *Playboy* and *Mayfair* and publications that were dedicated to hobbies such as fishing, sport and DIY; the US magazine *Esquire* was not published in the UK until the summer of 1991. *Arena* and *GQ* were bold in their contrasting editorial style which, Sean Nixon notes, not only focused on fashion, grooming and health but also offered 'a more sexualised representation of the male body' that drew on visual codes and conventions traditionally associated with representations of femininity.[3] These magazines were 'serious and aspirational' in tone, foregrounding fashion, grooming and health and including what Benwell describes as 'feminist friendly' material.[4] In this regard, these magazines were in keeping with the discourses of the proto-feminist new man of the late 1980s, and, similarly to the new man, occupied a clearly middle-class position.

When *loaded* magazine was first published in 1994, the rebuff to the discursively reconstructed masculinities of *Arena* and *GQ* was rendered explicit in the tag line 'for men who should know better'. Where *Arena* and *GQ* were polite and deployed a debonaire, gentlemanly style, *loaded* and its marketplace counterpart *FHM* adopted a rather different editorial style. They combined fashion with music, sport and light-hearted articles, and where women were featured in the magazines the emphasis was on interviews accompanied by soft-porn-style images of scantily clad celebrities.

The phenomenon of lad culture has attracted considerable academic interest since the end of the 1990s, suggesting that, despite its irreverence and deliberately juvenile performative tendencies, its significance in terms of the gender politics of British media is important and demands thorough critical investigation. Often cast as a rejoinder to the proto-feminist sensibilities of the new man, lad culture and the new lad were discursively constructed, as Rosalind Gill describes, as 'refreshingly honest and free from artifice' and as offering a more 'authentic' or 'natural' mode of masculinity.[5] As such, new lad culture was characterised by a nostalgic, populist reassertion of traditional masculinity which mobilised a performative white, working-class identity in order to create an affective authenticity. Bethan Benwell sees the deliberate performance of working-class masculinity as a crucial factor in the appeal of lad culture, explaining that the appropriation of its identities functioned to create a discourse of authenticity around lad culture and the figure of the 'new lad'.[6] The laddish Britpop band Blur were a case in point, a group of middle-class boys who went through a reinvention as 'geezers' replete with mockney accents in an attempt to disavow their original habitus. Their lack of authenticity was at the heart of their rivalry with Manchester band, Oasis, fronted by the (authentically) working-class Noel and Liam Gallagher. As Benwell suggests, the performative working-classness that is intrinsic to lad culture further appears to call the figure of the 'new man' into question, undermining the credibility of his apparent 'challenge to traditional, binary notions of gender' and implying that his feminist reconstruction was nothing more than a cynical and disingenuous media invention.[7]

Imelda Whelehan as well as scholars such as Benwell and Rosalind Gill all suggest that nineties lad culture is symptomatic of the broader discursive context of masculinity in crisis.[8] What is distinctive, and thus significant, about nineties lad culture is the way in which it responded to and negotiated issues around shifting ideas and practices of male identities. New lad culture rejected the tendency to position men as victims of socio-economic and gender shifts, offering instead a deliberately blithe riposte to the kinds of angst-ridden narratives seen in *The Full Monty* and *Brassed Off* in the previous chapter. Where these films were framed by melancholic and at times eulogistic tones, new lad culture was brash, bold and hedonistic, celebrating and legitimising an unabashed and unreconstructed version of masculinity. One of the most persistent criticisms of magazine iterations of new lad culture was that they invariably promulgated an explicitly sexist demotic that deployed irony not only as a rhetorical and linguistic device but as a fundamental mode of its evasive identity.[9]

Given the defiantly provocative tone of lad culture, it is unsurprising that it has attracted a significant amount of academic scholarship and critique. There is, for example, a body of work on the cultural politics of lad culture and magazines and there are a number of studies of lad literature that focus on the works of writers such as Nick Hornby.[10]

Until the release of Matt Glasby's book, *Brit Pop Cinema: From Trainspotting to This is England*, Claire Monk's essay, 'Men in the 90s', and

Steve Chibnall's chapter, 'Travels in Ladland', there was little in the ways of sustained analysis of the ways in which lad culture infiltrated and then evolved within British cinema.[11] I suggest that, in order to understand the specificity of the cinematic new lad culture and its legacy in British culture since the 1990s, it needs to be seen within the context of a postfeminism that was also beginning to emerge during the same time. In this regard I agree with Rosalind Gill's suggestion that lad culture was both informing and was informed by what she terms the postfeminist sensibility.[12] Further, her mobilisation of postfeminism as a 'sensibility' is productive in examining the role of irony in creating the affective misogyny of cinematic new lad culture.[13] I explore how films such as *Trainspotting*, *Lock, Stock and Two Smoking Barrels* and *Human Traffic* can be understood within an increasingly neoliberal cultural environment dominated by pastiche, irony and the 'double entanglement' of postfeminist gender politics. Within this context, performances of incompetence are mobilised as strategic mechanisms which function to obfuscate the regressive gender politics that are being played out through the characters and narrative. Through the analysis of my case studies, I argue that the convergence of postfeminism, postmodernism and a millennial reworking of British national identity created a cultural space in which anxieties about white, British masculinity were simultaneously opened up and closed down.

The cultural phenomenon of Cool Britannia provides a further contextual dimension for my analysis of these films; *Trainspotting* and *Lock, Stock and Two Smoking Barrels* in particular were part of this cultural moment of the mid-1990s. Situating my analysis of these films within the broader context of Cool Britannia, I suggest a further level of double entanglement in terms of national identity that draws on the Blairite rhetoric of Britain as youthful, socially progressive, tolerant, open-minded and multicultural, while simultaneously deploying an ironic and ambiguous nostalgia for a seemingly lost white, working-class masculinity. Following on from my analysis of films dating from the latter end of the 1990s, I consider the ways in which lad culture evolved to produce a representational legacy exemplified by the football film cycle that emerged in the early years of the 2000s. While lad culture waned post-2000 after a series of controversies associated with newer but more openly misogynistic lad magazines, *Nuts* and *Zoo*, however, its affective influences remained highly visible within British cinema and British culture more broadly. Indeed, I would suggest that these newer forms of lad culture are the origin point for some of the more insidious forms of misogyny and toxic masculinity that remain in evidence nearly two decades later, exemplified in cinematic terms by the likes of *Pimp* (Robert Cavanagh, 2010), a mock documentary starring lad icon Danny Dyer that was critically vilified for its portrayal of women sex-workers and the brutally misogynistic men that own and control them.

Cool Britannia and the Emergence of Lad Culture

While lad culture was initially a product of the men's magazine market, it quickly proliferated and found cultural purchase across a range of other mainstream media. DJs such as Chris Moyles and Chris Evans became known for their 'zoo radio' programmes which were dominated by laddish banter between the main host and his production team. Frank Skinner's and David Baddiel's hugely successful *Fantasy Football League* (BBC 2, 1994–1996) provided a television equivalent which capitalised on the increasing cultural prominence of football fandom. The show featured celebrity guests discussing their personal 'fantasy football teams' with the hosts and often included lad icons such as Damon Albarn, the lead singer with Blur, and the author Nick Hornby. Although borrowing from the conventions of the chat show, *Fantasy Football League* was deliberately informal and spontaneous; its studio set designed to look like the kind of flat that the audience might themselves live in. Arguably the most successful example of new lad culture on British television was the comedy series *Men Behaving Badly*. Initially broadcast on ITV, the series switched to BBC 1 in 1994 after two series and occupied a prime-time slot for several series. The sitcom centered on a pair of housemates, Gary (Martin Clunes) and Tony (Neil Morrissey), and their hapless exploits. Irony was a key discursive strategy in the series, enabling the characters to present sexism and male irresponsibility through a comedic lens, foreclosing critique by reclaiming the characters' behaviour as endearing immaturity.

Writers such as Nick Hornby and Tony Parsons were key figures in the development of the subgenre of literature, dubbed 'lad-lit'.[14] Hornby's novels, *Fever Pitch*, *High Fidelity* and *About A Boy* were adapted as feature films in the late nineties and early 2000s and are discussed in more detail in Chapter 5. Both Hornby and Parsons worked for the *NME* during the mid- and late 1990s and thus, unsurprisingly, lad culture had strong connections to music, particularly the emergent genre of Britpop. In many ways, the Gallagher brothers' 1960s style, mod-style haircuts and clothing evoke a longer history of machisimo within rock music and a nostalgia for 1960s working-class youth culture. The feud between Oasis and fellow Britpop band Blur is indicative of the centrality of authenticity to lad culture, with Damon Albarn, Blur's middle-class lead singer, invariably dismissed for his inauthentic appropriation of lad culture, the implication being that Albarn's class identity meant that he was only ever 'playing' with laddism and could never lay claim to a position as an authentic cultural icon. Despite the rhetoric of authenticity and class that was central to Oasis's brand, Noel Gallagher accepted an invitation to a post-election reception at Downing Street to celebrate Tony Blair's election, an event that is significant in terms of demonstrating the extent to which lad culture had become part of established, mainstream popular culture while also functioning to endorse Blair's authenticity as a harbinger of political and cultural change. The emergence of lad culture seemed to coincide with a moment of significant cultural and political change in Britain. Lad culture and Cool Britannia emerged out of the same cultural context and were informed by similar ideological and discursive impulses; both can be understood as a repudiation of the form of Britishness espoused by former Prime Minister John Major and, as such, part of a broader pre-millennial cultural zeitgeist.

Britain's cultural industries played a key role in negotiating and articulating this process of renewal and reconfiguration, and in line with this British cinema was enjoying a renaissance with numerous commercially successful films released in the period 1995–1998. Some of these films fall within what might be termed 'traditional' British cinema output; for example *Emma* (Douglas McGrath, 1996) and *Jane Eyre* (Franco Zefferelli, 1996) are period adaptations, while *Secrets and Lies* (Mike Leigh, 1996), *Stella Does Tricks* (Coky Giedroyc, 1996) and *My Name is Joe* demonstrate the importance of British social realism, and the release of *GoldenEye* (Martin Campbell) in 1995 saw the revival of James Bond, one of the most enduring, if problematic, icons of British masculinity.[15] Films such as *Trainspotting* and *Lock, Stock and Two Smoking Barrels* offered a clear departure from the established generic repertoire associated with British cinema. Where heritage films in particular relied upon the kind of nostalgia for the kind of timeless rural Britain invoked by John Major, films such as *Trainspotting* were much more in keeping with the trend for the conscious refashioning of British national identity.

Cinematic Specificities: Irony, Nostalgia and the Performance of 'New Lad' Culture in the Nineties

As in his manifestation in other media forms, the cinematic new lad can be understood as a reaction against and a rejoinder to the 'new man' trope of masculinity that was rejected for being contrived and inauthentic. Lad culture adamantly and consistently repudiated the supposedly 'feminised' new man in favour of a celebratory reclamation of a clearly demarcated form of heteronormative masculinity. A nostalgic impulse is clearly evident in cinematic iterations of lad culture with a number of films from the era deliberately and knowingly referring back to historical modes of masculinity from British cinema. There are, for example, traces of the double entendres of James Bond, the 'saucy' comedy of the *Carry On* films and the seventies *Confessions* series of films, as well as reverence for the iconography of the ultra-masculinity of Michael Caine's characters in *The Ipcress File* (Sidney J. Furie, 1965), *Alfie* (Lewis Gilbert, 1966), *The Italian Job* (Peter Collinson, 1969) and *Get Carter* (Mike Hodges, 1971), the last of which was adapted into a comic strip in the lad magazine, *loaded*, as an explicit endorsement of its iconic or cult status. While cinematic lad culture often draws on this specific national history and its iconographies of masculinity, it also operates within global postmodern media cultures and these influences are frequently deployed. Quentin Tarantino's films *Reservoir Dogs* (1992) and *Pulp Fiction* (1995) are particularly noticeable influences in the formal construction of *Lock, Stock and Two Smoking Barrels*, while *Human Traffic* contains multiple references to cult Hollywood films including the *Star Wars* Trilogy (George Lucas, 1977, 1980, 1983) for example.

The discourses of lad masculinity appear to sit adjacent to hegemonic masculinity in many ways: the irreverence, immaturity and ironic celebration of 'low' culture, for example, relies upon a tacit understanding of neoliberal, postfeminist hegemonies of masculinity in order to make sense. However, I would argue that lad culture has a complex relationship with hegemonic masculinity and, as the case studies that follow will show, it invariably mobilises its own distinct versions of counter-hegemonic masculinity and offers specific value systems and attendant hierarchies of race, class and region. In this regard, the forms of lad culture that we see in British cinema operate as specific codifications of hegemonic masculinity which operate in conjunction with other media forms as well as in relation to broader cultural discourses of neoliberal, postfeminist masculinity: Benwell's description of the magazine new lad as offering a 're-embrace of a very rigid conformist and conservative model of masculinity including an adherence to misogyny and homophobia'. for example, might equally be applied to certain versions of the cinematic new lad.[16]

The ironic and self-referential nature of films such as *Lock, Stock and Two Smoking Barrels*, *Trainspotting* and *Human Traffic* is very much in keeping with the kind of postfeminist, postmodern ironic posturing that was characteristic of other lad media. This led Michael Kimmel to describe lad culture as paradoxically 'deeply shallow' for the ways in which the performance of apolitical posturing becomes codified as a form of gendered politics in and of itself.[17] Indeed, the subcultural settings of each of these films deliberately brings into play politics of irony and ambivalence in the performances of masculinity that they facilitate.

Lad culture is, I argue, characterised by a distinctly postfeminist politics, which is then mediated specifically within the context of cinema; new lad culture can be seen as operating in a similar way to postfeminist culture and so, following Rosalind Gill's approach, I position it as a 'sensibility', a frame of reference that allows a productive amount of dexterity through which to analyse and make sense of its manifold manifestations.[18] Lad culture developed from being a media paradigm into an intrinsic part of postfeminist culture and its influence functioned in more diffuse ways permeating beyond films, magazines and media texts and into the gender politics of our day to day lives.[19] While in this chapter I focus deliberately on films that I consider to be emblematic of new lad culture, I also argue that lad culture as a sensibility can be seen to operate across a large number of other films, ranging from the irreverent comedy of *The Full Monty* to the social realist *Nil By Mouth*, as well as being a clear influence in a number of gangster films from the late 1990s and early 2000s such as *Final Cut* (Dominic Anciano and Ray Burdis, 1999), *Rancid Aluminum* (Edward Thomas, 2000), *Love, Honour and Obey* (Dominic Anciano and Ray Burdis, 2000) and *The Rise of the Footsoldier* (Julian Gilbey, 2007). In various ways all of these films are indebted to and contribute to the discourses of new lad culture simultaneously. Take, for example, Gary Oldman's bleak *Nil By Mouth*: the film presents a homosocial world dominated by pubs, strip clubs, alcohol and recreational drug use and the male characters are resolute in maintaining a strictly demarcated cultural environment away from their wives, mothers and girlfriends. The resurgence of the gangster film in the wake of *Lock, Stock and Two Smoking Barrels* is similarly bound up with a commercially viable postmodern and ironic nostalgia for the days of Swinging London replete with marketable soundtracks, catchy sound bites and proudly unreconstructed 'hard' men. Films such as *Snatch* (Guy Ritchie, 2000) and *Love, Honour and Obey* pay homage to the dominant masculinities of a gangland culture that has since been mythologised in British literature by writers such as Jeremy Cameron (*Vinnie Got Blown Away*, *It Was An Accident* and *Brown Bread in Wengen*), Nicholas Blincoe (*Manchester Slingback* and *The Last Call*) and Ken Bruen (*The Hackman Blues* and *The White Trilogy*), as well as in film.

Lad culture's key influence in terms of cinema is evidenced in a number of ways. At a general level films such as those mentioned above are distinguished by their ironic tone, offering moments of deliberate and knowing parody of both gender performance and genre exemplified by characters such as Nik 'the Greek' (Stephen Marcus) in *Lock, Stock and Two Smoking Barrels*, Spud (Ewen Bremner) in *Trainspotting*, whose amphetamine fuelled interview in is one of the iconic set pieces of the film, and Moff's (Danny Dyer) police superintendent father (Terence Beesley). At a representational level we see the normalisation of recreational drug taking, drinking and the positioning of (hetero)sex as key preoccupations of the male characters, while at the level of narrative and performance the films are, for the most part, dominated by banter, bravado, swagger and a playful machismo.

Cinematic lad culture, like these other media forms, is characterised by irony and self-parody, both of which are mobilised to generate ambiguity and contradiction in terms of gender politics. However, there are, I suggest, notable points of distinction between films and magazine media. Where magazines such as *loaded* are clearly and explicitly positioned as being part of consumer culture, films such as *Trainspotting*, *Twin Town*, *Human Traffic* and *Late Night Shopping* are much more ambivalent about the growth of consumerism. Indeed, with their ironic anti-aspirationalism *Trainspotting* and *Twin Town* can be understood as offering an opposition to consumer culture. The Lewis twins of *Twin Town* describe themselves as idealised consumers and entrepreneurs; while the nature of the goods that they consume might not be socially acceptable and their drug dealing might not be conventionally entrepreneurial, they still operate within the broader commodity culture that they appear to be trying to escape. *Trainspotting*'s infamous opening monologue (which ironically became a popular poster for university students across the UK in the late 1990s) offered a nihilistic critique of the banalities of hegemonic consumer habits:

> Choose Life. Choose a job. Choose a career. Choose a family. Choose a fucking big television, choose washing machines, cars, compact disc players and electrical tin openers. Choose good health, low cholesterol and dental insurance. Choose fixed interest mortgage repayments. Choose a starter home. Choose your friends. Choose leisurewear and matching luggage. Choose a three-piece suite on hire purchase in a range of fucking fabrics. Choose DIY and wondering who the fuck you are on a Sunday morning. Choose sitting on that couch watching mind-numbing, spirit-crushing game shows, stuffing fucking junk food into your mouth. Choose rotting away at the end of it all, pishing your last in a miserable home, nothing more than an embarrassment to the selfish, fucked up brats you spawned to replace yourself. Choose your future. Choose life . . . But why would I want to do a thing like that? I chose not to choose life . . . I chose something else.

As the sardonic tone of the famous opening monologue from *Trainspotting* demonstrates, the eschewal of sincerity in favour of irreverence, irony and 'banter' is one of the defining characteristics of lad culture. Despite seeming to constitute performances of what Claire Monk has termed

'post-political' masculinity, irony and insincerity function at an intrinsically political level, creating something akin to McRobbie's 'double
entanglement' of post-feminist culture.[20] The very fact that *Lock, Stock
and Two Smoking Barrels* features just two female characters (one is Gloria,
Winston's perpetually stoned girlfriend and the other is the croupier at the
card game between Ed and Harry) is seen by film scholar, Steve Chibnall,
as regressive but not necessarily misogynistic. However, the very fact
that Chibnall says that women are irrelevant to 'the stories Ritchie wants
to tell' is, in itself, tellingly indicative of the workings of postfeminist
gender politics in the film.[21] *Lock, Stock and Two Smoking Barrels* simply
relinquishes responsibility or complicity in its regurgitation of regressive gender discourses. The film draws, self-consciously, on a cinematic
heritage of gangsters, spivs and hard men, both in its characters and in its
aesthetic style, paying homage to films such as *Get Carter*, *The Long Good
Friday* (John MacKenzie, 1980) and *The Italian Job* in order to create a
particularly contemporary form of nostalgia described by Samir Ibrahim
as 'retro-macho'.[22] The referential and extra-textual layers of the film
are consolidated by having a cast that includes a rock star (Sting), an ex-
footballer known for his propensity to violence both off and on the pitch
(Vinnie Jones) and a one-time East End gangster turned bare knuckle
fighter (Harry McLean). There are, then, two connected hierarchies of
masculinity at play within the film: the diegetic hierarchy of elders, fathers
and godfather figures, represented by JD, Big Chris and Harry respectively, and the intertextual hierarchy of cultural icons.

   Lock, Stock and Two Smoking Barrels provides a number of tropes
of masculinity drawing on the rich heritage of character archetypes of
British crime capers and comedy heist films. The various gangs and
their members are introduced in a series of opening vignettes which ape
Tarantino's fragmented narrative style. Each group has its own aural
leitmotif and colour palette to provide differentiation: a discordant electric
guitar accompanies the images of the gangster group that represents the
main rivals to protagonist Ed's cohort, whilst a reggae track is used over
images of the middle-class cannabis growers. Colour is also used as a
mechanism for identification, Ed's group, for example, is dominated by
greys and browns, and the desaturated palette which echoes that of the
1960s and 1970s forms a nostalgic connection between the group and the
heydays of the 1960s gangster.

   Ed's voice-over is used to introduce the members of his group; couched
in 'mockney' patois and rhyming slang, his vernacular quickly establishes
both his own laddish identity and that of the group as affable (and, thus,
essentially harmless) chancers. The only member of the group whose job

is legitimate is Soap (Dexter Fletcher), so named because of his lack of criminal record. Soap is the only member of the group to be introduced against the brightly lit background of his professional kitchen; the bright white light and the gleaming stainless steel surroundings contrast with the earthier tones used for the other group members. In many ways, the group is precisely those 'men who should know better' and who are on the cusp of a somewhat belated maturity. Ed introduces Bacon (Jason Statham), explaining that he knows that 'his days of selling stolen goods on street corners are numbered!' Bacon's introduction pays ironic homage to the traditional East End wide-boy market trader. Shown on a makeshift market stall, he proudly proclaims the jewellery that he is selling as 'hand-made in Italy, hand stolen in Stepney!' His quick speech is full of rhyming slang and market stall patter echoing the linguistic style of lad magazines, replete with cultural references and 'jokey' sexism and the kind of double entendre associated with traditional forms of British comedians as he pro-nounces 'I took a bag home last night, and she cost me a lot more than a tenner . . .'. *Lock, Stock and Two Smoking Barrels* draws on a familiar para-digm of 'traditional', East End, 'rough diamond' masculinity epitomised by the likes of Del Boy (David Jason) and Rodney (Nicholas Lyndhurst) in the 1980s BBC sitcom *Only Fools and Horses* (BBC 1, 1981–1991), in order to establish Ed and his friends as likeable, well-intentioned jack-the-lads who get out of their depth. While the lads in *Lock, Stock and Two Smoking Barrels* occupy a socio-economic position that is distinct from Gary and Tony in *Men Behaving Badly*, irony is used, in both examples, as a mecha-nism that not only renders their various misdemeanours as harmless but actively functions to endorse the performance of strategic immaturity to provide what Benwell might term an 'evasive politics' of masculinity.[23]

As such, the role of irony within *Lock, Stock and Two Smoking Barrels* functions in at least two ways. It is used as a discursive mechanism which functions to anticipate and deflect critique by playing off the plurality of meaning and inflection. This strategy is used, as both Whelehan and Benwell argue, to effectively close down critique and to reinforce the boundaries between those who are 'in' on the joke and those (feminists) who fail to get it.[24] This form of rhetorical irony mobilises ambiguity and deliberately obfuscates certainty in ways that serve to reinforce the kinds of regressive gender politics that are endemic within lad culture and to reinscribe a strict gender binary. However, irony also functions in a broader way, which might be better understood in terms of Gill's notion of a sensibility.[25] In many ways, *Lock, Stock and Two Smoking Barrels* 'moves out of the realm of the true and false and into the realm of the felicitous and infelicitous',[26] deliberately and playfully activating moments of double-speak and parody in order to allow offensive ideas to be articulated or enacted. From the use of the Zorba the Greek soundtrack that accompanies Nik the Greek's appearance on screen, to the language used by Dog's (Frank Harper) gang of petty criminals when they raid the middle-class drug dealers, irony is used to foreclose critique. To this extent, irony is fundamental to the 'mode of existence' of the film using a knowingly humorous tone to a particularly evasive effect. The extent to which this is in fact evidence of the newness of new lad culture is debatable, within film at least, where self-parody has a longer lineage exemplified by the innuendo-filled dialogue of the James Bond films in particular. As is the case with Bond, irony and innuendo-led double-speak function as a mechanism to evade critique or challenge.

Irony, however, is also used at a more general level to facilitate the use of otherwise crudely constructed stereotypes; from the white, middle-class, dreadlocked, trustafarian drug growers to the various 'hard men' and the organised criminal gang comprised of heavily built Black men, all dressed in black hooded tops. There is a deliberate eschewal of political integrity which divests these images of their racial and gendered significance, rendering them, to borrow from Yvonne Tasker's critique of gender and race in American action cinema, nothing more than 'superficial differences of style'.[27] The political function of irony in this regard is perhaps most apparent in relation to the character of Nik 'The Greek' an apparently slow-witted fence, who is presented as clumsy, sly and stupid. Occupying the lower strata of the criminal fraternity and serving as a go-between for the various groups, he unwittingly ends up trying to sell the drugs that have been stolen from the diminutive but ferocious gang leader Rory Breaker (Vas Blackwood) back to him. When Breaker discovers that he has been double-crossed he is furious. His face is shot in close-up as he commands his men to find 'that greasy, wop, shistos, pezevengi, gamouri, Greek bastard'. The aim here seems to be deliberately provocative: to critique this as racially offensive would be to fail to 'get' the joke. Using the character of Breaker to deliver these lines provides a further level of laddish irony to the scene: the image of the diminutive Black racist and the lumbering white man plays off multiple contradictions of race, body and gender with an absurdity that functions to curtail critique. A similar case can be made with regards to the portrayal of the Liverpudlian thieves, Gary (Victor McGuire) and Dean (Jake Abraham), the petty criminals whose be-permed, tracksuit-wearing style is a cultural reference to the 'scouser' stereotype found in cartoon strips in *The Sun*, as well as in the Carla Lane sitcom *Bread* (BBC 1, 1986–1991) and as characters in *Harry Enfield's Television Programme* (BBC 1, 1990–1998). Like their cultural forebears, Gary and Lenny are portrayed as hopelessly dim-witted; in a particularly notable exchange, Gary admonishes Lenny for torturing the elderly owners of a stately home, exclaiming: 'you twat! . . . can't you see they've got no money, they can't even afford new furniture!' In the ironic, postmodern, postfeminist world presented by *Lock, Stock and Two Smoking Barrels*, the peripheral characters are only ever stereotypes and caricatures; their crudeness is deliberately immured by irony, which enables a range of problematic and regressive cultural politics around race, gender, class and regionality to persist.

I Choose Not to Choose Life: Appropriating Disempowerment

Trainspotting and *Human Traffic* were released in the years either side of *Lock, Stock and Two Smoking Barrels* and both present rather different narratives of young men emerging into adulthood in the post-industrial economy. Instead of nostalgia for a glamourised and mythical gangland, these films place a greater emphasis on the kinds of 'ordinary', or unspectacular men that Benwell describes as being the audience for many lad magazines.[28] These films share the kind of ironic detachment seen in *Lock, Stock and Two Smoking Barrels* but are more explicitly engaged with exploring the gendered identities of the main characters. *Trainspotting* does this via the character of Renton (Ewen McGregor) and his voice-overs which provide points of identification and continuity throughout the film, and *Human Traffic* employs the character of Jip (John Simm) in a similar way. Both films, and the slightly later *Late Night Shopping*, appear to respond to and negotiate questions of male gendered identities within the contemporary post-industrial landscape but do so in a manner that is clearly influenced by lad culture. As such, they sit in contrast to social realist films such as Shane Meadows's debut, *TwentyFourSeven* and Ken Loach's *My Name is Joe* and the later *Sweet Sixteen* (Ken Loach, 2002) also, circulating at the time when films exemplify a more despondent vision of young masculinity in the 1990s and early 2000s. In many ways, the films that I focus on here explicitly refute the oppressive stasis of their social realist counterparts: *Trainspotting* and *Human Traffic*, for example, seem to take the socio-economic precarity of their characters as an inevitable if not political point; poverty, in these films, is not mobilised as a structuring device in the same way that it is in *TwentyFourSeven*. Where Monk sees this as evidence of the post-political detachment of the generation, I suggest that these films are very much part of their political and cultural moment.[29] Moreover, it is irony that operates as a key mechanism by which disempowerment is reappropriated and reconfigured as a lifestyle choice. As such, these films have much to offer in terms of understanding the complexities of masculinity within new lad culture. In this way, films such as *Human Traffic* and *Trainspotting* can be seen as central in forging new canons of British cinema that respond to shifting discourses around gender and national identity.

Trainspotting mobilises the kinds of rhetorical irony that are characteristic of *Lock, Stock and Two Smoking Barrels* but also uses it as a narrative device through which questions of gender, poverty and national identity can be negotiated and evaded simultaneously. Playful generic hybridity seems central to the operation of irony in *Trainspotting*, creating moments where elements of realism and surrealism are juxtaposed. This is in order to accommodate the contradiction inherent in the film's attempt to portray the pleasurable psychic effects of taking heroin as well as the devastating consequences of addiction to it. Where *Lock, Stock and Two Smoking Barrels* openly glamourises gangster characters, *Trainspotting* incorporates elements of social realism, as demonstrated by the scene immediately following Tommy's (Kelvin McKidd) death or the grim state of the rooms Renton and his friends use as 'shooting galleries' for example, alongside moments of heightened or surreal humour: such as Spud's amphetamine-driven job interview and 'The Worst Toilet in Scotland' sequence. These combine to produce a film that presents a deliberately ambiguous narrative of heroin addiction. The juxtaposition of the depravity of heroin addiction with Renton's description of heroin as 'the best orgasm you ever had, multiply it by a thousand and you're still nowhere near' illustrate the ideological and stylistic juncture that the film tries to balance. Writing at the time of the film's release in the *British Medical Journal*, Declan McLoughlin contends that *Trainspotting* is misconstrued as pro-drugs, arguing that it 'is certainly not a film that will induce you to start using heroin'.[30] Despite this, the film courted controversy for a perceived failure to explicitly condemn drug taking; the right-wing press, including the *Daily Mail*, admonished it for an irresponsible refusal to 'judge or condemn heroin addiction'.[31] To some extent, then, *Trainspotting* can be understood as yoking the celebratory laddishness of *Lock, Stock and Two Smoking Barrels* to the ethos of social realist films analysed elsewhere in this book. *Trainspotting*'s blurring of generic conventions shows the complexity and potential contradictions that can be inherent in a cinematic text. It is not an outright social treatise, but neither is it an uncritical celebration of the subcultural milieu of the heroin addict, and, as such, the film exemplifies the kind of cultural double-speak that characterised British film culture (and postfeminist gender discourses) at this time.

Renton is the nihilistic narrator of the film, his anti-consumerist monologue providing not only the ambivalent political framework for the film but also a cultural touchstone for the generation coming of age in the 1990s. In centralising the discourses of consumerism and choice from the very outset, the film presents Renton's heroin addiction as a matter of choice but it simultaneously acknowledges that the impoverished social and economic environment of post-industrial Edinburgh circumscribed his choices. Scotland, like the north of England, was hit particularly hard by post-industrial poverty and the social and economic policies of the Thatcher government, and as Duncan Petrie explains, Irvine Welsh's novel was 'an angry backwards glance at the social exclusion, stagnation and decay that characterised great swathes of Thatcher's Britain'.[32]

As with the lads in *TwentyFourSeven* or Liam in *My Name is Joe*, the young male characters of *Trainspotting* already exist in a cultural space where traditional notions of masculinity (and consumerism) have no relevance. High unemployment, limited opportunities and narrow horizons mean that the likelihood of Renton and his friends ever being in a position to 'choose a starter home' or any of the other culturally sanctioned markers of successful consumerist masculinity that Renton references in his opening monologue are infinitesimally meagre, although he does eventually escape his friends and move to London, so the film hints at the possibilities of escape, maturation and conformity. Whereas *TwentyFourSeven* and *My Name is Joe* mobilise a discourse of victimhood regarding the disempowerment and marginalisation of the young male characters, *Trainspotting* rejects this device and instead presents the addict lifestyle as an alternative 'choice' and a conscious rejection of an emasculatory form of consumer culture. As Duncan Petrie explains, 'the film depicts poverty realistically, but in a way that encompasses the possibilities of escape as well as stories of entrapment. Moreover, *Trainspotting* exploits the aesthetics of film [. . .] to draw a kind of vitality from grinding poverty'.[33] In this way, *Trainspotting* acts as a cultural counterpoint to Loach's *My Name is Joe* which is much more in keeping with traditional forms of social realism; where Liam could only escape the tragic cycles of addiction, crime and violence through death, *Trainspotting*'s formal and stylistic qualities facilitate a more positive conclusion that is in keeping with the dictates of neoliberal selfhood without losing credibility.

As Petrie observes, *Trainspotting* deliberately rejects the conventions of the kind of social realism that is associated with films such as *My Name Is Joe*, eschewing naturalistic lighting for a gaudy colour palette inspired by the drug and club culture, with more highly stylised editing and by using a more intrusive soundtrack than is usual for social realist cinema;[34] the intertextual qualities and the generic hybridity of the film mark it out as a postmodern narrative. In this way the film contrasts with both *My Name is Joe* and *TwentyFourSeven*; from its opening seconds it is obvious that this is not the typically downbeat treatment of drug addiction that might be expected. The pounding beat of Iggy Pop's 'Lust for Life' punctuates Renton's opening diatribe while the rapid editing and mix of camera angles create a style that was, at that time, novel in British cinema. The scene cuts to a medium close-up of Renton; he is thin and pale, the tight-fitting jeans and vest top draw further attention to his emaciated body and the shot is close enough for the red circles that encase his eyes to be obvious. The shot changes to a longer one which shows him standing alone in an almost empty room, a cigarette in hand and a tourniquet tied around his arm. The walls are bare, one has a large hole punched through it, and the colour scheme is dominated by browns and greys that serve to emphasise the drabness. There is no furniture and no carpet. In many ways, this shot echoes *TwentyFourSeven*'s sparse, bleak domestic spaces. Certainly, it draws on a lexicon of images associated with poverty. However, where *TwentyFourSeven* uses these images to create a more tangible sense of despair and disempowerment, *Trainspotting* juxtaposes images of poverty with dialogue extolling the pleasures of heroin in ways that create a deliberate tension and ambiguity around intent.

The camera pans round from Renton's prone, intoxicated body to reveal the wider space of Swanney 'Mother Superior's' (Peter Mullan's) gallery; the walls are graffitied and there is no furniture in any of the rooms. A baby plays, unattended, among the detritus of the floor while her mother and other adults inject heroin in the next room. Although the film refrains from passing judgement on the characters, or indeed heroin addiction more broadly, the juxtaposition of the neglected baby in the heroin den with Renton's pro-heroin testimony creates a contradiction between what the audience sees and hears. This purposeful discord continues as the shot moves into the action in the adjacent room where Sick Boy (Johnny Lee Miller), Spud and Alison (Susan Vidler) are preparing for their next hit of heroin. Sick Boy is talking about Sean Connery as Bond in *Thunderball* and *Dr. No*, saying 'people think it is all about the misery and desperation and death and all that shite . . . which is not to be ignored . . . but they forget the pleasure of it'. The polysemic potential of his speech is deliberate, referring as much, if not more, to mainstream discourses on heroin and heroin addiction than to the Bond movies. The visual images of Spud collapsing onto the floor, eyes closed, with a euphoric grin, underline the pleasure to which Sick Boy and Renton both refer. In many ways these opening scenes correspond to the wider cultural context of 'heroin chic' which dominated the fashion scene in the mid-1990s. The overt sexualisation of drug culture, which is shown in the exchanges between Sick Boy, Spud, Alison and Swanney, gesture to the increased visibility of sexual fluidity that was emerging at the time. Where the lads of *Lock, Stock and Two Smoking Barrels* or *TwentyFourSeven* were defensively heterosexual, heroin enables a breakdown in rigid heteronormative strictures of masculinity. Sick Boy, Spud, Alison and Swanney inject each other, close-ups of needles penetrating the skin emphasising the intimacy of the situation. Renton and Sick Boy stare into each other's eyes as a high takes hold, rendering them both united and yet separate. In the film, heroin is seen to blur the boundaries between reality and fantasy, thus enabling forms of behaviour and expressions of affection that might otherwise be stigmatised for contravening the heteronormative codes of hegemonic masculinity. However, these moments of affection remain emphatically *not* queer, occupying a clearly non-sexual space that separates love from sex – similar moments are seen in *Human Traffic* when characters have taken ecstasy. Despite the fact that *Trainspotting* draws on relatively new codes of representing male sexuality, these remain within an explicitly heterosexual framework in which the boundaries between the homosocial and the homoerotic, which can never be entirely dismissed, are only fleetingly blurred by a narcotic high.

Although sometimes interpreted as a pro-drug film, *Trainspotting* deploys the iconography of social realism as a way of counterpointing the potential glamourisation of drug addiction. To attribute a straightforward reading of the film as being either for or against drug use is problematic because of this contradiction. By contrast, *Human Traffic*, which did not garner as much media attention as *Trainspotting*, can be seen as articulating a less ambiguous message in its presentation of club and drug culture in nineties Britain. The film engages with recreational drug use in club culture (none of the key characters is addicted to 'hard' drugs) in a lighthearted way. The drugs in question are cannabis, cocaine and ecstasy which are seen as integral to the subculture in which the film is set and to lad culture more broadly – although they bring their own discursive problems and moral panics. Ecstasy had been rising in popularity since the early 1990s had become a popular clubber's drug but had led to several deaths.[35] In 1992, the Shamen's track 'Ebeneezer Goode' became the focus of controversy on account of the apparent endorsement of drug taking, an issue that would also come to impact on the Britpop band, Pulp, whose 'Sorted for E's and Wizz' was considerably less subtle than its predecessor and was banned, indefinitely, by BBC Radio 1 for encouraging drug use. While it would seem that the recreational nature of both cannabis and ecstasy enables a mode of representation that is less inevitably tied to addiction, the level of drug taking in youth culture, and the potential for this to be 'glamourised' in film, remained a key site of moral panic. During this period, cocaine became increasingly affordable and available, and it is in the football hooligan films discussed later in this chapter where we see a cinematic engagement with the intersections of white, working-class masculinity and cocaine culture.

Human Traffic takes a satirical approach to the issue, presenting a parody of a drug education lesson just as Nina's (Nicola Reynolds's) younger brother Lee (Dean Davies) is about to take ecstasy for the first time. Lee's voice-over is used to present his thoughts and anxieties about what will happen, he ponders his fate and hopes that the drugs aren't fatal. The film cuts to a classroom scene where an authoritarian white male doctor (Eilan Wyn), wearing a white lab coat, stands in front of a blackboard and begins to deliver a stern lecture about the mental and physical side effects of taking ecstasy. However, his speech is punctuated by interjections from Jip (John Simm) who counters his arguments with a range of positive effects of the drug. Lee, confused by the two opinions that are being presented to him, is pictured looking from one to the other as he tries to make up his own mind on the issue. This scene characterises the ambiguity with which several lad films from the late nineties treat issues of drug taking. This refusal to adopt a particular or fixed standpoint on contentious issues is characteristic of lad culture, with irony being key to this. *Human Traffic* is typical of this in the way that it oscillates between different aspects of popular discourse around drugs and club culture, but, whereas *Trainspotting* appears to use irony as a mechanism for creating ambiguity, *Human Traffic* uses irony to point to the contradictions at play in medical and political narratives about drug taking. Jip takes on the role of the drug educator, advising that 'statistically you are more likely to die by becoming involved in a fight in a pub than you are from taking ecstasy . . . alcohol kills 30,000 people a year in Britain, but that's alright because it's a taxable drug'.

The contradiction surrounding social attitudes to alcohol, for example, is presented in the opening sequence of *Trainspotting*, where Begbie and Tommy both admonish Renton, Sick Boy and Spud for their heroin addiction while sitting drinking and smoking in a pub, apparently unable or unwilling to acknowledge the hypocrisy of their position. *Trainspotting* alludes to this paradox at several other moments in the film; Renton's father draws on a cigarette while reproaching his son for wasting his life 'filling yer veins wi' that shite' and his mother's valium consumption means that she is, in Renton's words, also a drug addict 'in her own socially

Figure 3.1 *Trainspotting:* The decor in Renton's room suggests his infantalisation

acceptable way'. These moments do not seem to promote a pro-heroin message; rather they underline the point that numerous other drugs, substances and addictions remain legal despite causing emotional and physical damage to those who are addicted. As such, both *Trainspotting* and *Human Traffic* use comedy and irony as a mechanism through which to draw attention to the complexities and contradictions of drug culture without preaching or becoming worthy.

A case in point is the way in which *Trainspotting* presents the overdose that forces Renton's parents to take him home and nurse him. While this narrative might echo that in *TwentyFourSeven* when the paternal character of Darcy (Bob Hoskins) cares for Fag Ash (Matt Hand), the style and form in *Trainspotting* are very different. Like Fag Ash, drug addiction has rendered Renton childlike, incapable of looking after himself. Renton's father carries him into his bedroom where his parents undress him and put him to bed; his dependent, infantilised position is accentuated by the children's wallpaper and small, single bed.

The message is unambiguous: heroin has rendered Renton incapable of sustaining a mature, independent adulthood within systems of capital, and the only means by which his recuperation into mainstream society can be achieved is through his literal removal from his circle of friends. What stands in stark contrast is the nature of the damage inflicted in in its active and passive stances; with the damaging sobriety acting within contexts of macro events rather than the damaged inflicted when Renton is in the throes of addiction. The damage inflicted through Renton's addiction remains passive and explicitly non-corporal: a television is quietly and calmly removed from a nursing home and CDs are stolen from a chain store that is successful enough to employ security staff. In contradistinction, sober Renton's opus of destruction crescendos at three key points. One is the shooting of a dog (which reacts by mauling its innocent owner); the second is the unapologetic sexual relationship with Diane (Kelly MacDonald), an under-age schoolgirl. The third and closing action of Renton's sobriety – which causes a fall out that leads to the implosion of his friendship group (and the incarceration of Begby (Robert Carlyle), who is on the run) – is his theft of the profits from a collective drug deal of wholesale heroin. This event neatly bookends Renton's journey with a reprised and altered version of his 'Choose Life' monologue which runs over the top of the ethereal and glistening opening synthesiser refrain of Underworld's 'Born Slippy'.

In this way, Renton is more fortunate than Liam (David McKay) in *My Name is Joe*, whose entrapment within the toxic environment of the Glasgow tenements proves fatal. After making it through his 'cold turkey' ordeal, Renton leaves the impoverished confines of Leith, much like a contemporary Dick Whittington, for a new life in London, not only the capital city of England (the hated colonisers referred to immediately before Renton's first relapse) but a symbol of post-industrial neoliberalism. This final segment of the film adopts a markedly distinct style of cinematography and visual tone which function to reinforce and romanticise London as a contemporary geocultural landscape of promise, wealth and opportunity in direct contrast to the drab tenements and poverty-stricken landscape of the Leith docklands. Renton's escape and apparently seamless transition from heroin addict to estate agent would be unthinkable for characters such as Fag Ash or Liam and, in many ways, demonstrates how *Trainspotting* functions as mediating a market position that draws heavily on neoliberal ideologies of self-betterment and self-determination. Renton's escape, however, is not straightforward; his friends arrive and he becomes drawn back into the cycles of crime and suspicion that he had tried to leave. Renton's final break from his friends comes when he decides to leave without splitting the proceeds from the heroin deal. It can be seen that Renton draws a moral line in the sand between those who are damaged, and those who are evil. Spud is a self-destructive mess, seemingly possessed with his own downfall, Begby is a sadistic sociopath, who glasses young females for the sake of inciting a pub brawl. Renton himself is an accidental, if not repentant, statutory rapist; whereas Sick Boy proactively tries to groom Diane. It is in this spectrum that we see an allusion to a moral spectrum that sits over and above a braid of toxicity and sobriety. Sick Boy's remorse at his child's death while he was on heroin acts as a counterpoint to Begby's acts of violence towards an innocent bystander while sober (albeit hungover) whom he blames for the loss of a pool game. At no point do we see any male character who is part of the immediate narrative nucleus – other than Renton – engage with unenforced emotional or physical journeys towards maturation out of their current sphere. This sets Renton apart; his character holds a moral compass that only undermines the welfare of this friendship network of junkies when it serves to improve Renton's standing within a wider societal one of domestic normativity. Again, the film strikes a contradictory note; on the one hand, Renton would appear to be disloyal, selfish and immoral, but in leaving £2,000 for Spud the concluding scene confounds a straightforward reading of the character. Renton is inherently contradictory; he is selfish, narcissistic and nihilistic at times, but sensitive and decent at others. The two competing discourses which are articulated in this character are, in this instance, presented as an ironic contradiction within contemporary ideologies of masculinity.

Where *Trainspotting* deploys irony at certain points in the narrative to produce a film that refuses to either condone or condemn heroin use, the Welsh film *Twin Town* presents an ironic portrayal of drug use and underclass masculinity that refuses to accord any sense of gravitas to the situation, thus typifying the kind of film that Monk terms 'post-political'.[36] The film's central characters, the Lewis twins (Lhyr and Rhys Ifans) are represented as immature and irresponsible; their drug-fuelled antics are presented as (relatively) harmless juvenile rebellion rather than symptoms of disenfranchisement. They strike drug deals with pensioners, swapping magic mushrooms for prescription pills, and they smoke a bong while sharing a bath, debating football trivia and daring each other to take bigger and bigger hits until they are almost delirious. Crucially, they are not heroin addicts; their drug taking is confined to softer 'recreational' drugs such as cannabis, enabling a more light-hearted note than *Trainspotting*. Moreover, the twins have a contradictory relationship to lad culture. While they might perform laddish personas in many ways (their rejection of adult masculinity enables them to embrace a life free from responsibility and commitment, they celebrate trivia and silliness), they are socially and economically marginalised, and their ability to access or attain mainstream norms of hegemonic masculinity appears severely curtailed. Like their counterparts in *Trainspotting*, *My Name is Joe* and *TwentyFourSeven*, they are trapped within cycles of poverty and lacking in social mobility. The Lewis family live in a mobile home, their sister works as a receptionist in a brothel and their father is a local builder. *Twin Town* turns the twins' alienation from the norms of masculinity into an ironic comedy aimed at the same post-political audience as *Trainspotting*. The pre-Oedipal characterisation of the Lewis twins legitimises their lack of responsibility as liberating and indulges the anarchic humour of the boys by juxtaposing it with the corruption of the masculine authorities represented by a range of unappealing characters such as detectives Greyo (Dorien Thomas) and Terry Walsh (Dougray Scott) and immoral local businessman Bryn Cartwright (William Thomas). In many ways, this film capitalises upon the discourses of laddism and the celebratory endorsement of an extended or perpetual adolescent mindset that indulges fantasies of irresponsibility.

At the end of the 1990s, cinematic lad culture appeared to be shifting into a more reflexive moment with the release of *Human Traffic*, notable at least in part for being the cinematic debut of new lad par excellence, Danny Dyer. Although the film did not achieve massive commercial success it seemed to mark a turning away from the unashamedly sexist, boorish characteristics of the lad towards a more sensitive incarnation. The central protagonist, Jip, is, in many ways, a reconfiguration of the bolshie and arrogant new lad figure that had proliferated to the point of ubiquity since the middle of the decade. Much like *Trainspotting* and *Lock, Stock and Two Smoking Barrels*, *Human Traffic* is very clearly influenced by postmodern, postfeminist sensibilities and the film draws on contemporary discourses of girl power as much as it reflects upon the gendered identities of its male characters. Jip's distinction from the more established trope of new lad is evidenced early in the film through a piece to camera in which he talks about being impotent. This sequence functions not only to position him as far less self-assured than the new lad but also to augment his laddish identity (as evidenced through his friends and his involvement in club/ecstasy culture) with a more sensitive, introspective side. However, this sensitivity and his sexual impotence is symbolically connected to both a lack of social power and the feminising effects of the neoliberal service economy. *Human Traffic* mobilises the ideological tension between the celebratory discourses and swagger of new lad culture with the ongoing anxieties about masculinity at the end of the twentieth century, thus suggesting that the era of the knowingly and unashamedly offensive new lad might be drawing to a close, and it offers potential for a new median to emerge: a form of masculinity that amalgamates both the sensitive new man rhetoric with those aspects of lad culture that were hedonistic and playful.

However, any proclamations regarding the demise of the more misogynistic forms of lad culture were premature. Although lad culture appeared to wane during the earliest years of the 2000s, with the readership of both *loaded* and *FHM* showing sharp reductions of around 70,000 readers in the six months prior to January 2004, lad culture was far from over.[37] In early 2004, two new weekly magazines were launched which revitalised the market. *Nuts* (Emap) and *Zoo* (IPC) magazines exaggerated the quasi-pornographic style and editorial irreverence of their predecessors and their commercial success demonstrated the extent to which sexist forms of lad culture retained, and indeed extended, their popularity as a cultural trope of masculinity. In terms of British cinema, films such as the remake of *Alfie* (Charles Shyer, 2004) in which Jude Law takes on the role that had become synonymous with lad icon Michael Caine, the low-budget *Sex Lives of the Potato Men*, and a slew of (often straight to DVD) Danny Dyer exploitation films continued to proliferate. It is in relation to this consolidation of certain kinds of laddism that I explore the emergence of a cycle of football films that emerged in the early 2000s in the next section.

The Legacy of New Lad Culture: The Rise of the Football Film

From Nick Hornby's 1992 novel, *Fever Pitch*, football was a cornerstone of nineties lad culture and this continued into the early years of the 2000s, as the interest in football and football culture continued to grow exponentially. From the rise of celebrity footballers such as David Beckham, the ongoing obsession with the 1966 world cup, Frank Skinner and David Baddiel capitalising on their *Fantasy Football* success to release the single *Three Lions* in the run up to the 1996 European Championships, to the growing body of biographical books documenting both the lives of famous footballers as well as the men involved in the supposed 'glory years' of English football hooliganism, the early 2000s marked the consolidation of a particularly contemporary configuration of an increasingly commodified football culture and fandom. It is perhaps unsurprising, then, that the first decade of the millennium should be one in which films about football and football fandom should come to such prominence. While British cinema history has been punctuated by football films (for example, *Escape to Victory* (John Huston, 1981), *Arsenal Stadium Mystery* (Thorold Dickinson, 1939) and *Yesterday's Hero* (Neil Leifer, 1979)), the cycle of films that emerged in the 2000s was notable for the ways in which ideas about masculinity and male communities were explicitly foregrounded and for the ways in which the figure of the football hooligan came to be a crucial site through which these ideas could be explored.

It is Alan Clarke who is credited with bringing the first British football hooligan film to the screen with the 1989 BBC television drama, *The*

Firm. Starring Gary Oldman and Phil Davis as rival gang leaders, Bex and Yeti, *The Firm* caused considerable media consternation upon broadcast, coming just a few years after the Heysel stadium disaster and the Bradford stadium fire, and just a few weeks before ninety-six fans were killed at the FA Cup semi-final in Hillsborough. *The Firm* is characterised by Clarke's anti-Thatcher politics and was deliberately ambivalent in its portrayal of the 'English disease' of football hooliganism. Within a cultural context marked by the spectre of violent, rampaging football hooligans, Clarke's film was equally praised and reviled for its unflinching portrayal of inter-firm warfare. While David Hare asserted that the film was 'the best implicitly anti-Thatcherite film of the 1980s', *The Sun*'s TV critic, Garry Bushell, condemned both Clarke and the BBC as 'irresponsible'.[38]

Despite the fact that the Hillsborough stadium disaster of 1989 (in which ninety-six Liverpool fans were crushed to death) was caused by police mismanagement and not by firms or their members, it was a tragedy that led to a series of reforms that would fundamentally change English football culture. The most significant of these changes came about as a result of the Taylor Report, which was commissioned to investigate what happened at Hillsborough.[39] Lord Justice Taylor's report led to the abolition of traditional terraces, which were replaced with all-seater stadia, sparking what Anthony King would come to term the social revolution of football.[40] The confluence of redesigned stadia which led, in turn, to increased ticket prices, new patterns of television coverage and the establishment of a new league structure changed the political and social economy of English football irrevocably. While these developments were part of a conscious modernisation process, designed to eradicate, or at least better manage, the problem of football hooliganism, they changed the cultures of football fandom and participation in fundamental ways, leading to the seemingly inexorable embourgeoisement and commodification of a cultural form that had, for generations, signified a bastion of unreconstructed, working-class masculinity. Although, as King argues, to understand the transformation of English football cultures during the 1990s as being 'a smooth and technocratic procedure' the neoliberal gentrification of football that was ongoing during this time is an essential factor in the emergence of what Emma Poulton terms 'fantasy football hooliganism'.[41] Films such as *Awaydays* (Pat Holden, 2009), *Cass* (Jon S. Baird, 2008), *Green Street* (Lexi Alexander, 2004) and *The Football Factory* all clearly operate within a cultural context which has been shaped by nineties lad culture. Thus, the proliferation of the hooligan film comes out of a particular point in British cultural history but also emerges out of specific moment in British cinema history as well. The confluence of lad culture and the resurgent British film during the late 1990s created a cultural zone in which films representing, and sometimes celebrating, the homosocial cultures of football hooliganism make perfect sense.

While *The Firm* provides a thematic precursor to the films that I examine here, the cultural and cinematic impulses for hooligan films were set in motion earlier in the 1990s, with the emergence of lad culture. Indeed, it was during this time that *ID* (Phil Davis, 1995) was released. Directed by Phil Davis, who played the role of Yeti in Clarke's *The Firm*, *ID* is the story of an undercover police officer who is investigating a firm associated with Shadwell FC, a fictional inner-London club, loosely modelled on Millwall FC. Like the hooligan films that come later on, *ID* is notable for its provocative ambiguity. Despite the fact that John (Reese Dinsdale) is an operational police officer, the boundaries between his worlds and his identities are blurred. Throughout the film, John's hooligan persona increasingly intrudes into his domestic life as the character becomes, according to Davis, 'the thing that he is pretending to be'. The ending of the film is explicitly ambiguous as John is seen infiltrating neo-Nazi gangs and the film seems to deliberately call into question the boundaries and identities, particularly in relation to men and male communities. The hooliganism seen in *ID* is arguably more extreme than that seen in the more recent iterations of the hooligan film such as *Green Street* and *The Football Factory*; it doesn't quite sit within the same realm of fantasy hooliganism as these more contemporary films, not least because it came out at a time in which the threat of hooliganism remained high in both domestic and international footballing arenas. While *ID* appears to take a more realist and less ironic approach to its subject than is seen in the later films, it is influential for the ways in which it sets up questions of masculinity in terms of identity, performance and belonging.

It was Nick Love's film *The Football Factory* which seemed to invigorate the more recent cycle of hooligan films. Released in 2004, *The Football Factory* came out at a time when fantasy hooligan media was emerging across a range of media platforms including a spate of autobiographical accounts written by former hooligans.[42] These books variously offer a nostalgic exposition of what Sean Redhead terms the 'golden age' of football violence; the informal tone, the celebration of male camaraderie and the coarsely recalled anecdotes signifiying the working-class authenticity of their male authors, who transform from malignant symbols of male deviance to 'self-styled oral historians'.[43] Indeed, *The Football Factory* is couched in similar terms, with much press attention given to the fact that Nick Love himself was an erstwhile member of Millwall's Bushwhackers firm, and sports a club tattoo on his lower lip. While Love has been quick to position himself as an authentic member of the hooligan fraternity, his background was relatively privileged and he explains how, as a middle-class boy in a working-class area of South London he had 'much more to prove to everybody . . . more drugs, more violence'.[44]

The Football Factory was the first of a number of films released between 2004–2009 which took football hooliganism and the homosocial bonds of hooligan culture as their central focus. The film was released just before England travelled to Portugal for the European Championships and it caused considerable consternation in the press. *The Guardian's* Richard Williams proclaimed that the film 'further legitimises' a particularly pernicious problem within English football, functioning to incite violence amongst travelling fans because 'whether the film's director, Nick Love, admits it or not, it's the way popular culture works on society'.[45] Putting aside some of the problematic assumptions on media effects, Williams's objections to the film appear to perpetuate the kinds of class discourses that emerged during the early years of the 2000s as well as functioning to uphold a hierarchy of British cinema which, as Andrew Higson suggests, 'writes' British cinema into cultural memory as a realist cinema.[46] Lad culture's typical modes of irony and postmodernism are in evidence throughout the film and are most apparent in the ways in which the film plays with conventions of realism and laddish fantasy throughout the narrative. The opening moments of *The Football Factory* appear to anticipate the critical rhetoric that shaped its reception. A parodic news report, replete with a patronising male anchor wearing a pristine West Ham scarf folded neatly

Figure 3.2 *The Football Factory:*
Tommy looms large in the frame as he breaks the fourth wall

around a suit jacket and espousing the death of the football hooligan, is cut short by a swift punch delivered from the peripheries of the screen. As the journalist staggers backwards, Tommy Johnson, played by new lad icon Danny Dyer, is revealed as the assailant and the image of his face, close-up, is captured in freeze frame while his voice-over delivers an expletive-laden riposte to the hackneyed, self-righteous report. Johnson's/Dyer's opening gambit sets the tone for the film. His proclamation that it is 'in man's nature' to fight rehearses the idea of a feminised consumer culture being antithetical to authentic masculinity, containing and restraining men's 'natural' aggression.

Tommy and his friends are Chelsea supporters and are part of a 'firm' which, according to both the narration and received cultural history, is one of the most fearsome hooligan groups in England. Although Harris is the firm's 'top dog' it is Billy Bright (Frank Harper) who functions as the operations manager of the group, making arrangements with rival firms on his mobile, barking orders at his subordinates and leading the men into battle. Harper imbues Bright's character with an unashamedly unreconstructed masculinity which draws on the actor's extra-textual reputation as an established 'hard man' of British cinema. Moreover, Harper's status as a self-confessed football hooligan and erstwhile 'top boy' of Millwall's 'Banta Boys' lends a further authenticity to Bright's character. At first appearances Bright is arrogant and boastful but this is soon revealed to be a precarious and defensive performance of a damaged man whose violence is presented as a misguided mechanism of self-protection. A flashback shows an unhappy childhood in which Bright is bullied by his peers and learns violent, racist behaviour from his father. To an extent, then, the film draws on familiar discursive territory in which violence is presented and understood as a symptomatic response for men who have previously been victimised. As is the case with many of these characters, Bright's rage constantly simmers just below the surface: the 'quiet one with his missus' who Tommy refers to is juxtaposed with an image of Bright head-butting another man in a pub. Further sequences – such as the imaginary outbursts in the courtroom where Bright delivers an expletive laden tirade at a stony-faced judge, and the encounter with his Millwall supporting nemesis Fred (Tamer Hassan) at a children's football match – explicitly illustrate Bright's violent temperament. Tommy's voice-over explains that Bright remains a frustrated and bitter character who resents his position as Harris's deputy. In many ways, Bright's character is typical of what Andrew Spicer might term a 'damaged' man: acutely aware of his own place in the social hierarchy, defensive of his middling position, and bound by a strict sense of the cultural codes of behaviour and protocol that govern his environment.[47]

Tommy's voice-over tells us that it is only out of respect for the established hierarchy of the firm that Bright doesn't immediately retaliate when the firm's youngsters, Zeberdee (Roland Manookian) and Raff (Calum McNab) burgle his home – instead, he waits and exacts a less violent revenge, making the youngsters stand in for targets for his children to practice darts on. Bright's character is inherently contradictory; he is described by other characters as being a 'bully' and a 'psychopath' but his witty and sharp dialogue, along with his troubled backstory, complicate such a straightforward categorisation. Indeed, the character appears to exemplify the evasive politics that are at play in the film more broadly. Just as *Trainspotting* was criticised for its failure to condemn heroin use, *The Football Factory* not only refuses to offer a denunciation of violence but explicitly gestures to the pleasures of belonging to a firm. However, Bright does not escape the film without punishment; he is jailed for seven years for his role in the climactic fight between Chelsea and Millwall. Incarceration notwithstanding, the film vacillates between endorsement and critique to the end, refusing to offer any kind of stable or predictable moral certitude.

It is Danny Dyer's character, Tommy, who is effectively the main protagonist of the film and it is his voice that is privileged throughout. Tommy is haunted by a recurrent dream in which he lies bloodied but conscious in an underpass; during these visions he encounters another man whose face is bandaged. The two have a conversation which reveals that Tommy is still alive although the anonymous bandaged man is dead; in their final exchange the mysterious figure reveals himself as Zeberdee, the young lad who represents the next generation of the firm's family. Even a perfunctory analysis of Tommy's narrative trajectory demonstrates the ambivalent ideological stance on hooliganism and football gang culture. The moral conundrum with which the film is preoccupied is, at times, explicit and heavy-handed. Tommy's erstwhile comrade turned florist challenges his friend, asking 'is it [the fun of the violence] worth it?' and the film contains several images of billboards and posters posing questions such as 'What are you doing?' This question is asked explicitly again in the final sequence of the film as Tommy returns to his friends; his voice-over recounts the extent of the injuries suffered in the clash with Millwall and he asks 'Was it all worth it? I'll leave you to decide.' Love approaches this final scene with characteristic ambivalence; Tommy's return to jubilant friends, the warmth of the bonds shared between these men seems to suggest that, yes, it was worth it, but the optimism is short-lived as Zeberdee is gunned down in the pub toilet in front of Tommy. Thus, Love rejects the allure of a celebratory ending and opts for a conclusion that seems to undermine the suggestion that the film offers a straightforwardly glamourised and inconsequential account of football hooliganism, opting instead for the kind of ambiguity that is so characteristic of lad culture.

Both *The Football Factory* and Love's remake of *The Firm* articulate the director's ongoing preoccupation with communities of men and the rites of passage, which are central to these subcultural groups. The sense of community and belonging that binds these men together is set against the individualist rhetoric of post-Thatcher neoliberalism and thus is part of a wider cinematic preoccupation with these same cultural outcomes. In *Brassed Off* it is the iconic colliery band that is invested in as the last bastion of industrial male communities; in *The Full Monty* the men form an unlikely community through their dislocation; *The Football Factory*, then, can be seen as part of this wider recent history of masculinity in British cinema.

Positioning the new lad as a specifically postfeminist idiom of masculinity this chapter has examined the specific ways in which lad culture was manifest in British cinema and how the legacies of lad culture continue into the twenty-first century. Using the example of *Lock, Stock and Two Smoking Barrels*, *Trainspotting* and *Human Traffic* I examine how the various masculinities in the films mobilise irony as part of a specifically postfeminist lexis and explore the regional and national complexities of these debates. The second half of the chapter focuses on the ways in which the legacy of lad culture can be seen to operate within the cycle of football hooligan films from the early 2000s. Drawing attention to the style and form of the film, I examine the various hierarchies and systems of fraternal friendship and enmity that structure the narrative, exploring the specific cultural and moral codes that create this homosocial environment. In so doing, I suggest that *The Football Factory* draws on familiar discursive territory in which violence is understood as symptomatic of male culture, as characterised by the likes of *The Guardian*'s Richard Williams who found it to offer a problematically glamourised portrayal of football violence,[48] suggesting that such readings were not only bound up with regressive class politics but also appeared to overlook the moral ambiguity of the film's conclusion.

Notes

1 Penman, Ian, 1997, in Whelehan, Imelda (ed.), 2000, *Overloaded and the Future of Popular Feminism*, The Women's Press, London.

2 McRobbie, Angela, 2004, 'Post-feminism and popular culture' in *Feminist Media Studies*, Vol. 4, No. 3, p. 255.

3 Nixon, Sean, *Hard Look: Masculinities, Spectatorship and Contemporary Consumption*, UCL Press, London, p. 3.

4 Benwell, Bethan, 2002, 'Is There Anything New About These Lads? The Textual and Visual Construction of Masculinity in Men's Magazines' in Litosseliti, Lia and Sunderland, Jane (eds), *Gender Identity and Discourse Analysis: Discourse Approaches to Politics, Society and Culture*, John Benjamins Publishing Company, Amsterdam, p. 150.

5 Gill, Rosalind, 2003, 'Power and the Production of Subjects' in Benwell, Bethan (ed.), *Masculinity and Men's Lifestyle Magazines*, Blackwell Publishing, London, p. 48.

6 Benwell, Bethan, 2002, 'Is There Anything New About These Lads? The Textual and Visual Construction of Masculinity in Men's Magazines' in Litosseliti, Lia and Sunderland, Jane (eds), *Gender Identity and Discourse Analysis: Discourse Approaches to Politics, Society and Culture*, John Benjamins Publishing Company, Amsterdam.

7 Ibid.

8 Ibid. Gill, Rosalind, 2003, 'Power and the Production of Subjects' in Benwell, Bethan (ed.), *Masculinity and Men's Lifestyle Magazines*, Blackwell Publishing, London. Whelehan, Imelda, 2000, *Overloaded: Popular Culture and the Future of Feminism*, The Women's Press, London.

9 Benwell, Bethan, 2002, 'Is There Anything New About These Lads? The Textual and Visual Construction of Masculinity in Men's Magazines' in Litosseliti, Lia and Sunderland, Jane (eds), *Gender Identity and Discourse Analysis: Discourse Approaches to Politics, Society and Culture*, John Benjamins Publishing Company, Amsterdam.

10 Ibid. Benwell, Bethan, 2003, 'Introduction: Masculinity and Men's Lifestyle Magazines' in Benwell, Bethan (ed.), *Masculinity and Men's Lifestyle Magazines*, Blackwell Publishing, London. Benwell, Bethan, 2004, 'Ironic Discourse: Evasive Masculinity in Men's Lifestyle Magazines' in *Men and Masculinities Journal*, Vol. 7, No. 1, pp. 3–21. Crewe, Ben, 2003, *Representing Men: Cultural Production and Producers in the Men's Magazine Market*, Berg, Oxford. Jackson, Peter, Stevenson, Nick and Brooks, Kate, 2001, 'Introduction' in Jackson, Peter, Stevenson, Nick and Brooks, Kate (eds), *Making Sense of Men's Magazines*, Polity Press, Cambridge.

11 Monk, Claire, 2000, 'Men in the 90s' in Murphy, R. (ed.), *British Cinema of the 90s*, BFI Publishing, London. Chibnall, Steve, 2009, 'Travels in Ladland: The British Gangster Film Cycle, 1998–2001' in Murphy, Robert (ed.), *The British Cinema Book* (3rd edn), BFI Publishing, London.

12 Gill, Rosalind, 2007, 'Postfeminist Media Culture: Elements of a Sensibility' in *European Journal Of Cultural Studies*, Vol. 10, No. 2, pp. 147–166.

13 Gill, Rosalind, 2003, 'Power and the Production of Subjects: A Genealogy of the New Man and the New Lad' in *Sociological Review*, Vol. 51, No. 1, pp. 34–56.

14 Showalter, Elaine, 2002, 'Lad-Lit' in Zachary Leader (ed.), *On Modern British Fiction*, Oxford: Oxford University Press, pp. 60–76.

15 For a useful discussion of *Elizabeth* as an 'anti-heritage' film see Andrew

Higson, 2003, *English Heritage, English Cinema: Costume Drama Since 1980*, Oxford University Press, Oxford.

16 Benwell, Bethan, 2002, 'Is There Anything New About These Lads? The Textual and Visual Construction of Masculinity in Men's Magazines' in Litosseliti, Lia and Sunderland, Jane (eds), *Gender Identity and Discourse Analysis: Discourse Approaches to Politics, Society and Culture*, John Benjamins Publishing Company, Amsterdam.

17 Kimmel, Michael, 2008, *Guyland: The Perilous World Where Boys Become Men*, Harper Perennial, New York.

18 Gill, Rosalind, 2003, 'Power and the Production of Subjects: A Genealogy of the New Man and the New Lad' in *Sociological Review*, Vol. 51, No. 1, pp. 34–56.

19 Gill, Rosalind, 2007, 'Postfeminist Media Culture: Elements of a Sensibility' in *European Journal of Cultural Studies*, Vol. 10, No. 2, pp. 147–166. doi: 10.1177/1367549407075898

20 Monk, Claire, 2000, 'Men in the 90s' in Murphy, Robert (ed.), *British Cinema of the 1990s*, BFI Publishing, London. Angela McRobbie, 2004, 'Post-Feminism and Popular Culture' in *Feminist Media Studies*, Vol. 4, No. 3, pp. 255–264.

21 Chibnall, Steve, 2009, 'Travels in Ladland: The British Gangster Film Cycle, 1998–2001', in Murphy, Robert (ed.), *The British Cinema Book* (3rd edn), BFI Publishing, London.

22 Ibrahim, Samir, 2006, 'A Cultural Studies Analysis of Guy Ritchie's *Snatch*'. https://www.grin.com/document/129441

23 Benwell Bethan, 2004, 'Ironic Discourse: Evasive Masculinity in Men's Lifestyle Magazines' in *Men and Masculinities*, Vol. 7, No. 1.

24 Ibid. Whelehan, Imelda, 2000, *Overloaded: Popular Culture and the Future of Feminism*, The Women's Press, London.

25 Gill, Rosalind, 2007, 'Postfeminist Media Culture: Elements of a Sensibility' in *European Journal of Cultural Studies*, Vol. 10, No. 2, pp. 147–166. doi: 10.1177/1367549407075898

26 Hutcheon, Linda, 1994, *Irony's Edge: The Theory and Politics of Irony*, Routledge, London.

27 Tasker, Yvonne, 2005, 'Fantasizing Gender and Race: Women in Contemporary Action Cinema' in Williams, Linda Ruth and Hammond, Michael (ed.), *Contemporary American Cinema*, Open University Press, Maidenhead, p. 424.

28 Benwell, Bethan, 2003, 'Introduction: Masculinity and Men's Lifestyle Magazines' in Benwell, Bethan (ed.), *Masculinity and Men's Lifestyle Magazines*, Blackwell Publishing, London.

29 Monk, Claire, 2000 'Men in the 90s' in Murphy, Robert (ed.), *British Cinema of the 1990s*, BFI Publishing, London.

30 McLoughlin, D., 1996, 'A Palpable Hit' in *British Medical Journal*, Vol. 312, No. 7030, 2 March, p. 585. http://www.bmj.com/cgi/content/long/312/7030/585 (accessed 20 October 2020).

31 Cited in ibid.

32 Petrie, D., 2010, '*Trainspotting*: The Film' in Schoene, B. (ed.), *Edinburgh Companion to Irvine Welsh*, Edinburgh University Press, Edinburgh, p. 43.

33 Petrie, D., 2004, *Contemporary Scottish Fictions: Film, Television and the Novel*, Edinburgh University Press, Edinburgh.

34 Ibid., p. 101.

35 Leah Betts was a particularly public example after her parents released pictures of their 18-year-old daughter on her death bed after taking ecstasy for the first time.

36 Monk, Claire, 2000, 'Men in the 90s' in Murphy, Robert (ed.), *British Cinema of the 90s*, BFI Publishing, London.

37 Dickinson, F., 2004, 'Publishing: What Does Your Magazine Say About You?' in *The Independent on Sunday*, 15 August 2004. http://www.independ ent.co.uk/news/media/publishing-what-does-your-magazine-say-about-you-556603.html (accessed 20 October 2020).

38 Rolinson, Dave, 2005, *Alan Clarke*, Manchester University Press, Manchester.

39 Lord Justice Taylor, 1989, *The Hillsborough Stadium Disaster Inquiry Report*, HMSO, London. Presented to parliament in January 1990.

40 King, Anthony, 2002, *The End of the Terraces: The Transformation of English Football*, Leicester University Press, Leicester.

41 Ibid. Poulton, E., 2006, '"Lights, Camera, Aggro!": Readings of Celluloid Hooliganism' in *Sport and Society: Cultures, Commerce, Media, Politics*, Vol. 9, No. 3.

42 Examples include *Naughty* by Mark Chester, *The Men in Black* by Tony O'Neill, *The Boys from the Mersey* by Nicholas Allt and *Cass* by Cass Pennant.

43 Redhead, Steve, 2009, 'Hooligan Writing and the Study of Football Fan Culture: Problems and Possibilities' in *Nebula*. www.nobleworld.biz/images/ Redhead2.pdf

44 Love, Nick, 2007, *The Guardian*. https://www.theguardian.com/film/2007/ mar/01/features.questiontime

45 Williams, Richard, 2004, 'The Football Factory: Irresponsible, Ill-timed and Risible' in *The Guardian*. https://www.theguardian.com/football/2004/ may/12/sport.comment (accessed 20 October 2020).

46 Higson, Andrew, 1984, 'Place, Space, Spectacle' in *Screen*, Vol. 81.

47 Spicer, Andrew, 2003, *Typical Men: Representations of Masculinity in Popular British Cinema*, I. B. Tauris, London, p. 195.

48 Williams, Richard, 2004, 'The Football Factory: Irresponsible, Ill-timed and Risible' in *The Guardian*. https://www.theguardian.com/football/2004/ may/12/sport.comment (accessed 20 October 2020).

CHAPTER 4

Social Exclusion, Poverty Culture and Marginalised Masculinities: Narratives of Youth and Race

With a narrative focus on social issues and political critique, social realism has been, if not quite an 'unbroken tradition' in British cinema, then one of its most established forms with a historical lineage stretching back to the documentary filmmaking of the 1930s and 1940s.[1] Indeed, as Andrew Higson has claimed in his influential analysis of British New Wave cinema of the 1960s, the narrative and aesthetic form of films such as *Saturday Night and Sunday Morning* (Karel Reisz, 1960) draw on stylistic conventions of documentary. Further, as Higson suggests, realism became a defining quality of British cinema in opposition to what he terms the 'melodramatic fantasies' of Hollywood cinema.[2]

Despite the plurality of form, style and genre of British film during the 1990s and 2000s, a significant number of films explicitly engaged in political and social critique. Alongside established directors such as Ken Loach and Mike Leigh, both of whom are renowned for films that are often explicit in their political intentions, new filmmakers such as Shane Meadows emerged appearing to continue this rich tradition of British cinema. While Claire Monk has rightly critiqued films such as *The Full Monty* for what she sees as their cynical, profit-driven commodification of marginalised masculinities, I argue that critically and politically informed films remained a significant part of British cinema and retained a steady, if sometimes less commercially visible, presence across the period.[3] Taking forward Higson's suggestion that British social realism is not necessarily always an expression of a collective working-class consciousness but is instead about the 'attempts of individuals to escape from their conditions' I argue that realist films remained a key site through which narratives of young masculinities in particular were mediated.

Drawing specifically on case studies of Shane Meadows debut feature, *TwentyFourSeven* (1997) and Ken Loach's *My Name is Joe* (1998) I examine the ways in which the cultural legacy of Thatcherism and the succession of Conservative governments in the 1980s and 1990s are used to present socially and politically critical narratives with a specific focus on young, working-class men. Over the course of the 2000s, representations of marginalised masculinity continued to proliferate in a range of genres including horror and comedy but the image of marginalised youth remained a central trope within social realist films in particular. Unlike the regional and northern focus seen in the previous decade, films such as *Bullet Boy* (Saul Dibb, 2004), *Kidulthood* (Menhaj Huda, 2006), *Shifty* (Eran Creevy, 2008), *1 Day* (Penny Woolcock and Michèle Nuzzo, 2009) and *4321* (Noel Clarke and Mark Davis, 2010) are all located in and around the multicultural communities of Greater London. While these films appear to give space to a greater diversity of narratives of marginalised young masculinities, they might also be understood, as Sarita Malik and Clive James Nwonka suggest, as reaffirming normative ideologies around race, class and gender and in particular the cultural narrative of the working-class, inner-city Black British youth as a pressing social problem in need of a political and social resolution.[4] Moreover, I suggest that the fact that the majority of the directors of these films are white and middle class demands investigation, and that although they may be well-intentioned, the fact that these films are directed, for the most part, by white filmmakers, is indicative of the ongoing systemic and structural racial inequalities of the British film industry. Moreover, there are questions to be asked regarding the ways in which these films commodify Black masculinity and Black subcultures in the service of upholding normative and invariably reductive discourses of urban Black youths. I draw on *Bullet Boy*, *Kidulthood* and *1 Day* as three different examples of social realist engagement with multicultural communities, examining the ways in which they perform problematically normative iterations of young Black British and Asian masculinities.

Debates about class, poverty and marginalisation had also shifted since the turn of the millennium, exemplified by the emergence of 'chav' culture, which, as Imogen Tyler demonstrates, functioned to pathologise poverty as evidence of a personal choice, or failing.[5] I suggest that while 'the chav' might be a logical endpoint in the socio-economic/-political project of British neoliberalism, British cinema offers a distinctive intervention into questions of marginality and poverty that demands a more complex analysis of the intersections between gender, race and class in order to better understand the cultural politics at play within these films. As Matthew Adams and Jane Raisborough point out, 'the chav' is most commonly represented as white,[6] but, as Sarita Malik and Clive James Nwonka suggest, race is a key absent presence within these debates.[7] They argue that the intersections between gender, class, race and media are 'intertwined with political, legislative and cultural agendas tied to post-multiculturalist and neoliberal tendencies' that were developing during this time.[8] As such, the films that I consider in this chapter have a necessary relationship with the emergence of 'chav' culture in the early 2000s and the particular ways in which young, poor, Black British masculinities are triply pathologised via mechanisms of race, class and gender. In extending these arguments in relation to British cinema, I extend the arguments put forward by Malik and Nwonka and Imogen Tyler to suggest that films such as *TwentyFourSeven*, *My Name is Joe*, *Bullet Boy* and *1 Day*, among others, occupy a contested political and discursive space that invariably functions to 'produce and reaffirm normative cultural meanings' around gender, class and race via a 'pervasive discourse of inclusivity'.[9]

Shifting Parameters of Realism

Perhaps unsurprisingly, given the predominance of cultural and political concern with questions around masculinity during this period, a large number of the films that might fall under the broader generic category of British social realism focused explicitly on issues around the behaviour and cultures of young men, exploring questions of structural and economic marginalisation with particular frequency. The films that I focus on in this chapter offer an identifiable mode of narrative and representation within the increasingly heterogeneous landscape of British cinema in the 1990s and 2000s, with an emphasis on impoverished and unemployed young men who are, as Andrew Spicer puts it, 'adrift in a society represented as hopelessly rundown'.[10] Films such as *TwentyFourSeven*, *Bullet Boy* and *Shifty* offer a differently configured palette of young masculinity from that commonly associated with 'new' lad culture and, I argue, they are also politically and discursively distinct from the crossover underclass films such as *The Full Monty*, as discussed in Chapter 1.

The focus on the deprivation and personal struggles of the marginalised young men that I focus on in this chapter also diverges from the more commercially successful genres of heritage film and romantic comedy and their predominant focus on more affluent and middle-class men. In contrast to the international success of films such as *Bridget Jones's Diary* (Sharon Maguire, 2001) or *Atonement* (Joe Wright, 2007) many of the films that I focus on in this chapter had a limited domestic release, and even those that garnered critical acclaim invariably remained a niche segment of the domestic film market. Even those films made by established directors such as Ken Loach or Mike Leigh rarely secured a general release, meaning that they were confined to independent, regional, art house cinemas, and the film festival circuits and the audiences that attend these events.

The films in this chapter connect with the traditions of British social realism in that they are firmly embedded within specific spatial and temporal locations. They are, as Samantha Lay describes, 'fixed in and by their contemporaneous elements' focusing upon social issues and questions born of their context.[11] Films such as *My Name is Joe*, *TwentyFourSeven*, *Bullet Boy*, *Kidulthood*, *1 Day* and *Sweet Sixteen* (Ken Loach, 2002) dramatise the distinct cultural dynamics of local spaces in which they are set. The kinds of *'local* practices' that Lisa McKenzie identifies in her ethnographic study of the St Anne's estate in Nottingham are shown to operate similarly (emphasis in original).[12] The characters in *TwentyFourSeven* are very much 'the products of their physical environments' with the dislocation of their community emphasising what Sarah Petrovic describes as their 'isolation from the hegemonic majority', creating a micro-culture with 'an autonomous, alternative value system defined in opposition to the norms of wider society'.[13] Similar microcosms are evident in *Sweet Sixteen* and *My Name is Joe*, both of which are part of Ken Loach's so-called Scottish Trilogy along with *Ae Fond Kiss* (2004).[14] Both *Sweet Sixteen* and *My Name is Joe* draw upon a rich iconography of the once vibrant and industrial but now rundown landscapes of Glasgow and the satellite docklands of Greenock to create parallels between the neglected, dereliction of the city with the marginality of their central characters.[15]

During the early years of the 2000s there was a distinct proliferation of films loosely defined by Malik and Nwonka as 'urban'.[16] These films tend to be based in and around the more deprived parts of London and feature a multicultural range of young characters; furthermore, and in distinction to the earlier films under discussion, they feature more prominent female characters alongside male protagonists. Films such as *Kidulthood* and its sequel, *Adulthood* (Noel Clarke, 2008), for example, include Black British, Asian British and white British characters, and a similar multicultural range of characters can be found in *Shifty*, *4321*, *Attack the Block* (Joe Cornish, 2010) and *Shank* (Mo Ali, 2009). *Bullet Boy* is notable as a film which focuses on an exclusively Black British cast in its narrative about inner-city gang culture and the codes of masculinity that dominate within it, often leading to comparisons with John Singleton's *Boyz N The Hood* (1991). Even though all of these films offer moments of social critique, they rehearse the familiar discursive construction of inner-city, poor boys as social problems and as 'active agents, deliberately and wilfully engaging in anti-social behaviour'.[17]

While films such as *Sweet Sixteen* and *TwentyFourSeven* work within the established narrative strategies of naturalism, and thus are, in many ways, quite traditional iterations of social realism, this period was one of creative development and innovation in British cinema within the broader genre of socially located/critical films. As noted by David Forrest among others, the visual styles and narrative forms of socially engaged filmmaking morphed during this period, pushing the established boundaries of naturalism in new directions visually and aurally, as well as in terms of genre and the structural organisation of the narrative.[18] Developing a trend that can be traced back to the 2006 American film, *Step Up* (Anne Fletcher), a number of films including *1 Day* and *4321* augment their naturalism and social realist themes with musical performances that draw on the thriving urban music culture of the time. The *Streetdance* (Maz Giwas and Dania Pasquini, 2010) films are similar in this regard, although the images of London in these more upbeat and aspirational terms offer a rather different kind of cultural politics that seems more in keeping with the hegemonies of neoliberalism via individual hard work and self-determination. Other films, such as *Shank* and *City Rats* (Steve Kelly, 2009) adopt a Tarantino-esque style of multi-strand storytelling and non-linear narratives, departing from the linear naturalism of traditional social realism. *Shank* and *Kidulthood* are also notable for the use of stylised editing which is a striking and conspicuous juxtaposition against the more naturalistic aspects of the films. These various formal and stylistic developments within films whose narratives concerns and characters clearly belong to a realist tradition demonstrate some of the creative developments within the genre during this period of the 2000s. Despite these formal and aesthetic departures from the traditional conventions of naturalism as one of the defining features of social realism, these films share an emphasis on socially embedded and informed filmmaking that focuses in particular on young, marginalised male characters and the implications of their economic and social marginality. As such, these films act as a counterpoint to the irreverent playfulness of nineties lad culture, as explored in the previous chapter, by making visible the psychosocial consequences of economic marginalisation and unemployment on young men who have grown up in post-industrial Britain.

In many ways, the focus on the social exclusion and marginalisation of unemployed, poor, young male characters positions them in ways that Imogen Tyler might describe as abject. They are the 'symbolic and material scapegoats' who function as 'ideological conductors mobilised to do the dirty work of neoliberal governmentality'.[19] This trend is something that becomes more pronounced at the latter end of the 2000s, where films such as *Kidulthood*, *Attack the Block* and the so called 'hoodie horror' *Eden Lake* (James Watkins, 2008) draw on the racial, gendered and classed paradigms of 'chav' culture. *Kidulthood*, for example, brings together two of the most familiar contemporary paradigms of social deviance: violent, drug-dealing Black adolescents and white, promiscuous and loud teenage girls who illustrate and perform the discourses of social and moral decay that were being rehearsed by politicians and news media alike. Moral panics over youth culture during this period focused intensely on the behaviour of young men, with Jack Straw, the Home Secretary, responsible for developing the Anti-Social Behaviour Orders (or ASBOs as they were commonly known), arguing that 'the behaviour and role of young men' was *the* main social issue of the 1990s and early 2000s.[20] His comments were not directed at *all* young men but implicitly gesture towards socially and economically marginalised young men who, as Linda McDowell suggests, become discursively constructed as 'social problems' on account of declining educational attainment, rising criminal convictions and a populist conflation of young poor men with drug taking.[21] Thus, poor (and invariably urban) young men became the defining symbol of the 'moral vacuum' of 'Broken Britain'.[22]

With young, high school-aged boys and girls taking drugs, having casual sex, drinking, shoplifting and becoming embroiled in violent gangs, films such as *Kidulthood*, *1 Day* and *Bullet Boy* appear to draw on the political iconography of 'Broken Britain' whilst also reaffirming it as a state of being for the young, urban poor. In this regard, the political discourses at play in these films are complex; on the one hand they are critically informed and engaged in the cultural work of criticism but on the other hand they rehearse a familiar populist narrative of young boys, and young, working-class Black youths in particular, as a social problem in need of management.

Cultures of Class, Race and Social Exclusion

In addition to the continued growth of the post-industrial economy and the concomitant decline of industry, the economic and ideological dominance of neoliberalism was increasingly consolidated during the period, impacting on the politics and discourses of class and gender. The 'problems' of poverty and unemployment were repositioned as the result of personal shortcomings that could be rectified by individual determination and making the 'right' choices. The steady economic growth of the 1990s lent false credibility to the myth of poverty as a self-induced state even though the wave of premillennial prosperity was less universally distributed than the political rhetoric suggested. The Poverty and Social

Exclusion in Britain report produced by the Joseph Rowntree Foundation in 2000 found that poverty had in fact increased from 14 per cent in 1983 to 21 per cent in 1990 and had risen further to over 24 per cent by 1999, and that the gap between the richest and poorest people in the UK was continuing to grow.[23] The findings of this report led Sir Peter Barclay, the then Chair of the Rowntree Foundation, to conclude that social exclusion and economic poverty remained endemic in Britain, 'despite the huge increase in affluence seen over the last two decades'.[24] After the recession of 1990–1991, the UK entered a lengthy period of growth, which strengthened steadily under the Labour government, assisted by low levels of inflation and a constantly solid growth in GDP. The increasingly global economy continued to flourish in the first part of the new millennium. In the UK, the so called 'dot-com bubble', the growth of a multinational economic infrastructure, and the buoyant creative and cultural economy were all signifiers of this wave of post-industrial and technologically driven prosperity. However, this period of stability and growth came to an abrupt end with the 2007/2008 global financial crisis, which plunged Britain back into a protracted period of recession and austerity, the effects of which have lasted well beyond the period with which this book is concerned.

Younger men have endured most of both the economic recession that marked the end of the 1980s and early part of the 1990s and the shift from an industrial to a service-based economy.[25] As Beverley Skeggs points out, the physicality of young, working-class men has 'little worth in a predominantly service economy',[26] rendering, as Linda McDowell suggests, 'pathways to employment . . . less available'.[27] In many ways, the 'crisis' of masculinity was symbolised by the figure of the poor, working-class adolescent who had been born into an industrial economy but who had come of age in a service economy for which he was inadequately equipped. As McDowell explains, the demands for deference that are central within the service economy are in distinct opposition to the 'street bravado and machismo' of working-class young men.[28]

One of the fundamental discursive cornerstones of British neoliberalism has been to generate a consensus which consistently positions class as irrelevant and anachronistic. As Imogen Tyler puts it, 'at the very moment that economic inequalities were deepening, "class" was to be expunged from mainstream political vocabularies'.[29] While the language of a meritocratic and classless Britain became a defining characteristic of Tony Blair's New Labour project, it had a longer historical legacy that began in the 1980s Thatcher government. It was John Major who proclaimed a vision of a classless society as one in which 'not everyone is the same, or thinks the same, or earns the same. But a tapestry of talents in which everyone from child to adult respects achievement; where every promotion, every certificate is respected; and each person's contribution is valued.'[30] Indeed, Blair's capacity to co-opt and continue the imagery and language of his Conservative predecessor illuminates the evolution of neoliberalism within the British socio-political context. But this emphasis on the ideology of meritocracy belies a fundamental paradox at the heart of the rhetoric of classlessness; as sociologist Stephanie Lawler explains, 'class is *built into* the idea of classlessness', and this is, in turn, evidenced by the emergence of the disparaging discourse of the abject underclass during this period.[31]

The paradoxical nature of the neoliberal goal of a society unfettered by class is particularly evident in those films that come out of the traditions of politically critical filmmaking associated with British social realism. Whether set in the past, contemporary times or the future, such as *Young Soul Rebels* (Isaac Julien, 1991), *TwentyFourSeven* and *Welcome II the Terrordome* (Ngozi Onwurah, 1995), the social effects of class were an ongoing theme within British cinema and provided a damning indictment of the myth of classlessness. This cinematic counterpoint to the hegemony of consumerism continues into the 2000s with a raft of films including *Bullet Boy*, *Kidulthood* and *Shank* among examples of representations of young men that emphasise the interdependent connections between class, race, region and gender.

Getting Shit 24:7:
Marginalised Young Men in 1990s British Films

Shane Meadows had begun to attract critical attention on the back of his sixty-minute film *Small Time* which had been screened alongside the thirteen-minute short *Where's the Money Ronnie!* (Shane Meadows, 1996) at the Edinburgh and Toronto Film Festivals in 1996. He had, by this stage, begun to build an impressive catalogue of around thirty short films, including *King of the Gypsies* (Shane Meadows, 1995), a ten-minute documentary about a bare-knuckle boxer from Uttoxeter which was broadcast on Channel 4 in 1995, giving Meadows his first broadcast credit. *TwentyFourSeven* was Meadows's feature-length debut; it was produced by Stephen Woolley and co-written with Paul Fraser who would go on to work with Meadows on *A Room for Romeo Brass* (Shane Meadows, 1999), *Once Upon a Time in the Midlands* (Shane Meadows, 2002), *Dead Man's Shoes* (Shane Meadows, 2004) and *Somers Town* (Shane Meadows, 2008). It was Woolley who persuaded Meadows and Fraser to develop *TwentyFourSeven* from a short film into what would become Meadows's debut feature. With an established producer on board in the shape of Woolley, Meadows secured funding of £1.4 million from BBC Films and Scala Productions and was able to secure Bob Hoskins as the lead character of Darcy.

Filmed in black and white, *TwentyFourSeven* only had a limited cinema release but garnered significant critical acclaim, securing nominations for the 1998 BAFTA Alexander Korda Award for Best British Film and in the Best British Independent Film category at the British Independent Film Awards, and winning both the Douglas Hickox Award at the 1998 British Independent Film Awards and the FIPRESCI Prize at the 1998 Venice Film Festival. Although not autobiographical, *TwentyFourSeven* is inspired by Meadows's experiences growing up in the impoverished, post-industrial Midlands during the Thatcher years, and in many ways the film is a riposte to the emphatic individualism of the era. In contrast to Thatcher, 'for Meadows, there *is* such a thing as society',[32] and the intense focus on the community in which Darcy, Tim (Danny Nussbaum) and Fag Ash live and the networks of friendships, rivalries and relationships within that micro-cosmos offer a politically critical treatise on the structural issues of poverty, marginalisation and their impact on the post-industrial, working-class men of central and northern England. *TwentyFourSeven* is a story about the men and the boys who 'get shit, 24:7', foregrounding themes of social dereliction and impoverishment from the opening frames.

The opening image of a disused, overgrown railway provides a visual indication of the social context and political agenda of the film; moreover, it conveys the sense of absolute stasis and entrapment that stifles the films various characters. The camera is static while a young man and his dog meander along. We follow Tim as he pursues his errant dog into the overgrown sidings. Hidden in a burnt-out wooden hut is a dirty, unkempt man. This man is Alan Darcy an erstwhile lynchpin of the local community who has fallen on hard times. Realising that all is not well with his old friend, Tim takes Darcy home. As the film cuts to the interior of Tim's house the poverty of the characters is emphasised: the furniture is sparse and old-fashioned, the decor is dated and the dark, drab kitchen is rendered even bleaker by the low lighting which casts foreboding shadows across the already dull room.

Passages in Darcy's diary provide the voice-over that returns us to the recent past in which the problems besetting the young men of the community first took hold. Darcy's words openly place the blame for the contemporary deprivation in the eighties on the social and economic policies of Thatcherism. A younger looking, better-groomed Darcy is seen busily renovating the same wooden structure in which Tim would find him years

Figure 4.1 *TwentyFourSeven:* The black and white cinematography
is used to emphasise the bleakness of Tim's house

later. His words, however, belie his industrious activity; 'the eighties, a
time in which', he proclaims, 'everything was a boom, a transaction . . .
money was God'. The resurgent affluence to which he refers, however, did
not reach the post-industrial heartlands of the Midlands regions; while
certain economic sectors were driving economic growth in some regions
of the UK, areas such as Nottingham, where the film is set, were being left
behind. The serious ramifications of this on heavy industries that had not
only provided employment but also social and economic stability would
affect several generations. As Darcy puts it, 'when our town died, we, with
our young in hand, were just beginning, but we weren't living'. Thus, by
highlighting the 'brutalising consequences of unemployment and poverty'
on Darcy and his neighbours, Meadows's film harks back to the traditions
of 1960s social realist films.[33]

The political intervention in Darcy's opening monologue sets the
tone for the film and contextualises the narrative of male disenfranchisement within a very specific social and economic climate shaped by the
deleterious legacy of the Conservative Thatcher government. Moreover,
it positions Meadows firmly within the lineage of British social realism,
politically and cinematically aligned with the likes of Ken Loach; the
use of non-actors further consolidates his position within this tradition.
Darcy labels himself and his neighbours as the 'forgotten casualties' or
'victims' of the hegemony of greed and aspiration of the 1980s in which
neoliberal individualism replaced collective working-class politics.[34] The
result of the disestablishment of the collective working-class community

is decay: poverty is embedded within the buildings and the spaces and it is inscribed on and performed by the bodies of the 'demoralised inhabitants' who happen to live there. Darcy's ongoing critique of 'progress' is accompanied by images of small rows of rundown terrace houses before cutting to the interior space. The shot changes to show the prone body of a man (Bruce Jones) sleeping on an old, worn-out sofa while his world-weary wife (Annette Hill) stands at an ironing board, providing further visual evidence of the damage of the interminable unemployment and concomitant poverty about which Darcy speaks. The Nottingham suburb in which the film is set symbolises the decline and poverty that have blighted once prosperous industrial communities all over the Midlands and northern parts of England. The extent of the broken promises of industrialisation is underlined by Meadows's choice of location: Nottingham was the setting for *Saturday Night and Sunday Morning* amongst other adaptations of Alan Sillitoe's novels. Despite the disillusionment of that title's central protagonist Arthur Seaton, the young men of his generation are more fortunate than their nineties counterparts. Seaton and his generation are employed and the film posits the possibilities of social mobility and potential escape. Thus Meadows's film contextualises the narratives of working-class masculinity within a wider cinematic and social continuum, drawing a parallel between the 'broken promises' of post-war reconstruction and those of the post-industrial neoliberalism for the lads in Darcy's town.

While Darcy's monologue explains how his generation was affected by the cultural and economic changes of the eighties it soon becomes evident that it is the next generation who are the real victims. The world that these (predominantly white) lads inhabit could not be further from the consumerist and hedonistic milieu of the new lads or the multicultural affluence that led to London being proclaimed 'the coolest city on Earth' by Newsweek in 1996.[35] The young men in Darcy's community appear destined to remain lost; they have no hope, no aspiration and no chance of success; they are marginalised and abject objects whose presence disrupts the neoliberal narrative of self-betterment and aspiration via consumption. Darcy is used as the political mouthpiece of the film as he describes how the young men in his community have been let down by the various 'broken promises' of economic progress ('progress', he ponders 'is a dodgy word, a bit like "fresh-frozen"'). This idea is evidenced further by the lads themselves, whose conversations demonstrate the shortcomings of their education with greater poignancy and delicacy than an explicit political statement. From the confusion over the salmonella outbreak to the debate between Knighty (James Hooton) and Gadget (Justin Brady) about whether wasps bite or sting the lads are shown to be harmless but hampered by a lack in their general knowledge and understanding of the world. While Meadows plays these snippets of dialogue for dark comedic value the more serious point is never far from the surface; the young men of this fictitious suburb on the outskirts of a Midlands town suffer from the build-up of multiple and interconnected deprivations. They were failed by Thatcher's economic policies, failed by the education system and, despite their young ages, they have ended up unemployed and trapped in the same cycles of deprivation, drug taking and subsequent criminalisation that their fathers appear ensnared in.

In many ways, then, these young men can be understood as prefiguring the emergence of 'chav' culture and complicating the pathologisation of poverty because of individual, wilfully made 'wrong' choices. Darcy's monologue emphasises precisely the opposite argument: the entrapment of the young men within both the geographical and economic location is indicative of a lack of individual and collective agency. As Darcy's opening monologue concludes, the image shifts from the figure of the defeated father to a group of young men hanging around in a park, smoking. They are socially, economically and culturally marginal. and they are trapped in a transgenerational cycle of poverty and social exclusion. Thus, Meadows's film rejects the postmodern style of the new lad films both politically and aesthetically. He refuses to turn the issue of male disempowerment into a light-hearted comedy in which the lads have chosen to reject employ-ment (as is the case in *Twin Town*), or follow a narrative in which their shambolic attempts at enterprise land them in trouble (as in *Lock, Stock and Two Smoking Barrels*). Instead, Meadows presents the narrative of this Nottingham suburb and the people within it as emblematic of the wider social problems caused by recent social and economic change. Aesthetically the film also counterpoints the slick stylisation of *Trainspotting* or *Lock, Stock*; not only is *TwentyFourSeven* filmed in black and white but the sequences are dominated by long, static shots with unobtrusive editing and, as such, the film harks back to the style of an older social realist tradition. Further, this style also situates Meadows as a politically driven director more in line with contemporary socialist filmmakers such as Mike Leigh and Ken Loach rather than his own generational cohort. Paul Dave suggests that *TwentyFourSeven* in particular is a film that brings 'the protective, reciprocal and collective aspects of working class culture' to the fore, emphasising the 'tenderness and mutuality' of the various relationships.[36] Indeed, there are moments throughout the film where Meadows draws attention to the complexities of these relationships, the lads make fun of Darcy at times but there is a deep-seated respect for him, as is shown in the funeral scenes. In this regard, Shane Meadows is one filmmaker who specifically challenges Monk's argument that the return to class consciousness in British cinema of the 1990s was 'superficial' and 'deceptive'.[37] Meadows's work during the nineties consciously takes on an unfashionably socialist sentimentality and I would suggest that there were a number of other directors, including both Mike Leigh and Ken Loach, who continued to make films that engaged critically and explicitly with issues of class and working-class cultures.

The town's lads are split into two rival groups and one of Darcy's main motivations in establishing the boxing club is to reunite them and lay their quarrels to rest. The issues that dominate the rivalry between the two groups revolve around the persistent need to appear to conform to a socially sanctioned performance of masculinity and to be respected within the community. Within this community the codes of hegemonic masculinity are clearly defined; as Darcy explains, 'Reputations are so important in a town like this . . . if your father was a hard man then you're obliged to operate with muscle. Librarians don't pull a lot of sway round here.' In this regard, the lack of work-based identities results in a heightened investment in the performative aspects of hegemonic masculinity, not least amongst which is to retaliate to any perceived slight with violence. The two groups of lads are continually engaged in a performative face-off, each member of the group occupying a defined role within the broader hierarchy and working collectively to maintain their dominance (whether perceived or actual) over the other. In many ways, this is evidence of exactly the kinds of collectivity and reciprocity described by Dave (2006).[38] Moreover, this is strikingly similar to the alternative values systems described by Lisa MacKenzie in her ethnographic study of the St Anne's estate in Nottingham (where *TwentyFourSeven* was filmed), whereby the detachment from neoliberal, white, middle-class hegemonies of aspiration leads to a local and insular cultural structure with its own value systems and hegemonic hierarchies.[39]

Much like the men that MacKenzie interviews for her research, the young men in *TwentyFourSeven* and in many of the other films that I look at in this chapter are more concerned with the immediate, the local and their position within it.[40] Their insularity is symptomatic of their literal and existential entrapment. The fractious interactions that ensue between the groups are banal and mundane; the ordinariness of the encounters speaking to the mundanity of the character's lives, the lads in *TwentyFourSeven* chatter without ever saying anything of substance. The codes of hegemonic masculinity that structure the communities of lads in *TwentyFourSeven* are implicitly heteronormative. In much the same way that the lads are compelled to display and perform forms of macho masculinity, so too heterosexuality remains assumed and unquestioned as the dominant sexual identity. In one scene, set in the toilets of their local pub, two of the more peripheral characters, Daz (Darren O'Campbell) and Stuart (Karl Collins), exchange friendly, laddish banter regarding their (hetero) sexual conquests. It transpires, however, that this performance of heterosexuality is a masquerade and both men are gay and, at the close of the film, they are seen together, as a couple. That Daz and Stuart are among the more peripheral characters in the narrative means that the film is able to include a gay relationship (which demonstrates a progressive politics of male sexuality) without being seen as a queer film. The breakdown of the heterosexual masquerade of both Daz and Stuart and the process by which they come to reveal their sexuality, to discover that they are attracted to one another and to embark upon a relationship, is conducted off-screen and thus remains contained, apparently extraneous to the main narrative. Much like the relationship between Lomper and Guy in *The Full Monty*, *TwentyFourSeven* acknowledges homosexuality in a way that gestures towards sexual inclusivity while relegating it to the margins of the narrative and the screen. Furthermore, in focusing on the fact that recovered drug addict Fag Ash is attending Darcy's funeral ensures that heteronormative masculinities remain privileged.

The consequences of drug addiction on marginalised young men is dealt with in *TwentyFourSeven* and also in *My Name Is Joe*. Offering a departure from the laddish, subcultural drug taking of *Trainspotting*, *Human Traffic* and *Twin Town*, both *My Name is Joe* and *TwentyFourSeven* offer more traditional and cautionary tales of drug use and addiction for their characters. While *TwentyFourSeven* allows Fag Ash to recover from his addiction and take on a socially sanctioned form of adult masculinity in becoming a father, thus validating Darcy's qualities as a surrogate father figure in the process, *My Name Is Joe* refuses to allow the palatable outcome of a happy resolution, using Liam's eventual demise as part of its pessimistic and often coruscating indictment of Thatcher's legacy. Liam (David McKay) is a recovering heroin addict who lives in one of Glasgow's deprived housing projects; he is a father to Scott (Scott Hannah) and is in a relationship with Sabine (Anne-Marie Kennedy). Like Fag Ash, Liam is symbolically trapped and, despite his best efforts, he is unable to break the cycles of deprivation and addiction that surround him.

In many ways the character of Liam has many of the qualities that are often seen as central to the figure of the postfeminist father (discussed in the following chapter) and his devotion to Sabine and baby Scott are frequently alluded to by Sabine and other characters in the film and emphasised by the 'combination of social observation and melodrama'.[41]

The young father is seen playing with his son in the park, and his wife, Sabine, extols his parental dedication to the health visitor, Sarah (Louise Goodall). Where Liam is trying his best to break his heroin addiction and make a life for his family, Sabine steals prescription pads, verbally abuses the medical professionals who try to help her and works as a prostitute in order to fund her addiction. Because of Sabine's addiction, Liam becomes indebted to a group of local drug dealers, finding himself forced into working off Sabine's debt because he has no other options. The character of Liam is trapped. Even when Joe gives him money to escape from the threats of the dealers he has nowhere to go, much like his counterparts in *TwentyFourSeven* he is both socially and literally immobile. He is reluctant to take Scott from his mother but he knows that the cycle of addiction and precarity and the dangers associated with them will inevitably continue if Sabine is with them. Liam, much like Fag Ash, is entirely dislocated. He appears to have no family and no support network beyond Joe, who by this stage in the narrative has started drinking again and, consumed by his own addiction, is unable to support the young father. As the gang members pull up outside Joe's tenement block, Liam runs out of options. The image switches from close-ups of Liam's trembling hands and fluid hand-held shots of his frantic movements around the darkened flat to static images of Joe, slumped in his chair in a vodka-induced stupor. Joe's failure to protect and help Liam when he needs it most functions as a symbol for the wider systemic and institutional failures that have left Liam desperate. In contrast to earlier parts of the film where Liam plays outside with his young son, these scenes are poorly lit. In a similar cinematic style to *Nil By Mouth* a low angle is used to heighten the sense of claustrophobia and entrapment as Liam prepares to take his own life rather than have it taken from him by the pursuant gang.

Similarly, to the lads in *TwentyFourSeven*, Liam is part of a cohort that has been most severely affected by the economic changes of recent years. None of the lads in the football team that Joe has set up is employed; as is the case in Meadows's film, they are simply drifting through life at the margins of society without the skills or resources to escape; they are all, as Darcy puts it, 'living the same day all their lives'. The only central character with a stable job is Sarah, a community health care worker who looks after Liam, Sabine and baby Scott. While Joe does his best to provide a role model for the lads in the football team, his position as a role model is precarious; he is as alienated from normative versions of masculinity as are the young lads. Joe is unemployed and at one point in the narrative he gets into trouble with the Benefits Agency after it is revealed that he undertook some casual work while claiming unemployment benefit. He has no family ties and is himself struggling to break free from the cycles of deprivation and alcoholism with little external support. Like Liam, Joe is unable to fully extricate himself from the local gang culture. Even though Joe's re-entry into the gang is undertaken in a misguided attempt to protect Liam from harm, his failure to break the links with the past effects a cautionary tone about the difficulties of escaping the destructive cycles that frequently go hand in hand with social and economic disempowerment. In this respect, *My Name is Joe* takes the sentiments expressed in *TwentyFourSeven* even further by harnessing, as John Hill suggests, 'the fatalistic logic of melodrama (. . .) to the socially-deterministic impulses of naturalism'.[42] In situating the central characters as victims and denying any positive resolution to their narrative, Loach's film is steeped in his typically belligerent socialist politics; it is made explicitly clear that Joe's actions are not the result of moral failings or personal shortcomings as much as they are a direct result of a desperate situation.

Liam's death is used to accentuate the extent to which young men have been let down by the convergent forces of Thatcherism, deindustrialisation and economic poverty and the fateful and fatal consequences therein. Drawing on the emotive iconography of poverty, Loach makes explicit the connection between Liam's situation and his fate; to this end we might read Liam's suicide as exemplifying Higson's arguments around the motif of individual escape within social realist films.[43] Where the lads in *TwentyFourSeven* lack the means to break the cycles of poverty and marginalisation, Liam's status as a father is mobilised as a motivation for the character's desire to build a better life. In some ways, *My Name Is Joe* tries to imbue fatherhood with the kind of recuperative potential, which, as the next chapter will show, is more frequently associated with middle-class fathers. Being a father gives Liam the kind of hope that is lacking in *TwentyFourSeven* but, ultimately, it does not save him. Liam's struggle represents the futility of trying to escape from the cycles of poverty and social marginalisation in which he and his young family are caught. In many ways, the focus on the psychosocial problems and marginalisation faced by young, white, unemployed men in *TwentyFourSeven* and *My Name Is Joe* continues a longer lineage in British cinema. The cinematography and editing construct a naturalism that emphasises the poverty and hopelessness of the characters; the political critique of both films is embedded in the deliberate lack of what Higson describes as the 'visual pleasure' of cinematic imagery associated with heritage, romantic comedy and, of course, Hollywood films.[44]

Despite the fact that the trope of the marginalised young man is a prominent trope in British cinema in the 1990s, social realist films from the era are far from monolithic in terms of the form, style and narrative focus. Both films articulate a clear and explicit political critique on the post-industrial poverty and the associated socio-economic marginalisation of young white men in particular and demonstrate that socially committed, politically aware filmmaking retained an important position in British filmmaking in the 1990s, even if it was less commercially profitable on account of issues such as poor distribution and marketing strategies and a lack of exhibition.[45] In the next section I examine two films that sit broadly under the auspices of social realism in the 2000s and suggest that an increasing creative diversity around the narratives, the form and the style of social realism took place during the period while a focus on the lives of dislocated and disenfranchised young people was retained.

Marginal Young Men of the 2000s: From *Bullet Boy* to *1 Day*

The cinematic obsession with films about poor young men continued into the 2000s and indeed into the 2010s. While the familiar narratives of rivalry, drug taking, violence, friendship and belonging continued, there seemed to be an increased diversity in the representation of films set within Black British, Asian and multicultural communities. In many ways, this makes sense given the centrality of multicultural inclusivity to the New Labour government which had been in power since 1997. The UK Film Council was established in 2000 with the key aim of supporting the growth of the industry, and diversity and inclusivity were key components of its mandate. The 2003 Creative Skillset Workforce Survey demonstrated the extent to which the British film and media industries remained dominated by affluent, white, able-bodied and London-based people.[46] The extent to which the attempts of the UKFC to create and promote a more diverse and inclusive culture within the film industry were successful remains questionable; indeed, the 2009 Creative Skillset report reveals a decline in the percentage of BAME people within the British production industries, from 6 per cent in 2003 to 5.3 per cent. As such, then, the extent to which Kwesi Owusu's ambition for Black British film to intervene in and challenge the structure of cultural hegemonies around Black British identities was fulfilled is debateable.[47] Thus, it seems that despite the long-established mainstream success of Black British popular culture encompassing music, television, art and literature, British film and the British film industry remains predominantly, and sometimes in terms of on-screen representation, exclusively, white. Given that 'British cinema has failed to reflect this hybridisation so evident in other areas of British cultural life', the relatively sudden and expansive rise in films that placed young Black and Asian British men at the centre of their narratives during the middle of the 2000s might be readily celebrated as indicative of progress.[48] However, as Karen Alexander argues, simply 'having interesting Black characters does not make the films Black'.[49] Indeed, *Bullet Boy*, a film with an entirely Black cast but with an overwhelmingly white crew, would seem to illustrate Lola Young's point that a film that is 'made under the artistic control of a predominantly white creative team' cannot be designated as 'Black British'.[50] The tensions around the ethnic constitution of the creative crew, the authorial roles and the content or form of the film produced, is, of course the subject of long and complex debates in film studies. It is particularly significant both in the context of the enduring structures of white cultural dominance and the consistent marginalisation of Black British people within the British film industry, but also because of the ways in which *Bullet Boy* positions Ricky (Ashley Walters), Curtis (Luke Fraser) and their long-suffering single mother, Beverley (Claire Perkins), in direct relation to a set of connected social difficulties and crises which reinforce problematic discourses of Black British people. In so doing, the film appears to reproduce long-held normative discourses around young, poor, Black men and boys, confirming a lazy and derogatory stereotype of 'Black criminality and, specifically, the contemporary Black gang, gun and knife crime consensus'.[51]

In some ways, *Bullet Boy* functions as a kind of cinematic juncture between the form and style of 1990s social realism and that which has emerged during the latter years of the 2000s. Narratively and stylistically, *Bullet Boy* is very much in keeping with the traditions of British social realism in terms of both cultural and generic verisimilitude. Set in the London borough of Hackney, one of the most deprived areas of London, *Bullet Boy* offers images of urban streets and high-rise flats, the clichéd iconography of impoverished inner-city landscapes. The story follows the events that take place upon Ricky's release from prison for an unnamed crime and, much like *My Name is Joe* and *TwentyFourSeven*, it follows a narrative trajectory that seems almost predestined. The film rehearses a familiar tale of poverty, exclusion, marginalisation and young Black British male violence. That Ricky's death and his socio-economic position as a poor, young Black man from a deprived area are so readily and intrinsically connected appears to reinforce, rather than challenge, dominant discursive conceptualisations around race, class and gender.

Despite a formal and stylistic connection with traditional British social realism, *Bullet Boy* does not appear to offer a particularly politicised engagement with class, poverty or racial inequality; instead it offers an individualised narrative which takes the marginalisation of its central characters as a background context and not as a theme for political interrogation or comment. While, as discussed above, Higson notes that the narrative of individual escape has been a long-established trope within British social realism, I would argue that in the case of *Bullet Boy* this does, in fact, undermine any sense of political critique.[52] Decontextualising the intersecting and multiple sites of marginalisation of the key characters functions as a means of depoliticising them, reducing 'inequality to a behavioural rather than a socio-political consequence'.[53] Moreover, it would seem that the aesthetic presentation of the film and its use of soundtrack invite the audience to take pleasure in the iconography of violence and poverty. Despite his best intentions, Ricky is unable to escape from the culture and violence of his surroundings, and his death, at the hands of a rival gang leader, seems almost inevitable from the start. Upon release from prison, Ricky is a reformed character who is desperate to move on from his violent past but is acutely aware of the difficulties of doing so; in scenes with his girlfriend, Ricky talks about his need to move away, literally to escape his culture and his reputation within it. In this way, *Bullet Boy* might not foreground a politically critical meta-narrative, but it does use the character of Ricky as a device through which to mediate questions of entrapment and the practicalities of escaping the toxic conditions of cultures with limited means. The difficulties of escape become particularly apparent when Ricky's best friend, Wisdom, accidentally knocks off the wing mirror of a local gang leader's car, sparking a series of violent altercations which culminate in both young men being murdered by Godfrey (Clark Lawson) and his gang. In many ways, Ricky's situation echoes that of Liam's, and both films gesture to the difficulties that appear to be blithely encapsulated in a political rhetoric of social mobility that operates in contradistinction to Mark Featherstone's assertion that 'the poor have nowhere to go and nothing to lose'.[54] Both Ricky and Liam discuss the possibility of moving away but these are never more than naïve dreams; their fates are respectively predestined, despite their best efforts.

One of the common discursive tropes around Black British culture as a social 'problem' centres on the notion of familial dysfunction exemplified by the well-worn tropes of struggling single mother and absent father. The ideological implication of this configuration is to suggest that despite her best efforts, a lone Black mother is unable to raise her son successfully and safely, a narrative trope that is also evident in Hollywood representations of the Black solo mother.[55] Indeed, contra to the dominant discourse of young Black and Asian masculinities which hold peer groups as 'the compensatory "family"' the family unit within *Bullet Boy* is presented as close-knit with Beverley positioned as the single mother, desperate to save Ricky from returning to a life of crime and prison and anxious to protect her younger son from following his brother's path.[56] The extent to which Ricky represents a risk to his twelve-year-old brother is frequently alluded to in the film; the closeness of the fraternal bond coded as inherently contradictory, holding positive and restorative potential for Ricky but negative and damaging implications for Curtis. The extent to which Ricky presents a risk to his younger brother is highlighted when Curtis finds the gun that Ricky had hidden in their shared bedroom and takes it to show his best friend, Rio (Rio Tison). Curtis and Rio share a gleeful excitement as they act out a shoot 'em up scenario in the local woodland, until Curtis accidentally shoots a bullet, injuring his young friend. This moment illustrates the extent to which Ricky's past has the potential to damage Curtis's future and reaffirms a narrative in which young, Black masculinity is once more configured as being 'the epitome' of marginalisation that is coded as dangerous as it is desirable.[57]

Rio's shooting leads Beverley to demand that Ricky move out of the family flat. Meeting with Ricky in the area outside their block of flats, Beverley calmly explains that she has to do what she can to prevent Curtis from following in his older brother's tracks; she gives Ricky a key to the flat before driving off. Left to fend for himself, Ricky decides to collect his money from Wisdom (Leon Black) in order to allow him to leave. Throughout the film, Ricky frequently talked about his desire to escape Hackney in order to extricate himself from the local gang culture and at this point in the narrative the promise of escape is tantalisingly close. The naïvety of this dream is proven, however, when Ricky finds Wisdom dead in his house, murdered by Godfrey's gang. Ricky's fate seems uncertain at this point and he makes his way to the station but, as he waits alone for his train, Godfrey and his gang close in, shooting Ricky multiple times and leaving his body abandoned on the platform. Shortly after accompanying their mother to identify Ricky's body, Curtis retrieves the gun from where he hid it after his accidental shooting of Rio. Curtis retreats out of sight but the camera holds the vacant frame, almost encouraging an audience to ponder the potential outcomes of this moment and whether Curtis will attempt to avenge his brother's death (thus reigniting the cycle of violence and death for the next generation of boys) or whether he will manage to resist the allure of gang culture machismo. Once more, *Bullet Boy* presents a neoliberal narrative in which the choices of the individual are presented as unencumbered and straightforward; the structural cultural codes of gang masculinity that demand respect, loyalty, support and a fierce conflict with rivals are effaced here.[58]

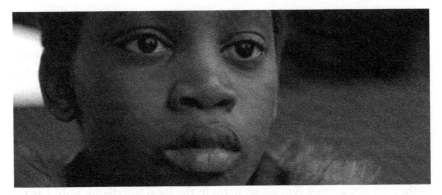

Figure 4.2 *Bullet Boy:* Curtis contemplates his future as he
throws his brother's gun into the river

The closing scene of the film presents an iconography, familiar within
contemporary realist British cinema: Curtis stands at a riverside, the City
of London is in the distance and he pauses before throwing the gun into
the water, symbolically freeing himself from his brother's path. Despite
offering, on the one hand, a restorative and positive conclusion that suggests Curtis will reject the cycles of violence and crime that ensnared his
brother, *Bullet Boy* promulgates an intrinsically neoliberal resolution in
which a life trajectory becomes reduced, simply, to individual choice as
opposed to proffering an understanding of the nature of intersectional
socio-economic and structural issues. Similar scenes are used in the Shane
Meadows film *This is England* (2006), where Shaun (Thomas Turgoose)
throws the St George flag into the sea in a symbolic rejection of Combo
(Stephen Graham) and his racist ideologies, and also in *Shifty*, where the
eponymous character (Riz Ahmed) and his friend Chris (Daniel Mays)
throw their gun and Shifty's mobile phone into the Thames estuary. In
this instance the gesture is as much practical as it is symbolic, preventing
any of Shifty's clients from contacting him and so safeguarding him from
being pulled back into the world that he had only just managed to escape.

In much the same way, *Kidulthood*, too, appears to 'produce and affirm
normative cultural meanings' around race, gender, poverty and criminality.[59] In focusing on the lives of inner London teenagers, the film brings
together two of the most prevalent symbols of the 'feral' youth discourse
– the 'chavvy' white girl and the often, but not always, Black male 'hoodie'.
Written by Noel Clarke and directed by Menhaj Huda, the film follows a
loose grouping of teenagers who are given a day off school following the
bullying-induced suicide of one of the girls. In many ways the film replicates a familiar repertoire of impoverished, urban teenage culture; the

narrative includes an under-age pregnancy, drinking, smoking, drugs and sex, and presents a scenario in which the girls are equally but differently as 'at risk' as their male counterparts.[60] For girls, 'risk' is coded in the form of Alisa's (Red Madrell) unplanned pregnancy and Becky's (Jamie Winstone) use of sexual favours to procure drugs, to cite two examples. While sex does not necessarily evoke the same kinds of dangers for the adolescent male characters in the film, a range of common-or-garden risks is presented as intrinsic to their culture and their experiences including drink, drugs, thievery, violence and, for Trife (Aml Ameen), initiation into the street gangs run by elder family members. Although *Kidulthood* does not draw on the familiar tabloid narrative of knife crime, it nevertheless rearticulates and reaffirms popular preconceptions around young, poor, urban men as what Imogen Tyler might term, 'failed citizens', who are discursively constituted via their perpetual marginality.[61] *Kidulthood*, therefore, appears, much like *Bullet Boy*, to offer a conventional rendition of young Black masculinity appearing to play to a dominant paradigm of cultural verisimilitude but offering little in the way of socio-political critique or progressive cultural intervention into the broader contextual debates with which it is concerned. Moreover, in leaving the relationship between the individual and culture unexplored, *Kidulthood* appears to inadvertently adhere to a neoliberal model of gender and class that obfuscates both the diffuse and multiple structural and institutional mechanisms at play within British society.

Kidulthood appeared to spark a series of films about impoverished and marginalised young inner-city inhabitants, not least of which is its sequel, *Adulthood*, which takes up the story of Sam (Noel Clarke) upon his release from prison for Trife's murder. In the wake of the success of both *Kidulthood* and *Adulthood* a raft of films including *Shifty*, *4321*, *Shank*, *Rollin' With the 9s* (Julian Gilbey, 2006) and *1 Day* emerged, each of which offered a variant on the theme of impoverished, marginalised, urban youth. Indeed, the films became so well-known as cultural touchstones that a good-natured parody *Anuvahood* (Adam Deacon and Daniel Toland, 2011) was released, featuring, among a number of well-known Black British and Asian actors, Jaime Winstone who had starred in the original film. While films such as *1 Day*, *Rollin' With the 9s* and *Life and Lyrics* (Richard Laxton, 2006) presented familiar narratives of young, disenfranchised, Black British masculinities and drew influence from social realism, they juxtaposed this with an emphasis on music and, as in the opening scene of *1 Day*, a form and aesthetic derived from music videos. In this way, the emergence of grime as the prime musical genre for the multicultural millennial generation became increasingly integrated within films, augmenting a realist aesthetic and pushing the boundaries in new directions. On television, Malik and Nwonka note, there was a steady increase in drama programming that they describe as 'Black urban crime' typified by their case study, *Top Boy*, the Channel 4 series that tells the story of disenfranchised Black youths living in Hackney. On the other side of the legal colliery is a rise in the figure of the hard-boiled, streetwise Black cop, exemplified by characters such as Luther (Idris Elba), the eponymous detective of the award winning BBC series.[62]

While films such as *1 Day* break away from the more traditional social realist approaches to representing urban deprivation, departing from continuity editing and naturalism in their cultural verisimilitude, *4321*, is an example of a non-linear narrative in ways that draw attention to the constructed and ideological function of realism, drawing on familiar urban iconography and cinematography associated with realist films while abandoning the conventional linear narrative of traditional realist cinema. Whilst the majority of these later films are set in and around London and draw on the attendant lexicon of metropolitan multiculturalism, they are often less explicit in their political critique and more ambivalent in their discursive construction. The familiar iconography of decaying and derelict urban spaces, tower blocks, local shops and rundown pubs functions to define and demarcate the cultural spaces of the narrative, creating a cultural verisimilitude of poverty and marginalisation. These images invariably bring to bear what Beverley Skeggs terms 'value formations', in which value judgements and connotations are implied but disconnected from questions of structure and politics.[63] In Penny Woolcock and Michèle Nuzzo's *1 Day*, characters such Flash (Dylan Douffas), Angel (Yohance Watson) and Evil (Duncan Tobias) exemplify symbols of persistent cultural anxieties around poor, urban Black masculinity, and their narratives rehearse familiar discursive conjectures around crime, violence and drug culture in ways that reinforce persistent and pernicious racial stereotypes. By decontextualising the characters and their actions from the socio-economic or institutional structures that perpetuate various forms of inequality, films such as *1 Day* perform and 'strengthen hegemonic narratives of Black criminality'.[64] For all that *1 Day* appears to offer innovation and creativity – incorporating group-based grime performances as a means of storytelling, offering critical commentary and reflection on gang culture and the various hegemonic forms of masculinity within it, it offers a rather typical narrative of marginal Black masculinity.

Conclusion

Each of the films discussed in this chapter connect with and draw from ongoing cultural anxieties about the 'social problem' of poor, young men. I argue that *TwentyFourSeven* is a particularly powerful counterpoint to the cinematic version of the new lad and that the film uses its cinematography and mise-en-scène as a mechanism to refute the irreverent irony of lad culture, and in so doing the film offers a politically critical treatise on the shortcomings of British neoliberal culture. I suggest that *TwentyFourSeven* was fundamental in setting up some of the thematic concerns that have gone on to shape Shane Meadows's future work and argued that the explicit critique of neoliberal culture and its impact on young working-class men drew on traditional forms of social realism and offered an ideological contrast to the political irreverence of lad culture. Against Meadows's debut, I examined *My Name is Joe* by Ken Loach, one of the most prolific and consistent directors in British cinema with a career spanning more than fifty years. I argue that *My Name is Joe* is typical of the kind of politically incisive film that has characterised his oeuvre.

In the second half of the chapter I turned my attention to the rise of urban crime films and paid particular attention to *Bullet Boy*, *Kidulthood* and *1 Day* to show how these films ranged from *Bullet Boy*'s conventionally social realist presentation of young Black British culture to those that pushed the formulaic boundaries of the genre, producing a transmedia intersectionality with emergent grime culture. In line with Clive James Nwonka and Sarita Malik, I suggested that these films tended to rehearse normative (and implicitly white) critiques of young Black masculinity that invariably affirmed a range of problematic assumptions around urban, poor, Black masculinity and violence.[65] Furthermore, in considering the institutional and authorial politics of these films, I suggest that the predominance of white directors producing these films is indicative of the ongoing structural racial inequalities of the British film industry, which, when taken in conjunction with Walter's critique regarding class, paints a particularly damning situation for the ways in which contemporary Black British and Asian British cultures are mediated.

Notes

1 Lay, Samantha, 2002, *British Social Realism: From Documentary to Brit Grit*, Wallflower Press, London, p. 1.
2 Higson, Andrew, 2016, 'Space, Place, Spectacle: Landscape & Townscape

in the Kitchen Sink Film' in Higson, Andrew (ed.), *Dissolving Views*, Bloomsbury Press, London, p. 136.

3   Monk, Claire, 2000, 'Men in the 90s' in Robert Murphy (ed.), *British Cinema of the 90s*, BFI Publishing, London, p. 227.

4   Malik, Sarita and Nwonka, Clive James, 2017, 'Top Boy: Cultural Verisimilitude and the Allure of Black Criminality for UK Public Service Broadcasting Drama' in *The Journal of British Cinema and Television*, Vol. 14, No. 4, pp. 423–444.

5   Tyler, Imogen, 2013, *Revolting Subjects: Social Abjection and Resistance in Neo-Liberal Britain*, Zed Books, London.

6   Adams, Matthew and Raisborough, Jayne, 2011, 'The Self-control Ethos and the "Chav": Unpacking Cultural Representations of the White Working Class' in *Culture and Psychology*, Vol. 17, No. 1, p. 83.

7   Malik, Sarita and Nwonka, Clive James., 2017, 'Top Boy: Cultural Verisimilitude and the Allure of Black Criminality for UK Public Service Broadcasting Drama' in *The Journal of British Cinema and Television*, Vol. 14. No. 4, pp. 423–444.

8   Ibid., p. 424.

9   Ibid. Tyler, Imogen, 2013, *Revolting Subjects: Social Abjection and Resistance in Neo-Liberal Britain*, Zed Books, London.

10 Spicer, Andrew, 2000, *Typical Men: Representations of Masculinity in Popular British Cinema*, I. B. Tauris, London, p. 188.

11 Lay, Samantha, 2009, *British Social Realism: From Documentary to Brit Grit*, Wallflower Press, London, p. 1.

12 MacKenzie, Lisa, 2013, 'The Stigmatised and De-Valued Working Class: The State of a Council Estate' in Will Atkinson, Steven Roberts and Mike Savage (ed.), *Class Inequality in Austerity Britain: Power, Difference, Suffering*, Palgrave Macmillan, London, p. 133.

13 Petrovic, Sarah, 2013, 'Changing Spaces of "Englishness": Psychogeography and Spatial Practices in *This is England* and *Somers Town*' in Fradley, Martin, Godfrey, Sarah and Williams, Melanie (eds), *Shane Meadows: Critical Essays*, Edinburgh University Press, Edinburgh, p. 127.

14 Johnston, Sheila, 2004, *Ae Fond Kiss*, in Screenonline. http://www.screenon line.org.uk/film/id/1408654/index.html

15 Martin-Jones, David, 2009, *Scotland: Global Cinema: Genres, Modes and Identities*, Edinburgh University Press, Edinburgh, p. 180.

16 Malik, Sarita and Nwonka, Clive James, 2017, 'Top Boy: Cultural Verisimilitude and the Allure of Black Criminality for UK Public Service Broadcasting Drama' in *The Journal of British Cinema and Television*, Vol. 14, No. 4, pp. 423–444.

17 McDowell, Linda, 2003, *Redundant Masculinities: Employment Change and White Working-Class Youth*, Blackwell Publishing, Oxford, p. 287.

18 Forrest, David, 2013, *Social Realism: Art, Nationhood, Politics*, Cambridge Scholar's Press, Newcastle upon Tyne.

19 Tyler, Imogen, 2013, *Revolting Subjects: Social Abjection and Resistance in Neoliberal Britain*, Zed Books, London, p. 9.

20 Straw, Jack, 2003, *The Anti-Social Behaviour Bill*. https://api.parliament.uk/historic-hansard/lords/2003/jul/18/anti-social-behaviour-bill (accessed 20 October 2020).

21 McDowell, Linda, 2003, *Redundant Masculinities: Employment Change and White Working-Class Youth*, Blackwell Publishing, Oxford, p. 4.

22 McRobbie, Angela, 1994, *Postmodernism and Popular Culture*, Routledge, London, p. 200.

23 Barclay, Peter, 2000, *Poverty and Social Exclusion in Britain*, Joseph Rowntree Foundation. https://www.jrf.org.uk/report/poverty-and-social-exclusion-britain (accessed 20 October 2020).

24 Ibid.

25 See McDowell, Linda, 2003, *Redundant Masculinities: Employment Change and White Working-Class Youth*, Blackwell Publishing, Oxford, p. 4.

26 Skeggs, Beverley, 1997, *Formations of Class and Gender: Becoming Respectable*, Sage, London, p. 9.

27 McDowell, Linda, 2003, *Redundant Masculinities: Employment Change and White Working-Class Youth*, Blackwell Publishing, Oxford, p. 4.

28 Ibid., p. 278.

29 Tyler, Imogen, 2013, *Revolting Subjects: Social Abjection and Resistance in Neoliberal Britain*, Zed Books, London, p. 153.

30 Major, John, 1991, Leader's Speech, Conservative Party Conference. http://www.britishpoliticalspeech.org/speech-archive.htm?speech=137 (accessed 20 October 2020).

31 Lawler, Stephanie, 2005, 'Introduction: Class, Culture and Identity' in *Sociology* Vol. 39, No. 5, p. 800.

32 Fradley, Martin, Godfrey, Sarah and Williams, Melanie, 2013, 'Introduction: Shanes' World' in Fradley, Martin, Godfrey, Sarah and Williams, Melanie (eds), *Shane Meadows: Critical Essays*, Edinburgh University Press, Edinburgh, p. 14.

33 Hill, John, 1999, *British Cinema in the 1980s*, Clarendon Press, Oxford, p. 167.

34 Godfrey, Sarah, 2013, "'I'm A Casualty But It's Cool'": *TwentyFourSeven* and British Masculinity of the Nineties' in *The Journal of British Cinema and Television*, Vol. 10, No. 4, pp. 846–862.

35 *London Reigns*. http://www.newsweek.com/id/103313

36 Dave, Paul, 2006, *Visions of England: Class and Culture in Contemporary Cinema*, Berg, Oxford.

37 Monk, Claire, 2000, 'Underbelly UK: The 1990s Underclass Film, Masculinity and the Ideologies of "New" Britain' in Ashby, Justine and Higson, Andrew (eds), *British Cinema Past & Present*, Routledge, London.

38 Dave, Paul, 2006, *Visions of England: Class and Culture in Contemporary Cinema*, Berg, Oxford, p. 85.

39 MacKenzie, Lisa, 2013, 'The Stigmatised and De-Valued Working Class: The State of a Council Estate' in Atkinson, Will, Roberts, Steven and Savage, Mike (eds), *Class Inequality in Austerity Britain: Power, Difference, Suffering*, Palgrave Macmillan, London.

40 Ibid.

41 Hill, John, 2000, 'Failure and Utopianism: Representations of the Working Class in British Cinema of the 1990s' in Robert Murphy (ed.), *British Cinema of the 90s*, BFI Publishing, London, p. 281.

42 Ibid., p. 282.

43 Higson, Andrew, 2016, 'Space, Place, Spectacle: Landscape & Townscape in the Kitchen Sink Film' in Higson, Andrew (ed.), *Dissolving Views*, Bloomsbury Press, London.

44 Ibid.

45 It is worth noting that the 2016 Ken Loach film, *I, Daniel Blake*, which was a scathing critique of the Conservative Party's project of austerity, was shown in ninety-four screens across the UK on its opening weekend, and grossed £404,000, suggesting that, with appropriate marketing and distribution, social realist films can find a place within the multiplex-dominated environment of contemporary cinema. https://www.theguardian.com/film/2016/oct/25/i-daniel-blake-ken-loach-uk-box-office-trolls-top-spot (accessed 20 October 2020).

46 https://www.screenskills.com/media/1394/workforce_survey_report_2003.pdf (accessed 20 October 2020).

47 Korte, Barbara and Sternberg, Claudia, 2004, *Bidding for the Mainstream: Black British and Asian Film Since 1990s*, Rodopi Press, New York.

48 Alexander, Karen, 2000, 'Black British Cinema in the 90s: Going, Going, Gone' in Murphy Robert (ed.), *British Cinema of the 90s*, BFI Publishing, London, p. 112.

49 Ibid., p. 112.

50 Young, Lola, 1995, *Fear of the Dark: Race, Gender and Sexuality in the Cinema*, Routledge, London, p. 1.

51 Malik, Sarita and Nwonka, Clive James, 2017, '*Top Boy:* Cultural Verisimilitude and the Allure of Black Criminality for UK Public Service Broadcasting Drama' in *Journal of British Cinema and Television*, Vol. 14, No. 4, p. 424.

52 Higson, Andrew, 2016, 'Space, Place, Spectacle: Landscape & Townscape in the Kitchen Sink Film' in Higson, Andrew (ed.), *Dissolving Views*, Bloomsbury Press, London.

53 Nwonka, Clive James, 2014, '"You're What's Wrong with Me": *Fish Tank, The Selfish Giant* and the Language of Contemporary British Social Realism' in *New Cinemas: Journal of Contemporary Film*, Vol. 12, No. 3, p. 206.

54 Featherstone, Mark (2013), 'Hoodie Horror: The Capitalist Other in Postmodern Society' in *Review of Education, Pedagogy and Cultural Studies*, Vol. 35, No. 3, pp. 178–190.

55 FitzGerald, Louise, 2009, *Negotiating Lone Motherhood: Gender, Politics and Family Values in Contemporary Popular Cinema*, unpublished PhD thesis, available at https://ueaprints.uea.ac.uk/10577

56 Alexander, Claire, 2004, 'Imagining the Asian Gang: Ethnicity, Masculinity and Youth after "the Riots"' in *Critical Social Policy*, Vol. 24, No. 4, p. 356.

57 Alexander, Claire, 2002, 'Beyond Black: Re-thinking the Colour/Culture Divide' in *Ethnic and Racial Studies*, Vol. 25, No. 4, p. 557.

58 O'Donnell, Mike and Sharpe, Sue, 2000, *Uncertain Masculinities: Youth, Ethnicity and Class in Contemporary Britain*, Routledge, London.

59 Malik, Sarita and Nwonka, Clive James, 2017, '*Top Boy:* Cultural Verisimilitude and the Allure of Black Criminality for UK Public Service Broadcasting Drama' in *Journal of British Cinema and Television*, Vol. 14, No. 4, pp. 423–444.

60 Harris, Anita, 2004, *Future Girl: Young Women in the 21st Century*, Routledge, London.

61 Tyler, Imogen, 2013, *Revolting Subjects: Social Abjection and Resistance in Neoliberal Britain*, Zed Books, London, p. 162.

62 Malik, Sarita and Nwonka, Clive James, 2017, '*Top Boy:* Cultural Verisimilitude and the Allure of Black Criminality for UK Public Service Broadcasting Drama' in *Journal of British Cinema and Television*, Vol. 14, No. 4, p. 423.

63 Skeggs, Beverley, 2011, 'Imagining Personhood Differently: Person Value and Autonomist Working-Class Value Practices' in *Sociological Review*, Vol. 59, No. 3, p. 503.

64 Malik, Sarita and Nwonka, Clive James, 2017, '*Top Boy:* Cultural Verisimilitude and the Allure of Black Criminality for UK Public Service Broadcasting Drama' in *Journal of British Cinema and Television*, Vol. 14, No. 4, p. 429.

65 Ibid.

CHAPTER 5

Framing Fatherhood: Class, Race and Discourses of Dysfunction and Redemption

Definitions and configurations of 'the family' underwent significant change during the twenty-year period of 1990–2010, slowly but clearly moving away from the exclusively visible and predominant heteronormative, nuclear model predicated on a gendered division of economic and domestic roles that had dominated since the Industrial Revolution. Foremost amongst these shifts were the rising number of women working in paid employment outside of the home and the concomitant decline of heavy industries that resulted in widespread economic redundancy for the men who had once been employed in them, as discussed in greater detail in Chapters 1 and 2. These developments had a profound impact on both the economic and domestic organisation of family units and the roles of gendered individuals therein; not least being the tension between male unemployment and the centrality of the breadwinner (or financial provider) role to hegemonic discourses of masculinity.[1] Alongside this, the increasing acceptance of gay partnerships and families continued, albeit at a rather slow pace. The Civil Partnerships Act of 2004 provided same-sex couples with many of the same rights and responsibilities as those in heterosexual marriages. This was followed in 2013 by the Marriage (Same Sex Couples) Act which legalised gay marriage in the UK (from 2014 onwards), finally according same-sex couples the same status and rights as those in heterosexual unions.

A rather different trend saw rising numbers of people getting divorced and often remarried during this societal shift, leading to greater diversity in terms of extended and 'blended' families. These challenges to the traditional conceptualisation of family directly addressed the supremacy of a family being defined by biological relationships – family ties no longer being necessitated by genetic connections. The increased acceptance of family diversity was not, however, universally equitable, and the tendency for family courts to favour maternal custody when families break up led to a rise in fathers having part-time contact with their children. The end of the 1990s and early part of the 2000s saw a rise in what was termed father's rights activism, with some groups, such as Fathers4Justice, attracting news coverage for increasingly outlandish protests.[2] The father's rights groups within the UK were not, as Richard Collier explains, a coherent or coordinated network so much as a 'loosely based coalition of men' who believed that the family court system was unfairly biased against them, to the detriment of their children as much as themselves.[3] These disparate coalitions in the UK were often characterised by animosity towards both the family court systems that they saw as instrumental in putting barriers between men and their children, and also towards women more generally.[4]

In line with developments in sociology, cultural studies and gender studies, there was a move away from conceptualising 'the family' as a naturally occurring entity and a greater understanding of it as socially and culturally constructed, in line with the hegemonic and ideological politics of patriarchal culture. Patriarchal culture is, as has been established, premised on a series of ideological investments in presenting gender as naturally occurring and pre-ordained; this in turn underpins the heteronormativity of patriarchal culture. Following this line of thinking, which comes out of a long lineage of feminist scholarship stretching back to the ground-breaking work of scholars including Ann Oakely, Kate Millett and their contemporaries, it became increasingly clear that 'the family' was not natural and pre-ordained, nor was it culturally or historically universal; it was an organisational category that emerges out of the socio-political requirements of a patriarchal, capitalist culture.[5] Deborah Chambers explains further that the reification of the nuclear family as normative and natural relies on it being 'treated as if it were a real and tangible object' when it is, in fact, an ideological construct that is 'elevated as a norm through a range of official and informal discourses'.[6] It is within this specific historical context that the cultural politics of cinematic mediations of British postfeminist fatherhood must be understood and analysed.

This chapter proceeds from the perspective that the hegemony of the nuclear family that had developed since the Industrial Revolution was not just culturally specific but also racially and ethnically codified as white. The diversity of family practices that emerged within the increasingly multicultural landscape of late twentieth-century Britain created an increasingly heterogeneous range of family lives, structures and practices within the UK during this time, and these two intersected with and impacted upon cultural understandings and practices of men's roles within families.

It is within this socio-political context that my investigation of the gendered politics of fatherhood in British cinema is situated. I explore the ways in which discourses of fatherhood operate within the postfeminist, neoliberal context of Britain during the 1990s and 2000s, examining the ways in which British cinema constructed paternal characters and narratives of fatherhood and how the intersections of race and class, in particular, function as structuring devices for these cinematic father figures. The case studies in this chapter are organised differently than in other chapters. Where I have used a broadly chronological structure for organising and analysing case study films elsewhere, this chapter adopts a thematic structure in order to provide a more precise analysis of the intersections between race, class and the gender politics of British postfeminist fatherhood in film. The first section focuses on the ways in which class functions as a structuring device for the representation of fathers and father figures in British cinema during the period and draws on the 1996 film *When Saturday Comes* (Maria Giese) and the 2002 film *About A Boy* (Chris Weitz and Paul Weitz). The former presents a number of issues that are germane to the discussion of the representation of working-class fathers in British cinema at the time, with its acrimonious relationship between Joe (John McEnery) and Jimmy (Sean Bean) demonstrating the shifting parameters of male parenting within a post-industrial context. *About A Boy* is the story of an avowed bachelor, Will Freeman (Hugh Grant), an independently wealthy man in his mid-thirties who, having made a cynical decision to only date single mothers, forms an unlikely friendship with a twelve-year-old social misfit, Marcus (Nicholas Hoult). In a narrative that deploys the typical postfeminist trope of fatherhood as recuperative, Marcus is the key to Will's reconstruction and maturation into an appropriate and hegemonic form of postfeminist masculinity, while it is Will (and not Marcus's mother) who is positioned as better understanding how to help the youngster.

About A Boy and *When Saturday Comes* offer a productive coupling through which to explore the class dyad at play within representations of fatherhood in British cinema during the period, in which narratives of recuperation and restoration appear more readily available to middle-class, affluent men. The two films that make up this section of the chapter are also of interest for the ways in which their respective male stars of Sean Bean and Hugh Grant function with respect to region, class and performances of masculinity and fatherhood therein. Bean's northern star image is described by David Forrest and Beth Johnson as constructed around the white working-class qualities of 'grit, resilience, emotional reserve, charm and candour'.[7] Grant's stardom, on the other hand, is described by Gael Sweeney as 'stumbling but endearing' and 'a good looking but naïve upper class twit'.[8] These two films offer an opportunity to understand and explore the discursive politics of white masculinity, class and fatherhood in Britain during the period and engage with the question of stardom and star images within British cinema during this time.

The second half of the chapter draws on *My Son the Fanatic* (Udayan Prasad, 1997) and *East is East* (Damien O'Donnell, 1999), both of which narrativise and represent British Asian identities via familiar 'culture clash' narratives which revolve around the fathers' relationships with their children. *East is East* is perhaps the more familiar version of the culture clash narrative, presenting the father as struggling to make his children see the value of the cultural traditions that he practices. The situation in *My Son the Fanatic* is inverted. Here Farid (Akbar Kurtha) is the son who comes to loathe his father for rejecting his cultural heritage. Farid becomes increasingly invested in the religious and cultural practices that his father had turned away from. In the course of the narrative, issues are raised about both configurations of power and the discursive machinations of masculinity within nineties British culture. Although *East is East* is set in the seventies, the ways in which it raises and negotiates the tensions between fathers and sons through the prism of cultural heritage, nostalgia and belonging connects with the cultural context of late nineties Britain, and discourses of multiculturalism and cultural diversity that character-ised the pre-millennial years of the New Labour government.

Postfeminist Fatherhood and British Context: Culture and Politics

More than any of the other chapters in this book this one is necessarily engaged with both cultural politics and formal politics; that is to say that, in following my methodological approach of contextually located analysis of British cinema's representations of masculinity, fatherhood and the roles of men within family units pertain as much to state politics as they do to cultural politics. This section seeks to give an overview of some of the key debates and issues at play within both of these arenas; drawing con-nections and comparisons that will inform the critical analysis of the films that follow. Given the ideological investment in the family as a hegemonic unit of society it seems sensible to begin by providing a brief examination of the ways in which fathers and fathering were constructed within the rhetoric of state politics before moving on to questions of cultural politics.

Despite the cultural shifts outlined at the outset of this chapter, the (nuclear) family retained significant cultural and political purchase as *the* hegemonic norm, intertwined within a heteronormative, patriarchal ideological framework that ascribes it as 'a moral domain'.[9] Within this context, media and cultural studies scholar Deborah Chambers suggests that the father in particular functions as 'a powerful ideological device' which serves to both recuperate and reinstate patriarchal values and thus the dominance of the heterosexual, nuclear family as the hegemonic form.[10] In this way, 'the family' becomes understood as a core component of civilisation and thus of 'the nation'. The breakdown of the family unit, whether in media discourse or political rhetoric, becomes synonymous with the breakdown of the nation state. It was to these exact concerns that John Major's 'Back to Basics' election campaign spoke in the early 1990s; and while Tony Blair's 1997 manifesto tagline was 'education, education, education', family policy took a central role. Stephen Driver and Andrew Martell draw attention to the similarities between the 'New' Labour manifesto and established conservative ideologies with respect to the family, arguing that Blair's first government gave 'much greater promi- nence [. . .] to the family as a factor in shaping an individual's propensity to criminality' and that this drove Blair's and Gordon Brown's active support for 'the two-parent family as the basic moral unit of society'.[11] Once more, in the 2010 election, the family became a key site of concern, subsumed under the rhetorical banner of 'Broken Britain' – a phrase that became synonymous with David Cameron over the course of his election campaign, backed up with evidence from Iain Duncan Smith's Centre for Social Justice (CSJ). The CSJ explicitly extolled the benefits of hetero- sexual marriage and committed relationships as safeguards for individuals, communities and society at large; warning that family breakdown led to an ultimately downward trajectory of poverty, educational failure, economic dependency on the state, indebtedness and addiction.[12]

In this regard we can see how the political rhetoric over the course of the 1990s and 2000s can be understood as intrinsically shaped by the discursive impulses of postfeminism, described by Angela McRobbie as comprising 'the coexistence of neoconservative values in relation to gender, sexuality and family life . . . with processes of liberalisation in regard to choice and diversity in domestic, sexual, and kinship relations'.[13] Within the context of the UK, there was a continued promulgation of a conservative notion of both family and fathering which relied upon extolling the absolute importance of the heterosexual two-parent family. Alongside this was an increasing recognition of same-sex partnerships and families, a reduction in the social stigmatisation of divorce and single parenthood, and a gradual reorientation of men's roles within the domestic sphere and their patterns of fathering which, according to Joseph Pleck, had been developing slowly since the middle of the 1980s.[14]

In thinking through modern fatherhood within a British context, there has been a long sociological and cultural interest in family cultures which exists in dialogue with policy. Articles such as 'The Problem of Fathers: Policy and Behaviour in Britain' and 'From Fatherhood to Fathering: Transmission and Change among British Fathers in Four Generations of Families' have presented quantitative and qualitative data; tracing how shifting family patterns have affected social practices of fatherhood and men's familial roles.[15] As scholars including Deborah Chambers and Estella Tinknell have shown, the effects of a postfeminist reconstructed masculinity had considerable impact on discourses about fatherhood and social practices of fatherhood.[16] Tinknell, for example, demonstrates how gendered practices of masculinity changed the ways in which men operated within family units, while Chambers suggests that, following on from the reconstructed 'new man' of the 1980s, fatherhood became 'recast as a newly acceptable form of emotional empowerment for men'.[17] Moreover, this reconstruction of men's familial roles invested in the idea that involvement in parenting and domesticity could be potentially liberating, or even fulfilling for men. These apparently new practices of fatherhood can be traced back to the end of the 1980s, the period in which the 'new man' proliferated as the predominant trope of reconstructed masculinity. In terms of fatherhood, he was epitomised with the Athena poster, L'enfant, in which a bare-chested, muscular man, looks down, tenderly, at the baby he is cradling.[18]

Turning to the cinematic representation of fatherhood within British cinema, there has been little scholarly work, with James Leggott's essay 'Like Father? Failing Parents and Angelic Children in Contemporary British Social Realist Cinema' being a notable exception, as is the study of father figures within Shane Meadows's films by Martin Fradley and Sean Kingston.[19] However, the representation of fatherhood has been more extensively theorised in relation to contemporary Hollywood and US cinema, and Hannah Hamad's book, *Postfeminism and Paternity in Contemporary US Film* provides a useful theoretical framework though which to consider recent patterns in film.[20] She notes how fatherhood has become *the* dominant marker of hegemonic masculinity within postfeminist film and culture more broadly.[21] Taking a lead from Tania Modleski, who cautioned against superficially progressive discourses of fatherhood emerging in films such as *Three Men and a Baby* (Leonard Nimoy, 1987) and suggested that their focus on reconstructed father figures served to marginalise women and reify the primacy of the patriarchal father through a process she terms the 'derealisation' of the mother,[22] Hamad's work builds on Modleski's influential foundations in assessing more recent examples of paternal supremacy and maternal derealisation in Hollywood film.[23] Similar trends can be discerned across British media culture,

Figure 5.1 'L'Enfant' by Spencer Rowell captures the emergence of postfeminist fatherhood. © Spencer Rowell

creating what Bruzzi terms 'active discourses of fatherhood', with fathers becoming increasingly central to cinematic narratives.[24]

However, there are important cultural differences between British and American representations. While I adopt Hamad's phrase, postfeminist fatherhood, I augment it with a national prefix in order to account for the specific ways in which British forms of postfeminism, and thus its articulations of fatherhood, are distinct from American forms.[25] As Hamad notes, Hollywood cinema has become dominated by narratives of:

> a model of fatherhood which is (or becomes) emotionally articulate, domestically competent, skilled in managing the quotidian practicalities of parenthood and adept at negotiating a balance and/or discursive confluence of private sphere fatherhood and public sphere paternalism.[26]

But while there are certainly examples of British postfeminist fatherhood that can be understood in these terms, they tend to be limited to films with middle-class, affluent protagonists. The British film that comes closest, perhaps, to Hamad's model is *Jack and Sarah* (Tim Sullivan, 1995). The eponymous couple are expecting their first baby, they live in an affluent part of London and are presented as possessing all the trappings of upper middle-class life. From the outset of the film, parenting is specifically mobilised as being Sarah's (Imogen Stubbs) domain of expertise. Her calmness is juxtaposed with Jack's (Richard E. Grant) nervousness, which culminates in him falling down the stairs and knocking himself unconscious as Sarah goes into labour. When Jack wakes up, he discovers that Sarah died during childbirth, a literalisation of Modleski's notion of derealisation.[27] Sarah's death leaves Jack and their newborn daughter alone. Crucially, Jack has to 'learn' fatherhood. Neither the practical aspects of looking after a baby nor the emotional job of nurturing appear to come naturally to him. After his mother and mother-in-law intervene, Jack awakens to find his new daughter asleep with him and from this moment he begins to actively engage with the processes of fatherhood; not only does he learn to look after baby Sarah, her very existence provides his life with new purpose and meaning. The unambigious investment in father-hood as restorative and recuperative that we see in *Jack and Sarah* may be more in keeping with the dominant cultural discourses around masculinity and fatherhood during the 1990s; however, it is something of an anomaly within British cinema. It appears that restorative narratives of fatherhood such as that of *Jack and Sarah* and my case study *About A Boy* are only available to middle-class fathers. By contrast, working-class and unem-ployed fathers are often positioned as abusive, violent or otherwise failing their children, which is, I suggest, a symptomatic precursor to the class politics that Imogen Tyler has described as being central to twenty-first-century neoliberalism in which those people who fall below the middle class norm are marginalised and rendered abject.[28]

Class and Conflict in *When Saturday Comes*

When Saturday Comes bears several similarities to *Brassed Off*. Both are set in mining communities which remain active albeit precarious, within the context of post-industrialisation, both feature generational tensions between fathers and sons, and both reiterate a notion of inherited pat-terns and practices of working-class masculinity that passes from father to son. *Brassed Off* appears to lament the passing of the spaces and cultures of industrial working-class masculinity, suggesting that their demise has created a cultural and economic schism between generations of men. In contrast, *When Saturday Comes* provides a distinctly contemporary fantasy of post-industrial, working-class masculinity, culminating in the unlikely success of Jimmy in escaping the confines of the brewery by securing a contract as a professional footballer. When Jimmy's girlfriend Annie (Emily Lloyd) discovers that she is pregnant, part way through the film, it becomes mobilised as a device that is used as a motivating mechanism for Jimmy's reconfiguration and subsequent recuperation from his working-class, unreconstructed masculinity to something closer to a hegemonic paradigm of British postfeminist masculinity. This film, then, is of interest to me here for a number of reasons: firstly, the contrasting masculinities of Joe and Jimmy, the father and son relationship at the heart of the film, and secondly because of the way in which impending fatherhood is used as a narrative mechanism that facilitates Jimmy's personal transformation out of his proletarian, macho culture and his transcendence into a more affluent and esteemed position of a professional footballer. This social transformation, within this dominant paradigm, takes an everyman and morphs their occupational status into one of the most celebrated and glamourised male roles within neoliberal celebrity cultures. However, in order to realise his ambition of becoming a professional footballer, he has to actively resist and overcome the damaging cultural legacy of his father's gendered identity. Finally, I am interested in analysing the ways in which Sean Bean's star image is deployed as a mechanism through which working-class narratives of fatherhood can be mediated.

From the beginning of the film, Jimmy's father, Joe, exemplifies the negative characteristics of the working-class father in many ways. Where Danny (Pete Postlethwaite), the patriarch in *Brassed Off*, exemplifies 'respectable' working-class masculinity, as discussed in Chapter 2, Joe represents a more problematic if equally familiar counterpart. Joe smokes and is a heavy drinker, he also has a gambling addiction and is physically and verbally abusive to his wife, Mary (Ann Bell), as well as to his children. He leads the family into debt and continually mocks Jimmy's attempts to break free from the cultural confines of the community. Joe's outdated practices of fatherhood are unequivocally positioned as problematic by the film; his gruffness, his authoritarian rule, his emotional remoteness and his bullying attitude towards his wife and children are frequently depicted, emphasising the ways in which his behaviour is as much about this own damage as it is about the damage that he does to his family.

The opening flashback sequence contextualises the narrative and sets up the main characters and the various points of connection and tension between them. The young Jimmy is in a careers interview at school. As the career adviser sets out Jimmy's career options (working in the pit like his father, or working in a local factory) he protests, arguing that he wants to be a professional footballer. The be-suited adviser's accent and clothing point to him unambiguously as a middle-class member of the education establishment, whose job it is to channel young boys like Jimmy into the factory or industry where they are most needed. The careers adviser dismisses Jimmy's ambition with a mocking sarcasm. In a complete inversion of the aspirational attitudes and of social mobility that are central to neoliberalism, the implication of Jimmy's meeting with the careers adviser was that working–class lads like Jimmy have a pre–defined place within society and they should not seek to challenge or change it. It seems from this scene that within the confines of the industrial northern town, hierarchies of class and belonging are firmly entrenched. Much like Arthur Seaton before him, Jimmy is confined and contained within the limited options of his geocultural place and is left to rail against the structural authorities that keep him there. The film cuts to the present day where the adult Jimmy is, as predicted by the school careers adviser, working in the local brewery. Jimmy's ambivalence to the job is demonstrated as he runs through the gates, clocking into work with seconds to spare, much to the irritation of his floor manager.

Joe's shortcomings as a father are also presented from the opening scenes of the film, in which a careers teacher reproaches Jimmy for his parents' absence at an important meeting. Shortly after this, Joe finds Jimmy and Russell (Craig Kelly) in the pub. He chases them out, shouting and swearing at them, before clipping Jimmy around the head for his audacity. When Jimmy retaliates with a quip about his careers interview his father slaps him again and sneers 'I don't need to go to no careers office to know what will become of you!' This opening encounter sets the tone for the rest of the film. Joe is temperamental and often abusive. The differences between father and son are further highlighted in other family interactions. When Jimmy returns home from working in the brewery, he kisses his mother and compliments her on the smell of the meal that she is cooking. He is shown looking after his younger brother, Russell, buying him football programmes to cheer him up. Joe, on the other hand, is disrespectful and abusive to them all, his tone invariably laden with sarcasm and a bitter, cruel edge, admonishing Jimmy in particular for an array of supposed misdemeanours. He assumes an authoritarian role in the family, which is clearly exacerbated by his heavy drinking.

The relationship between Joe and Jimmy is mobilised in order to foreground how father/son relationships are bound up with gendered cultural inheritance and the maintenance and/or negotiation of masculinity as a social practice. In this instance, Joe's masculine legacy is presented negatively – something to be resisted. Indeed, there are several instances where Jimmy is a likened to his father and explicitly cautioned against following his legacy. The extent of the similarities between father and son become clear during Jimmy's second trial at Sheffield United when it is revealed that, like Jimmy, Joe had been offered multiple trials at the club but his heavy drinking thwarted his progress, causing him to squander his otherwise prodigal talent. This revelation accomplishes two purposes: reminding viewers of the dangers of the father's legacy, and what is at stake should Jimmy fail to resist it. In this regard, Joe's continual presence functions as a Dickensian ghost of Christmas future, a constant reminder of what Jimmy's life might become should he fall at the same hurdles as his father and fail to break free from his cultural inheritance. But, secondly, and perhaps more importantly, the revelation that Jimmy is on the precipice of achieving where Joe failed functions to explain, if not to legitimate, Joe's attitude towards his son. While Joe serves to remind Jimmy of what is at stake should he follow the wrong path, Jimmy functions as a constant reminder of what Joe's life *could* have been. In this regard, *When Saturday Comes* might be understood as a contemporary, classed-based Oedipal narrative, in which the son must overcome his father's legacy in order to successfully negotiate his way to adulthood, or, in Jimmy's case, his journey to hegemonic postfeminist masculinity.

The cinematography and framing of scenes of the two men separately and together further highlight the distinction between the characters. In scenes where Jimmy is not with his father, he is typically centre of frame and often surrounded by other people, either family, friends or his girlfriend. Framing emphasises his affection towards his mother and brother and his popularity within the friendship group. Joe, however, is invariably alone in the frame, emphasising his isolation from family and friends. In contrast to Joe's embittered and isolated character, Jimmy enjoys his social position as the alpha male in his friendship group, and the markers of working-class masculinity are explicitly embodied by the character. Jimmy's life revolves around a familiar triptych of working-class male culture: football, the pub and an exclusively male friendship group. His language is coarse, his gender politics are unreconstructed, and he articulates a range of old-fashioned notions around gender roles and behaviour, blatantly ogling the bar maid and passing comment on her breasts (comments that she seems to dismiss but indulge as harmless fun) and joining in with sexist 'banter'.

Jimmy's alpha male identity places him at the centre of attention on the shop floor of the factory, another macho environment inhabited exclusively by men. The unreconstructed gender politics of the shop floor is evidenced as the men gather around the newspaper to ogle the daily 'page 3' image of a bare-breasted female model; they exchange banter about sexual prowess and tell lewd jokes. While at work Jimmy appears to

Figure 5.2 *When Saturday Comes:* Joe Muir is invariably positioned alone in the frame

be central to the machismo of the shop floor, at home he is shown to be a caring son, shown to be invested in familial relationships with his mother and brother. Here lies a further contrast between father and son; where Jimmy is seen invariably surrounded by his friends, his family or with his girlfriend, Annie, his father is typically framed alone – his addiction to alcohol and gambling have alienated him from friends and family alike.

When Joe is interacting with both friends and family, his tone is brusque and blunt; the only time he is shown as trying to be pleasant is when he is trying to borrow money from Jimmy and Russell. When Jimmy refuses, saying that he will pass the money directly onto his mother, the veneer of niceness evaporates, replaced by a scowl and a curt reply. The precarious line between the similarities and differences of the father and son are highlighted in the sequence where, having found out that Joe has taken £25 from his wife's purse, the boys decide to go to the bookies. Once there they take Joe's money from his friend and put the bet on themselves. Jimmy decides to add a further £25 to the bet. The race is a photo finish between the favourite, who Joe wanted to bet on, and an outsider called No Chance. When No Chance is declared the winner, Jimmy hugs his brother and plants a firm kiss on his forehead. Rather than following his father's tip, Jimmy had placed £50 on No Chance and won £1,000. Joe enters the bookies just as Russell and Jimmy are collecting their winnings. He is downcast when he discovers the result, immediately asking his friend for some more money to try and recoup his losses. An ebullient Jimmy returns the original £25 to his father, who is humiliated in front of his friends, before he returns home to give a substantial portion of his winnings to his mother to clear the debts his father had accrued. Jimmy's victory is both material and symbolic. His success positions him in contrast to his father who would have backed another losing horse. In rejecting his father's choice of horse, Jimmy is symbolically rejecting his father's legacy. His victory not only validates this rejection but, more importantly, is also used as a means of highlighting the similarities and differences between the two men. Where Joe had taken money from the family and got them into debt because of his gambling, Jimmy returned money and cleared the debt. Despite the fact that he won, and that he gave money to his family, the potential for the father/son cycle repeating is clear and is voiced by Jimmy's mother who cautions him, reminding him of how his father's gambling habit grew out of winning.

A particularly crucial narrative juncture for Jimmy comes the evening before his football trial. Joe goads Jimmy into another argument, this time about Jimmy's decision to stay in and have an early night in preparation for his trial, a decision that means he misses out on his best friend's birthday. Joe taunts Jimmy for being a 'rubbish' best friend for choosing to stay home when he should be out celebrating; father and son exchange verbal blows, with Jimmy suggesting that his father is jealous because Jimmy is on the verge of succeeding where his father had failed. Having endured his father's taunts for some time, Jimmy takes his leave. The camera stays focused on Joe as the door closes behind Jimmy; he gives a self-satisfied smirk, saying 'Ah, I knew he couldn't stop in, not just for one night!'

The scene cuts to Jimmy, be-suited, at the flat viewing that Annie had set up. While Annie looks round, enthusiastically, Jimmy appears distant and ambivalent. In a conversation that frames the characters separately, cutting between them for reaction shots, Annie finally reveals that she is pregnant. Jimmy, who has recently been sacked from the brewery after punching his floor manager, does not share her happiness. The two of them argue, culminating in Jimmy telling Annie 'I'm not ready yet' and 'I just don't want a fucking kid.' At this, Jimmy turns and walks out of the flat, leaving Annie crying; her hopes of sharing the flat and having a baby together seemingly dashed. In the next scene, Jimmy joins his friends at the pub, where the celebrations appear to be in full swing. Although Jimmy does, initially, appear to honour his intention of staying sober in preparation for his trial, his commitment wavers in the face of the cultural expectations of drinking, and his recent argument with Annie, and he downs a shot of whiskey. This inevitably leads him to continue drinking with catastrophic consequences and he ends up in bed with a stripper. He wakes up at the exact time of his final trial. Not only does Jimmy fail to impress the coaches at Sheffield United, he also embarrasses his Hallam coach Ken (Pete Postlethwaite), who happens to be Annie's uncle, while his infidelity destroys his relationship with Annie.

At this point in the film Jimmy seems to reach his lowest point; he is unhappily single, unemployed and living in a sparsely furnished flat, having been thrown out of the family home after another argument with his father. Just as Jimmy seems to be at the bottom of his narrative trajectory, his younger brother, Russell, is killed in a mining accident. Jimmy's grief leads him to the edge of suicide. He walks along a railway track, a train coming up behind him. He flips the lucky coin that Russell had given him previously. The shot shows the train speeding along the track. It is only as the train clears the frame that Jimmy's fate is revealed: he appeared to jump out of the way at the last second. A close-up shows the coin clasped tightly in his hand.

It is from this moment that Jimmy begins his to negotiate his redemption, from unfaithful, unemployed, unreconstructed working-class masculinity into a more acceptable iteration of hegemonic masculinity. Shortly after he decides not to commit suicide, Jimmy returns to see his coach, Ken, to ask him for another chance. Initially Ken is hostile, berating Jimmy for letting himself down, and for proving to the Sheffield management that he is too similar to his father to make a successful professional footballer. Jimmy begs for a second chance, tears glinting in his eyes, as he admits that a lack of courage led him to mess everything up with Annie and his football career. The older man appraises his protégé silently for a few seconds before agreeing to help. From this moment on, the film focuses much less on Jimmy's relationship with his own father and more on his transformation into an appropriate version of postfeminist fatherhood. This process of transformation begins with a clichéd training montage which serves to indicate the passing of seasons and thus functions as a testament to his commitment to himself, to Ken and, by implication, to Annie. The heavy rain in which some of his training is performed provides further proof of Jimmy's renewed commitment. The montage also depicts Jimmy's commitment to Annie and his persistence in trying to redeem himself; he runs the same route every day, and on each occasion he posts a letter through Annie's door. As such, the montage is used to connect Jimmy's commitment to training with his desire to prove himself as a partner to Annie and a father to their unborn child. On the final instance, Jimmy sees Annie's mother and asks after her; Mrs Doherty promises to pass his message on. He is about to leave when Annie appears and the two of them share an awkward exchange. Annie confirms that all is well with the baby before bidding a friendlier goodbye.

With renewed hope that Annie might forgive him Jimmy attends his second trial at Sheffield United where he lives up to his promise, impressing the managers enough to secure a professional contract. In so doing, Jimmy's transformation from an unreconstructed working-class man is complete. Jimmy's transition from brewery worker to professional footballer also coincides with a cultural moment in which 'New Labour' was in ascendance, and, with it, attendant neoliberal discourses of social mobility and classlessness in Britain. Moreover, the film is prescient in this respect, having been released just a few months before England was due to host the 1996 European Cup Finals, and just at the moment in which the celebrification of football was beginning to take hold in British culture. This brought with it the rise of the super-rich celebrity football players, with players such as David Beckham beginning to feature more heavily in media culture, becoming a central fantasy of working-class masculinity.

By casting an icon of white, northern, working-class masculinity in the figure of Sean Bean, *When Saturday Comes* taps in to a range of contemporary cultural impulses, not least among which is the increasingly reconstructed social practices of fatherhood. By presenting a character that is able to transcend the punitive financial constrictions of his classed and regional location via the specific combination of 'natural talent', hard work and the persistence of self-determination, the film invests in the recuperative potential of postfeminist fatherhood. Further, it does so in ways that consolidate the contemporary fantasies of classlessness to the discourses and representations of postfeminist masculinity. Despite the distinctly uninspiring beginning to his time on the pitch, Jimmy goes on to score the winning goal in a cup match, and after the final whistle he and Annie reunite on the pitch, leaving the film to close with the assumption that Jimmy will consolidate his career as a professional footballer, and that the couple will remain together and will begin an idealised neoliberal nuclear family. In this regard the film encapsulates a specific moment in terms of class, gender and familial practices of masculinity in British cultural history: a country on the verge of political and cultural rejuvenation. While Jimmy's redemption is unequivocal, Joe's is less clear-cut. He makes a tentative peace with Jimmy when he returns the football programmes that he had taken from Russell; Jimmy grants his father peace of mind, reassuring him that Russell was unaware of his father's actions. Joe is only seen once more thereafter, in the pub, apparently alone but at the margins of the men who have gathered to celebrate Jimmy's debut. While Jimmy's winning goal appears to endorse the notion that he has been successful in breaking free from his father's legacy, by showing Joe in the pub and Jimmy's mother and sister in the family living room, watching the match on the television, it suggests that both the relationship between Joe and the women is ambiguous and that Joe remains entrapped by his own socio-cultural position. Ultimately, the ending implies that while Jimmy might have been able to transcend his cultural legacy having acquired the agency to break the cycles of destructive paternalism via his success as a professional footballer. Joe's position, however, remains less clear; he remains isolated and apart from his family and watches his son's victory from the homosocial familiarity of the local pub.

About A Boy and a Middle-Class Man

Despite the fact that *About A Boy* and *When Saturday Comes* are both male-centred romantic comedies they offer very different narratives of fatherhood. This is bound up with issues of class and stardom, as well as the different production contexts of the films. *When Saturday Comes* was Maria Giese's directorial debut and was produced through a collaborative network of small independent production companies, for some of whom this represented their sole project. Although picked up by New Line for distribution, it did not benefit from the same production and distribution advantages that *About A Boy* enjoyed, having been produced by Working Title Productions, one of the biggest independent British film producers, and distributed by Universal. Likewise, while Sean Bean had an extensive catalogue of both film and television roles, including playing Boromir in the *Lord of the Rings* (Peter Jackson) films of the early 2000s, he never had the same level of transatlantic visibility and thus marketability as Hugh Grant, established through his roles in *Four Weddings and A Funeral* (Mike Newell, 1994), *Notting Hill* (Roger Michell, 1999) and a variety of other rom-coms and heritage films. The iteration of British masculinity in which Grant specialised was both recognisable and appealing to American audiences; arguably more so than the more proletarian type with which Bean tended to be associated, and exemplified through his role in *When Saturday Comes*.

One further advantage *About A Boy* enjoyed was its provenance as an adaptation of a novel by Nick Hornby, the best-selling 'new lad' author whose previous books *Fever Pitch* and *High Fidelity* had already been made into commercially successful films.[29] All three books focus on performances and practices of masculinity and share a preoccupation with male characters who are unwilling, or unable, to divest themselves of their boyhood hobbies and who are also, invariably, insecure and emotionally immature. Much like *Fever Pitch* and *High Fidelity*, *About A Boy* is a belated coming-of-age narrative in which a central male character transitions from a state which might be described as over-extended adolescence into a more mature embodiment of masculinity. The protagonists of all three narratives have had a series of failed romantic relationships. They are depicted as showing a fundamental lack of understanding of women; they represent a version of unreconstructed masculinity (the lad paradigm) which is tempered, through their middle- and upper middle-class status, into something that is benign and endearing, as opposed to violent and threatening, in spite of its occasionally predatory or self-centred aspects.

The protagonist of *About a Boy* is Will Freeman, played in the film version by Grant. His father composed a popular Christmas hit record and the ongoing royalties enable Will to live very comfortably, unencumbered by the demands of work, bills and budgets; he is free to indulge in what Murray Pomerance and Frances Gateward describes as the 'unending consumer dream state' of affluent adolescence.[30] In many ways the character chimes with a wider cultural phenomenon particularly associated with masculinity. Variously described as kidults, adultescents and rejuveniles, the cultural trope of masculinity as defined by a protracted period of immaturity and adolescence stretching well into the early twenties took hold in British popular media culture. Conservative commentators such as Laura Nolan were particularly concerned about the consequences of what she termed 'a generation of man-boys' on their more mature female counterparts; she expresses her anxieties for the women who are looking to these men as potential husbands and fathers and finding them emotionally stunted, juvenile and tedious.[31] Her colleague at *The Times*, Kate Muir, goes further, bemoaning that 'the generation who first became addicted to Pac-Man and Super Mario would turn out to be boys who never grew up . . . man teens sitting before their kiddy consoles like huge manatees'.[32] The men described here are British iterations of the American 'dude' paradigm and, much like him, they are predominantly white and belong to the affluent middle classes, invariably inheriting their wealth rather than earning it. Where Pomerance and Gateward suggest that the cultural trade-off for the extended adolescence is a 'denial of the full responsibilities of adult citizenship', Will welcomes this, actively embracing a lifestyle of underachievement, resisting and rejecting any transition into the hegemonic role of adult masculinity, and is able to do so because of his inherited financial independence.[33] Measuring his day in terms of half-hour 'units', Will explains that he has an aversion to the cultural practice of measuring in hours on account of the fact that they are too long and require too much commitment. Indeed, Will's surname, Freeman, is a none-too-subtle indicator of his attitude and status at the outset of the narrative.

The film opens to show Will in his London apartment; it is a bright and open space, with floor-to-ceiling shelves housing his collection of music, books, video games and media alongside an impressive array of high-end gadgets and devices, providing unequivocal visual evidence of his afflu-ence, his lifestyle and his cultural inclinations. Arguing against John Donne's famous dictum that 'no man is an island', Will states that not only is he an island, he would describe himself as Ibiza, best known as a hedon-istic, designer-obsessed party destination, as popular with celebrities and fashionistas as it is with partygoers and clubbers. As the array of high-end apparel appears to imply, Will is a man for whom appearance matters. It is not just the expression of identity provided by branded goods that matters, Will is equally concerned with his own appearance, checking out his reflection in the stainless steel kitchen surfaces, reading men's lifestyle and fashion magazines, and maintaining regular hairdresser and grooming appointments. In this regard, Will epitomises the postfeminist paradigm of metrosexual masculinity; a gendered identity that appropriates and re-masculinises consumption as a contemporary expression of heterosexual masculinity.[34] As Helen Shugart explains, drawing on the foundations of scholars including Sean Nixon, Anthony Easthope and Tim Edwards, there has been an ongoing tension between consumer culture and mascu-linity, with regards both to the ways in which the male body is objectified and commodified, and also in the way that the act of consuming has been traditionally designated as either feminine or queer. In this regard, metro-sexuality emerges as a mechanism through which acts of consumerism and commodification can be incorporated within new scripts of normative, heterosexual masculinity.[35] In this regard, Will defines himself in accord-ance with the terms of metrosexual masculinity; rejecting the feminised implications of 'shopping', Will proclaims himself 'an arbiter of style and taste!' The noun in this instance is deployed to confer an appropriately normative authoritative and expert quality to his role as a consumer.

In many ways, *About A Boy* can be read as a meditation on Hugh Grant's changing star image. The work that put him on the map as a star con-structed an image that was posh and charming but vulnerable and lovably self-deprecating, 'the quintessence of diffident, old world charm'.[36] His arrest for soliciting a prostitute in America complicated that image some-what, although Grant managed to retain his popularity and his commercial appeal. Elements of a more rakish image which Grant displayed in *An Awfully Big Adventure* (Mike Newell, 1995) and *Small Time Crooks* (Woody Allen, 2000) were then developed with the character of Daniel Cleaver, the caddish, womanising book publisher in the *Bridget Jones's Diary* films (2001, 2004). The character of Will in *About a Boy* retains the class and economic privilege of several of his previous characters while also giving voice to similar kinds of gendered insecurities as they are embodied. But the film marks an important juncture in Grant's career, drawing on a narrative of postfeminist fatherhood as a mechanism through which Grant's particular iteration of British masculinity is renegotiated in order to allow a transition from the bumbling, diffident ingénue of his earlier roles into a more mature and middle-aged masculine identity. Despite the fact that he now has five children, Grant's star image had never been bound up with fatherhood; his age, however, meant that he was less suited to the role of the hapless bachelor, and increasingly suited to more paternalised roles. Indeed, the character of Will enables the various threads of Grant's star image to converge and to be reconfigured in keeping with the cultural ideologies of affluent, middle-aged men in postfeminist culture.

Will's initiation into paternal masculinity is unplanned and initially unwelcomed. From the film's outset, he is shown explicitly as both physically and emotionally uncomfortable with children. He declines the invitation to be godfather to his niece, emphasising his lack of suitability for the role to his sister and her husband by proclaiming that the minute she turned eighteen he'd most likely 'try to take her out, get her drunk and try to shag her!' Holding the small baby in his arms, Will's brother-in-law needs no further persuasion, while his sister, apparently used to Will's tendency towards inappropriate comments, shakes her head. While played for awkward comedy, Will is clearly anxious to avoid what he sees as a potentially dangerous quasi-parental commitment; his self-deprecation functions as an evasive strategy that allows him to avoid what he sees as an unwelcome burden of responsibility; but more significantly, it is also an expression that exemplifies the postfeminist gender politics of the film. Will's comments clearly rely on an awareness of the boundaries of propriety, and a tacit understanding that while he is contravening these boundaries deliberately and provocatively in his speech, he would not literally do this. Will's performance, therefore, is an expression of strategic incompetence paired with strategically deployed inappropriateness, mobilised in order to avoid being coerced into something that he does not want to do.

Will continues to perform this kind of gendered performance throughout the film, playing with the cultural codes and conventions of reconstructed and unreconstructed masculinity, depending on which best suits his agenda at any one moment. In this way, his character might be described as the ultimate in bricolage masculinity, and a postmodern simulacrum of postfeminist masculinity, completely comfortable with the neoliberal project of the self that enables him to adapt his performance according to his audience or, as we might describe it, his market. The personal capital that Will gains from his ability to manipulate various codes and performances of masculinity makes him a rather cynical protagonist for a romantic comedy and, thus, it is imperative that he undergoes a significant transformation, or reconstruction, in order to be moulded into an appropriately paternalised, postfeminist masculinity that is required of the generic form.

Having shut down the potentially dangerous quasi-parental commitment of being a godfather Will agrees to go on a date, arranged by his sister. According to his voice-over, all is going well until his date Angie (Isabel Brook) tells him that she is a mother to a three-year-old child. From here on in, voice-over is used as a recurrent device through which Will's inner thoughts are expressed, invariably in direct contrast to the situation he finds himself in. This technique is used to draw attention to the performative nature of gender, sexual politics and dating, but also, in this particular instance, to reveal the disparity that Goffman refers to when discussing how the social demands of performance can demand inauthenticity.[37] In this instance, the voice-over explains, 'I wanted to run!' in contrast to the gushing response that he delivers to his date: 'wonderful, I mean, I love kids, I mean, I would have been disappointed if you didn't have kids . . .'. In this instance the voice-over positions Will as a character who is able to mobilise and perform a range of behaviours associated with postfeminist masculinity for his own cynical gains; it is not so much that his performance is inauthentic rather that it is deliberately so – Will's expertise in consumerism enables him to commodify himself in accordance with the needs of his target. As such, the contrast between external performance and internal voice-over highlights the extent to which Will's postfeminist masculinity is little more than a performative masquerade beneath which lies an unreconstructed and, in terms of gender politics, problematic identity. A further layer of complexity is added, however, by Will's ongoing reflexivity regarding what he sees as the ridiculous transparency of his performance. He smiles at her, voice-over questioning 'she can't be buying this, surely?!'

The first time that we see Will in action as a postfeminist father figure (after his clumsy handling of his niece) is at the zoo where he is looking after Angie's toddler, having successfully secured a further date, despite his anxiety that she would have seen through his completely inauthentic performance. Left alone with the child, Will attempts to entertain him, holding him upside down and swinging him from side to side. Although the child squeals with delight, clearly enjoying Will's attempt at emulating fatherly behaviour, the cinematography reveals Will's discomfort and the performative requirements of paternalised postfeminist masculinity. A close-up of Will's face shows his bemused and uncertain expression while the following long shot emphasises the tense and mechanical physicality of his performance: his shoulders are hunched up as he jolts rather than swings the child from side to side. Despite his initial reservations, revealed through the second-date voice-over, Will admits, as the day draws to a close, that he was surprised at the extent to which he enjoyed the emotional connections with both Angie and her child. He continues to revel in his position of 'Will, the good guy', relishing Angie's adoring compliments on his exemplary performance of paternal, postfeminist masculinity and, of course, the physical relationship that this affords.

However, he soon admits uncertainty and boredom, commenting both on the difficulties of 'being wonderful all the time' and on the limitations that come with dating someone who has parental commitments: he has to pretend not to mind when Angie is late for their date at IMAX and bemoans the lack of media technology in her house. For Will, a man who is unaccustomed to having to work around the constraints that come with young children, the experience and the compromises prove too demanding, and before long Will decides that he needs to end the relationship. He reflects on the forthcoming conversation in which he will terminate the relationship and, as he does, it appears that he has changed in some way, explaining that 'I didn't really relish going back to unreliable, emotionally stunted asshole', once more appearing to acknowledge, internally at least, the limits of unreconstructed bachelor masculinity. Thus, the maintenance of his position as a hegemonic and desirable postfeminist man as well as his integrity as a character in whom the audience can invest necessitates a careful negotiation of the separation. The montage of crying ex-girlfriends serves as a reminder of the extent to which, despite his recent performances, Will is the far from the sensitive, postfeminist, romantic leading male. However, Will's integrity and thus his narrative function in this regard are saved when Angie is the one to bring the relationship to an end, leaving Will absolved of blame. The end of Will's relationship with Angie brings him to an initial juncture on his transition from unreconstructed cad, or man about town, as Spicer terms him, into a paternal version of postfeminist masculinity.[38] Despite proclamations of the extent to which the relationship with Angie had caused Will's attitudes to change, his subsequent decision to deliberately pursue single mothers – motivated by what he perceives as the various sexual 'benefits' that they afford – is another example of his performative bricolage masculinity that he constructs via curation and commodification.

Will's deliberate deception continues when he decides to join 'Single Parents Alone Together' (SPAT), a group that he describes as being a prime 'hunting ground' for 'desperate' but 'gorgeous' single mothers. Will's facial expressions suggest that he is rather unpleasantly surprised when the women attending the meeting do not live up to his expectations of physical attraction. The majority of them are distinctly unglamor-ous, tired, make-up free and sceptical with regard to men. Despite this initial shock Will decides to stay. He meets Suzi (Victoria Smurfit), the one woman in the group to come close to his physical ideal. The layout of the room in which SPAT meets further emphasises the dramaturgic requirements of postfeminist fatherhood. As the only male in the room, Will listens to the women recount their tales of abandonment and post-separation parenting, becoming increasingly reflexive over the gender politics of heterosexual relationships and the role of masculinity therein. Despite being aware of his own predatory motivation for attending, and his own personal relationship history (as recounted by the montage of crying women), upon hearing the various tales of betrayal tendencies with respect to relationships, upon hearing the women's stories, Will proclaims 'Men are bastards!' He concludes that the women's experiences at the hands of their former partners made him want 'to cut my own penis off with a kitchen knife'. Despite this moment of apparent awareness, there is little in the way of contrition for his own previous behaviour, nor for being an imposter within a support group in which members have had their trust abused and broken by men. Indeed, when it is Will's turn to speak, he concocts a heart-wrenching story about how his partner aban-doned himself and their son, Ned, leaving them for his imaginary best friend. Despite the far-fetched details – the inclusion of the model of the Ferrari that the fictitious wife and friend absconded in – Will offers an accomplished performance of postfeminist fatherhood. He appears to be sensitive, caring and clearly devoted to his son, he is also vulnerable and emotionally intelligent, and is apparently open and honest in his communication. As such, Will's masquerade in the group demonstrates the performative potential of postfeminist fatherhood as *the* heteronor-mative hegemonic paradigm of masculinity for middle-aged men. Will's performance is deliberately deceptive and deployed consciously as a tool through which to attract and seduce women. In this respect his character's behaviour is not that far removed from the kinds of strategic 'studied cha-risma' advocated by the misogynistic 'seduction communities' of online PUA's (pick-up artists), a movement that began in the 1990s but that grew exponentially with the rise of the internet in the 2000s. Will's narrative contrasts the postfeminist father with the uncaring, absent and material-istic mother. He regurgitates some of the more reactionary gender politics of postfeminism as detailed by Modleski, in which women and mothers who pursue careers and personal fulfilment over traditional family roles in particular are denounced, while fathers are lauded when they undertake regular, mundane parenting tasks.

It is when on a date with one of the SPAT women that Will meets Marcus (Nicholas Hoult), the young boy who facilitates Will's narrative transition from unreconstructed cad to postfeminist father figure. Upon discovering that the date with Suzi was to feature not only her toddler but also this other, older boy, Will was disgruntled, his voice-over contemplating whether Marcus's presence was some kind of punishment for his predation of a single mother. Against the odds, Will and Marcus begin to bond after Will covers up for the boy after he accidentally killed a duck by throwing a loaf of his mother's homemade wholemeal bread into the pond. The developing relationship between Will and Marcus is facilitated by the suicide attempt of Marcus's mother, Fiona (Toni Collette). Upon finding Fiona unconscious in the sitting room of the house, Suzi springs into action, apparently knowing exactly what to do; Will, on the other hand, is stunned and dithers around when Fiona tells him to call an ambulance. In this situation, Will is re-positioned as an immature and incapable man-child who needs a woman for leadership and guidance. As Will and Marcus follow the ambulance to the hospital there is an awkward silence between them; the audience, on the other hand, is engaged by a further voice-over monologue that switches capriciously from sensitivity to immaturity and inappropriate frivolity. 'It was horrible, horrible!' he says, as he looks over to the young boy in the passenger seat, appearing genuinely concerned about the events and their impact upon Marcus, but this readily gives way to immaturity, as he breaks into a grin as he quips 'but driving fast behind the ambulance was fantastic!' Once more this creates an ambivalent and unstable politic that appears to be deliberately incoherent in order to obfuscate any sense of certitude with regard to the character, with such narrative sleights of hand enabling Will to switch position depending on the context. He is never just unreconstructed and manipulative, nor is he simply an underdeveloped man-child, he is all of these things at different moments, with various aspects of his identity interwoven in ways that appear to provide and undermine coherence at the same time.

Once Fiona has returned home, the family is, as far as Will is concerned, no longer part of his life and so, when his regular hairdressing appointment is interrupted by a call from Marcus, he is taken aback. Will eventually agrees to Marcus's suggestion of an outing, not because of a sudden altruism but because he sees an opportunity to once more perform the 'Cool Uncle Will' role that he enjoyed during his brief relationship with Angie. Marcus, however, is not satisfied with Will's initial agreement to a day out telling him that they will be taking his mother as well; he adds that on account of their lack of wealth he expects Will to pay. Marcus hangs up abruptly, leaving Will confused but intrigued. The following sequences, set in a café and then in Marcus's and Fiona's home, invoke the ongoing disparity between Will's inner personality and his outwardly performed version of masculinity. Will's opening gambit: 'Hi, er, are you feeling better?' is delivered with the social awkwardness that has become one of Grant's signature characteristics but, unlike the genuine awkwardness it denotes in Charles in *Four Weddings and a Funeral*, in this instance it appears to be more cynically deployed as a deliberate performance of diffidence.

Throughout the scene Will's voice-over and his facial expressions contradict his performed humility. He mocks Fiona's outfit, describing her jumper as 'yeti-style', for example. His façade is punctured, albeit momentarily, when Marcus proudly announces their vegetarianism. Upon learning this, Will turns to the waiter with a knowing smirk, commenting 'you don't say?' and without missing a beat 'and I'll have a steak sandwich, thanks, mate!' Fiona's eye-roll at Will's arrogance is the only indicator that she has picked up on the discrepancy between his performances thus far and his apparent arrogance. Marcus, on the other hand, is naïvely oblivious, his voice-over is used to detail his hope for romance to blossom between Will and his mother, with Will's voice-over following almost instantaneously to shut down any such aspirations. The voice-over not only shuts down Marcus's naïve hopes of a relationship between Will and Fiona, it also functions to emphasise the contrast between Will's insincerity and Fiona's earnestness. Arriving back at Fiona's and Marcus's house, Fiona takes to the piano. Will and Marcus are at the table. Marcus looks to Will frequently, as if to gauge his appreciation of his mother's musical talent. While Will smiles at the boy, his voice-over reveals his true feelings, recalling it as unbearable. Fiona invites Marcus to join her and the two commence a mother-and-son duet of 'Killing Me Softly'. As Will's voice-over moans 'I hate it when they close their eyes!' the pair, obviously, close their eyes, immersed in the emotional vulnerability of the moment. The camera cuts back to show Will's face, horrified, trapped and wondering if he will ever be able to escape. Unable to bear any more, Will does eventually make his excuse and departs, lamenting on his way out that 'the trouble with charity is that you have to mean it' – the implication being that he saw spending the afternoon with Marcus and Fiona as a good deed, endured despite its tedium.

Thus, when Marcus turns up at Will's flat one afternoon he is taken aback. The two sit in silence as they watch *Countdown* in the winter twilight and then, as the credits for the programme roll, Marcus gets up, bids Will goodbye and takes his leave, as abruptly as he arrived. The visits soon become more regular, as a montage sequence of the pair on Will's sofa demonstrates, and gradually a friendship seems to develop. Against Will's anti-paternal instincts, the pair inevitably begin to talk over more serious issues, including Will's father and Fiona's mental health. In an exchange which marks a key moment in Will's narrative development, Will discovers that Marcus visits him to avoid going home and that the trauma of Fiona's suicide attempt remains very fresh. Unable to provide anything more meaningful than 'fucking hell!' by way of support or understanding, Will's emotional immaturity and his shortcomings as a reconstructed and emotionally articulate postfeminist father figure are highlighted in direct comparison to Marcus's maturity when the younger boy is shown to have the resilience and maturity that the older man lacks.

In this regard the film upholds another prominent trope of cinematic postfeminist fatherhood in which a younger character takes on the role of teacher or facilitator to the older man's narrative journey. This dynamic is mobilised in the scene where Will and Marcus discuss the problems that the youngster is having at school; once more the younger boy demonstrates levels of fortitude and psychological understanding that remain beyond Will's grasp. While Will does not have the emotional articulacy that is central to the postfeminist father, he does have the financial means and cultural capital to try to resolve the situation through his own area of expertise: consumption and the associated demonstrations of 'good taste' that accompany it. When an attractive shop assistant assumes that Will is Marcus's father, she compliments him, apparently impressed by a father taking his son shopping, as well as by the fact that Will appears to contravene traditional ideas about British masculinity as being unconcerned with appearance and style. Having purchased a pair of trainers for Marcus, Will reveals via voice-over the 'extraordinary rush of well-being' that the act gave him despite the fact that it 'only cost me sixty quid!' Here we see a further step in Will's transition from unreconstructed male island to postfeminist father figure, as he discovers the emotional fulfilment of an entirely selfless act. The point is emphasised when Will looks down affectionately at the young boy stood close beside him.

Immediately after this, the same bullies who had earlier chased Marcus to Will's house steal his brand-new trainers, forcing him to walk home barefoot in the rain. This leads to an argument in which Fiona discovers the extent of Will's and Marcus's friendship. She heads out to confront Will, who happens to be having dinner with his sister at a local restaurant. Unperturbed by the public setting, Fiona challenges Will to explain why a man in his late thirties would pursue a friendship with a young boy such as Marcus, demanding to know 'what does a single *childless* man in his thirties want with a twelve-year-old boy?' It takes a moment for Will to fully grasp Fiona's meaning, and in the ensuing argument it transpires that it is Will and not Fiona who understands Marcus more fully. Will disabuses Fiona of her illusions regarding her son; rising from the table to face Fiona, he admonishes her as a 'daft fucking hippy!' explaining that Marcus 'comes round every night of the week . . . because he's had the shit bullied out of him at school and you haven't got a clue! You're sending him out there like a lamb to the slaughter, he's being torn to pieces every day of the week!' In his takedown of Fiona, Will is positioned as the more aware and informed parent figure, a revelation that Marcus observes via his voice-over, 'Wow! Will really gets it! It should be mum, but it's Will!' In this moment, Will's credentials as an appropriate parent figure are put beyond question but also, crucially, so is his superiority over Fiona. The emotionally stunted and cynical Will, who has no experience of bringing up children and no relationship to Marcus, is shown to have a 'natural' kinship.

Despite the revelations of the restaurant scene, Will remains reluctant to relinquish his solitude entirely. The scene cuts to an exterior of a busy London street where Will is shown to be walking against a tide of pedestrian traffic, literally going against the flow of everybody else, suggesting that his attempt to march against the tide of postfeminist fatherhood is futile and ultimately untenable. Marcus asks Will to spend Christmas with them; the symbolic significance is not lost on Will – after all it is the ritualistic repetition of Christmas traditions that affords his leisurely lifestyle. Walking into a shop, Will reflects on his personal approach to Christmas, 'my intention is to spend Christmas as I always do, getting drunk and stoned and watching videos!' His moment of reflection is brought to a halt by the sudden intrusion of 'Santa's Sleigh', the song that made Will's father rich and thus facilitates Will's own lifestyle. The cold lighting used to show Will alone in his minimalist and undecorated apartment, drinking a bottle of beer and re-watching *Frankenstein* (James Whale, 1931) departs from the more typical lighting used in scenes depicting Christmas celebrations. The heavy-handed critique of masculinity as being isolated and disconnected is further emphasised by the soundtrack of the film, in which Frankenstein bemoans his loneliness and his monster proclaims 'friends, good!'

Thus, it seems, initially, that Will has resisted the allure of friendship and connection and retains his belief in a solitary existence, and so, when the scene cuts once more to show Will, ensconced in an armchair in the warmly-lit living room of Fiona's and Marcus's house, the hegemonic value of a form of masculinity that is emotionally connected and involved is once more proclaimed. When Marcus receives a pair of socks from his father and a tambourine from his mother, a number of close-up shots of Will's face seem to suggest a genuine affection and admiration for Marcus who enthusiastically thanks his parents for what Will describes as 'truly crap presents'. Will's gift is a CD player and CD by a contemporary hip hop act, showing him to be more naturally in tune with Marcus than any of his family. His gesture both points to his affluence and his capacity to provide the kinds of material items that are desired by teenage boys, but also his effortless understanding of Marcus and his role as a postfeminist father figure. This positioning is emphasised even further when Marcus defends Will in an argument with Suzi and his mother, objecting that not only is Will his friend but 'he also knows what kids really need!'

About A Boy functions as an exemplary tale of postfeminist father-hood; taking on the role of surrogate father enables Will to see beyond the shallow and superficial values of neoliberal consumerism within which he was previously so entrenched. The extent of his journey is demonstrated when he rushes to Marcus's school to 'save' him from 'social suicide'. Throughout the film, Fiona has reiterated how happy it makes her when Marcus sings and so, after she has bought him a tambourine for Christmas, he promises her that he will perform in the school talent show. When Will realises that the performance will, inevitably, be another painful rendition of 'Killing Me Softly', he rushes to intervene. He arrives just as Marcus has gone on stage. The hall is silent, full of cool, cruel kids willing him to fail. Marcus's voice wobbles; the audience begins to jeer. Grabbing an electric guitar from one of the other pupils, Will saunters out onto stage, joining Marcus in a rock-inspired interpretation of the song; not only does he close his eyes as the song culminates, but he also provides a hugely over-the-top performance that makes him, and not Marcus, the focus of any ridicule. The pay-off, for Will, is, of course, the relationship with Marcus and Fiona, but his new-found emotional maturity also leads him to forming a relationship with Rachel (Rachel Weisz). The final scene takes place the following Christmas; opening the scene to the familiar imagery of Will, on the sofa, watching *Frankenstein*, the camera zooms out to reveal a very different scene – it is a very contemporary family Christmas featuring Will, Rachel and her son, Marcus and Fiona, and Will's former Amnesty colleague, who he has clearly invited along in a matchmaking attempt for Fiona. Drawing once more on the warm imagery of the con-temporary family Christmas scene, Will has completed his narrative arc and has transitioned from boy to man.

Fathers, Sons and Questions of Belonging and Inheritance

Throughout the 1990s and 2000s, a number of films engaged with questions about ethnicity and identity. The political and cultural reflexivity that occurred in the aftermath of the racially motivated murder of Stephen Lawrence, the reworking of national identities within a multicultural nation state, and the increasing awareness of the cultural diversities in the period were key cultural concerns. Films such as *East is East* and *My Son the Fanatic* appeared, on the surface at least, to be part of an emergent cycle of British Asian filmmaking.[39] The political tone of these films varied considerably, with films like *East is East* and *Bend it Like Beckham* (Gurinder Chadha) both appearing to celebrate the polymorphous possibilities of hybridity and belonging within multicultural Britain. The case study film, *My Son the Fanatic*, however, adopted a rather different tone. Released in 1997, the film is contemporaneous with the wave of Cool Britannia, but despite opening with Dreadzone's 'Little Britain', a track that was explicit in its celebration of Britain as a multicultural and forward-looking nation, the film refuses to conform to the upbeat, rhetoric of Cool Britannia, instead offering a more circumspect narrative of cultural tensions and diaspora that it navigates via the father–son relationship.

In contrast to *East is East* and *Bend it Like Beckham* in which it is the older, diasporic generation who yearn for the traditions and cultural practices of their homeland, *My Son the Fanatic* appears to invert generational and familial tensions around cultural practices, performances of identity and expressions of belonging. George (Om Puri), the patriarch in *East is East*, invests in actively maintaining his Pakistani identity; listening to Pakistani news on the radio and adhering to cultural and religious practices associated with his Pakistani Muslim identity, all while attempting to make his British Pakistani children follow suit. Meanwhile Parvez (Om Puri), the father in *My Son the Fanatic*, is presented as having assimilated into British culture and working to dissuade his son Farid (Akbar Kurtha) from embracing Islamic fundamentalism. As with *East is East* the narrative revolves around the tensions and incompatibilities between father and son. Farid views his father's assimilation into British culture as distasteful and immoral, whereas in *East is East* the Khan children are quick to subvert their father's authority, cooking bacon while he is at the mosque, smoking, sneaking out to go drinking, and having pre-marital sexual relationships. Where the Khan children rail against what is presented as the restrictive prohibitions placed upon them, seeing their father's insistence on cultural and religious adherence as being incumbent on their mixed-race identities, Farid is more sceptical about his position within British culture.

The differences between Parvez and Farid are constructed not only through their narrative trajectories but also symbolically through the visual representations of their respective private spaces within the family home. Ensconced in the underground basement is Parvez's den-like room, it is cluttered with his possessions, including a television, a record player, record collection, ashtrays and bottles of whiskey; he retires alone to this room to drink whisky and listen to Americana and Blues music. Farid, by contrast, is seen ridding himself of Westernised possessions, including his guitar, an enduring symbol of Western masculinity, and items of clothing. Against the dark, cluttered basement room inhabited by his father, Farid's bedroom is spartan and sterile, a place where he retreats to pray and study the Qur'an. Farid rejects his father's integration into British culture and sees his embrace of Westernised liberalism as evidence of a corruption of spirit as well as being a denial of his 'true' heritage. Farid and his friends reject the possibilities of hybrid identities in which Britishness and Pakistani identities, practices and beliefs are merged, and instead turn to religious doctrine in order to recreate what they perceive as being an authentic and coherent sense of identity. In this regard, *My Son the Fanatic* is a product of its time. Made before the horror of the US terror attacks on 11 September 2001, the film is able to explore issues around cultural belonging, alienation and religious fundamentalism in ways that have been more difficult since the event. Indeed, the lack of British films interrogating questions about cultural belonging and the complexities of multiculturalism is testament to the difficulty; *Four Lions*, released in 2010 and directed by the controversial satirist Chris Morris, told the story of religious fundamentalism and British jihad through black comedy; suggesting that Islamic fundamentalism remained a contentious topic for British film.

In much the same way as *East is East* and *Bend it Like Beckham*, the opening scenes of *My Son the Fanatic* set up the central questions about hybridity and cultural identities, and the potential tensions that can arise between them. The film's opening offers a pointed critique of some of the central myths of Cool Britannia; juxtaposing the opulent mansion of the Fingerhut family over the Dreadzone track draws attention to the disparity between discourses of social mobility and classlessness and the lived reality, in which the gap between rich and poor continues to widen. Further, the narrative of progress, belonging and social mobility espoused in the soundtrack is at odds with the image of the mansion as a symbol of inherited wealth, accrued and passed on through generations. Parvez, his wife Minoo (Gopi Desai) and their son Farid are at the mansion to celebrate the impending engagement between Farid and Chief Inspector

Fingerhut's daughter, Madeline (Sarah Jane Potts). Even this supposedly happy union between the two families is a source of tension between Farid and Parvez. For Parvez, the engagement is evidence of his family's successful integration within the higher echelons of British society, whereas Farid appears unconvinced by his father's optimism. Throughout the scene Parvez's demeanour is obsequious as he seeks to ingratiate himself with the pompous, white Fingerhut (Geoffery Bateman). Parvez assumes a servile role throughout the gathering, either unaware of, or choosing to ignore, his host's barely concealed disdain. Parvez's offer to bring 'our food' to the police headquarters for the white man to 'enjoy' not only draws on an orientalist association of 'exotic' food with South Asian-ness but also highlights the racial politics and power relations of the relationship. Parvez's insistence on taking a photograph of the two families together juxtaposes a reductive, (Western) discourse of South Asian-ness with Fingerhut's obvious investment in white supremacy.

Parvez busily arranges the various family members, fussing around them and getting them in order; Fingerhut, however, looks on, his facial expressions scarcely hiding his contempt. By drawing attention to the white man's facial expressions, the film highlights the broader cultural issues of institutional and culturally embedded racism, and, by association, the frailty of multiculturalism as a socio-political rhetoric. Parvez's desperation to be accepted as an equal appears to make him unaware of Fingerhut's behaviour, or at least to ignore it. In contrast to his father, Farid does not accept or ignore their host's sleights; he sees Fingerhut's attitude and his contemptuous treatment of his family as symptomatic of the wider prejudices that South Asian Britons face on a daily basis, as he remonstrates later on in the film. Further, Farid sees his father's treatment at the hands of Fingerhut and his white clientele as exemplifying what he sees as the toxic hierarchies of race in nineties Britain. These experiences provide Farid with evidence of what he sees as the intractable differences between East and West, and between Muslim and Christian cultures.

Where Parvez sees the union between Farid and Madeleine as symbolic of the family's cultural integration, Farid comes to view it as an inappropriate and unfeasible symptom of assimilation in which he and his family are expected to modify their behaviour and their religious and cultural practices. While the film does not show any explicit acts of racism, the likes of which are shown in *Ae Fond Kiss* (Ken Loach, 2004), the familiarity of ideas such as institutional, structural and everyday racism, alongside the legacy of racially motivated attacks and murders, means that the film does not necessarily have to show the character being subject to racial abuse for the audience to understand that this is likely to be a key part of his lived experiences as a Pakistani Muslim living in Britain. Parvez's occupation as a taxi driver makes him a more obvious target for racially motivated abuse, and we see this happen at the hands of Herr Schitz, the German business-man. Much like Fingerhut, Schitz (Stellen Skarsgård) is not explicitly or physically violent in his racism, but the dynamic between the white German and the Pakistani taxi driver is fraught with tense power relations. Schitz frequently belittles and patronises Parvez, describing him as 'my little man'. Schitz's manner and language function to maintain a clear hierarchy between the men and to contain Parvez on account of his race and his occupation. For Farid, the ongoing everyday racism that he and his father encounter leads him to conclude that there can be no reconciliation between two opposing cultures and that, within British culture, there can never be full equality and acceptance for people of colour, and particularly for those who identify as Muslim. This point is picked up in the pointed post-9/11 and post-7/7 satire of *Four Lions* several years later. It is this experience that appears to lead to Farid's renunciation of cultural integra-tion and his desire to return to the traditions of his ancestors and, in so doing, reclaim his cultural identity. The tension between father and son hinges on this point. Farid sees his father as being too quick to assume a servile role in order to oblige both Fingerhut and his white clients. Parvez, on the other hand, relishes what he sees as the benefits of a secular culture and the freedom from religious doctrine that it entails. The ideological gulf between father and son appears to be almost insurmountable and, indeed, the generational nature of the conflict is confirmed by one of the imams at the local mosque who bemoans the orthodoxy of the younger generation to a bemused Parvez, saying that they dismiss the older genera-tion of men as 'corrupt and foolish'.

The confrontations between Farid and Parvez confirm this generational shift, which is caused by tensions around diasporic cultures and integra-tion and assimilation between different generations. Parvez remonstrates as Farid rids himself of an array of material possessions including his guitar, squash racquet and Western clothes, many of which Parvez has bought him. The fault line between father and son appears to be at a fun-damental level of belief. In his opinion Parvez has worked hard to provide for his son, and to give him the material and financial support to facilitate the best quality of life possible. However, as Bettina (Rachel Griffiths), the prostitute who Parvez escorts in his taxi, explains, this is not the only func-tion that a father needs to fulfil, and that while Parvez has clearly tried to do his best in terms of material provision, he also needed to help guide his son and 'give Farid a better philosophy'. While Bettina's suggestion perplexes the secular Parvez, it appears that this is exactly what Farid is looking for in a father figure. Indeed, Parvez's inability to fulfil his son's spiritual needs is further emphasised in the scene that follows this conversation. The scene cuts from the exterior of Bettina's house to the interior of Parvez's cab; seated in the back of the car are two men in salwar kameez; their traditional clothing functioning to connote their cultural and spiritual distinction from the secular taxi driver, who is, as ever, dressed in a shirt and jacket. The men pass comment on the 'disease-ridden, filthy whore' who is standing on the street, her whiteness and her revealing Western clothing providing further evidence of what they see as the corrupt and impious British culture. Their commentary continues as the shot changes to foreground Parvez, in the front of his cab, toying with a pink comb that Bettina had previously left behind. The focus on Parvez's resigned expression suggests that he is painfully aware of the gulf between himself and Farid and his inability to bridge the ideological schism between them. This inability to bond across generations is a common theme in cinematic narratives about fathers and sons, and at the heart of this tension lies the question of cultural practice and identity. Despite his apparent assimilation, and the pride he expresses when describing Britain to passengers in his taxi, Parvez appears to remain indoctrinated by a legacy of colonial discourses of power and subservience. He describes himself as driven by a code of gentlemanliness, when questioned by his German client, Herr Schitz. Indeed, throughout the exchange with Schitz, Parvez is unflinchingly gracious, even when his client is condescending and mocking towards him.

One of the central points of discord between father and son is around what Farid sees as the corrupt and immodest sexual permissiveness of British culture. Farid's distaste for the more ignominious aspects of British culture and Parvez's job, which involves driving prostitutes and clients, means that Farid sees his father as being complicit in the parts of British culture that he finds most objectionable. The fractious relationship between father and son is evidenced in their different perspectives on British culture. Where Parvez regales his passengers with tales of British history, architecture and success, providing a proud tribute to British culture, Farid's narration when he accompanies the visitors on their journey from the airport to the family home that Farid and Parvez share strikes a rather different tone. His monologue is marked out by its indictment of what he sees as an impoverished and immoral culture, which is saturated with sex and stripped of moral and spiritual value. Where Parvez sees beyond the material dereliction of the area, Farid sees it as symbolic of the wider cultural decay that he is seeking to escape through his religious practice. Ultimately, Parvez becomes symbolic of that which

Farid feels compelled to escape from; his father's involvement in the seedy world of prostitution is evidence of the corrupt nature of Western culture that Farid rejects.

In contrast to father characters such as Geoff in *TwentyFourSeven* or Joe in *When Saturday Comes,* and a host of other working-class fathers in 1990s British film, Parvez is constructed as a sympathetic character. Certainly, his pronouncement that he works in order to provide the best for his son distinguishes his character from many of the cinematic father figures of the era who relinquish responsibility for their families or who themselves are trapped in cycles of abuse and self-destructive behaviour from which they are unable to escape. Despite this, father and son are constantly presented in opposition to one another. Where Parvez drinks and listens to American music in the cellar of their house, Farid is upstairs with his friends from the mosque studying the Qur'an. It is not just Farid who appears to be less enamoured with the allure of British culture; Parvez's wife Minnoo is, in many ways, resistant to assimilation, not least because of her lack of English. In some ways she is a rather reductive stereotype of Asian femininity, accorded very little agency within the film and, for the most part, her lines are little more than perfunctory. What is particularly interesting about this is the ways in which this is used in the film to endorse Parvez's progressive character. When Parvez discovers that Minoo has been relegated to the kitchen to eat while Farid and his friends from the mosque eat together, Parvez breaks the orthodox edicts of Farid and his cohort by refusing to join them and instead having food with his wife, in the kitchen, thus making an explicit statement with regard to both religious and gender practices. By positioning himself in this way, Parvez is able to lay claim to a more progressive mode of masculinity than his son and his son's friends. In this regard, Parvez can be understood as the site through which the intercultural tensions both converge and separate, becoming, in Farid's words, 'like oil and water'. During the reconciliation dinner, the distance between the two men becomes self-evident. In one way Farid sees his father's material motivations as symptomatic of his corruption by Western culture, and he is clearly rebelling against this (he asserts that his father has been duped by the 'white and Jewish conspiracy'). However, Farid's apparent rebellion against his father is also a misinterpreted defence of his father. The son tries to explain to his father that one of the reasons why he rejects British culture so vehemently is because of the attitudes of people like Chief Inspector Fingerhut. Where Parvez's pronounced sycophancy towards Fingerhut in the opening scenes demonstrates the strength of his desire to be accepted, Farid is more perceptive and sees the reaction of his fiancée's family as indicative of their repulsion that Madeline should be engaged to a Pakistani. Thus, at this stage in the film at least, Farid's return to Islam can be understood as born out of pride for his heritage and that of his father. *My Son the Fanatic* does not allow the reconciliation of father and son and indeed concludes with the breakdown of the whole family unit. After Farid and his cohort attack Bettina and the other prostitutes in the name of Islam, Parvez turns on his son. The two have a furious fight in which Farid admits to being ashamed of his father. The details of Parvez's affair with Bettina are revealed and Farid and Minoo return to Pakistan, leaving Parvez alone in England, unsure what the future will hold.

One of the overriding thematic concerns of *My Son the Fanatic* is the ways in which two different generations relate to their inherited culture and navigate their way through new territories. In many ways this film's portrayal of the father–son relationship corresponds to dominant dis-courses within 1990s British cinema, presenting them as fraught with difficulty and disidentification, with the generational divide becoming an important site at which issues of identity, gender and power are negoti-ated. Although *East is East* is set in the 1970s, its intervention into debates about cultural plurality, gendered identities and the role of the father is very much in keeping with broader cultural narratives produced around the time of the millennium. This is a time in which the father is positioned as a central yet ambivalent figure through whom issues about national and gender identities within a changing cultural context can be negotiated. *East is East* presents a familiar story in which the children rebel against their culturally conservative father, George (Om Puri). George is repre-sented as a strict, authoritarian father who, like many of the other fathers seen in nineties British cinema, has a propensity towards physical violence when challenged or disobeyed. His character is also similar to a host of other father characters in that he is consistently positioned as being emo-tionally removed and ultimately isolated from his family.

Despite knowing the repercussions of disobedience, the attitudes of George's white British wife Ella (Linda Basset) and the behaviour of his mixed-race children are characterised by ambivalence towards him. For example, the children openly flout their father's adherence to Islamic dietary rules, cooking and eating sausages while George attends mosque. The opening scenes of the film show the Khan children taking part in a Christian parade through the streets of Salford. Meenah (Archie Panjabi) carries a crucifix while her brothers carry a statue of the Virgin Mary on a sedan bedecked with flowers and church banners. The family group is far from taking the religious sentiment of the parade seriously, as they laugh and joke between themselves; the older brothers clearly have ulterior motives for their participation in the parade as they use the opportunity to flirt with some of the female participants. The family are enjoying themselves until they realise that their route will intercept their father as he makes his way home from the mosque. Upon this realisation the family take flight from the procession, cutting through the back alleyways and rat runs that connect the terrace houses in the area in order to prevent George from discovering them before they rejoin the parade safely out of his sight. This opening scene establishes the ambivalence with which the children view their father; the act of running confirms that they are unwilling to risk incurring his wrath by being blatantly disrespectful of his religion, but they do not identify his beliefs or value systems as being appropriate or meaningful for them. As Barbara Korte and Claudia Sternberg explain, 'the film's disputes and clashes are caused by George's determination to enforce Muslim customs on his offspring and marry within the Pakistani-British community'.[40] In rejecting their father's religious identity the younger generation also reject aspects of their own identity but do not put anything positive in its place. In *East is East* this loss is not refracted around nostalgia; rather it is celebrated as a positive, even though the film has been criticised by scholars such as Sanjay Sharma for a regressive representation that posits traditional South Asian-ness as 'backwards-orientated' while leaving 'whiteness intact'.[41]

Despite the initial signals that George's primary identification is as a Pakistani Muslim the sequence goes on to establish the extent of his integration and belonging within the local community. George is clearly enjoying the parade, and this is made evident through the sequence of shots that show him smiling and waving as he greets the various friends and acquaintances who pass by in the parade. The camera zooms out from a shot of George smiling at the passing parade to a large, wide shot that reveals the children's proximity to their father. The evasive actions of his wife and children are designed to leave no doubt that while George is able to enjoy watching his friends in the parade, his reaction would be markedly different if he were to discover his children's involvement. Although George performs or adopts many of the signifiers of cultural integration, these are represented as superficial markers that are often at odds with his personal views, and they are certainly contrary to his wishes for his children. George's identity is presented as fundamentally fractured; although he has married a Caucasian woman, dresses in Western fashion, smokes and even signals his credentials as an Anglicised Pakistani through the name of his business, 'George's English Chippy', he identifies first and foremost as a Muslim and a Pakistani. The two elements of George's identity appear to be constantly in conflict throughout the film; while his wife, children and customers call him George, the imam and other men in the mosque use his birth name, for example, and he is frequently shown to be more interested in news from Pakistan than he is in the events in his immediate surroundings. Furthermore, the fact that it is revealed that, in addition to Ella, George has a second wife who remains in Pakistan marks his identity as 'other'. The children's lack of connection to their father is notably evidenced when Tariq declares that he is 'not marrying a fucking Paki'.[42]

Despite the superficial markers of Anglicisation, George is presented as believing in traditional Pakistani ideas about gender and his role as a father. Central to George's ideas are the conjoined issues of family honour and individual conduct. The narrative is set in motion when George's eldest son, Nazir (Ian Aspinall) absconds from his own wedding. The perceived shame that Nazir's behaviour brings on the family is too much for George; the father disowns the son and proclaims him to be dead. Nazir's refusal to go through with the marriage is because he is gay; while in this way the film signals the disruptive potential of gay masculinity in terms of patriarchal norms, *East is East* subsequently confines this gay character to the margins. Indeed, it is only when the Khan children embark on a mission to see their estranged brother that they discover his sexuality. When Nazir returns his siblings to Manchester, he sees his mother who implores him to leave without seeing his father; thus, homosexuality is represented as a spectre which must be contained and denied. It is these attitudes which cause the breakdown of his family and his expulsion from the unit. The problems that beset the Khan family thus seem to be the clash between the father's desire to inculcate a certain belief system in his children and their rejection of the ethnic identity that this implies. The estrangement of father and children that the opening scene of *East is East* establishes continues through the film; where Ella and the various children are presented as unified, George, like Joe in *When Saturday Comes*, is more typically at the margins. George is an outsider both in the country and in the domestic space of his family; the questions of belonging are thus posited as central to the narrative preoccupation with how cultural identities and ideas about gender are passed on and negotiated from one generation to the next, and in many ways the film maps the familial tensions onto the wider cultural tensions between assimilation, multiculturalism and hybridity. The rift in the family is presented visually by the frequent use of shots that frame Ella and the children together, where George is more often presented alone in the frame. This codifies the breakdown in the family relationship and amplifies the ambivalence that the younger generation feel towards what they see as the imposition of an alien cultural heritage upon them. George and Ella's children revel in their hybrid identities, seeing them opening up opportunities for transgression, and the transcendence that this affords them. In many ways the central crisis that besets the Khan family, and George in particular, is the conflict between cultural identities; where George is desperate for his children to retain their Pakistani heritage, they see themselves as integrating into British society and culture. Despite the apparent rejection of restrictive traditions on the part of the younger generation, *East is East* deploys a stereotypical perception of Asian families and, moreover, Asian fathers as being dominant, rigid and despotic, as Korte and Sternberg explain, 'what almost destroys the family in this film is not rejection by a Britain that insists on remaining white, but Muslim patriarchalism'.[43]

The ambivalence of the younger generation to embrace the cultural heritage represented by their father is most apparent in the scenes where George introduces his family to the Shah family. In keeping with his traditional status George believes that it is his role to select appropriate spouses for his children, despite their protests. When Ella challenges George's plans to arrange marriage matches for Tariq and Abdul, he forecloses any discussion by counselling that 'Pakistanis believe that if a father wants a son to marry then the son marries'. Tradition is further deployed as a means of circumventing Ella's involvement; the business of arranging marriages is something that is conducted by the fathers, friends and religious elders. George's insistence on the marriage of Tariq and Abdul to the Shah sisters (Tallat Nawaz and Sharmeen Rafi) is presented as motivated by his need to ensure that the traditions that shaped his own life are made meaningful to his sons; furthermore, it is presented as being about preserving the specificities of these diasporic traditions in order to prevent them from being lost. The hybrid identities of his children cause George considerable consternation, and his insistence that Tariq and Abdul marry women who live by the traditional dictates of Islam becomes a matter of ensuring that they – his sons – understand and honour the traditions of their forefathers. When Tariq refuses to comply with his father's demands, George remonstrates that the only way for him to teach his children their true identity is by ensuring that they marry within the Pakistani community. The hypocrisy of his declaration about English women being 'no good' is seized upon by Tariq who responds by saying that he will conform to his father's wishes and proceed with the marriage but that he will take a second wife who is white 'just like my dad!' George thus comes to represent a cultural inheritance that is meaningless to his children.

The traditions, customs and ideas that he believes in are without value or resonance to them, and his insistence that the children should accept and respect them results in his eventual alienation from the family group. George's beliefs are manifested in an authoritarian approach to his family; he is positioned as a self-appointed patriarch who demands respect and obedience. On several occasions throughout the film George reminds Ella that he, as the husband and father, is the head of the family and that she is duty bound to obey him; when she is insubordinate or defies his demands, he hits her. On one occasion he loses control, hitting and punching her while screaming that if she is unable to obey him then she should 'fuck off and take your bastard kids too'. Through George and Ella's relationship, *East is East* develops a specifically postfeminist trajectory that is mediated through ethnicity. The deference that he demands is presented as problematic and as such the implication is that British culture favours women and has begun working towards greater equality. George's grip on authority over his family is ridiculed during the Shah visit and leads to the final confrontation of the film. After the visitors have gone, George rages about the way in which Ella and the children have undermined his authority and bought shame on him and the whole family; the fight that ensues appears to hasten his expulsion from the family unit as his children all turn against him. During this scene, the familiar camera angles that isolate George from the rest of the family return as Ella retaliates to his remonstrations with the charge that his insistence upon the arranged marriages and the standards of behaviour that he demands have nothing to do with ensuring that his children are happy; rather they are used to compensate for the shame he feels at his own family's miscegenation. *East is East* continually appears to straddle a contradictory line; on the one hand it celebrates the liberatory potential of cultural hybridity, but in order to do so it must cast the racial identity of the father as a problematic obstacle to integration. Moreover, as Korte and Sternberg suggest, George's refusal to acknowledge the schism between his ideas and the social milieu in which his family live and work is increasingly seen by his family as 'the disavowal of his own marriage and the negotiation of his children's dual heritage'.[44]

The film ends with an uneasy reconciliation between George and Ella as she returns to work in the chip shop. In this final scene George appears to be abashed and humble; he is hesitant and less arrogant than before as he fidgets uncomfortably behind the counter of the chip shop. Despite his apparent contrition, it is Ella and not George who extends the symbolic offer of peace by asking him if he would like a cup of tea. George's remorse is apparent in the more gentle tone of his response; this kinder timbre is in marked contrast to his earlier manner, and seems to indicate a genuine desire to recompense for his treatment of her and their children although the extent to which this is meant to be understood as translating into a permanent transformation is left unclear. Moreover, that it is Ella who makes the conciliatory gesture appears to suggest that the patriarchal hierarchy remains intact. The questions that remain posed but unresolved in this tentative reconciliation underscore the instability of George's position as family patriarch, while also appearing to articulate the ongoing negotiation that his diasporic identity requires. The scene cuts to show the children outside in the street going about their day-to-day activities: Tariq chases after Stella (Emma Rydal) trying to win her back, Saleem (Chris Bisson) is chased by his white girlfriend, Peggy (Ruth Jones) after she finds Sajid (Jordan Routledge), the youngest of the Khan clan, and his friend Earnest Moorhouse (Gary Damer) running round with the model of her groin that Saleem had made as part of his art course. Meena comes charging out of the house to join in the fun and pulls Maneer into the fray with her while Abdul looks on smiling at the ensuing chaos. The individual articulations of cultural identity are embodied in the diverse clothes of the group; Saleem wears a flowery shirt and flared jeans, Abdul and Tariq are dressed in suits, Sajid is wearing a shirt, a tie and trousers, Meena wears a sari, and Maneer wears a thobe and skull cap. Each of the children has negotiated their own individual cultural identity embracing or rejecting the inheritance and traditions that their father represents to varying degrees. The shrieks and laughter of the group as they run down the street merge with the closing song to produce an upbeat ending. The implication of these two concluding scenes is that the father will be reconciled with the family unit, but that his authoritarian grip has been somewhat curtailed; further, he has understood the hybrid identities and ideas of his family, he has accepted them and is no longer ashamed by them.

Conclusion

In comparing the 1996 film, *When Saturday Comes* with the 2002 Hugh Grant vehicle, *About A Boy*, I demonstrated the ways in which class and privilege are seen to determine forms of paternal engagement. I argued that Jimmy's (Sean Bean's) successful escape from his industrial working-class origins is motivated by his impending fatherhood and a desire to break away from the cultural legacies of his own father. Contra to this, I argue that it is Will's affluence that enables him to retain a life of extended adolescence, revolving around consumption and self-fulfilment. Much like *When Saturday Comes*, however, the film posits fatherhood (albeit in this instance, surrogate fatherhood) as key to Will's redemption and restoration into a more appropriately hegemonic form of masculinity. In this regard, I suggest that *About A Boy* is an exemplary tale of postfeminist fatherhood in which the protagonists come to see beyond the superficial values of neoliberal consumerism as a direct result of discovering the emotional engagement and fulfilment of fatherhood. The comparison between *My Son the Fanatic* and *East is East* is useful as a mechanism for examining the ways in which narratives about fathers and sons in particular can be used as a narrative device through which issues of gender and national identity can be negotiated. The ambivalent position of the two father figures in the films draws attention to the dissonance of generational identities and the cultural practices of masculinity therein.

Taken together, the various films examined in this chapter provide a number of examples of the ways in which cinematic discourses of post-feminist fatherhood are specifically negotiated via the lens of class and race in British cinema.

Notes

1 Connell, R. W., 1985, *Masculinities*, Polity Press, London.
2 Examples of some of the publicity stunts undertaken by members of Fathers4Justice include dressing up as Santa Claus to deliver leaflets in London; one of their members also dressed as Batman and traversed Buckingham Palace.
3 Collier, R., 2006, 'The Outlaw Fathers Fight Back: Father's Rights Groups, Fathers 4 Justice and the Politics of Family Law Reform – Reflections on the UK Experience' in Collier, Richard and Sheldon, Sally (eds), *Father's Rights Activism: Law Reform in Comparative Perspective*, Bloomsbury, London.
4 Dragiewicz, Molly and Mann, Ruth (eds), 2016, 'Special Issue: Fighting Feminism: Organised Opposition to Women's Rights' in *International Journal for Crime, Justice and Social Democracy*, Vol. 5, No. 2.
5 Oakely, Ann, 2015, *Sex, Gender & Society*, Routledge, London. Millett, Kate, 1977, *Sexual Politics*, Virago, London.
6 Chambers, D., 2012, *A Sociology of Family Life: Change and Diversity in Intimate Relations*, Polity Press, London.
7 Forrest, David and Johnson, Beth, 2016, 'Northern English Stardom' in *Journal of Popular Television*, Vol. 4, No. 2, pp. 195–198.
8 Sweeney, Gael, 2001, 'The Man in the Pink Shirt: Hugh Grant and the Dilemma of British Masculinity' in *Cineaction*, Issue 55, p. 55.
9 Chambers, Deborah, 2001, *Representing the Family*, Sage, London, p. 1.
10 Ibid.
11 Driver, Stephen and Martell, Luke, 1999, 'New Labour: Culture and Economy' in Ray, Larry and Sayer, Andrew (eds), *Culture and Economy after the Cultural Turn*, Sage, London.
12 Slater, Tom, 2012, 'The Myth of "Broken Britain": Welfare Reform and the Production of Ignorance' in *Antipode*, Vol. 46, No. 4, p. 954.

13 McRobbie, Angela, 2007, 'Postfeminism and Popular Culture: Bridget Jones and the New Gender Regime' in Tasker, Yvonne and Negra, Diane (eds), *Interrogating Postfeminism: Gender and the Politics of Popular Culture*, Duke University Press, London, pp. 27–39.

14 Pleck, Joseph H., 1987, 'American Fathering in Historical Perspective' in Kimmel, Michael (ed.), *Changing Men: New Directions in Research on Men and Masculinity*, Sage, London.

15 Lewis, J., 2002, 'The Problem of Fathers: Policy & Behaviour in Britain' in Hobson, Barbara (ed.), *Making Men into Fathers: Men, Masculinities and the Social Politics of Fatherhood*, Cambridge University Press, Cambridge. Brannen, J. and Nilsen, A., 2006, 'From Fatherhood to Fathering: Transition and Change among British Fathers in Four Generations of Family' in *Sociology*, Vol. 40, No. 2, pp. 335–352.

16 Ibid.

17 Ibid. Chambers, Deborah, 2001, *Representing the Family*, Sage, London, p. 55.

18 https://en.wikipedia.org/wiki/L%27Enfant_(poster)

19 Leggott, James, 2004, 'Like Father? Failing Parents and Angelic Children in Contemporary British Social Realist Cinema' in Powrie, Phil, Davies, Ann and Babbington, Bruce (eds), *The Trouble with Men: Masculinities in European and Hollywood Cinema*, Wallflower Press, London. Fradley, Martin and Kingston, Sean, 2013, 'What Do you Think Makes a Bad Dad? Shane Meadows and Fatherhood' in Fradley, Martin, Godfrey, Sarah and Williams, Melanie (eds), *Shane Meadows: Critical Essays*, Edinburgh University Press, Edinburgh, pp. 171–185.

20 Hamad, Hannah, 2013, *Postfeminism and Paternity in Contemporary US Film: Framing Fatherhood*, Routledge, London.

21 Ibid.

22 Modleski, Tania, 1991, *Feminism Without Women: Culture and Criticism in a Postfeminist Age*, Routledge, London, p. 82.

23 Hamad, Hannah, 2013, *Postfeminism and Paternity in Contemporary US Film: Framing Fatherhood*, Routledge, London.

24 Modleski, Tania, 1991, *Feminism Without Women: Culture and Criticism in a Postfeminist Age*, Routledge, London. Bruzzi, Stella, 2006, *Bringing Up Daddy: Fatherhood and Masculinity in Post-war Hollywood*, BFI Publishing, London, p. ix.

25 Ibid.

26 Ibid.

27 Modleski, Tania, 1991, *Feminism Without Women: Culture and Criticism in a Postfeminist Age*, Routledge, London, p. 82.

28 Tyler, Imogen, 2013, *Revolting Subjects: Social Abjection and Resistance in Neoliberal Britain*, Zed Books, London.

29 *Fever Pitch* (David Evans, 1997) starred Colin Firth as the lead protagonist, while *High Fidelity* (Stephen Frears, 2000) was relocated from London to Chicago in order to maximise the international audience.

30 Pomerance, Murray and Gateward, Frances, 2005, 'Introduction' in Pomerance, Murray and Gateward, Frances (eds), *Where the Boys Are: Cinemas of Masculinity and Youth*, Wayne State University Press, Detroit, p. 3.

31 Nolan, Laura, 2008, 'Where Have All the Men Gone?' in *The Sunday Times*, 1 February.

32 Muir, Kate, 2008, 'The Dark Ages' in *The Times*, 4 February. https://www.thetimes.co.uk/article/the-dark-ages-zxtcp9jlbpr

33 Pomerance, Murray and Gateward, Frances, 2005, 'Introduction' in Pomerance, Murray and Gateward, Frances (eds), *Where the Boys Are: Cinemas of Masculinity and Youth*, Wayne State University Press, Detroit, p. 3.

34 Shugart, Helen, 2008, 'Managing Masculinities: The Metrosexual Moment' in *The Journal of Communication and Critical/Cultural Studies*, Vol. 5, No. 3, pp. 280–300.

35 Ibid.

36 Spicer, Andrew, 2004, 'The Reluctance to Commit: Hugh Grant and the New British Romantic Comedy' in Powrie, Phil, Davies, Ann and Babbington, Bruce (eds), *The Trouble with Men: Masculinities in European and Hollywood Cinema*, Wallflower Press, London, p. 80.

37 Goffman, Erving, 1990, *The Presentation of the Self in Everyday Life*, Penguin Psychology, London.

38 Spicer, Andrew, 2006, *Typical Men: The Representation of Masculinity in Popular British Cinema*, I. B. Tauris, London.

39 Korte, Barbara and Sternberg, Claudia, 2004, 'Asian British Cinema Since the 1990s' in Murphy, Robert (ed.), *British Cinema Book* (3rd edn), Palgrave Macmillan–British Film Institute, London.

40 Ibid.

41 Sharma, Sanjay, 2000, '*East is East*' in *Black Media Journal*, Vol. 1, No. 2, pp. 32–34.

42 Korte, Barbara and Sternberg, Claudia, 2004, 'Asian British Cinema Since the 1990s' in Murphy, Robert (ed.), *British Cinema Book* (3rd edn), Palgrave Macmillan–British Film Institute, London.

43 Ibid.

44 Ibid.

CHAPTER 6

Violence and Victimhood: Representations of Excessive Masculinities

The aim of this chapter is to examine a selection of films that feature forms of violent masculinity and to locate them within their cinematic and cultural context so as to better understand the ways in which they occupy a particularly complex relationship with hegemonic notions of masculinity. To this end, I begin the chapter with a section in which I outline the theoretical impetus for labelling these films as examples of 'excessive' masculinity. I argue that it is important to distinguish the kinds of representations under discussion in this chapter from the more generic forms of 'crisis' masculinity discussed in previous chapters. Moreover, I suggest that the term 'excessive' is productive because it simultaneously invokes the ways in which these forms of masculinity are inextricably connected with hegemonic discourses of masculinity while also signalling the ways in which they are distinct from what has been termed 'hypermasculinity'. In particular, I am interested in the ways in which these male characters often occupy complex, or at times paradoxical, subject positions that revolve around articulating forms of disempowerment and victimhood that are expressed via violence and displays of physical dominance.

With the aim of exploring the cultural and discursive politics of violent masculinity in British film from 1990–2010, this chapter seeks to make sense of some of the more complex and contentious representations of masculinity from the era in order to understand the ways in which tensions between agency and disempowerment are mobilised in cinematic narratives in order to provoke a sense of contradiction, instability and ambiguity around their male protagonists. Each of the case study films presented in this chapter features central male characters who are the perpetrators of violence, abuse and misogyny but who are, with the exception of Charles Bronson (Tom Hardy), positioned within the narrative as victims themselves. Drawing on *Naked* (Mike Leigh, 1993), *Nil By Mouth* (Gary Oldman, 1997), *Enduring Love* (Roger Michell, 2004) and *Bronson* (Nicolas Winding Refn, 2008), I examine the ways in which violence is used as an affective strategy in order to destabilise a straightforward understanding of these characters as perpetrators or victims and to consider the ways in which this operates via class discourse. I argue that by emphasising the ways in which these various male characters are 'damaged' victims of cultural disempowerment and emasculation, these films elide the issue of the damage done *by* these men and thus efface questions of culpability and agency.

I suggest that the postfeminist, neoliberal, socio-cultural context within which these films are produced further functions to mitigate and explain male violence in ways that obfuscate the materiality of social class cultures and the specific practices of masculinity therein. There is, I suggest, a paradox connecting the four male characters under discussion in this chapter in which cultures of masculinity are mobilised as explanations for male violence. However, this mobilisation renders opaque the systemic and material aspects of class and their intersections with material practices of masculinity. In this regard, questions of male agency and male disempowerment create a narrative paradox that reconstitutes violence, intimidation and abuse as expressions of disempowerment and, as such, re-inscribes the subjective position of these men as victims.

I begin this chapter by elaborating on my use of the term 'excessive' masculinity and go on to unpack some of the key theoretical issues that are central to the analysis of these complex and often contentious representations. I argue that critical analysis needs to adopt dexterous methodological frameworks in order to navigate a continuum of violence within contemporary hegemonic masculinity and to understand the function of class and culture within this. I use the case study films to analyse four iterations of male characters who might be understood as different iterations of excessive masculinities, arguing that, in addition to the role of class and culture, the films in which these characters appear are characterised by stylistic and formal ambiguities that serve to emphasise the contradictory and paradoxical male characters therein. Each of the case study films engages with challenging content, including graphic scenes of rape and physical violence as well as multiple instances of intimidation and emotional and psychological violence. This opening section thus draws important lines of distinction between the films under discussion in this chapter and those equally violent films discussed in previous chapters. I argue that the films in this chapter occupy a different cinematic and cultural position to the laddish violence of films such as *Lock, Stock and Two Smoking Barrels* or *The Football Factory*, and that they offer a distinctive rendition of violent masculinity. This iteration of violence gives rise to specific issues around gender and class in particular; where the laddish gangster films and the cycle of hooligan films were subject to considerable critical opprobrium, each of the films considered in this chapter received critical, if not commercial, acclaim.

Directed by Mike Leigh, *Naked* won the Best Actor and Best Director awards at the Cannes Film Festival and was nominated for the BAFTA Alexander Korda award for Best British film in 1994. *Nil By Mouth* was nominated for the Palme d'Or at the Cannes Film Festival while Kathy Burke won the Best Actress award. The film also won the BAFTA Alexander Korda award for Best British Film in 1998 and director Roger Michell, better known for his transatlantic romantic comedy *Notting Hill* before he made *Enduring Love*, was nominated for Best Director at the British Independent Film Awards, while also receiving a nomination for Outstanding Directorial Achievement in British Film by the Directors Guild of Great Britain. Daniel Craig and Samantha Morton were nominated for Best Actor and Best Actress respectively at the British Independent Film Awards. *Bronson* was nominated for the Grand Jury Prize at the Sundance Film Festival and was nominated for the category of Best Achievement in Production in the British Independent Film Awards where Tom Hardy won Best Actor. Each of these demonstrates how films *about* masculinity were not just commercially viable but were able to garner significant critical acclaim over the course of the twenty-year period. They exist on a cinematic continuum with the representations of crisis and marginalisaton presented in previous chapters but they challenge creative, generic and discursive boundaries in the process.

Defining the Parameters:
Toxic, Damaged and Excessive Masculinities

In the period since 2010, the term 'toxic masculinity' has gained considerable traction in both popular and academic discourses as a means of describing the ways in which certain hegemonic discourses and practices of cis-gendered patriarchal masculinity are damaging, dysfunctional and detrimental to men themselves as well as to those of other genders and sexual identities.[1] Much like the notion of 'masculinity in crisis', toxic masculinity has become something of a catch-all, used in a vast array of contexts and to describe a range of male behaviours including violence, aggression, homophobia and misogyny, and while it has become particularly germane as a means of describing dominant narratives and patterns of masculinity, in light of Donald Trump's presidency and the multitude of revelations regarding the behaviour of powerful men in a range of industries including entertainment, politics and business, it is, I suggest, not a particularly new phenomenon.[2] Discussions about the prevalence of retrosexism and unreconstructed masculinity in the 1990s and 2000s have much in common with these more recent debates.[3]

Toxic masculinity denotes how established forms of patriarchal masculinity are pervasive and enduring despite being destructive and damaging; indeed, as Terry Kupers usefully explains, the idea of 'toxic' masculinity functions to 'delineate those aspects of hegemonic masculinity that are socially destructive [from] those that are culturally accepted and valued'.[4] Indeed, the idea of toxic masculinity can be traced back to the early days of the New Men's Studies; writing in 1987, Michael Kauffman and Gad Horowitz described how masculinity and male sexuality were 'cast in terms of aggression, objectification, domination, and oppression'.[5] A decade later, Jeff Hearn identified what he described as the 'toxic discourses of masculinity' operating at the intersections between gender, patriarchy and male sexuality.[6] Thus, while there is an historical precedent for using the term toxic as a means of describing masculinity, I argue that a straightforward transposition of a term that has evolved to have a particular set of meanings within a specific context to an earlier moment in history has the potential to elide important temporal specificities, and thus it is not necessarily the most appropriate concept through which to analyse the cinematic representations of masculinity from the 1990s and 2000s.

In his 2003 book, *Typical Men*, Andrew Spicer uses the term 'damaged' to describe a number of the cinematic masculinities of the 1990s that were marked by 'social and psychic disorder'.[7] Spicer describes the men in this group as 'aggressively misogynistic', 'chronically unstable', 'violent abusers' who have been 'irreparably damaged by social disintegration'.[8] Positioning these men as victims serves to legitimise their violence and palliate their culpability by offering a causal and external explanation for their actions. The notion of masculinity as damaged positions men as victims, which functions to limit any sense of individual agency and culpability by explaining (and thus potentially legitimising) their violence in terms of their disempowerment. These claims to victimhood echo the terminology of lower-class, white, heterosexual men in crisis discourse, which asserts that these men have been disproportionately affected by the economic shift into a post-industrial, neoliberal landscape. Describing men as damaged thus functions to legitimise their violence on account of their own status as disempowered victim. However, such an argument fails to acknowledge the damage that these men cause. The construction of these men as damaged masks an important paradox which is central to understanding these representational strategies: these men are not just damaged victims of cultural change, they are the perpetrators of violence, abuse, rape and misogyny and they often occupy both positions simultaneously.

In rejecting the term damage, I seek to refocus the emphasis away from notions of victimhood and the damage done *to* these men and instead to highlight the damage done *by* them. For these reasons I suggest that the term excessive is a more appropriate one to employ in the analysis of the cinematic representations of violent masculinities in the period. The discursive connection between masculinity and violence is perhaps inevitable, given that violence is deeply embedded within normative scripts of masculinity; indeed, as Kimmel and Mahler suggest, violent behaviour is not so much symptomatic of excessive deviance as it is evidence of excessive over-conformity to a particular normative construction of masculinity. This normativity being one that 'defines violence as a legitimate response to a perceived humiliation'.[9] Violence, then, is normalised to an extent within discourses of hegemonic masculinity and intrinsically connected to those aspects of hegemonic masculinity that insist on strength, domination, holding social power, demanding respect, denying vulnerability and suppressing all emotions except for anger. As psychologist Jane Garde suggests, violence is 'a consequence of the cultural demands of being male'.[10] Garde's conceptualisation, then, implies that male violence operates on a continuum of hegemonic masculinity.[11] In this regard, the term excessive is particularly useful for the ways in which it allows a 'blurring of the distinctions between acts of violence and everyday behaviour'.[12]

Male violence is complex because it is simultaneously legitimate and deviant; the extent to which it is seen as socially acceptable or unacceptable depends upon the context in which it happens, the means by which it is expressed, and who is the target.[13] Indeed, as the tension between victimhood and violence seems to suggest, the excessive masculinities that I explore in this chapter are often paradoxical and unstable, contentious and contradictory. Employing the concept of excessive masculinities as a means of analysing the discursive construction of a range of dysfunctional, violent or abusive representations of masculinity illuminates multiple points of connection and overlap between ideas of crisis, damage, and toxic and hegemonic masculinities; providing a framework through which to acknowledge the complex intersections of the continuum of male violence.[14]

The relationship between violence and patriarchal masculinity has been the subject of extensive academic scrutiny in gender studies, sociology, criminology and psychology. This extant research produces a multidimensional understanding of masculinity, power and violence and their connection within contemporary patriarchal culture. Moya Lloyd suggests that the connections between patriarchy, masculinity, power and violence are almost inevitable, given that 'patriarchy is a *system* of male power that permeates *all* aspects of life at all times and in all places' (emphasis in original).[15] The centrality of power within the cultural infrastructure of patriarchy functions, then, to codify notions of male dominance over women and to perpetuate patriarchal systems of male domination.[16] Further, as criminologist Steve Hall posits, patriarchal discourses of masculinity invariably 'reproduce[s] the belief that it is *legitimate* and *natural* for men to use violence as a means of oppressing women and less belligerent males' (emphasis added).[17] Given this, then, violence then can be 'potentially invoked as a resource for successfully accomplishing masculine identity'.[18] Violence, then, appears to persist as part of normative masculinity; indeed, as gender scholar Melanie McCarry notes, masculinity is the 'one constant in most interpersonal violence'.[19]

Given this, I suggest that understanding violent and abusive masculinities requires particular attention to the language used in order to take into account the function of violence within discourses of normative masculinity and how this perpetuates patriarchal modes of hegemonic masculinity. Violence occupies a paradoxical position: it is simultaneously imbricated into normative discourses of masculinity but also socially unacceptable and legally prohibited. In this regard, the term excessive is particularly useful for the ways in which it accommodates the more liminal and ambiguous status of male violence: excessive masculinity is connected to hegemonic masculinity but is also an excessive aberration of it.

Excessive Masculinities in *Naked* and *Nil By Mouth*

Those male characters in 1990s British cinema who might be described as excessive are those who seem least able to cope with the apparent reduction in their patriarchal power and who subsequently respond with a combination of self-destructive behaviour and physical or psychological violence towards other people. Key to their construction is an ambiguity brought about by the constant slippage between agent and victim. While men such as Raymond (Ray Winstone) in *Nil By Mouth* and Johnny (David Thewis) in *Naked* might be violent, misogynistic and abusive they are also presented as victims of economic, social and cultural change as well as victims of inherited cycles of destructive and abusive behaviour. In this way, both characters are representative of the paradox that is central to the representations of excessive masculinity during this era. Both films use the tension between the contradictory positions of victim and agent in order to deliberately destabilise any certainty around the characters. Further uncertainty is created through the nuanced performances that are delivered by Winstone and Thewlis. Winstone, in particular, brings to bear his image as an authentic East End hard man, erstwhile boxer and barrow boy while Thewlis presents a very different iteration of excessive masculinity. Not only is Thewlis of considerably slighter stature than Winston, but the characters of Ray and Johnny are markedly different. As Glen Creeber observes, the title, *Nil By Mouth* is somewhat ironic, referring to Raymond's verbal performance of an emotionally illiterate masculinity that is continually talking but saying nothing of substance; in contrast, Johnny is quite the opposite, he is erudite and quick-witted, his speech characterised by linguistic dexterity.[20]

For all their differences, Johnny and Raymond are situated at the socio-economic margins of society, they are chronically unstable, switching from jovial 'banter' to menacing threat without warning or provocation. They are simultaneously vulnerable and vicious. Where Raymond is surrounded by friends and acquaintances, and assumes a central role within the hierarchy of his homosocial community, Johnny is positioned as a loner. While Raymond is defined by his social dominance and the subsequent need to protect and maintain this position, Johnny is defined by his lack of social role. Unable to fit in he becomes increasingly dysfunctional and estranged from society; the tenuous connections that he forms with others are characterised by their transient and precarious nature. Johnny turns his marginality into an opportunity to indulge his nihilism through increasingly caustic encounters. This section will focus first on the character of Johnny, and will draw on his interactions with the various female characters, as well as on other key scenes, in order to explore the cultural significance of his excessive masculinity. Although Johnny's behaviour towards other men is unpleasant, it is his misogynistic attitude to women that is particularly notable, but his is not the only excessive masculinity that is on display in the film. Indeed, in a 2013 interview, Mike Leigh stated that one of the things he wanted to achieve with *Naked* was to make a film about 'unacceptable male behaviour'.[21] In this regard, he certainly succeeded; all of the male characters, to a greater or lesser extent, present versions of misogynistic masculinity; security guard Brian (Peter Wright), for example, refers to women as 'whores and harlots' in an early conversation with Johnny, he also spies on the woman who lives in the flat opposite his workplace. In the final part of my discussion of *Naked*, I turn my attention to a much less discussed character in the film, that of the yuppie landlord, Jeremy (Greg Crutwell). If there is any ambiguity surrounding Johnny's status as a rapist (as will be discussed further below), there is no doubt around Jeremy's actions; not only does he rape two women in the film, he visibly relishes the physical and psychological torment that he inflicts.

Naked opens with a tracking shot of a dark alleyway to focus in on a couple at 'almost exactly the moment when consensual sex . . . becomes something else instead'.[22] As the shot closes in, Johnny is revealed pinning a woman against a wall, one hand on her throat. She is visibly uncomfortable and complaining that Johnny is hurting her, before managing to push him away and run off. While both Mike Leigh and David Thewlis have defended the scene – with the latter arguing that it was not rape, 'it's sex that gets out of hand', in a 1993 interview[23] – and the dim light in the alleyway combines with the cinematography to enhance the ambiguity of what we are seeing, it is clear that Johnny and the woman are having sex and it is obvious that, at this point, she is no longer a willing participant. Despite both Leigh and Thewlis's insistence that *Naked* is an exploration of unacceptable male behaviour, journalists and academics alike have expressed concern over the extent of the 'directorial misogyny' present in the film.[24] Leigh defended the character of Johnny, arguing that he was intended to be deliberately provocative and contentious but, as Gary Watson points out, not only is the audience asked 'to identify with a man whom we have just seen hurting a woman', but there is a lack of natural justice in the film.[25]

If this opening scene is troubling for the ways in which it presents Johnny's excessive misogyny, then his treatment of Sophie (Katrin Cartlidge) does little to quell the unease regarding Johnny's treatment of women. Having fled Manchester, Johnny is waiting for his ex-girlfriend Louise (Lesley Sharp) to return home. While he is waiting for her, Sophie, one of her flatmates arrives and invites Johnny inside. The two of them spend the afternoon smoking cannabis and flirting. Not only does the flirting continue even after Louise returns, but Johnny actively enjoys the opportunity to humiliate her, singing 'halitosis' to the tune of Handel's 'Hallelujah' when she kisses him. Not only does Johnny continue to torment Louise throughout the rest of the scene, offering sarcastic and often caustic responses to her questions, but he repeatedly integrates Sophie into the dynamic, looking to her for reaction and approval. Johnny's and Sophie's relationship quickly escalates from flirting to sex, although there are early indications that Johnny is not as sincere in his affection as Sophie is, withdrawing his hand from hers as they walk along a street, shutting down her playful attempts to engage with him and striding along, hands in pockets, leaving her to skip behind him in an attempt to catch up.

The second sex scene follows on from this. Johnny and Sophie are on the sofa, Sophie plays with Johnny's hair and tells him that she really likes him. Her affection annoys Johnny; once more, he rebuffs her, telling her that she does not 'even know' him. As he says this he grabs her by the hair, as if to emphasise the fact that she really does not know him. Sophie protests, pledging her affection once more, to which Johnny tightens his grip and pulls her closer to him. Holding her hands behind her back he mocks her, asking '[d]o you still like me?' to which she confesses her love. He laughs. At this point, the wide shot which frames the couple on the sofa begins to zoom in slowly to focus on Johnny's smirking face. In the next shot, Johnny is on top of Sophie, they are both fully clothed but having sex. In a reprisal of the imagery from the opening scene, Johnny has his hands around Sophie's neck and he holds her head, banging it against the arm of the sofa. Despite her protestations, Johnny not only continues but bangs her head even harder. Later that evening, Johnny rebuff's Sophie's insistent affections, pushing her away when she follows him and flinging her to one side to get round her and return to the living room. Without saying a word, he takes Louise's cigarette, flicks ash on to the floor, kisses Louise passionately on the lips, much to Sophie's despair, then he walks out. The close-up shot as he exists the room emphasises his satisfied smirk, underlining the pleasure he takes in Sophie's anguish.

Johnny encounters a number of women during his travails of London. The nameless 'woman in the window' (Deborah McLaren) is the first of the women that he meets. He visits the woman purely to antagonise Brian, who he knows will be watching. Having charmed his way in to her flat, Johnny kisses the woman, softly at first, before grabbing her hair in an act that appears to become his leitmotif. When she objects to him pulling on her hair he mocks her and continues to do it, violently jerking her head from side to side, sneering, 'What? You don't like that? [pulls hair] Or that? [pulls hair].' Despite this, the woman begins to unbutton her top. He looks down at her, a shot of his face shows him looking bored and dispassionate. When she demands that he bites her, he gets up, checks in the window, knowing that Brian will be watching, before taking a seat in an old armchair next to the bed. There is silence over a close mid-shot which shows the woman's face and naked décolleté as she stares desperately over at Johnny while draping an elaborate necklace around herself. Johnny is quick to turn her desperation in to an opportunity to reject and humiliate her, callously responding to her attempts at beautification by saying 'I can't love, sorry . . . you look like me mother!' The close-up on her face, crumpling at his cruelty, emphasises her humiliation. The next shot is a wider shot, the woman is lying in bed, back to the camera, and to the left of the frame Johnny is seen, slumped in the armchair. He jerks awake; once he has come to, he carefully unzips his bag, steals a pile of books and slips away before his victim wakes up. This scene draws attention to what I would describe as Johnny's iteration of excessive masculinity; although he is not physically violent, the humiliation of the woman is driven both by misogyny and also by a desire to taunt Brian and contain him within a subordinate position.

Johnny goes on to manoeuvre his way into the café girl's house after this. The disparity between the two is marked. Café girl (Gina McKee), as she is credited, fails to understand Johnny's jokes and his references. Johnny seems to genuinely appreciate the kindness that she has shown him in letting him come to the house where she is staying in and use the bath. However, the burgeoning friendship quickly deteriorates when she asks Johnny to leave. In a monologue that has been likened to Shakespeare's *Hamlet*, Johnny turns on café girl, cursing her and her future children. Here we see the extent of Johnny's capricious personality. Although he does not humiliate café girl in the same way that he does the woman in the window, Sophie and Louise, he does subject her to a tirade of verbal abuse. Like many of the other excessive masculinities in this chapter, Johnny is continually teetering on an emotional precipice; his frustration and rage continue to simmer beneath the surface even during moments of relative calm. Johnny is, of course, distinct from the likes of Bronson or Raymond; he is not physically imposing, indeed, quite the opposite, he is tall and skinny with long, sinewy limbs. His slightness of stature is further underlined in various moments of the film: he stumbles and staggers, he is easily overpowered by the man in the van and the street gang who beat him up. Unlike Raymond, Bronson and many other excessively violent masculinities, Johnny's pathology manifests in a more cerebral or psychological way; he uses his intellect and his quick wit as a 'buffer to his own near psychotic condition and as a weapon of subordination'.[26]

The final scenes of the film focus on Johnny's ultimate betrayal. Having returned to Louise and Sophie's house after being beaten up, Johnny spends the night being looked after by both women. Much to Sophie's devastation, Johnny and Louise appear to retain their bond; Johnny asks Sophie to leave him alone with his ex-girlfriend so that they can talk. Together they hatch a plan to leave London and return to their hometown of Manchester. Having made their plans, Louise goes into her office to hand in her resignation. They kiss before she departs and her final image in the film is of her standing in the doorway, smiling contentedly at Johnny, apparently secure in their reignited relationship. However, with her gone and their other flatmate Sandra (Claire Skinner) taking a bath, Johnny slips Jeremy's money into his pocket and exits the house. The final shot sees him limping away from the house, towards the camera. His destination, his future and the impact of his actions are all unknown.

Despite the fact that we, as an audience are, in Claire Monk's words, 'inevitably complicit' with Johnny's actions, he is not a point of positive identification in the film. His lack of redeeming characteristics makes it difficult to form anything other than a circumspect reading of the character; that he is never fully held to account for his actions, with the beating being the closest he comes to punishment, further alienates him, not only from the diegetic world within the film itself but also from the viewer. Such a position entraps him in a seemingly perpetual cycle of dislocation, transience and marginality which, in turn, feeds his nihilism and alienation further. Unlike many of Leigh's other films, *Naked* is not a sociological treatise but a psychological consideration of excessive masculinity; where *Naked* is distinct from many other films from the decade is the lack of a causal link between the economic marginalisation of the character and his misogynistic, abusive behaviour. Johnny's behaviour and his attitudes towards women are neither explained nor reflected upon. The journalist Suzanne Moore notes, 'to show a misogynist and surround him with walking doormats has the effect, intentional or not, of justifying this behaviour'.[27] Andy Medhurst goes further, suggesting that the film 'indulges' Johnny's excessive misogyny both by rendering the women 'peripheral' but also through the prism of class politics: 'he might be a rapist but at least he's not posh'.[28]

Class politics remain a central theme in *Naked*, and it is the yuppie character of Jeremy who rivals Johnny for the position of antagonist. Our first glimpse of Jeremy positions him unequivocally as Johnny's opposite. Where the latter is dressed in scruffy, ill-fitting black clothes and is seen against the drab background of Sophie's and Louise's rented house, Jeremy is positioned in a brightly lit gym, wearing a white polo shirt, his hair coiffed while he works out. His sneering expression is inescapable in the close-up shot. The shot then cuts to one of Jeremy lying prone on a massage bed, naked with the exception of his underwear. His accent emphasises his sense of superiority. He asks the masseuse (Carolina Giammetta) if she would like to have dinner with him that evening, to which she replies with a swift and emphatic 'No!' Unperturbed, he continues, 'Do you think women like to be raped?'; he gets no response, but she refocuses her attention on the forcefulness of her massage as she slaps his back. The camera cuts to Jeremy's face, he smirks, clearly enjoying antagonising her and revelling in her dislike of him. The next time that we see Jeremy is at a posh restaurant. He is accompanied by the masseuse, although her facial expression and closed body language are used to ensure that we understand that she does not really want to be there. The couple sit in frosty silence, in complete contrast to the easy conversations between

Johnny and Sophie at this stage in the film. 'You've got wonderful breasts!' he proclaims, seemingly without provocation and with no regard for his companion's feelings. Jeremy wears his privilege openly and unapologetically. He stares brazenly at her chest and leers at the waitress (Elizabeth Berrington) as well. 'Don't you mean tits?' his dinner companion retorts, a close image used to emphasise her repulsion. The conversation continues to develop in a disturbing direction, with Jeremy continuing to question his companion about her breasts as he tears meat from the bone, the juices from which smudge around his mouth. His companion, on the other hand, uses her fork, and her face, and fingers, remain clean. Every retort earns her a sneer and Jeremy tries harder to intimidate her, enjoying her discomfort. She responds to his impertinent questions by asking if he is sexually frustrated, a comment that visibly angers him. He retorts, sneering, 'are you feminist?' followed by 'do you like fucking?' She meets his challenge each time, refusing to subordinate herself to him, responding with 'do you like wanking?' His reply, 'not on my own, no . . .', seals his victory. She looks down, beaten. Jeremy sneers as he licks the chicken juices from his fingers, enjoying her defeat more than his own victory.

The woman manages to escape from Jeremy, taking her leave in a taxi shortly after this incident. The next time we see Jeremy is inside his home, replete with designer furnishings and minimalist décor. The waitress from the restaurant does the splits while Jeremy looks on, dispassionately. She attempts conversation but with little success. Eventually she asks 'don't you wanna know me name?' After a lengthy and uncomfortable silence in which it becomes obvious that he is not going to comply with her agenda, she gives in and reveals it. He looks at her and demands that she kisses him. She is eager to oblige and so leans in. As they kiss Jeremy bites her, causing her to squeal in pain and shock. He laughs out loud at the reaction as she looks at him, uncertain and wary. In the next shot, Jeremy is tormenting her with a stuffed reptile that he rubs over her body. Despite the fact that she isn't enjoying the experience, she continues, asking, 'are you glad I came?' Her question seems to provoke him. He thrusts the reptile up to her neck and into her hair. She squirms and pleads with him to stop. A close-up on Jeremy's face emphasises the extent of his enjoyment. He stares, his eyes dispassionate, with the familiar sneer returning to his lips. The image is cut, abruptly, and replaced with a wider shot of Jeremy throwing the waitress onto his bed. She cries, but he holds her down. He torments her, asking if she had ever considered committing suicide and enjoys her struggling against his grip. She is pinned down and crying. The camera positioned above them to show Jeremy's back and her face. He lunges in and bites her, she screams. Her scream carries on into the final shot in the scene, a wider shot that reveals the pair to be clothed still, but with Jeremy holding firmly on top of her. Although we do not see what happens next, the inference is clear; he intends to rape her.

From the very outset Jeremy is positioned as an excessive misogynist whose socio-economic privilege is a mechanism through which he can demand the subordination of women, but it is not until his encounter with Sophie that the extent of his sadistic misogyny is fully realised. The first clue for Sophie that suggests all is not as it should be is when she opens the fridge to find an expensive bottle of champagne in the door and a can of beer missing. Confused she wanders into the living room where she discovers Jeremy, who introduces himself under a pseudonym of Sebastian Hawks. Jeremy notices the tattoo on Sophie's shoulder and asks her if it hurt; when she confirms that it did, he snorts and replies 'good!' The next scene shows Jeremy on the bed, wearing only his underpants. Sophie is topless, he commands her to whip him with her hair, a task which clearly causes her physical discomfort. She pauses to catch her breath, but he admonishes her and grabs her hair, forcing her to recommence. A jump cut presents Sophie, topless and sitting on Sandra's bed. Jeremy demands that she puts on Sandra's nurse's uniform. She complies at first before stopping. She appeals to Jeremy: 'I've had a tough week, I just don't think I can go through with this . . .'. Jeremy grabs hold of Sophie, pinning her down, and rapes her. The camera is positioned by Sophie's head, foregrounding her pain and anguish while allowing Jeremy to dominate the other half of the frame, showing him sneering with satisfaction and contempt. That Jeremy stays in the flat, sleeping in Sophie's bed after the event emphasises his sadistic nature. The next morning, Jeremy wanders into the kitchen, wearing just his underpants, and still exercising his dominance over Sophie and Louise, demanding a coffee. His cover is blown when Sandra returns home and reveals him to be their landlord. As Sophie cringes on the floor. Jeremy pulls out his wallet and flings a handful of £20 notes at her, laughing as he says 'for services rendered!'

Naked presents two different forms of excessive masculinity along the class spectrum; while neither character is held to account for his actions, Leigh's class politics appear to come into play, with Jeremy being rendered unambiguously unpleasant. It is harder to dismiss the ways in which the film positions the viewer in relation to Johnny; the lack of repudiation and critique continues to render the gender politics ambiguous and ambivalent.

As the characters of Johnny and Jeremy illustrate, excessive masculinity is a classed and raced category. Jeremy's misogyny is emphasised by the sneering entitlement afforded by his affluence, whereas Raymond's violence in *Nil By Mouth* is presented as less an act of deliberate and calculated cruelty but rather more as a manifestation of primal rage and frustration at the brutality of his marginalisation. *Nil By Mouth* is framed as a semi-autobiographical account of Oldman's violent upbringing at the hands of an alcoholic, abusive father, conferring an authorial authenticity to the violent, excessive masculinities that dominate the film. Raymond is violent, abusive and tyrannical but he is also presented as a victim of his own abusive and violent father. In this regard the film complicates a dichotomy of agent/object of violence and attempts to 'explain' the ways in which toxic masculinities can be the result of self-perpetuating cycles of violence and abuse. As such, in *Nil By Mouth*, excessive masculinity is simultaneously damaged and damaging; both victim and agent of violence.

From the opening moments of the film, it is apparent that Raymond represents a defiantly unreconstructed form of masculinity; his heavy-set body fills the frame as he stands at the bar ordering a large round of drinks. He delivers the drinks to his wife and her family before returning to his male friends. Raymond is at his most comfortable in the homosocial world of bars and clubs, bragging about sexual conquests, drug and alcohol binges and scrapes with 'the old bill'. Even when he is at home he shows little enthusiasm for engaging with his wife (Kathy Burke) and their daughter. The opening scenes of the film present Raymond as being the alpha male of his group; the other men look to him for approval and use his reactions as a means of mediating their own responses to each other. The conversation is dominated by 'banter', and represents an explicitly masculinist culture in which women are only relevant as sexual objects or domestic servants. Toxic masculinity permeates the group, performances of machismo and bravado are overblown and clear codes of conduct and respect structure the hierarchy. Despite the extent to which the female characters suffer at the hands of the variously toxic masculinities in the film, their stories and their voices remain very much confined to the margins, secondary to the dominance of the homosocial world of Raymond and his associates.

While *Naked* has been subject to controversy and critique, Claire Monk criticises *Nil By Mouth* for privileging the violent male voice over that of the female characters; arguing that while the masculinities of Raymond and his friends are 'marked as problematic' the film is also 'ambiguous and capable of multiple, perhaps less progressive readings, in its portrayal of Ray'.[29] The intense focus on male characters provides a particularly detailed representation of toxic masculinities and the extensive damage that they cause while simultaneously explaining them via narratives of victimhood. In so doing, the extent to which Raymond is culpable for his actions is questioned if not entirely negated. The visceral presentation of domestic violence and its horrific consequences force the audience to confront and engage with both the causes and the effects of Raymond's actions. As such, *Nil By Mouth* does not frame male violence as an inconsequential or even glamourous male fantasy in the same way that some British gangster and football hooligan film do, nor does it function to provide an entertaining spectacle of hypermasculinity as is seen in a number of football and gangster films from the era. Rather, in explicitly presenting the film as an autobiographical mediation, the film appears to be a more reflexive intervention into the complex issues of inherited cycles of excessive masculinity that are consistently damaged and damaging.

Raymond and his family live in the rundown district of Deptford in south-east London. The dockyards which had provided employment for generations of men are no longer in operation and there is little in the way of alternative employment. Indeed, the film draws upon a representational lexicon of poverty and marginalisation identified by Samantha Lay as an iconographic shorthand for the 'bad' working classes.[30] Raymond and his associates are situated at the bottom of the socio-economic hierarchy; they appear to lack legitimate employment, instead engaging in a range of illicit activities including small-scale drug dealing and fencing stolen goods. Their dominance over wives, partners, children and other men can thus be understood as an attempt to compensate for the lack of social and economic power.[31]

Raymond is fiercely jealous and proprietorial over his pregnant wife, Valerie, and their daughter, despite the fact that when they are at home Raymond all but ignores them. When Raymond finds Valerie playing pool with her mother (Laila Morse) and a group of friends, he orders her home, frog-marching her out of the pool hall. The scene cuts to an image of Valerie, asleep in bed. Raymond is seated at the kitchen table, dressed only in boxer shorts, nursing a drink and smoking a cigarette. A close-up shot of his face conveys the brooding anger that is simmering beneath the surface. He wakes Valerie and summons her downstairs where he accuses her of having an affair with one of the men from the pool hall. Valerie, who is heavily pregnant, denies any wrongdoing but Raymond's rage is unabated. Wearily, Val proclaims that she 'can't stand' the constant tension between herself and her husband. Raymond's retaliation is particularly brutal; he punches his wife to the ground and continues to kick her, screaming 'cunt!' until she lies, motionless, on the kitchen floor. The cinematography is a crucial factor in understanding the function of violence in the film. The viewer is placed with the characters and yet apart from them and the camera remains focused on Raymond throughout, forcing us to focus on him. The rage on Raymond's face is emphasised through tight close-up shots as he spits and screams obscenities at his wife; we see

Figure 6.1 *Nil By Mouth:* The framing emphasises the rage on Raymond's face

the physical force of his anger as he kicks her; the spit from his mouth and the sweat from his brow mingles together to exaggerate the savagery of the image. The camera angles are skewed and the movement is jumpy; walls and counters come into shot and obscure the view, defying either sadistic voyeurism or identification with Raymond on the part of the audience but still forcing an intimate proximity to his brutality.

The scene then cuts to a slightly longer shot which is framed by the stairwell; the kitchen is obscured by the distance. Raymond is standing over Valerie's supine, motionless body. He fiddles with the waistband of his boxer shorts in what Richard Williams describes as 'a kind of defiant uncertainty'.[32] The physical retreat of the camera does not work to ease the discomfort of the scene; in fact, it has the opposite effect. As the camera continues to zoom out from the main focus of the kitchen it becomes apparent that, sitting at the top of the stairs, just in view, is Michelle, Valerie and Raymond's six-year-old daughter. She appears to have witnessed the entire incident, just as we have. Raymond switches from brutal husband to father in a split second; having just beaten her mother unconscious, he reassures his daughter and urges her to return to bed. The sudden shift from raging wife-beater to caring father highlights the contrary and volatile instability of the character in the most disturbing fashion.

This paradox is further emphasised shortly after this sequence when more details about Raymond's backstory are revealed. Talking to his best friend Mark (Jamie Foreman), he recounts the violence that he and his mother experienced at the hands of his own alcoholic father. The cycles of violence and patterns of inherited behaviour are emphasised as Raymond drinks throughout the conversation; the implication being that recurrent paths of addiction, poverty and violence are inherited and therefore, potentially, inevitable. While this scene does not legitimise or condone Raymond's behaviour it does seem to function as a critical explanation for it. This scene might be understood in a Freudian sense; a therapeutic act of remembering and recalling the childhood trauma that Raymond suffered and is, therefore, compelled to repeat. In a rare moment of reflection, Raymond describes the lack of love he experienced as a child and the horror that he felt watching his father beating his mother; Michelle, of course, having just witnessed the exact same behaviour from Raymond. Raymond continues to work through his trauma with Mark, recalling how his father would get drunk and fall asleep in the armchair, only to have to be woken up to go to bed. The extent to which the cycle is being repeated is emphasised when Valerie describes Raymond's behaviour in exactly the same terms. The acts of recalling and remembering explain, but do not excuse, Raymond's actions. The emotional breakdown that Raymond experiences when Valerie leaves him and he learns about the loss of their baby is important in contributing to the film's political intervention into discourses of excessive masculinity. In both the opening scene of the film, and in the scene where he beats Valerie, Raymond's physical size and strength is emphasised by the way in which he fills the frame. This contrasts with the framing used during the scenes leading up to his breakdown, He is pictured alone in an empty pub, bereft of the homosocial banter and exuberance that has been central to his character thus far. He no longer commands his surroundings but, instead, appears to be lost within them. Continuing to take solace in alcohol, Raymond is alone is the family flat when he breaks down. He rants and raves to himself, pacing up and down the frame of vision like a caged animal in the trashed flat. In this moment the violent and controlling abuser becomes needy and pitiful, as the cycles of excessive masculinity that have been passed down from father to son continue to entrap another generation.

The conclusion of the film allows a tentative reconciliation between Raymond, Valerie and her family. The kitchen has been refitted by Raymond and, for the first time in the film, he engages with both Valerie and their daughter Michelle in their home. Indeed, he is actually there to look after Michelle while Valerie and her mother travel to visit his brother-in-law, Billy (Charlie Creed-Mills), in prison. The film refuses to provide false hope or romanticised fantasy and Raymond's apparently renewed commitment to his family functions as a reminder of the fragility of peace, rather than to suggest that a happy future is guaranteed. Indeed, the lack of resolution suggests that there is still much to work through; this moment is a lull 'in between moments of high tension' in which life takes on 'a semblance of normality' but, as explained at the outset of the chapter, the root causes of Raymond's violence remain unresolved.[33] In this regard, then, the lack of resolution suggests that respite from violence is never guaranteed and that the problems associated with inherited cycles of excessive masculinity are complex and difficult to resolve. This tentative and tenuous reconciliation does not function to negate Raymond's violence; the film tells his story, as opposed to the story of the women who suffer as a result of his inherited pattern of excessive masculinity. Through this masculine-centric position Raymond is a victim of this excessive inheritance, but it does not absolve him from the consequences of his actions.

Criminality and Insanity:
Excessive Masculinities in *Enduring Love* and *Bronson*

Enduring Love and *Bronson* provide two very different iterations of excessive masculinity in British cinema of the 2000s. *Enduring Love* features Rhys Ifans as Jed, a social misfit who ends up falling in love with and stalking Joe (Daniel Craig), a university lecturer of philosophy and exemplar of postfeminist masculinity, after the two of them are involved in a freak hot-air balloon accident in which a man falls to his death. I use *Enduring Love* as a point of comparison with *Bronson*, a dramatised biopic of Charles Bronson who has the dubious distinction of being Britain's most violent prisoner. The role was played by Tom Hardy, who famously underwent a daunting fitness regime in order to attain a similar physique. The film's Danish director, Nicolas Winding Refn established a reputation for making films that feature uncompromisingly violent men. His debut feature film, *Pusher* (1996) attained cult status, it was remade in Hindi and Louis Preto completed a British remake in 2012.

Enduring Love is a 2004 film adaptation of the Ian McEwan novel of the same name. It is directed by Roger Michell, a director whose films have engaged with a variety of different representations of masculinity ranging from the bumbling, middle-class man 'in crisis' in *Notting Hill* through to the paramilitaries of 1970s Northern Ireland in *Titanic Town*. His 2003 film, *The Mother*, featured Daniel Craig as Darren, a married handyman who has an affair with a woman that he is working for and her recently bereaved mother at the same time. *Enduring Love* was the second time that Michell worked with Daniel Craig, who takes on the lead role of Joe, the university lecturer who is stalked by Jed, played by Rhys Ifans. In many ways the film appears to offer a study of the continuum of male behaviour from hegemonic masculinity, as represented by Joe, through to excessive masculinity, as represented by Jed. Jed, like Johnny, is an outsider, but where Johnny relishes his marginality, Jed is desperate to belong. Jed's infatuation with Joe is represented as being increasingly excessive through-out the film and culminates in Jed stabbing Joe's partner Claire (Samantha Morton) in order that he and Joe can begin a romantic relationship. The film thus appears to imply a rather problematic connection between Jed's sexuality and his excessive masculinity; this link is emphasised by the ways in which Jed and Joe are positioned as diametrically opposed. Joe is the epitome of neoliberal, postfeminist, hegemonic masculinity: he is white, affluent, successful and in a heterosexual relationship. In other words, he is everything that Jed is not. In what follows, I suggest that because Joe occupies a position which is hegemonic, and thus normative, Jed is auto-matically 'othered' in multiple ways – class, accent and presentation of the self, for example, but it is his sexuality that appears to be the root cause of his excessive masculinity.

Enduring Love offers a very different version of England and Englishness than the other films in this chapter; it departs from the familiar terrain of the impoverished urban milieu in favour of the more provincial setting of Oxford. In so doing, the film invokes a history of academia and literature, rather than that of post-industrial deprivation; indeed, the film occupies resolutely middle-class spaces such as the art gallery and studio, the uni-versity lecture rooms, the airy and industrially classy apartment in which Claire and Joe live, and the suburban home of their friends, Robin and Rachel. In this way, *Enduring Love* appears to buy into the middle-class hegemony of post-industrial, neoliberal Britain, which might gesture towards liberal identity politics of inclusivity, but which remains predomi-nantly heteronormative and white. It is apparent very early on in the film that Jed does not belong in those spaces, his Welsh accent and unkempt appearance are at odds with Joe and his friends. Where Joe displays close bonds with his partner and their friendship group, sharing suppers and drinks at each other's houses, for example, Jed is presented very clearly as a loner. He is entirely dislocated from any human connection.

The distinction between Joe and Jed is made obvious from the outset. At first glimpse, Joe displays the markings of hegemonic masculinity on his body and in his demeanour; he is the perfect icon of postfeminist, neoliberal masculinity. He is white, able bodied and heterosexual, his accent-less middle England voice positions him as part of what Paul Dave terms the post-Thatcher 'working-middle-class'.[34] His clothes are casual but smart: a grey T-shirt and jeans, the epitome of an unmarked, normative masculinity that is always white. His position as a member of the neoliberal middle class is further consolidated by the bottle of Dom Perignon that he is trying to open. A lecturer at an unnamed Oxford college, Joe's profession is avowedly middle class, providing him with both cultural and economic capital, and Claire's work as an artist on the brink of breaking through also affirms their status. The markers of what Mike Savage describes as 'the unacknowledged normality' of middle-class culture are evident throughout the film, from the intimate dinner party with Rachel (Susan Lynch) and Robin (Bill Nighy), through to the visits to art galleries and bookshops, and, of course, through the apartment that Joe and Claire share.[35] Images such as those of Claire shaving Joe and of them sharing a cuddle while they brush their teeth romanticises their neoliberal, middle-class habitus. Both Rachel and Robin and Claire and Joe might be described as quietly acquisitive, but their choices are indicative of their middle-class sensibilities: the bookshelves, the piano in the living room, the bright and light space of the penthouse apartment all converge to construct a very particular image of middle-class identities in neoliberal, post-feminist Britain. They appear to belong to 'a particular faction of the white middle classes who both pride themselves on their liberal values and are still basking in the glow of cosmopolitan multiculturalism'.[36] Moreover, Joe is presented as an idealised version of postfeminist masculinity; he is emotionally articulate, invested in his relationships and friendships, and not afraid to show affection to either male or female friends.

Occupying the contrasting position is Jed, who over the course of the film develops an obsession with Joe. They two men are brought together when a hot-air balloon becomes untethered and begins to blow away with a young boy inside. Joe and Jed are among the group of men who try to bring down the balloon safely. They are in sight of success when a gust of wind pushes the balloon into another ascent. The camera focuses on Joe, who glances from the balloon to the ground before letting go. All but one of the men follow suit, landing heavily but safely on to the field; the man who we later discover to be Dr Lomax held on. As Lomax falls to his death a close-up of Joe's face brings the audience into direct proximity with Joe's emotion. Until this moment Jed had gone unnoticed. The focus of the action and the camera was on the balloon, the young boy and Joe, the other men were peripheral and anonymous. It is only when Joe decides to go and look for Dr Lomax that our attention is drawn to Jed. From the first moment it becomes obvious that he is very different from Joe. Physically, his hair is straggly and unkempt and, in contrast to Joe's clean-shaven face, Jed's face is covered in an unsightly regrowth that is too long to be stubble but not formed enough to be a beard. Joe's body has the healthy musculature of someone who works out and invests themself in the regimes of bodily maintenance that are espoused in neoliberal discourse. Jed, however, is skinny and his clothes are mismatched and shabby, locating him as outside of the normative dictates of neoliberal, middle-class masculinities. When Jed and Joe discover Dr Lomax's body in a nearby field Jed suggests, much to Joe's discomfort, that they join together in prayer. When Joe declines the offer, firmly but politely, Jed becomes increasingly adamant until Joe acquiesces; Jed kneels, hands clasped, head bowed and eyes closed, Joe kneels with his hands resting on his thighs and eyes open, staring at the twisted corpse of Dr Lomax.

The following scene is of Claire and Joe having supper with their friends, Robin and Rachel; although the balloon incident is the main topic of conversation, the scene seems to suggest that Joe's life has returned to its former normality. No more is seen or heard from Jed until a scene where Joe is at home, alone, trying to work out the mechanics of the accident and the phone rings. Joe is shocked to hear Jed on the line and questions how he came to have his telephone number. Jed insists that the two of them meet, promising Joe that he will never hear from him again if he agrees to meet. Throughout the scene Joe wanders around his flat, trying to bring the conversation to an end; he comes to a halt in the sitting room, with his back to the camera. He slowly turns to a prolife position and walks over to the window as he asks for Jed's whereabouts. A point-of-view shot is used to reveal Jed standing in the park on the opposite side of the road waiting for Joe; he gives an awkward wave. Joe acquiesces and agrees to go over to the park; as the men shake hands, Joe gets Jed's name wrong. During this encounter Joe's reluctance and discomfort is obvious. Although Jed's intentions at this point are unknown, close-up shots are used to draw attention to his facial expressions as he looks, longingly, towards Joe. His insistence that they need to talk, urgently and in private, is quickly shut down by Joe who makes a vague excuse about being busy before taking his leave. As Joe makes his way across the road, the camera stays focused on a close-up of Jed who is staring after him; as Joe disappears round the corner, Jed whispers a soft 'goodbye' which brings the scene to a close.

The following scenes restore the sense of Joe's normality and his fit within it. He is with his partner in an art gallery and although they discuss the encounter with Jed it is quickly dismissed by Claire, who suggests that 'he's probably just lonely, or something . . .'. Although the couple appear to be talking through the recent events, the cinematography hints at his dislocation. Standing some distance from Claire, Joe is gripped by a sculpture of a tree, replete with round red berries which recall the shape of the ill-fated balloon. His isolation is emphasised against the stark white backdrop of the gallery; that Claire can only look on from a distance emphasises the disconnect in their relationship. Over the course of the next few scenes, this sense of Joe's normality continues as we see him at work and at home with Claire. Jed's intrusion is abrupt and striking. Joe is perusing the shelves of a bookshop and a camera flash goes off behind him; startled, he turns round to see Jed. On this occasion, Jed follows Joe around the bookshop, eventually cornering him in an alcove. Here, as Jed coerces Joe into signing a copy of his book, the shots become very close-up, providing a sense of claustrophobia created by Jed's proximity to Joe. This proximity is maintained in a close-up two shot which shows Jed looking adoringly at Joe as he reluctantly signs his book. When Joe is finished he hands the book back and tries to make his escape; Jed follows him, pointing out the fact that Joe had, once more, got Jed's name wrong. That Joe continually gets Jed's name wrong emphasises the power dynamics of the relationship; for Joe, Jed is an unimportant inconvenience, but for Jed, Joe is much more. Jed continues to follow Joe around the bookshop, quoting the Bible and trying to engage him in conversation about religion. Joe finally manages to leave the shop, but Jed is close behind. The ensuing confrontation uses a series of extreme close-up shots, many of which are canted, in order to provide a sense of the unfolding action. Although Joe may well be the film's iteration of hegemonic masculinity, Jed is the taller of the two, and he leans in over Joe as he pleads with him to 'be honest about what happened between them'. Joe, clearly uncomfortable with Jed's capacity to turn up unexpectedly, is adamant in his refusal, demanding that Jed leaves him alone. Jed is quietly menacing as he proclaims himself a victim. He is manipulative in his attempts to ingratiate himself with Joe, accusing him of giving out 'mixed messages' and of refusing to acknowledge 'what passed between them' on the day of the balloon crash. It is clear, now, to the audience, if not to Joe, that Jed's interest is romantic. It is Jed's mental instability and his manipulative behaviour which create his deviation from hegemonic norms of masculinity and, thus, his position as excessive. In this regard it is implied that Jed's homosexuality is the root cause of his excessive masculinity. In other words, homosexual masculinity is deviant by implication.

Further emphasising the problematic connection between sexuality, hegemonic masculinity and excessive masculinity is the performance given by Rhys Ifans. From the outset, Jed is positioned as a different kind of masculinity to Joe, and this is emphasised by his performance and his facial expressions throughout the film. At times he adopts a coquettish demeanour, his head to one side, his eyes fixed firmly but adoringly on the object of his attention. Ifans's expressions are often emphasised by close-up shots that draw attention to Jed's simpering smile and the way he bats his eyelashes when he stares at Joe; where long shots are used they are, invariably, employed in order to draw attention to Jed's isolation and dislocation with the normatively middle-class world.

After the scene at the bookshop, Jed's behaviour becomes increasingly erratic and excessive and his stalking appears to become more intense. He turns up at the adjacent table at a restaurant in which Joe is having lunch with a colleague, he appears at the window of the pool where Joe is swimming, and then he appears at one of Joe's lectures. Jed has managed to get into the classroom unseen and has hidden himself at the back of the class. Joe's frustration and distraction is evident from the beginning of the scene. His classroom is full and the students look on, expectantly, but Joe stands by the window, looking out. When he becomes aware of the students' gaze he seems to snap back into lecturer mode as he opens the lecture by asking 'What happens when we fall out of love?' The camera follows Joe as he paces around the room talking, posing rhetorical questions. Jed begins singing, quietly at first, but soon he gains the attention of the students who turn round to look at the source of the disruption. Jed stands up, still singing 'God only Knows' by the Beach Boys. The camera tracks backwards and the mid-shot reveals enough of his body to show that he is almost sashaying down the aisle towards Joe as he performs his serenade. Joe is only seen in close-up at this stage; his panic and confusion are evident as is his discomfort at being put in a feminised position of being

Figure 6.2 *Enduring Love:* The close-up on Jed's face emphasises the intensity of his infatuation with Joe during the serenade

serenaded by another man. As Jed draws closer to him the shot switches to a closer one focusing on the emotion in Jed's face. He looks intensely at Joe, as he concludes his performance with a whisper 'God only knows what I'd be without you . . .'.

The next image we see is of Joe running down multiple flights of stairs and bumping into students as he tries to flee. Jed is, of course, close behind, shouting after him. The two come face to face in the plaza outside of the university building. Jed trails Joe as he tries to get away, the camera switching positions to create the sense of Joe's about-turn. Joe's frustration reaches its climax as he pins Jed against the wall, yelling '[I]f you ever, ever, ever fucking bother me again, if you ever come anywhere fucking near me, I will follow you, I will find you and I will gut you like a fucking fish.' Joe's violence is, of course, sanctioned within the discourses of hegemonic masculinity in this instance; he has been provoked and is being threatened. He lets go and begins to walk off but Jed is persistent. He shouts after him 'You started this, you made it happen, why don't you admit it?' As he catches up with Joe, he shouts his first explicit proclamation of love. His hands outstretched in joy, he proclaims 'I love you! I love you, and you're trying to destroy me!' In publicly 'outing' Joe, Jed not only implies that Joe is gay but also that he is somehow malicious and deviant. That this takes place in the vicinity of Joe's college serves to create maximum impact on Joe's personal and professional reputation, a consequence that is emphasised by the fact that several of Joe's students are clearly within frame and they are all looking over at the confrontation; one of them tries to stop Joe but he shrugs him off and heads out of the area.

From this moment on Joe's paranoia builds. When back at his flat, he begins to look into the curtain signals that Jed referred to. The sequence uses a series of quick cuts and close-up shots to create a sense of urgency. The ensuing conversation between Joe and Claire is interesting because of the ways in which typical gender roles are inverted. Joe's account of his experience and his findings is garbled, frantic and hysterical. Claire watches and listens but her facial expression is blank; throughout the film she has dismissed Joe's worries, even suggesting, in what could be considered an instance of victim blaming, that Joe might have led Jed on. Joe turns to the window to illustrate his findings, he opens and closes the curtains in quick succession before flinging them wide open only to see Jed, in the rain, sitting on top of the climbing frame at the park which faces the flat. Joe urges Claire to look, desperate for her to believe him but she turns away, telling Joe to go to bed. The following morning, Joe is looking around Claire's studio and he discovers not only a notebook full of sketches that Claire has made of him but also a sculpture of his face.

Having earlier explained that she couldn't sculpt him because she was too close to him, this appears to be an ominous sign. Indeed, as Claire appears in the doorway she informs Joe that their relationship is over. Her dispassionate and detached attitude contrasts with Joe's emotional reaction which culminates in him forcing an improvised ring onto her finger before storming out. Joe's paranoia and his breakdown thus appear to be bound up with the fact that his hegemonic masculine identity has been undermined. He is no longer in control and, moreover, he is vulnerable and emotional.

Having acquired Jed's address from Dr Lomax's widow, Joe makes his way over. Jed's flat is in a rundown area, graffiti covers the walls. It offers a stark contrast to the gentrified district in which Joe lives. Joe makes his way up to Jed's flat and, finding the door ajar, he lets himself in. The flat is dark and hazy, the soft focus of the frame adds to the sense of unfamiliarity. Gradually the images start to come into focus, as snapshots of the flat are revealed – the open packet of biscuits, the tie-dye curtain, the unmade bed, the wardrobe door covered in old, peeling newspaper cuttings, the dirty fish tank, and the floor, strewn with rubbish. These images provide us with a tableau representation of Jed's life and emphasise how different it is from Joe's. Joe's attention is drawn to a wall which is covered in pictures, newspaper cuttings and religious icons. On closer inspection it appears to be a shrine, dedicated to Joe; it includes a series of cigarette butts, pinned to a board, a ripped up rizzla packet, a series of receipts and a roughly torn heart-shaped piece of paper attached to the photograph of Joe in the bookshop. Joe begins to dismantle the shrine. Confirmation of Jed's excessive delusions appears to reinforce Joe's sense of self within the structures of hegemonic masculinity. It is only when he comes across a newspaper photograph of Claire with the eyes defaced that Joe loses his temper and begins to smash the rest of the shrine with a baseball bat.

Jed's voice comes from off-screen, attracting Joe's attention. Jed is on the floor, bare chested. He begs Joe, who is still holding the baseball bat, 'please, don't do this', before repeating his declaration of love. Close-up images of Joe's face render his fury palpable. He stands, baseball bat raised, ready to strike his tormentor. However, despite Jed's taunting, he does not hurt him, he drops the bat and leaves. The camera returns to a close-up of Jed, tears in his eyes as he begins to hit his head against the wall, slowly at first but with increasing ferocity. Having spent the rest of the day in the pub, Joe turns up at Rachel's and Robin's house where he spends the night. Claire rings, early the next morning, telling Richard that Jed is with her. Joe immediately heads back to his flat. When he gets there he finds Jed and Claire sitting on the sofa together, Jed, wearing a dressing gown, and nursing a severely bruised face. Jed recounts his story, admonishing Joe for attacking him. Despite Joe's insistent protests of innocence, Claire doubts him. Jed continues to explain the curtain signals. Claire's glance from Jed to Joe suggests that she is no longer sure who she believes. Despite her uncertainty, she returns to the sofa, although she shrugs off Jed's attempt at a hug. Joe is exasperated and leaves the room. Jed follows, explaining how he planned to make Claire 'so jealous that she would just go away'. He continues with his diatribe, proclaiming Claire 'a fucking manipulative bitch' as he follows Joe from room to room. A continuous succession of sudden, jerky panning shots between Joe and Jed increases the tension. Jed follows Joe back in to the living area. With his back to the camera we hear Jed say 'Look Joe, watch!' He grabs something, but it isn't clear what. All we see is Jed's back and all we hear is him grunting, followed by Claire, gasping, the camera zooms out to show Claire as she falls to the floor, clutching her stomach. The image reveals a mid-shot of Jed's torso, knife in hand, blood dripping on to the floor.

The tension continues to mount as Joe seems to be playing along with Jed, reassuring him that it is okay and offering to wash the knife. Despite initial reservations, Jed takes Joe's extended hand and the two of them embrace. A series of close-ups are used during their conversation, in which Joe declares his love for Jed and encourages him to let go of the knife. Jed leans in to kiss Joe and Joe responds, they kiss for several seconds before the silence is broken by a punching sound. The close-up on Jed's face shows his shock as he realises that Joe has stabbed him. Joe pulls him close momentarily before letting him drop to the floor and returning to Claire. The final scene of the film takes place a year later. Joe and Claire, still separated, meet at the field where the film began. Joe finally opens the bottle of champagne and the two drink. Joe tries to begin a conversation, but Claire smiles at him, saying 'don't say anything'. The image cuts to show them sitting together, backs to the camera. It cuts again, several times, each time to show them further in the distance. The ending is ambiguous. The potential for reconciliation is clearly implied but whether it will happen or not is entirely uncertain.

The screen cuts to black and the credits begin to roll, only to be interrupted by a fade into an image of a psychiatric hospital. Jed is in a bright white room, he is at a desk, writing, frantically. He looks up at the camera and smiles, the suggestion being that his narrative has not been resolved. The issue of his excessive masculinity remains ongoing. The credits recommence, leaving the ending open and ambiguous. *Enduring Love*, then, presents a narrative of hegemonic masculinity being disrupted by excessive masculinity. The blurring of the boundaries between normal and deviant are continually made explicit as the film progresses, with Joe's behaviour becoming increasingly marked by paranoia and instability. It is only in regaining control and his truthfulness being proved that his hegemonic status is retrieved. The character of Jed, however, remains more troubling because of the continual linkage between his sexuality and his mental instability, the open-ended nature of his narrative further suggests that neither will ever be fully resolved.

Released in 2010, *Bronson* is characterised by ambiguity and contradiction. It is a fictionalised biopic which openly 'takes creative liberties'[37] in telling the life story of Charles Bronson, one of Britain's most notorious prisoners, deliberately obscuring the boundaries between fact and fiction in ways that emphasise the contrary nature both of Bronson himself and of the media construction of his excessively violent masculinity. Much like *Naked* and *Nil By Mouth*, the film appears not to offer moral judgement, opting instead for nuance and ambiguity and in this way it is markedly different from earlier criminal biopics including *The Krays* (Peter Medak, 1990), *The Essex Boys* (Terry Winsor, 2000) and *Cass* (Jon S. Baird, 2008), all of which glamourise the violent and excessive masculinities of their central characters to a certain extent. *Bronson* is also formally distinct from these films, departing from the more mainstream crime films with realist scenes and moments juxtaposed alongside animated sequences which use (the real) Bronson's art work.

The film uses an array of styles and techniques including images from newspaper headlines covering Bronson's various crimes. Archival news footage is used as a mechanism for telling the story of Bronson's time at Broadmoor High Security Hospital during which he mounted three separate rooftop protests. This particular sequence is framed as a projection onto a screen behind Bronson and the images are accompanied by dramatic orchestral music. Bronson interacts with the projected image, he turns his back to the camera and pretends to conduct the orchestra using exaggerated gesticulation that draws attention to the various levels of performative masculinity that are merging in the scene. There is, of course, the 'real' Bronson, as depicted in the archival footage, then there is the performance of Bronson as a cultural icon of excessive masculinity, and then, finally, there is the performance of Tom Hardy performing the character of Bronson. Through the metaphor of the conductor within the space of the theatre, this segment of the film plays up the performative aspects of excessive masculinity and accentuates the ways in which, for Bronson, these various levels of performance and meaning converge.

From the opening shot, *Bronson* is markedly different from the aforementioned films and from the other crime-based films that proliferated in the wake of *Lock, Stock and Two Smoking Barrels*. The film opens with a close mid-shot of Bronson, framed against a plain black backdrop. He stares down, directly into the camera, commanding attention and appearing to challenge it at the same time. He introduces himself, 'My name is Charles Bronson and all my life I've wanted to be famous'; his speech is laconic and matter of fact, and notably lacking in emotion. His estuarine accent recalls numerous cinematic hard men who have preceded him, lending a menacing edge to the otherwise calm delivery of his opening gambit. The shot cuts to reveal Bronson, standing on a stage, appearing to address *his* audience. From the outset, the film appears cognisant of the tensions between literal and metaphorical performances; signalling a self-awareness of the fissures between Bronson as a real-life person, as a media construction, and as a subject for a film that has its own part to play in his mediated image. Prison is rendered, as Dario Llinares suggests, a 'theatrical space that is both darkly menacing and comically ironic'.[38] As his opening monologue continues the stage is replaced by a montage of still images showing him in a range of prison cells in which he appears entirely devoid of any emotion. The first three images show Bronson looking directly into the camera, his demeanour appearing to be both bored and yet defiant. In the penultimate image he is seated in a prison cell, gazing off camera, apparently deep in thought, while in the final image, a pair of blue-tinted Lennon-style glasses obscures his eyes, though his body language remains clearly insolent. The discordant opening strains of 'The Mechanic' by the Walker Brothers creates a menacing atmosphere. We return, briefly, to Bronson, the narrator, before the calm is brought to an abrupt halt. The soundtrack becomes louder and more intense as the image switches; the frame is dark, with red lighting, the central object is initially obscure but, as it comes more clearly into focus, it is Bronson, encaged, naked and bloodied; he is frantic and frenetic. He punches the walls of his cage, performs a series of press-ups and engages himself in a shadow boxing bout during which the camera emphasises his impressive musculature. As a number of guards approach, it becomes apparent that this was, in fact a warm-up to our first glimpse of Bronson's excessive violence. The guards enter the room in which Bronson is encaged, posturing, agitated and ready for a fight.

A high-angle shot shows Bronson pouncing the moment the cage door is opened, clearly undeterred by the extent to which he is outnumbered; this is followed by a series of images shot through the mesh of the cage, functioning both to obscure the action but also to position the viewers as onlookers to the almost primeval violence of Bronson and the brutality of the prison guards. The images of Bronson being restrained by two guards while another punches him repeatedly in his stomach make for uncomfortable viewing, particularly in a cultural environment in which police brutality (and by extension, prison officer brutality) is still known to be a pernicious and institutional problem. This scene is, thus, typical of the moral ambiguity that is characteristic of the entire film. Bronson is not presented as a helpless victim of institutional violence, he responds to his beating by head-butting the leading prison officer, momentarily regaining the upper hand, before once more being brought down. Even at this stage, Bronson still appears to be playing a game; he gestures surrender, only to charge, headlong into the waiting hands of the guards. The scene concludes with Bronson, bloodied and cornered; his sideways glance up at his opponents remains defiant, his half-smile seems to suggest a perverse enjoyment that is as much masochistic as it is sadistic. The construction of Bronson's excessively violent masculinity is consolidated in the montage which follows on from the opening fight. A series of images of Bronson and some of his victims in numerous fights is intercut with front pages from contemporary newspapers bemoaning his depravity. The penultimate shot is of a swastika, perhaps one of the most ideologically loaded symbols of reprehensible violence, daubed on a prison wall in blood; it is followed by a front cover of *The Sun* newspaper which reinforces Bronson's, and by extension, the film's raison d'être: the desire for fame.

The contrary nature of the character is key to his excessive masculinity; throughout the film the character confounds and contradicts expectations. The first such example comes early on when it appears that Bronson breaks down, having just returned to his cell following a visit from his first wife. With his back to the camera, Bronson bows his head and covers his face with his hands, appearing to sob, his head bobbing up and down with emotion. The scene switches back to the stage, where Bronson, as narrator and performer returns, donning a French clown-style outfit replete with white face make-up and white gloves. The 'audience' laughs along with Bronson as he exclaims, 'go on! I 'ad ya going!' suggesting that the apparent sobbing was, in fact, the opposite, it was hysterical laughter.

This kind of deliberate ambiguity recurs throughout the film, playing off Bronson's public image as a notoriously violent criminal in order to create moments of tension and paradox. For instance, upon his release from his first spell in solitary confinement, Bronson is seen in the prison kitchen, wheeling a tea trolley. He politely offers the guard a cup of tea, pouring it with a pronounced flourish. A new inmate enters; Paul Daniels (Matt King) is flamboyantly camp and smoking a cigarette as he saunters into the kitchen. Bronson watches, clearly both bemused and amused, head cocked to one side. He points and asks 'And would you like a cup of tea too, mate?' His apparently affable manner and his subservient pose, slightly bowed, over the trolley, belies his unpredictable character. We know from the film thus far that Bronson is capricious and entirely unpredictable. Daniels begins flirting with Bronson, commenting on his muscular physique, and his 'big guns! Bang bang!' as he takes the cup from Bronson's hand. Bronson remains, arms outstretched, his fists clench and he pulls his left arm back, as if to punch. Bronson's clenched fists remain in the foreground but Daniels remains oblivious, eyes closed, as he sips the tea. Holding this shot for several seconds emphasises the ever-present potential for violence, but Bronson's initial encounter with Daniels passes uneventfully, as the latter wanders off, leaving Bronson, still half-bowed and fists clenched, bemused.

It is perhaps during his sixty-seven days of freedom that the film's most significant use of deliberate ambiguity takes place. Bronson has begun a relationship with Alison (Juliet Oldfield); she is seated on the floor of a living room, flipping through a magazine, apparently oblivious to Bronson's intense and unwavering gaze, captured in a close-up shot. Bronson is seated on a sofa, dressed in his typical attire of shirt and tie, he fiddles with a pen as he confesses his love for her. The shot cuts back to Alison who pauses before looking up from the magazine and asking 'what?' A wider shot shows the two of them, facing each other. Bronson places the pen on the table, opens his arms and repeats 'I love you!' before breaking into a broad grin. The following few seconds of silence, in which Alison looks down, and back to her magazine, are uncomfortable. Bronson, remains, arms open and vulnerable, a position that is emphasised by a shot which is unusually wide for the film. Alison looks up again, eyes wide, and asks 'but what about Mark?' The image cuts back to the more familiar mid-close-up of Bronson, arms still open, asking 'who is Mark?' Mark, Alison reveals, is her 'proper' boyfriend – a man she describes as having more ambition and drive than Bronson. At this moment a violent outburst seems almost inevitable, the low shot accentuating Bronson's bulky physique and once again foregrounding the clenched fists as he takes in this apparently unexpected development. He does not, however, lash out. In fact, the next scene is of him entering a jewellery shop, dressed in a suit and tie. He smashes the male shop worker's head against a glass cabinet before helping himself to the ring that he had selected. He instructs the female shop assistant not to call the police for fifteen minutes, and he takes his leave of the shop. His next stop is the hairdressing salon where Alison works. The scratches and bloody patches on his face and head sit incongruously with his be-suited appearance. He presents her with the ring, smiling as she thanks him. His joy, much like his anger, appears to be intense as he smiles, bobbing up and down with apparent excitement. His happiness, however, is short-lived as Alison not only informs him that she is marrying Mark but that she can't stay with Bronson because of his apparent lack of ambition. Once more we have a long, silent mid-shot of Bronson, staring, jaws clenched, opening up an expectation of violence. However, rather than the predictable outburst, Bronson offers his congratulations. The final shot in the scene returns to the familiar mid-close-up, a shot which is wide enough to accommodate and accentuate Bronson's muscular physique but close enough to ensure that the intensity of his stare and the intense emotions that are simmering underneath are not lost. In robbing the jewellery shop Bronson knew that he would most likely be arrested and returned to jail; this might, in fact, be his ambition. As such, the intent behind the proposal is, I suggest, left deliberately ambiguous. The question of whether it functioned primarily as a device to facilitate his return to prison or not remains open.

The film continually draws attention to the performative elements of excessive masculinity and uses performance as means of emphasising the precarity of this kind of male identity. A notable example of this is the scene that replays a conversation between Bronson and the female governor at Rampton Hospital (a high-security psychiatric hospital in which Bronson was briefly held in 1978). In this scene Bronson's face is split in two; the right side of his face is natural but his left side is made up in a caricature of the prison governor, replete with painted on black hair, drawn in the style of cartoon character Betty Boop. The scene, in which the governor explains to Bronson that he won't be returning to mainstream prison and that his intended victim didn't die, shows Bronson playing both sides of the conversation. His exaggerated performance of the governor's femininity provides a camp quality to the scene which, in turn, draws attention to Bronson's masculine performance.

The final scene of the film is a dramatised version of the incident when he took his art teacher hostage. In the film, as in real life, Bronson is shown to be a talented painter. He is taking lessons with a young, slight instructor (James Lance) who extolls the untamed talent of the prisoner. However, when he begins talking about what will happen once Bronson is released, things take an unplanned turn, and Bronson takes the hapless teacher hostage. The teacher is tied to a pillar, an apple stuffed in his mouth as Bronson paints his face, including his closed eyes. Classical music blares in the background, in line with Bronson's demands. As Bronson stands back from the captive teacher we realise that he is totally naked, except for his glasses and a bowler hat; he is covered in the black boot polish that he uses to make it harder to catch him. Moving closer to the teacher, Bronson caresses his painted face, gently placing the glasses and hat on him. It is a self-portrait of sorts. Bronson is delighted, he smiles, admiring his work. A closer shot of the teacher's face reveals a tear running down his cheek. Bronson stands back, and in his characteristic booming voice he shouts 'All right! That's enough! 'e's 'ad enough, let's get out of 'ere!' He turns back to the teacher and winks as the guards come smashing through the door to the art room. The classical music reaches a crescendo as the fighting between Bronson and the guards intensifies. Two guards manage to hold him against a door, arms out to the side. Naked and vulnerable, another guard comes in and punches him. Eventually he goes down, the guards let go. The shot is a close-up mêlée of guards, punching and kicking Bronson. The scene cuts back to the silent stage with the un-made-up Bronson staring defiantly into the camera. The image is held for a couple of seconds before it changes once more to show a bloodied and swollen Bronson, naked, inside a cage that is designed for him to stand in. The red light emphasises the bloody, bruised colour of the prisoner. Two guards walk towards the large wooden doors and shut them. Shutting us back out of Bronson's life and returning him to the solitary confinement where we first met him at the beginning of the film.

Conclusion

This chapter examines one of the most problematic and contentious forms of masculinity in British cinema during the period. I use the term excessive to describe how the violent masculinities under discussion in this chapter might be understood as on a continuum with normative masculinity and how their deviation from more hegemonic versions of masculinity is often explained via recourse to discourses of 'damage' and victimhood. Each of the films examined in this chapter provides different representations of violent masculinities, many of which can be understood as being connected to extreme iterations of hegemonic masculinities via their emphasis on strength, domination, aggression and machismo. Although each of these representations shares common ground, and all of them can be considered under the broad umbrella of excessive or toxic masculinity, their distinctions and specificities demonstrate that there is much to distinguish them. *Naked*'s Johnny is the most obviously cerebral, although it becomes clear during the course of *Bronson* that Charles too shares a keen intellect, albeit one that is less articulate. The dramatised Bronson is also the only character to actively refute the temptation to explain his actions via recourse to victimhood. Johnny shares his misogyny with *Nil By Mouth*'s Raymond, and both of them commit violent acts towards women. Despite his notoriously violent streak, Bronson is never shown to be violent towards the women that he encounters. *Enduring Love*'s Jed is the least physically violent but is in some ways the most psychologically disturbed of the four. Looking across them all, we can see how many of these traits have developed into what is now understood as toxic masculinity. In examining *Nil By Mouth*, *Naked*, *Bronson* and *Enduring Love*, I find that the films consistently mobilise tensions between agency and disempowerment in order to provoke a sense of contradiction, instability and ambiguity around their male protagonists. While all the male characters discussed in this chapter are perpetrators of violence, abuse and misogyny, they are also positioned as victims themselves. I suggest that the semi-autobiographical framing of *Nil By Mouth* gives the character of Raymond the clearest claim to victimhood while, at the other end of the spectrum, the eponymous Bronson explicitly rejects any such suggestion.

Notes

1 Salam, Maya, 2019, 'What is Toxic Masculinity?' in *The New York Times*, 22 January. https://www.nytimes.com/2019/01/22/us/toxic-masculinity.html (accessed 14 June 2019).

2 The #MeToo campaign highlighted the extent of sexual assault and rape culture within the American film industry, There have been other high-profile accusations of rape and sexual assault against politicians, sportsmen, businessmen and men in the entertainment industries too. There is an ongoing police investigation, Operation Yewtree, which is looking into the behaviour of several high-profile men in the 1970s–1990s.

3 Imelda Whelehan's *Overloaded: Popular Feminism and the Future of Feminism*, The Women's Press, London (2000) has a useful discussion of retrosexism.

4 Kupers, Terry, 2016, 'Toxic Masculinity as a Barrier to Mental Health Treatment in Prison' in *Journal of Clinical Psychology*, Vol. 61, No. 6, p. 716.

5 Horowitz, Gad and Kauffman, Michael, 1987, 'Male Sexuality: Towards A Theory of Liberation' in Kauffman, Michael (ed.), *Beyond Patriarchy: Essays by Men on Pleasure, Power and Change*, Oxford University Press, Oxford.

6 Hearn, Jeff, 1998, *The Violences of Men: How Men Talk About and How Agencies Respond to Men's Violence to Women*, Sage, London, p. 33.

7 Spicer, Andrew, 2001, *Typical Men: Representations of Masculinity in Popular British Cinema*, I. B. Tauris, London, p. 161.

8 Ibid., p. 196.

9 Kimmel, Michael S. and Maher, Matthew, 2003, 'Adolescent Masculinity, Homophobia, and Violence' in *American Behavioural Scientist*, Vol. 46, No. 10, pp. 1439–1458.

10 Garde, Jane, 2003, 'Masculinity and Madness' in *Counselling and Psychotherapy Research*, Vol. 3, No. 1, p. 7.

11 Ibid.

12 Heartfield, James, 2002, 'There is no Masculine Crisis' in *Genders*, Vol. 35, p. 3. http://www.genders.org.g35/g35_heartfield.html

13 Hall, Steve, 2002, 'Daubing the Dregs of Fury: Men, Violence and the Piety of the "Hegemonic Masculinity" Thesis' in *Theorising Criminology*, Vol. 6, No. 1.

14 Kelly, Liz, 1987, 'Continuum of Sexual Violence' in Maynard, Mary and Hanmer, Jalna (eds), *Women, Violence and Social Control*, Macmillan, London. Nicholas, Kitty, 2018, 'Moving Beyond Ideas of Laddism: Conceptualising "Mischievous Masculinities" as a New Way of Understanding Everyday Sexism and Gender Relations' in *Journal of Gender Studies*, Vol. 27, No. 1, pp. 73–85.

15 Lloyd, Moya, 2005, *Beyond Identity Politics: Feminism, Power & Politics*, Sage, London, p. 74.

16 Keith, Thomas, 2017, *Masculinities in Contemporary American Culture*, Routledge, London.

17 Hall, Steve, 2002, 'Daubing the Drudges of Fury: Men, Violence and the Piety of the "Hegemonic Masculinity" Thesis' in *Theorising Criminology*, Vol. 6, No. 1.

18 Edwards, Tim, 2006, *Cultures of Masculinity*, Routledge, London, p. 59.

19 McCarry, Melanie, 2007, 'Masculinity Studies and Male Violence: Critique or Collusion?' in *Women's Studies International Forum*, Vol. 30, No. 5, pp. 404–415. https://doi.org/10.1016/j.wsif.2007.07.006

20 Creeber, Glen, 2000, 'Can't Help Lovin' Dat Man: Social Class and the Female Voice in *Nil By Mouth*' in Munt, Sally (ed.), *Cultural Studies and the Working Class: Subject to Change*, Cassell, London.

21 Hoad, Phil, 'Interview with Mike Leigh: How we Made *Naked*' in *The Guardian*, 18 November 2013. https://www.theguardian.com/film/2013/nov/18/how-we-made-naked

22 Morrison, Steven, 2013, 'Those Days Are Over: *Naked* and Something Rotten in the Early 1990s' in Cardinale-Powell, Bryan and DiPaolo, Marc (ed.), *Devised and Directed by Mike Leigh*, Bloomsbury Academic, London, p. 232.

23 Whitehead, Tony, 2007, *Mike Leigh*, Manchester University Press, Manchester, p. 90.

24 Monk, Claire, 2000, 'Men in the 90s' in Murphy, Robert (ed.), *British Films of the 90s*, BFI Publishing, London.

25 Watson, Gary, 2004, *The Cinema of Mike Leigh: A Sense of the Real*, Wallflower Press, London, p. 107.

26 Coveney, Michael, 1997, *The World According to Mike Leigh*, HarperCollins, London, p. 28.

27 Moore, Suzanne, 1993, 'Reel Men Don't Eat Quiche' in *The Guardian*, 4 November.

28 Medhurst, Andy, 'Mike Leigh Beyond Embarrassment' in *Sight and Sound*, Vol. 3, No. 11, pp. 5–12.

29 Monk, Claire, 2000, 'Men in the 90s' in Murphy, Robert (ed.), *British Films of the 90s*, BFI Publishing, London, p. 165.

30 Lay, Samantha, 2002, *British Social Realism: From Documentary to Brit-Grit*, Wallflower Press, London, p. 107.

31 Hill, John, 2004, 'A Working Class Hero is Something to be? Changing Representations of Class and Masculinity in British Cinema' in Powrie, Phil, Davies, Ann and Babington, Bruce (eds), *The Trouble With Men: Masculinities in European and Hollywood Cinema*, Wallflower Press, London, p. 106.

32 Williams, Richard, 1997, 'Cinema Doesn't Get Much More Real than This' in *The Guardian*, 10 October.

33 Westlund, Andrea, 1999, 'Pre-Modern and Post-Modern Power: Foucault and the Case of Domestic Violence' in *Signs: Journal of Women in Culture and Society*, Vol. 24, No. 4, p. 1047.

34 Dave, Paul, 2006, *Visions of England: Class and Culture in Contemporary Cinema*, Berg, Oxford, p. 60.

35 Savage, Mike, 2003, 'Review Article: A New Class Paradigm?', *British Journal of Sociology of Education*, Vol. 24, No. 4, p. 535.

36 Reay, Diane, Crozier, Gill and James, David, 2007, *White Middle Class Identities and Urban Schooling*, Palgrave Macmillan, London, p. 1043.

37 Shaw-Williams, Hannah, 2015, 'Bronson: A Retrospective with Director Nicolas Winding Refn' in *Screen Rant*, 9 September. https://screenrant.com/bronson-nicolas-winding-refn-tom-hardy/

38 Llinares, Dario, 'Punishing Bodies: British Prison Films and the Spectacle of Masculinity' in *Journal of British Cinema and Television*, Vol. 12, No. 2, p. 216.

Reflections on Representations of Masculinity in British Cinema, 1990–2010

Using a range of case studies from the twenty-year period of 1990–2010, this book offers a critical analysis of representations of masculinity in British cinema, and locates these readings within the broader social, cultural, political and economic context of their production and circulation. In so doing, I advanced an argument about the importance of understanding the specific ways in which both postfeminism and neoliberalism are inflected and manifest at a national level. In turn, I used the various case studies to demonstrate the ways in which these interface with and inform the cultural discourses of masculinity and their cinematic mediation. Exploring a range of paradigms of masculinity from the beleaguered post-industrial men of Chapter 2 to the presentation of privileged postfeminist fatherhood in Chapter 5, each of the case study chapters demonstrated the cultural formations of millennial masculinity within British cinema. These case study chapters were connected by a number of themes and threads – class, race, region, age and genre – which were all examined for the ways in which they interpellate and shape the presentation and narrativisation of male characters.

The case studies all demonstrate the ways in which discourses of gender are inextricable from their broader social, economic and political contexts and, as such, they demonstrate the rationale for examining seemingly transnational phenomena, such as postfeminism or neoliberalism within specific cultural and national or regional parameters. In this regard, the films selected for detailed analysis function as exemplars of the ways in which British cinema operates as a particular site at which gender discourse is continually produced. Moreover, they help to illuminate the nuanced ways in which neoliberalism and postfeminism operate within the specific milieu of British culture and how, invariably, they intersect with and inform the cultural discourses and cinematic representations of masculinity.

By focusing upon a twenty-year period, this book and the case studies herein have been able to balance detailed analysis and interrogation alongside a broader historical purview; this approach has enabled me to explore the ways in which particular themes, ideas and discursive formations of masculinity have developed over the period and to understand the ways in which cinema feeds into the cultural processes of gender politics. Furthermore, this historical era is one in which the discourses of and cultural ideas about masculinity have been undeniably shaped by the combined cultural forces of postfeminism, post-industrialisation and neoliberalism. As the case study chapters illustrate, there are substantial variations and nuances in the specific manifestations of postfeminism, neoliberalism and post-industrialisation across the cinematic spectrum: from the ironic and retrogressive figure of the new lad to the beleaguered men of the formerly industrial working class, and from the impoverished adolescents of *TwentyFourSeven* and *Bullet Boy* to the affluent father figure of Hugh Grant in *About A Boy*, to name a few examples. The nuances of the representational palette of masculinity during this time clearly have much to offer in terms of academic analysis of British film history but, as I have demonstrated throughout this book, they are also germane to creating a better understanding of both gender studies and British cultural history more broadly. My aim in this book was to produce a culturally specific theorisation of postfeminism and neoliberalism, which can be used as a basis for further studies of gender, culture and media within a British context. By focusing on British film, I have elaborated on one particular way in which these ideas can be mobilised and applied.

As the readings of the case study films have shown, tropes of masculinity are complex, multifaceted and changeable, albeit within the specific confines of a compulsively heteronormative, patriarchal context. I have used the critical reading of the case studies to interrogate the ways in which cinematic representations of masculinity are both products and producers of complex systems of cultural history. Over the course of the various chapters, I have sought to demonstrate the importance of understanding gender discourses and media representations of masculinity as dynamic, contingent and continually evolving, but also as shaped by ideological tensions and points of contradiction. In this regard, the case studies are just that – they function as exemplars of specific moments and mediations. They are focal points, selected for the ways in which they connect with or facilitate the illustration of specific tropes, trends and ideas

The period on which I have focused here came to a natural pause in 2010, both in terms of the chronological marking of decades and, more significantly, in cultural terms with the election of David Cameron's Conservative-Liberal Democrat coalition government which came to power after Gordon Brown was unable to form a majority cabinet following a tumultuous time as prime minister and an unsuccessfully flat election campaign. The cultural ramifications of this political change were wide-ranging. Just two months after securing their government, the Con-Lib coalition announced swathing cuts at the heart of the British film industry and the closure of the UK Film Council. Championing a post-recessionary fiscal policy of austerity, the government, led by David Cameron, proceeded to implement deep cuts in public spending across sectors including education, welfare, housing and public sector employment. This new and arguably darker period for the British Isles, which would ultimately lead to an embittered referendum on the UK's membership of the EU, brought with it a revision of these postfeminine, masculinised narratives. Actors, writers and directors still operated within this continuum, bringing the identity, socio-enconomic and racial politics presented within this publication as case studies under a new political lens. Ken Loach's *I, Daniel Blake* (2016) revisits the narrative of the Post-Industrial Male, in this iteration having to reckon its existence against an abjectly cruel benefits system. Tom Hardy's ascension to a Hollywood mainstay has seen him continue to operate within roles of excessive masculinity within natively produced films such as *Legend* (Brian Helgeland, 2015), the biopic of the Kray twins. This production can be seen as a novel interjection on Hardy's career, because he played both Ronnie and Reggie, whilst scenes very explicitly dealt with the previously forbidden subject of Ronnie's homosexuality. Much more recently, in an act of almost self-aware effacement, Hardy has featured as a story time host on the toddler-focused BBC channel CBeebies. It could be argued that the optimism that New Labour instilled and encouraged within the cultural psyche gave way during its own term of office with the events of 9/11, and the subsequent invasion of Afghanistan and Iraq, with an economic crisis closing off the decade in the later stages of the 2000s. The 2010s under a Con-Lib coalition cemented this malaise, whilst conjunctively politics and cultural attitudes towards homosexuality and the decentralisation of the compulsory heterosexual family unit, and ideas around the toxic male and masculinity as a health crisis, have begun to operate as a default dialogue. I argue that this discourse granted permission for male actors and genres that housed them to operate on more introspective, self-aware spectrums without the fear of losing a grounding of authenticity upon which they were built. Moreover, I argue that the cinematic landscape of the British Isles in the 2010s acted as a pressure valve for this political cruelty that took place; with the neoliberal optimism of the 1990s being reacquired within this more emotionally evolved and politically aware field.

Filmography

Films

1 Day (Penny Woolcock and Michèle Nuzzo, 2009)
4321 (Noel Clarke and Mark Davis, 2010)
About A Boy (Chris Weitz and Paul Weitz, 2002)
Adulthood (Noel Clarke, 2008)
Ae Fond Kiss (Ken Loach, 2004)
Alfie (Lewis Gilbert, 1966)
Alfie (Charles Shyer, 2004)
All or Nothing (Mike Leigh, 2002)
An Awfully Big Adventure (Mike Newell, 1995)
Anuvahood (Adam Deacon and Daniel Toland, 2011)
Archipelago (Joanna Hogg, 2010)
A Room for Romeo Brass (Shane Meadows, 1999)
Arsenal Stadium Mystery (Thorold Dickinson, 1939)
Attack the Block (Joe Cornish, 2010)
Atonement (Joe Wright, 2007)
Awaydays (Pat Holden, 2009)
The Battle of Orgreave (Jeremy Deller, 2001)
Bend it Like Beckham (Gurinder Chadha, 2002)
Blue Blood (Steven Reilly, 2006)
Body Song (Janine Marmot, 2003)
Boyz N The Hood (John Singleton, 1991)
Brassed Off (Mark Herman, 1996)
Bridget Jones's Diary (Sharon Maguire, 2001)
Bridget Jones: The Edge of Reason (Beeban Kidron, 2004)
Bronson (Nicolas Winding Refn, 2008)
Bullet Boy (Saul Dibb, 2004)
Cass (Jon S. Baird, 2008)
City Rats (Steve Kelly, 2009)
Crossing the Line (Daniel Gordon and Nicholas Bonner, 2006)
Dead Man's Shoes (Shane Meadows, 2004)
East is East (Damien O'Donnell, 1999)

Eden Lake (James Watkins, 2008)
Elizabeth (Shekar Kapur, 1998)
Emma (Douglas McGrath, 1996)
Enduring Love (Roger Michell, 2004)
Escape to Victory (John Huston, 1981)
The Essex Boys (Terry Winsor, 2000)
Faceless (Manu Luksch, 2007)
Fever Pitch (David Evans, 1997)
Final Cut (Dominic Anciano and Ray Burdis, 1999)
The Firm (Alan Clarke, 1989)
The Football Factory (Nick Love, 2003)
Four Lions (Chris Morris, 2010)
Four Weddings and a Funeral (Mike Newell, 1994)
Frankenstein (James Whale, 1931)
The Full Monty (Peter Cattaneo, 1997)
Get Carter (Mike Hodges, 1971)
GoldenEye (Martin Campbell, 1995)
Green Street (Lexi Alexander, 2004)
Harry Potter (various, 2001–2011)
High Fidelity (Stephen Frears, 2000)
Howards End (James Ivory, 1992)
Human Traffic (Justin Kerrigan, 1999)
ID (Phil Davis, 1995)
I, Daniel Blake (Ken Loach, 2016)
The Ipcress File (Sidnet J. Furie, 1965)
The Italian Job (Peter Collinson, 1969)
Jack and Sarah (Tim Sullivan, 1995)
Jane Eyre (Franco Zefferelli, 1996)
Kidulthood (Menhaj Huda, 2006)
King of the Gypsies (Shane Meadows, 1995)
The Krays (Peter Medak, 1990)
Late Night Shopping (Saul Metzstein, 2001)
Legend (Brian Helgeland, 2015)
Life and Lyrics (Richard Laxton, 2006)
Lock, Stock and Two Smoking Barrels (Guy Ritchie, 1998)
The Long Good Friday (John MacKenzie, 1980)
Love, Honour and Obey (Dominic Anciano and Ray Burdis, 2000)
The Mother (Roger Mitchell, 2003)
My Name is Joe (Ken Loach, 1998)
My Son the Fanatic (Udayan Prasad, 1997)
Naked (Mike Leigh, 1993)

Nil By Mouth (Gary Oldman, 1997)
Notting Hill (Roger Michell, 1999)
Once Upon a Time in the Midlands (Shane Meadows, 2002)
Pimp (Robert Cavanagh, 2010)
Pulp Fiction (Quentin Tarantino, 1995)
Rancid Aluminum (Edward Thomas, 2000)
Remains of the Day (James Ivory, 1993)
Reservoir Dogs (Quentin Tarantino, 1992)
The Rise of the Footsoldier (Julian Gilbey, 2007)
Rollin' With the Nines (Julian Gilbey, 2006)
Rubber Johnny (Chris Cunningham, 2005)
Saturday Night and Sunday Morning (Karel Reisz, 1960)
Secrets and Lies (Mike Leigh, 1996)
Sex Lives of the Potato Men (Andy Humphries, 2004)
Shakespeare in Love (John Madden, 1998)
Shank (Mo Ali, 2009)
Shifty (Eran Creevy, 2008)
Small Time Crooks (Woody Allen, 2000)
Snatch (Guy Ritchie, 2000)
Somers Town (Shane Meadows, 2008)
Star Wars Trilogy (George Lucas, 1977, 1980, 1983)
Stella Does Tricks (Coky Giedroyc, 1996)
Step Up (Anne Fletcher, 2006)
Streetdance (Maz Giwas and Dania Pasquini, 2010)
Sweet Sixteen (Ken Loach, 2002)
This is England (Shane Meadows, 2006)
Trainspotting (Irvine Welsh, 1996)
TwentyFourSeven (Shane Meadows, 1997)
Twin Town (Kevin Allen, 1997)
Welcome II the Terrordome (Ngozi Onwurah, 1995)
When Saturday Comes (Maria Giese, 1996)
Where's the Money Ronnie! (Shane Meadows, 1996)
Yesterday's Hero (Neil Leifer, 1979)
Young Soul Rebels (Isaac Julien, 1991)

Television Programmes

The Big Breakfast (Channel 4, 1992–2002)
Fantasy Football League (BBC 2, 1994–1996)
Men Behaving Badly (ITV 1992–1993, BBC 1993–1998)
Only Fools and Horses (BBC 1, 1981–1991)

Bibliography

Abele, Elizabeth and Gronbeck-Tedesco, John A. (eds). *Screening Images of American Masculinity In the Age of Postfeminism*. Lexington Books, New York. 2015.

Abrams, Fran. *Below the Breadline: Living on the Minimum Wage*. Profile Books, London. 2000.

Adams, Matthew and Raisborough, Jayne. 'The Self-control Ethos and the "Chav": Unpacking Cultural Representations of the White Working Class', in *Culture & Psychology*, 2011, Vol. 7, No. 1, pp. 81–97.

Alexander, Claire. 'Beyond Black: Re-thinking the Colour/Culture divide', in *Ethnic and Racial Studies*, 2002, Vol. 25, No. 4, pp. 552–571.

Alexander, Claire. 'Imagining the Asian Gang: Ethnicity, Masculinity and Youth After "The Riots"', in *Critical Social Policy*, 2004, Vol. 24, No. 4, pp. 526–549.

Alexander, Karen. 'Black British Cinema in the 1990s: Going, Going, Gone', in Robert Murphy (ed.) *British Film of the 90s*. British Film Institute Publishing, London. 2000.

Allt, Nicholas. *The Boys From the Mersey: The Story of Liverpool's Annie Road Crew: Football's First Clobbered Up Mob*. Milo Publishing, Preston. 2005.

Anderson, Eric. *Inclusive Masculinity: The Changing Nature of Masculinities*. Taylor & Francis, London. 2009.

Anonymous. 'Leading Article: John Major: Is he Up to the Job?' *The Independent*, 4 April 1993. https://www.independent.co.uk/life-style/leading-article-john-major-is-he-up-to-the-job-1453316.html (accessed 1 June 2019).

Anonymous. 'London Reigns'. *Newsweek*, 11 March 1996. https://newsweek.com/london-reigns-176148 (accessed 1 June 2019).

Anonymous. 'UK Economy Sidesteps Global Recession'. *The Guardian*, 20 December 2001. https://www.theguardian.com/business/2001/dec/20/uk economy.comsumerspending (accessed 1 June 2019).

Anonymous. 'UK Film Council to Be Abolished'. BBC News, 26 July 2010. https://www.bbc.co.uk/news/entertainment-arts-10761225 (accessed 1 June 2019).

Aschied, Antje. 'Safe Rebellions: Romantic Emancipation in the Woman's Heritage Film', in *Scope: An Online Journal of Film Studies*, 2006, No. 4. https://www.nottingham.ac.uk/scope/issues/2006/february-issue-04.aspx (accessed 1 June 2019).

Ashby, Justine. 'Postfeminism in the British Frame', in *Cinema Journal*, 2005, Vol. 44, No. 2, pp. 127–132.

Barclay, Peter. *Poverty and Social Exclusion in Britain*. Joseph Rowntree Foundation. 2000. https://www.jrf.org.uk/report/poverty-and-social-exclusion-britain

Barrett, Ciara. 'The Feminist Cinema of Joanna Hogg: Melodrama, Female Space and the Subversion of Phallogocentric Narrative', in *Alphaville*, 2015, Issue 10.

Bennett, Joe. '"*Chav-Spotting*" in Britain: The Representation of Social Class as Private Choice', in *Social Semiotics*, 2013, Vol. 23, No. 1, pp. 146–162.

Benwell, Bethan (ed.). *Masculinity and Men's Lifestyle Magazines*. Blackwell Publishing, London. 2003.

Benwell, Bethan. 'Introduction: Masculinity and Men's Lifestyle Magazines', in Bethan Benwell (ed.) *Masculinity and Men's Lifestyle Magazines*. Blackwell Publishing, London. 2003. pp. 6–29.

Benwell, Bethan. 'Ironic Discourse: Evasive Masculinity in Men's Lifestyle Magazines', in *Men and Masculinities*, 2004, Vol. 7, No. 1, pp. 3–21.

Benwell, Bethan. 'Is There Anything New About These Lads?: The Textual and Visual Construction of Masculinity in Men's Magazines', in Lia Litosseliti and Jane Sunderland (eds) *Gender Identity and Discourse Analysis: Discourse Approaches to Politics, Society and Culture*. John Benjamin's Publishing Company, Amsterdam. 2002. pp. 149–176.

Benyon, John. *Masculinities and Culture*. Open University Press, Maidenhead. 2002.

Bhavhani, Reena. *Barriers to Diversity in Film: A Research Review*. 2007. https://www.yumpu.com/en/document/view/18620874/barriers-to-diversity-in-film-a-research-review-aug-07

Bhopal, Kalwant. *White Privilege: The Myth of the Post Racial Society*. Policy Press, Bristol. 2018.

Blance, Andy. *Hibs Boy: The Life and Times of Scotland's Most Notorious Football Hooligan*. Fort Publishing, Ayr. 2011.

Bly, Robert. *Iron John: A Book About Men*. Addison-Wesley, Boston, MA. 1990.

Bonefield, Werner. *A Major Crisis: The Politics of Economic Policy in Britain in the 90s*. Dartmouth Publishing, Dartford. 1995.

Boyle, Karen. 'Feminism Without Men: Feminist Media Studies in a Postfeminist Age' in Charlotte Brunsdon and Lynn Spigel (eds) *Feminist Television Criticism: A Reader*. Open University Press, Maidenhead. 2007.

Brabon, Benjamin A. 'The Spectral Phallus: Re-Membering the Postfeminist Man', in Benjamin Brabon and Stephanie Genz (eds) *Postfeminism; Cultural Texts and Theories*. Edinburgh University Press, Edinburgh. 2009.

Brabon, Benjamin A. and Genz, Stephanie (eds). *Postfeminist Gothic: Critical Interventions in Contemporary Culture*. Palgrave Macmillan, London. 2007.

Brannen, Julia and Nilsen, Ann. 'From Fatherhood to Fathering: Transmission and Change among Fathers in Four Generation Families', in *Sociology*, 2006, Vol. 4, No. 2, pp. 335–352.

Brittan, Arthur. *Masculinity and Power*. Basil Blackwell, Oxford. 1989.

Brod, Harry (ed.). *The Making of Masculinities: The New Men's Studies*. Unwin Hyman, London. 1987.

Brooks, Gary. *Beyond the Crisis of Masculinity: A Theoretical Model for Male Friendly Therapy*. American Psychological Association, Washington, DC. 2006.

Brooks, Kate, Jackson, Peter and Stevenson, Nicholas (eds). *Making Sense of Men's Magazines*. Polity Press, Cambridge. 2001.

Brown, Colin. 'Why Two Years is a Long Time in Politics'. *The Independent*, 9 April 1994. https://www.independent.co.uk/news/uk/why-two-years-is-a-long-time-in-politics-early-in-1993-after-a-series-of-post-election-disasters-1368934.html (accessed 1 June 2019).

Brown, Patricia Leigh. 'Heavy Lifting Required: The Return of Manly Men'. *The New York Times*, 2001. http://www.nytimes.com/2001.10/28/weekinreview. ideas-trends-heavy-lifting-required-the-return-of-the-manly-men.html

Brunsdon, Charlotte and Spigel, Lynn (eds). *Feminist Television Criticism: A Reader* (2nd edn). Open University Press, Maidenhead. 2007. pp. 174–190.

Bruzzi, Stella. *Bringing up Daddy: Fatherhood and Masculinity in Post-War Hollywood*. British Film Institute Publishing, London. 2005.

Bruzzi, Stella. *Men's Cinema: Masculinity and Mise-en-Scene in Hollywood*. Edinburgh University Press, Edinburgh. 2013.

Bruzzi, Stella. 'Two Sisters, The Fogey, His Priest and his lover: Sexual Plurality in 1990s British Cinema', in Robert Murphy (ed.) *British Film of the 90s*. British Film Institute Publishing, London. 2000. pp. 125–134.

Butler, Judith. *Gender Trouble: Feminism and the Subversion of Identity*. Routledge, London. 1990.

Canaan, Joyce and Griffin, Christine. 'The New Men's Studies: Part of the Problem or Part of the Solution?', in Jeff Hearn and David Morgan, D. (eds) *Men, Masculinities and Social Theory*. Unwin Hyman, London. 1990. pp. 206–214.

Carey, Maggie. 'Perspectives on the Men's Movement', in Christopher McLean, Maggie Carey and Cheryl White (eds) *Men's Ways of Being: New Directions in Theory and Psychology*. Westview Press, Oxford. 1996.

Caterer, James. *The People's Pictures: National Lotter Funding and British Cinema*. Cambridge Scholar's Press, Cambridge. 2011.

Caterer, James. 'Carrying a Cultural Burden: British Film Policy and its Products', in *Journal of British Cinema and Television*, 2008, Vol. 5, No. 1, pp. 146–156.

Caterer, James. 'Reinventing the British Film Industry: The Group Production Plan and the National Lottery Franchise Scheme', in *International Journal of Cultural Policy*, 2011, Vol. 17, No. 1, pp. 94–105.

Chambers, Deborah. *Representing the Family*. Sage, London. 2001.

Champion, Tony. *The Population of Britain in the 1990s: A Social and Economic Atlas*. Clarendon Press, London. 1996.

Chawla-Duggan, Rita and Pole, Christopher, J. (eds). *Reshaping Education in the 90s: Perspectives on Primary Schooling*. Routledge, London. 2012.

Chester, Mark. *Naughty: The Story of A Football Hooligan*. Category C Publishing, London. 2011.

Chester, Mark. *Sex, Drugs and Football Thugs*. Category C Publishing, London. 2010.

Chibnall, Steve. 'Travels in Ladland: The British Gangster Film Cycle, 1998–2001', in Robert Murphy (ed.) *The British Cinema Book* (3rd edn). British Film Institute Publishing, London. 2009. pp. 375–386.

Christie, Ian. 'Where is National Cinema Today (and Do We Still Need It)?', in *Film History, An International Journal*, 2013, Vol. 25, No. 1, pp. 9–30.

Clare, Anthony. *On Men: Masculinity in Crisis*. Arrow Books, London. 2000.

Cohen, D. 'It's a Guy Thing, Men are Depressed and That's Official'. *The Guardian*, 4 May 1996.

Coleman, John and Warren-Adamson, Chris (eds). *Youth Policy in the 1990s: The Way Forward*. Routledge, London. 1992.

Collier, Richard. 'The Outlaw Fathers Fight Back: Father's Rights Groups, Fathers 4 Justice and the Politics of Family Law Reform – Reflections on the UK Experience', in Richard Collier and Sally Sheldon (eds) *Father's Rights Activism: Law Reform in Comparative Perspective*. Bloomsbury, London. 2006.

Connell, R. W. *Gender and Power: Society, the Person and Sexual Politics*. Stanford University Press, Stanford, CA. 1987.

Connell, R. W. *Masculinities*. Polity Press, Cambridge. 1995.

Connell, R. W., Hearn, Jeff and Kimmel, Michael. 'Introduction', in R. W. Connell, Jeff Hearn and Michael Kimmel (eds) *The Handbook of Studies on Men and Masculinity*. Sage, London. 2005.

Coveney, Michael. *The World According to Mike Leigh*. HarperCollins, London. 1997.

Coward, R. 'Whipping Boys Perspectives: Unemployed, Unmarriageable, Criminal and Above All, Male'. *The Guardian*, 3 September 1994.

Creeber, Glen. 'Can't Help Lovin' Dat Man: Social Class and the Female Voice in *Nil By Mouth*', in Sally Munt (ed.) *Cultural Studies and the Working Class: Subject to Change*. Cassell, London. 2000.

Crenshaw, Kimberle. 'Demarginalizing the Intersection of Race and Sex: A Black Feminist Critique of Anti-discrimination Doctrine, Feminist Theory and Anti–Racist Politics', in *University of Chicago Legal Forum*. 1989. https://chicagounbound.uchicago.edu/cgi/viewcontent.cgi?article=1052&context (accessed 30 May 2019).

Crewe, Ben. *Representing Men: Cultural Production and Producers in the Men's Magazine Market*. Berg, Oxford. 2003.

Croft, Stuart. 'British Jihads and the British War on Terror', in *Defence Studies*, 2007, Vol. 7, No. 3, pp. 317–337.

Crompton, Rosemary and Lyonette, Clare. 'The New Gender Essentialism – Domestic and Family "Choices" and their Relation to Attitudes', in *The British Journal of Sociology*, 2005, Vol. 56, No. 4, pp. 601–620.

Dave, Paul. *Visions of England: Class and Culture in Contemporary Cinema*. Berg, Oxford. 2006.

Dickinson, F. 'Publishing: What Does Your Magazine Say About You? *The Independent on Sunday*, 15 August 2004.

Dodd, Philip. *The Battle Over Britain*. Demos, London. 1995.

Dorey, Peter. 'Introduction: John Major – One of Us?', in Peter Dorey (ed.) *The Major Premiership: Politics and Policies Under John Major*. Macmillan, London. 1999.

Dow, Bonnie, J. 'The Traffic in Men and the Fatal Attraction of Postfeminist Masculinity', in *Women's Studies in Communication*, 2006, Vol. 29, No. 1, pp. 113–131.

Doyle, Gillian et al. *The Rise and Fall of the Film Council*. Edinburgh University Press, Edinburgh. 2015.

Dragiewicz, Molly and Mann, Ruth, M. (ed). 'Special Issue: Fighting Feminism: Organised Opposition to Women's Rights', in *International Journal for Crime, Justice and Social Democracy*, 2016, Vol. 5, No. 2.

Driver, Stephen. 'Welfare Reform and Coalition Politics in the age of Austerity', in Smon Lee and Matt Beech (eds) *The Cameron Clegg Government*. Palgrave Macmillan, London. 2011.

Driver, Stephen and Martell, Luke. 'New Labour: Culture and Economy', in Larry Ray and Andrew Sayer (eds) *Culture and Economy after the Cultural Turn*. Sage, London. 2011.

Ducat, Stephen. *The Wimp Factor: Gender Gaps, Holy Wars and the Politics of Anxious Masculinity*. Beacon Press, Boston, MA. 2005.

Easthope, Anthony. *What A Man's Gotta Do: The Masculine Myth in Popular Culture*. Routledge, London. 1990.

Edwards, Tim. *Cultures of Masculinity*. Routledge, London. 2006.

Edwards, Tim. *Men in the Mirror: Men's Fashion, Masculinity and Consumer Society*. Cassell, London. 1997.

Faludi, Susan. *Stiffed: The Betrayal of the Modern Man*. Chatto & Windus, London. 1999.

Farrell, Warren. *The Myth of Male Power*. Berkley Trade, New York. 1993.

Faucher-King, Florence and Le Galès, Patrick (eds). *The New Labour Experiment: Change and Reform Under Blair and Brown*. Stanford University Press, Stanford, CA. 2010.

Featherstone, Mark. 'Hoodie Horror: The Capitalist Other in Postmodern Society', in *Review of Education, Pedagogy and Cultural Studies*, 2013, Vol. 35, No. 3, pp. 178–190.

FitzGerald, Louise. *Negotiating Lone Motherhood: Gender, Politics and Family Values in Contemporary Popular Cinema*. 2009. Unpublished PhD thesis. https://ueaprints.uea.ac.uk/10577

FitzGerald, Louise and Godfrey, Sarah. '"Them over there": Motherhood and Marginality in Shane Meadows' films', in Martin Fradley, Sarah Godfrey and Melanie Williams (eds) *Shane Meadows: Critical Essays*. Edinburgh University Press, Edinburgh. 2013. pp. 155–170.

Follows, Stephen. www.stephenfollows.com/how-many-feature-films-are-shot-in-the-uk-each-year/ (accessed 1 June 2019)

Footman, Tim. *The Noughties: 2000–2009: A Decade that Changed the World.* Crimson, London. 2009.

Forrest, David. *Social Realism: Art, Nationhood and Politics.* Cambridge Scholars Press, Cambridge. 2013.

Forrest, David. 'Better Things (Duane Hopkins, 2008) and the New British Realism', in *Journal of Contemporary Film*, 2010, Vol. 8, No. 1, pp. 31–43.

Forrest, David. 'The Films of Joanna Hogg: The New British Realism and Class', in *European Cinema*, 2014, Vol. 11, No. 1, pp. 64–75.

Forrest, David. 'Shane Meadows and the British New Wave: Britain's Hidden Art Cinema', in *Studies in European Cinema*, 2009, Vol. 6, No. 2, pp. 191–201.

Forrest, David. 'Twenty-first Century Social Realism: Shane Meadows and New British Realism', in Martin Fradley, Sarah Godfrey and Melanie Williams (eds) *Shane Meadows: Critical Essays.* Edinburgh University Press, Edinburgh. 2013. pp. 35–49.

Forrest, David and Johnson, Beth. 'Northern English Stardom', in *Journal of Popular Television*, 2016, Vol. 4, No. 2, pp. 195–198.

Foucault, Michel. *The History of Sexuality* (Vol. 1). Penguin, London. 1978.

Fradley, Martin and Kingston, Sean. 'What Do You Think Makes a Bad Dad?: Shane Meadows and Fatherhood', in Martin Fradley, Sarah Godfrey and Melanie Williams (eds) *Shane Meadows: Critical Essays.* Edinburgh University Press, Edinburgh. 2013. pp. 171–185.

Fradley, Martin, Godfrey, Sarah and Williams, Melanie (eds). *Shane Meadows: Critical Essays.* Edinburgh University Press, Edinburgh. 2013.

Fradley, Martin, Godfrey, Sarah and Williams, Melanie. 'Introduction: Shane's World', in Martin Fradley, Sarah Godfrey and Melanie Williams (eds) *Shane Meadows: Critical Essays.* Edinburgh University Press, Edinburgh. 2013. pp. 1–20.

Fradley, Martin, Godfrey, Sarah and Williams, Melanie. 'Shane Meadows: Introduction', in *Journal of British Cinema and Television*, 2013, Vol. 10, No. 4, pp. 823–828.

Fukuyama, F. 'Who Killed the Family? *The Sunday Times*, 21 September 1997.

García-Favaro, Laura and Gill, Rosalind. '"Emasculation nation has arrived": Sexism Rearticulated in Online Responses to Lose the Lads' Mags Campaign', in *Feminist Media Studies*, 2016, Vol. 16, No. 3, pp. 379–397.

Garde, Jane. 'Masculinity and Madness', in *Counselling and Psychotherapy Research*, 2003, Vol. 3, No. 1, p. 7.

Genz, Stéphanie. *Postfemininities in Popular Culture.* Palgrave Macmillan, London. 2009.

Genz, Stéphanie (ed.). *Postfeminist Gothic: Critical Interventions in Popular Culture.* Palgrave Macmillan, London. 2007.

Genz, Stéphanie and Brabon, Benjamin A. *Postfeminism: Cultural Texts and Theories* (2nd edn). Edinburgh University Press, Edinburgh. 2018.

Giddens, Anthony. *The Third Way: A Renewal of Social Democracy*. Polity Press, Oxford. 1998.

Giddens, Anthony. 'The Rise and Fall of "New" Labour', in *New Perspectives Quarterly*, 2010, Vol. 27, No. 3, pp. 32–37.

Gill, Rosalind. *Gender and the Media*. Polity Press, Cambridge. 2006.

Gill, Rosalind. 'Culture and Subjectivity in Neoliberal and Postfeminist Times', in *Subjectivity*, 2008, Vol. 25, No. 1, pp. 432–445.

Gill, Rosalind. 'Mediated Intimacy: A Postfeminist Tale of Female Power, Male Vulnerability and Toast'. Working paper online. https://extra.shu.ac.uk/wpw/chicklit/gill.html or https://kclpure.kcl.ac.uk/portal/files/4680341/gill%20ladlit.pdf (accessed 28 May 2019).

Gill, Rosalind. 'Postfeminist Media Culture: Elements of a Sensibility', in *European Journal of Cultural Studies*, 2007, Vol. 10, No. 2, pp. 147–166.

Gill, Rosalind. 'Post-postfeminism?: New Feminist Visibilities in Postfeminist Times', in *Feminist Media Studies*, 2016, Vol. 16, No. 4, pp. 610–630.

Gill, Rosalind. 'Power and the Production of Subjects: A Genealogy of the New Man and the New Lad', in Bethan Benwell (ed.) *Masculinity and Men's Lifestyle Magazines*. Blackwell Publishing, London. 2003. pp. 34–56.

Gill, Rosalind. 'Powerful Women, Vulnerable Men and Postfeminist Masculinities in Men's Popular Fiction', in *Gender and Language*. https://s3.amazonaws.com/academia.edu.documents/34717347/Gender_and_language_final.doc?AWSAccessKeyId=AKIAIWOWYYGZ2Y53UL3A&Expires=1559238551&Signature=2lCzomkhqUOEleGxy74KIETdb10%3D&response-content-disposition=inline%3B%20filename%3DPowerful_Women_Vulnerable_Men_and_Postfe.doc (accessed 30 May 2019).

Gill, Rosalind. 'Sexism Reloaded. Or It's Time to get Angry Again', in *Feminist Media Studies*, 2011, Vol. 11, No. 1, pp. 61–71.

Gill, Rosalind and Scharff, Christina (eds). *New Femininities: Postfeminism, Neoliberalism and Subjectivity*. Palgrave Macmillan, London. 2011.

Gilroy, Paul. *Postcolonial Melancholia*. Columbia University Press, New York. 2005.

Ging, Debbie. *Men and Masculinities in Irish Cinema*. Palgrave Macmillan, London. 2012.

Godfrey, Sarah. 'The Hero of my Dreams: Framing Fatherhood in *Mamma Mia!*', in Louise FitzGerald and Melanie Williams (eds) *Mamma Mia! Exploring a Cultural Phenomenon*. I. B. Tauris, London. 2013. pp. 189–205.

Godfrey, Sarah. '"I'm A Casualty, but it's Cool . . .": 1990s British Masculinities in *TwentyFourSeven*', in *Journal of British Cinema and Television*, 2013, Vol. 10, No. 4, pp. 846–862.

Godfrey, Sarah. '"Taking the Temperature": Masculinities and Male Identities From *Bleak Moments* to *Happy–go–Lucky*', in B. Cardinale-Powell and M. DiPaolo (eds) *Devised and Directed by Mike Leigh*. Bloomsbury Press, London. 2013.

Godfrey, Sarah and Hamad, Hannah. 'Save the Cheerleader, Save the Males:

Resurgent Protective Paternalism', in Karen Ross (ed.) *The Handbook of Gender, Sex and Media*. Wiley Blackwell, London. 2012. pp. 157–173.

Godfrey, Sarah and Walker, Johnny. 'From Pinter to *Pimp*: Danny Dyer, Class, Cultism and the Critics', in *Journal of British Cinema*, 2015, Vol. 12, No. 1, pp. 101–120.

Goffman, Erving. *The Presentation of Self in Everyday Life*. Penguin, London. 1975.

Goodward, Catherine, Flintham, Neil and Spilsbury, Mark. *Skillset Workforce Survey Report 2003*. Skillset, London. 2004. www.screenskills.com/insight/research (accessed 20 May 2019).

Gordon, David and Pantazis, Christina (eds). *Breadline Britain*. Ashgate, London. 1997.

Gordon, David et al. *Poverty and Social Exclusion in Britain*. Report for Joseph Rowntree Foundation. Joseph Rowntree Foundation, York. 2000. https://www.jrf.org.uk/report/poverty-and-exclusion-britain (accessed 1 June 2019).

Grey, Clive. 'The Millennium Dome: Falling from Grace', in *Parliamentary Affairs*, 2003, Vol. 56, No. 3, pp. 441–455.

Hall, Steve. 'Daubing the Drudges of Fury: Men, Violence and the Piety of the "Hegemonic Masculinity" Thesis', in *Theorising Criminology*, 2002, Vol. 6, No. 1, p. 37.

Hall, Stuart. 'The Neoliberal Revolution', in *Cultural Studies*, 2011, Vol. 25, No. 6, pp. 705–728.

Hamad, Hannah. *Postfeminism and Paternity in Contemporary US Film: Framing Fatherhood*. Routledge, London. 2013.

Hamad, Hannah. 'Extreme Parenting: Recuperating Fatherhood in Steven Spielberg's *War of the Worlds*', in Hilary Radner and Rebecca Stringer (eds) *Feminism at the Movies: Understanding Gender in Contemporary Popular Cinema*. Routledge, London. 2011.

Hamad, Hannah. 'Hollywood Fatherhood: Paternal Postfeminism in Contemporary Popular Cinema', in Joel Gwynne and Nadine Muller (eds) *Postfeminism and Contemporary Hollywood Cinema*. Palgrave Macmillan, London. 2013.

Harris, Anita. *Future Girl: Young Women in the 21st Century*. Routledge, London. 2004.

Harris, John. *The Last Party: Britpop, Blair and the Demise of English Rock*. Harper Perennial, London. 2003.

Harvey, David. *A Brief History of Neoliberalism*. Oxford University Press, Oxford. 2005.

Hattenstone, Simon and Walker, Peter. 'Julie Walters: Lack of Working-Class Actors is Sad'. *The Guardian*, 23 January 2015. https://www.theguardian.com/culture/2015/jan/23/julie-walters-lack-working-class-actors-sad (accessed 10 August 2019).

Hearn, Jeff. *The Violences of Men: How Men Talk About and How Agencies Respond to Men's Violence to Women*. Sage, London. 1998.

Hearn, Jeff. 'Preface', in David Jackson (ed.) *Unmasking Masculinity: A Critical Autobiography*. Unwin Hyman, London. 1990.

Hearn, Jeff and Morgan, Dave (eds). *Men, Masculinities and Social Theory*. Unwin Hyman, London. 1990.

Hearn, Jeff and Morgan, Dave. 'Men, Masculinities and Social Theory', in Jeff Hearn and Dave Morgan (eds) *Men, Masculinities and Social Theory*. Unwin Hyman, London. 1990. pp. 1–20.

Heartfield, James. 'There is no Masculine Crisis', in *Genders*, 2002, Vol. 35, p. 3. http://www.genders.org.g35/g35_heartfield.html

Heffernan, Richard et al. *Developments in British Politics 10*. Palgrave Macmillan, London. 2016.

Heppell, Timothy and Seawright, David. 'Introduction', in Timothy Heppell and David Seawright (eds) *Cameron and the Conservatives*. Palgrave Macmillan, London. 2012.

Hey, Valerie. 'Be(long)ing: New Labour, New Britain and the "Dianaization" of Politics', in Adrian Kear and Deborah Lynn Steinberg (eds) *Mourning Diana: Nation, Culture and the Performance of Grief*. Routledge, London. 1999. pp. 60–76.

Higgins, Vaughn and Larner, Wendy. 'Introduction', in Vaughn Higgins and Wendy Larner (eds) *Assembling Neoliberalism*. Palgrave Macmillan, London. 2017. pp. 1–20.

Higson, A. *Dissolving Views: Key Writings on British Cinema*. Cassell, London. 1996.

Higson, A. *English Heritage, English Cinema: Costume Drama since the 1980s*. Oxford University Press, Oxford. 2003.

Higson, A. *Film England: Culturally English Filmmaking Since the 1990s*. I. B. Tauris, London. 2010.

Higson, A. *Waving the Flag: Constructing a National Cinema in Britain*. Oxford University Press, Oxford. 1997.

Higson, A. 'The Concept of National Cinema', in *Screen*, 1989, Vol. 30, No. 4, pp. 36–47.

Higson, A. 'Place, Space, Spectacle', in *Screen*, 1984, Vol. 25, No. 4–5, pp. 2–21.

Hill, John. *British Cinema in the 1980s*. Clarendon Press, Oxford. 1999.

Hill, John. 'Failure and Utopianism: Representations of the Working Class in British Cinema of the 1990s', in Robert Murphy (ed.) *British Film of the 90s*. British Film Institute Publishing, London. 2000. pp. 178–187.

Hill, John. 'Space, Place, Spectacle: Landscape & Townscape in the Kitchen Sink Film', in Andrew Higson (ed.) *Dissolving Views*. Bloomsbury Press, London. 2016.

Hill, John. 'A Working-Class Hero is Something to Be? Changing Representations of Class and Masculinity in British Cinema', in Phil Powrie, Ann Davies and Bruce Babington (eds) *The Trouble With Men: Masculinities in European and Hollywood Cinema*. Wallflower Press, London. 2004.

Hill, Sarah. *Young Women, Girls and Postfeminism in Contemporary British Film.* Bloomsbury Press, London. 2020.

Hill-Netterton, Pamela. 'Hanging with the Boys: Homosocial Bonding and Bromance Coupling in *Nip/Tuck* and *Boston Legal*', in Elizabeth Abele and John Gronbeck-Tedesco (eds) *Screening Images of American Masculinity in the Age of Postfeminism.* Lexington Books, London. 2016. pp. 120–135.

Hoad, Phil. 'Interview with Mike Leigh: How we Made *Naked.' The Guardian,* 18 November 2013. https://www.theguardian.com/film/2013/nov/18/how-we-made-naked

Hobson, Barbara (ed.). *Making Men into Fathers: Men, Masculinities and the Social Politics of Fatherhood.* Cambridge University Press, Cambridge. 2002.

Holloway, Kali. 2015. 'Toxic Masculinity is Killing Men: The Root of Male Trauma'. *The Salon,* 12 June 2015. https://www.salon.com/2015/06/12/toxic_masculinity_is_killing_men_the_roots_of_male_trauma_partner/ (accessed 4 April 2019).

Hornby, Nick. *About A Boy.* Riverhead, London. 1998.

Hornby, Nick. *Fever Pitch.* Riverhead, London. 1992.

Hornby, Nick. *High Fidelity.* Riverhead, London. 1995.

Horowitz, Gad and Kauffman, Michael. 'Male Sexuality: Towards A Theory of Liberation', in Michael Kauffman (ed.) *Beyond Patriarchy: Essays by Men on Pleasure, Power and Change.* Oxford University Press, Oxford. 1987.

Horrocks, Roger, *Male Myths and Icons: Masculinity in Popular Culture.* Macmillan, Basingstoke. 1994.

https://inews.co.uk/inews-lifestyle/women/what-is-toxic-masculinity-and-why-does-it-matter/ (accessed 4 April 2019).

Hutcheon, Linda. *Irony's Edge: The Theory and Politics of Irony.* Routledge, London. 1994.

Ibrahim, Samir. 2006. 'A Cultural Studies Analysis of Guy Ritchie's *Snatch'.* https://www.grin.com/document/129441

Jackson, Peter, Brooks, Kate and Stevenson, Nick (ed.). *Making Sense of Men's Lifestyle Magazines.* Polity Press, Cambridge. 2001.

Jackson, Peter, Brooks, Kate and Stevenson, Nick (ed.). 'Introduction', in Peter Jackson, Kate Brooks and Nick Stevenson (eds) *Making Sense of Men's Lifestyle Magazines.* Polity Press, Cambridge. 2001.

Jarvis, Lee. *Times of Terror: Discourse, Temporality and the War on Terror.* Palgrave Macmillan, London. 2009.

Jeffords, Susan. 'The Big Switch: Hollywood Masculinity in the Nineties', in Jim Collins, Ava Preacher Collins and Hilary Radner (eds) *Film Theory Goes to the Movies.* Routledge, London. 2012.

Johnson, Beth, 'Art Cinema and *The Arbour*: Tape Recorded Testimony, Film Art & Feminism', in *Journal of British Cinema and Television,* 2016, Vol. 13, No. 2, pp. 278–291.

Johnson, Shelia. '*Ae Fond Kiss'. Screenonline.* http://www.screenonline.org.uk/film/id/1408654/index.html (accessed 1st June 2019).

Kaufman, Michael (ed.). *Beyond Patriarchy: Essays by Men on Pleasure, Power and Change*. Oxford University Press, Oxford. 1987.

Kear, Adrian and Steinberg, Deborah Lynn (ed.). *Mourning Diana: Nation, Culture and the Performance of Grief*. Routledge, London. 1999.

Keegan, William. *The Prudence of Mr Brown*. Wiley Blackwell, London. 2003.

Keith, Thomas. *Masculinities in Contemporary American Culture*. Routledge, London. 2017.

Kelly, Lisa. 'Professionalising the British Film Industry: The UK Film Council and Public Support for Film Production', in *International Journal of Cultural Policy*, 2016, Vol. 22, No. 4, pp. 648–663.

Kelly, Liz. 'Continuum of Sexual Violence', in Mary Maynard and Jalna Hanmer (eds) *Women, Violence and Social Control*. Macmillan, London. 1987.

Kennedy, Melanie. '"Come on [. . .] let's go find your inner princess": (Post-)feminist Generationalism in Tween Fairy Tales', in *Feminist Media Studies*, 2017, Vol. 18, No. 3, pp. 424–439.

Kerr, Peter, Byrne, Christopher and Foster, Emma. 'Theorising Cameron', in *Political Studies Review*, 2011, Vol. 9, No. 2, pp. 193–207.

Kimmel, Michael. *Guyland: The Perilous World Where Boys Become Men*. Harper Perennial, New York. 2009.

Kimmel, Michael, 'Rethinking Masculinity', in Michael Kimmel (ed.) *Changing Men: New Directions in Research on Men and Masculinity*. Sage, London. 1987.

Kimmel, Michael, S. and Maher, Matthew. 'Adolescent Masculinity, Homophobia, and Violence', in *American Behavioural Scientist*, 2003, Vol. 46, No. 10, pp. 1439–1458.

King, Anthony. *The End of the Terraces: The Transformation of English Football*. Leicester University Press, Leicester. 1998.

Korte, Barbara and Sternberg, Claudia. *Bidding for the Mainstream: Black British and Asian Film Since the 1990s*. Rodophi Press, New York. 2004.

Korte, Barbara and Sternberg, Claudia. 'Asian British Cinema Since the 1990s', in Robert Murphy, Robert (ed.) *British Cinema Book* (3rd edn). Palgrave Macmillan, London. 2009.

Kupers, Terry. 'Toxic Masculinity as a Barrier to Mental Health Treatment in Prison', in *Journal of Clinical Psychology*, 2016, Vol. 61, No. 6, pp. 713–724.

Larner, Wendy. 'Neoliberalism, Policy, Ideology, Governmentality', in *Studies in Political Economy*, 2000, Vol. 63, No. 1, pp. 5–25.

Lawler, Stephanie. 'Introduction: Class, Culture and Identity', in *Sociology*, 2005, Vol. 39, No. 5, pp. 797–806.

Lawson, Christopher. 'Making Sense of the Ruins: The Historiography of Deindustrialisation and its Continued Relevance in Neoliberal Times', in *Historical Compass*, 2020, Vol. 18, No. 8. doi.10.1111/hic3.12619

Lay, Samantha. *British Social Realism: From Documentary to Brit-Grit*. Wallflower Press, London. 2009.

Leggott, James. *Contemporary British Cinema: From Heritage to Horror*. Wallflower Press, London. 2008.

Leggott, James. 'Like Father? Failing Parents and Angelic Children in Contemporary British Social Realist Cinema', in Phil Powrie, Ann Davies and Bruce Babington (eds) *The Trouble With Men: Masculinities in European and Hollywood Cinema*. Wallflower Press, London. 2004. pp. 163–175.

Leonard, Mark. *Britain™: Renewing Our Identity*. Demos, London. 1997.

Levy, Jonah. 'Foreword', in Florence Faucher-King and Patrick Le Galès (eds) *The New Labour Experiment: Change and Reform Under Blair and Brown*. Stanford University Press, Stanford, CA. 2010.

Lewis, Jane. 'The Problem With Fathers: Policy and Behaviour in Britain', in Barbara Hobson (ed.) *Making Men into Fathers: Men, Masculinities and the Social Politics of Fatherhood*. Cambridge University Press, Cambridge. 2002. pp. 125–149.

Lewis, Philip. *Islamic Britain: Religion, Politics and Identity among British Muslims: Bradford in the 1990s*. I. B. Tauris, London. 1994.

Littler, Jo. 'The Rise of the "Yummy Mummy": Popular Conservativism and the Neo-Liberal Maternal in Contemporary British Culture', in *Journal of Communication, Culture and Critique*, 2013, Vol. 6, No. 2, pp. 227–243.

Llinares, Dario. 'Punishing Bodies: British Prison Films and the Spectacle of Masculinity', in *Journal of British Cinema and Television*, 2015, Vol. 12, No. 2, pp. 207–228.

Lloyd, Moya. *Beyond Identity Politics: Feminism, Power & Politics*. Sage, London. 2005.

Longman, Philip. 'The Return of Patriarchy'. *Foreign Policy*, 20 October 2009, pp. 56–65. https://foreignpolicy.com/2009/10/20/the-return-of-patriarchy/

Love, Nick. *The Guardian*, 1 March 2007. https://www.theguardian.com/film/2007/mar/01/features.questiontime

Luckett, Moya, 'Image and Nation in 90s British Cinema', in Robert Murphy (ed.) *British Film of the 90s*. British Film Institute Publishing, London. 2000. pp. 88–99.

McCarry, Melanie. 'Masculinity Studies and Male Violence: Critique or Collusion?', in *Women's Studies International Forum*, 2007, Vol. 30, No. 5, pp. 404–415. https://doi.org/10.1016/j.wsif.2007.07.006

McDowell, Linda. *Redundant Masculinities: Employment, Masculinities and White Working-Class Youth*. Blackwell Press, Oxford. 2003.

McGuigan, Jim, 'The Neoliberal Self', in *Culture Unbound*, 2014, Vol. 6, pp. 223–240.

MacKenzie, Lisa. 'The Stigmatised and De-valued Working Class: The State of a Council Estate', in Will Atkinson, Steven Roberts and Mike Savage (eds) *Class Inequality in Austerity Britain: Power, Difference, Suffering*. Palgrave Macmillan, London. 2013. pp. 128–144.

McLoughlin, Declan. 'A Palpable Hit', in *The British Medical Journal*, 1996, Vol. 312, p. 585.

Macpherson, William. *The Inquiry into the Matters Arising from the Death of Stephen Lawrence: The Macpherson Report*. February 1999. https://www.gov.

uk/government/publications/the-stephen-lawrence-inquiry (accessed 1 June 2019).

McRobbie, Angela. *Postmodernism and Popular Culture*. Routledge, London. 1994.

McRobbie, Angela. 'Postfeminism and Popular Culture', in *Feminist Media Studies*, 2004, Vol. 4, No. 3, pp. 255–267.

McRobbie, Angela. 'Postfeminism and Popular Culture: Bridget Jones and the New Gender Regime', in Yvonne Tasker and Diane Negra (eds) *Interrogating Postfeminism: Gender and the Politics of Popular Culture*. Duke University Press, London. 2007. pp. 27–39.

Major, John. Speech to Conservative Party Conference, 1991. http://www.britishpoliticalspeech.org/speech-archive.htm?speech=137 (accessed 1 June 2019).

Major, John. Speech to Conservative Party Conference, Blackpool, 8 October 1993. http://www.johnmajorarchive.org.uk/1990-1997/mr-majors-speech-to-1993-conservative-party-conference-8-october-1993/ (accessed 1 June 2019).

Major, John. Speech to Conservative Group for Europe, 22 April 1993. http://www.johnmajorarchive.org.uk/1990-1997/mr-majors-speech-to-conservative-group-for-europe-22-april-1993/ (accessed 1 June 2019).

Malik, Sarita. *Representing Black Britain: Black and Asian Images on Television*. Sage, London. 2001.

Malik, Sarita. 'Beyond the "Cinema of Duty"? – The Pleasures of Hybridity: Black British Films of the 1980s and 1990s', in Andrew Higson (ed.) *Dissolving Views: Key Writings on British Cinema*. Cassell, London. 1996.

Malik, Sarita. 'The Dark Side of Hybridity: Contemporary Black and Asian British Cinema', in Daniela Berghahn and Claudia Sternberg (eds) *European Cinema in Motion: Migrant and Diasporic Film in Contemporary Europe*. Palgrave Macmillan, London. 2010. pp. 132–151.

Malik, Sarita. 'Race and Ethnicity', in Daniele Alertazzi and Paul Cobley (eds) *The Media: An Introduction*. Pearson, London. 2009. pp. 444–456.

Malik, Sarita and Nwonka, Clive James. '*Top Boy*: Cultural Verisimilitude and the Allure of Black Criminality for UK Public Service Broadcasting Drama', in *Journal of British Cinema and Television*, 2017, Vol. 14, No. 4, pp. 423–444.

Mansfield, Harvey. *Manliness*. Yale University Press, New Haven, CT. 2006.

Marr, Andrew. *The History of Modern Britain*. Pan Macmillan, London. 2009.

Martin, Ron and Townroe, Ron (eds). *Regional Development in the 90s: The British Isles in Transition*. Routledge, London. 1992.

Martin-Jones, David. *Scotland: Global Cinema: Genres, Modes and Identities*. Edinburgh University Press, Edinburgh. 2009.

Mather, Nigel. *Tears of Laughter: Comedy–Drama in 1990s British Cinema*. Manchester University Press, Manchester. 2006.

Millett, Kate. *Sexual Politics*. Virago, London. 1977.

Modleski, Tania. *Feminism Without Women: Culture and Criticism in a Post-Feminist Age*. Routledge, London. 1990.

Moller, Michael. 'Exploiting Patterns: A Critique of Hegemonic Masculinity', in *Journal of Gender Studies*, 2017, Vol. 16, No. 3, pp. 263–276. https://doi.org/10.1080/09589230701562970

Monk, Claire. 'Men in the 90s', in Robert Murphy (ed.) *British Film of the 90s*. British Film Institute Publishing, London. 2000. pp. 156–166.

Monk, Claire. 'Underbelly UK: The 1990s Underclass Film, Masculinity, and the Ideologies of "New" Britain', in Justine Ashby and Andrew Higson (eds) *British Cinema Past and Present*. Routledge, London. 2000. pp. 274–287.

Montero, Henry, A. 'Depression in Men: The Cycle of Toxic Masculinity'. 2019. https://www.psycom.net/depression-in-men/depression-in-men-toxic-masculinity/ (accessed 4 April 2019).

Mudge, Stephanie. 'What is Neoliberalism?', in *Socio-Economic Review*, 2008, Vol. 6, No. 4, pp. 703–731.

Muir, Kate. 'The Dark Ages'. *The Times*, 2 February 2008. https://www.thetimes.co.uk/article/the-dark-ages-tz7tkw95dk2

Mulvey, Laura. 'Visual Pleasure and Narrative cinema', in *Screen*, 1975, Vol. 16, No. 3, pp. 6–18.

Murphy, Robert (ed.). *The British Cinema Book* (3rd edn). Palgrave Macmillan, London. 2009.

Murphy, Robert (ed.). *British Film of the 90s*. British Film Institute Publishing, London. 2000.

Murphy, Robert. 'A Path Through the Moral Maze', in Robert Murphy (ed.) *British Film of the 90s*. British Film Institute Publishing, London. 2000.

Neale, Steve. 'Masculinity as Spectacle', in *Screen*, 1983, Vol. 24, Issue 6, November–December, pp. 2–17.

Negra, Diane. *What A Girl Wants: Fantasizing the Reclamation of the Self in Postfeminism*. Taylor & Francis, London. 2009.

Negra, Diane and Tasker, Yvonne. 'Introduction: Gender and Recessionary Culture', in Diane Negra and Yvonne Tasker (eds) *Gendering the Recession: Media and Culture in an Age of Austerity*. Duke University Press, London. 2014.

Neil, Calum. 'Masculinity in Crisis: Myth, Fantasy and the Power of the Raw', in *Psychoanalysis, Culture and Society*, 2020, Vol. 25, No. 1, pp. 4–17.

Netterton, Pamela. 'Hanging with the Boys: Homosocial Bonding and Bromance Coupling in *Nip/Tuck* and *Boston Legal*', in E. Abele and J. A. Gronbeck-Tedesco (eds) *Screening Images of American Masculinity*. Lexington Books, London. 2016.

Newsinger, Jack. 'British Film Policy in an Age of Austerity', in *Journal of British Cinema and Television*, 2012, Vol. 9, No. 1, pp. 133–142.

Newsinger, Jack. 'The Cultural Burden: Regional Film Policy and Practice in England', in *Journal of Media Practice*, 2009, Vol. 10, No. 1, pp. 39–55.

Newsinger, Jack. 'A Cultural Shock Doctrine? Austerity, the Neoliberal State and the Creative Industries Discourse', in *Media Culture and Society*, 2015, Vol. 37, No. 2, pp. 302–313.

Newsinger, Jack. 'The Politics of Regional Audio-Visual Policy in England: Or,

How we Learnt to Stop Worrying and "Get Creative"', in *International Journal of Cultural Policy*, 2012, Vol. 18, No. 1, pp. 111–125.

Nicholas, Kitty. 'Moving Beyond Ideas of Laddism: Conceptualising "Mischievous Masculinities" as a New Way of Understanding Everyday Sexism and Gender Relations', in *Journal of Gender Studies*, 2018, Vol. 27, No. 1, pp. 73–85.

Nicholls, Andy. *Scally: Confessions of a Category C Football Thug*. Milo Books, Preston. 2011.

Nixon, Darren. 'I Just Like Working With My Hands: Employment, Aspirations and the Meaning of Work for Low-Skilled Unemployed Men in the British Service Economy', in *Journal of Education and Work*, 2006, Vol. 19, No. 2, pp. 201–217.

Nixon, Sean. *Hard Looks: Masculinities, Spectatorship and Contemporary Consumption*. UCL Press, London. 1996.

Nolan, Laura. 'Where Have All The Men Gone?' *The Times*, 1 February 2008.

Noonan, Peggy. 'Welcome Back, Duke: From the Ashes of 9/11 Arise the Manly Virtues'. *The Wall Street Journal*, 12 October 2001.

Nwonka, Clive James. 'Diversity Pie: Re-thinking Social Exclusion and Diversity Policy in the British Film Industry', in *Journal of Media Practice*, 2015, Vol. 16, No. 1, pp. 73–90.

Nwonka, Clive James. 'Estate of the Nation: Social Housing as Cultural Verisimilitude in British Social Realism', in David Forrest, Grahame Harper and Jonathan Rayner (eds) *Filmurbia*. Palgrave Macmillan, London. 2017. Pp. 65–78.

Nwonka, Clive James. 'Hunger as a Political Epistemology', in *Studies in European Cinema*, 2016, Vol. 13, No. 2, pp. 134–148.

Nwonka, Clive James. '"You're What's Wrong With Me": *Fish Tank* and *The Selfish Giant* and the Language of Contemporary British Social Realism', in *New Cinemas: Journal of Contemporary Film*, 2014, Vol. 12, No. 3, pp. 205–223.

Nwonka, Clive James and Malik, Sarita. 'Cultural Discourses and Practices of Institutionalised Diversity in the UK Film Sector: "Just Get Something Black Made!"', in *Sociological Review*, 2018, Vol. 66, No. 6, pp. 1111–1127.

Oakely, Ann. *Sex, Gender & Society*. Routledge, London. 2015.

O'Donnell, Mike and Sharpe, Sue. *Uncertain Masculinities: Youth, Ethnicity and Class in Contemporary Britain*. Routledge, London. 2000.

O'Neil, Tony. *Men in Black: Inside Manchester United's Football Hooligan Firm*. Milo Books, Preston. 2005.

Osgerby, Bill. 'A Pedigree of the Consuming Male: Masculinity, Consumption and the American Leisure Class', in *Sociological Review*, 2003, Vol. 51, No. 1, pp. 57–85.

O'Sullivan, Sean. *Mike Leigh*. University of Illinois Press, Springfield. 2011.

Parekh, Bhiku. *The Future of Multi-Ethnic Britain: Report of the Commission on the Future of Multi-Ethnic Britain*. Runnymede Trust, London. 2000. https://www.runnymedetrust.org/projects/meb/report.html (accessed 1 June 2019).

Parker, Kathleen. *Save the Males: Why Men Matter and Why Women Should Care*. Random House, New York. 2009.

Peck, Jamie. 'Zombie Neoliberalism and the Ambidextrous State', in *Theoretical Criminology*, 2010, Vol. 14, No. 1, pp. 104–110.

Pennant, Cass. *Cass*. John Blake Publishing, London. 2008.

Perbedy, Donna. *Masculinity and Film Performance: Male Angst in Contemporary American Cinema*. Palgrave Macmillan, London. 2011.

Perkins, Sean, Maine, Nick and Little, Stephanie. *The BFI Statistical Year Book 2011*. British Film Institute Publishing, London. 2011. www.bfi.org.uk/sites/bfi.org.uk/files/downloads/bfi-statistical-yearbook-2011.pdf (accessed 1 June 2019).

Petrie, Duncan. *Creativity and Constraint in the British Film Industry*. Palgrave Macmillan, London. 1991.

Petrie, Duncan. *Contemporary Scottish Fictions: Film, Television and the Novel*. Edinburgh University Press, Edinburgh, 2004.

Petrie, Duncan. *Screening Scotland*. British Film Institute Publishing, London. 2000.

Petrie, Duncan. 'The New Scottish Cinema', in Mette Horte and Scott Mackenzie (eds) *Cinema and Nation*. Routledge, London. 2000. pp. 153–169.

Petrie, Duncan. '*Trainspotting:* The Film', in Bertold Schone (ed.) *The Edinburgh Companion to Irvine Welsh*. Edinburgh University Press, Edinburgh. 2010. pp. 42–53.

Petrovic, Sarah. 'Changing Spaces of Englishness: Psychogeography and Spatial Practices in *This is England* and *Somer's Town*', in Martin Fradley, Sarah Godfrey and Melanie Williams, Melanie (eds) *Shane Meadows: Critical Essays*. Edinburgh University Press, Edinburgh. pp. 127–141.

Pleck, Joseph H. 'American Fathering in Historical Perspective', in Michael Kimmel (ed.) *Changing Men: New Directions in Research on Men and Masculinity*. Sage, London. 1987.

Plumb, Steve. 'Politicians as Superheroes: The Subversion of Political Authority Using a Pop-Cultural Icon in the Cartoons of Steven Bell', in *Media, Culture and Society*, 2004, Vol. 26, No. 3, pp. 432–439.

Pomerance, Murray and Gateward, Frances (eds). *Where the Boys Are: Cinemas of Masculinity and Youth*. Wayne State University Press, Detroit, MI. 2005.

Pool, Hannah. 'Question Time: Nick Love'. *The Guardian*, 1 March 2007. https://www.theguardian.com/film/2007/mar/01/features.questiontime (accessed 1 June 2019).

Pope, Andrew. 'Thatcher's Sons: 1980s Boyhood in British Cinema 2005–10', in *Boyhood Studies*, 2015, Vol. 9, No. 1, pp. 22–39.

Poulton, Emma. 'Lights, Camera, Aggro!: Readings of Celluloid Hooliganism', in *Sport and Society: Cultures, Commerce, Media, Politics*, 2006, Vol. 9, No. 3, pp. 403–426.

Powrie, Phil, Davies, Ann and Babbington, Bruce (eds). *The Trouble With Men: Masculinity in European and Hollywood Cinema*. Wallflower Press, London. 2004.

Pulver, Andrew. 'Ed Vaizey Re-starts the Film Funding Merry-go-Round'. *The Guardian*, 29 November 2010. https://www.theguardian.com/film/film blog/2010/nov/29/bfi-film-council-arts-funding (accessed 1 June 2019).

Reay, Diane, Crozier, Gill and James, David. *White Middle Class Identities and Urban Schooling*. Palgrave Macmillan, London. 2011.

Redhead, Steve. 'Hooligan Writing and the Study of Football Fan Culture: Problems and Possibilities', in *Nebula*, 2009, Vol. 6, No. 3, pp. 16–41.

Robb, John. *The Nineties: What the F**K was that all about?* Ebury Press, London. 1999.

Robinson, Sally. *Marked Men: Masculinity in Crisis*. Columbia University Press, London. 2000.

Rollinson, David. *Alan Clarke*. Manchester University Press, Manchester. 2013.

Rottenberg, Catherine. *The Rise of Neoliberal Feminism*. Oxford University Press, Oxford. 2014.

Rumens, Nick. 'Postfeminism, Men, Masculinities and Work: A Research Agenda for Gender and Organisation Scholars', in *Gender, Work and Organisation*, 2016, Vol. 24, No. 3, pp. 245–259.

Salam, Maya. 'What is Toxic Masculinity?' *The New York Times*, 22 January 2019. https://www.nytimes.com/2019/01/22/us/toxic-masculinity.html (accessed 14 June 2019).

Savage, Mike. *Moving on Up? Social Mobility in the 1990s and 2000s*. Resolution Foundation, London. 2011. https://www.resolutionfoundation.org/publica tions/moving-social-mobility-1990s-2000s/ (accessed 1 June 2019).

Seidler, Victor (ed.). *The Achilles Heel Reader: Men, Sexual Politics and Socialism*. Routledge, London. 1991.

Seidler, Victor. *Rediscovering Masculinity: Reason, Language and Sexuality*. Routledge, London. 1989.

Seidler, Victor. *Urban Fears and Global Terrors: Citizenship, Multiculturalism and Belongings after 7/7*. Taylor & Francis, London. 2007.

Seidler, Victor. 'Men and Feminism', in Victor Seidler (ed.) *The Achilles Heel Reader: Men, Sexual Politics and Socialism*. Routledge, London. 1991.

Sharma, Sanjay. '*East is East*', in *Black Media Journal*, 2000, Vol. 1, No. 2, pp. 32–34.

Shary, Timothy (ed.). *Millennial Masculinity: Men in Contemporary American Cinema*. Wayne State University Press, Detroit, MI. 2012.

Shaw-Williams, Hannah. '*Bronson*: A Retrospective with Director Nicolas Winding Refn'. *Screen Rant*, 9 September 2015. https://screenrant.com/bronson-nicolas-winding-refn-tom-hardy/

Showalter, Elaine. 'Lad-Lit', in Zachary Leader (ed.) *On Modern British Fiction*. Oxford University Press, Oxford. 2002. pp. 60–76.

Shugart, Helen. 'Managing Masculinities: The Metrosexual Moment', in *The Journal of Communication and Critical/Cultural Studies*, 2008, Vol. 5, No. 3, pp. 280–300.

Skeggs, Beverley. *Formations of Class and Gender*. Sage, London. 1997.

Skeggs, Beverley. 'Imagining Personhood Differently: Person Value and Autonomous Working-Class Value Practices', in *Sociological Review*, Vol. 59, No. 3, pp. 496–513.

Slater, Tom. 'The Myth of "Broken Britain": Welfare Reform and the Production of Ignorance', in *Antipode*, 2012, Vol. 46, No. 4, pp. 948–969.

Spicer, Andrew. *Typical Men: Representations of Masculinity in Popular British Cinema*. I. B. Tauris, London. 2003.

Spicer, Andrew. 'The Reluctance to Commit: Hugh Grant and the New British Romantic Comedy', in Phil Powrie, Ann Davies and Bruce Babbington. (eds) *The Trouble With Men: Masculinity in European and Hollywood Cinema*. Wallflower Press, London. 2004. pp. 77–89.

Steans, Jill. 'Telling Stories about Women and Gender in the War on Terror', in *Global Society*, 2008, Vol. 22, No. 1, pp. 159–176.

Stearns, Peter N. *Be A Man! Males in Modern Society*. Holmes & Meier Publishers, London. 1979.

Storry, Mike and Childs, Peter. *British Cultural Identities* (5th edn). Routledge, London. 2016.

Straw, Jack. The Anti-Social Behaviour Bill. 2003. https://api.parliament.uk/historic-hansard/lords/2003/jul/18/anti-social-behaviour-bill (accessed 1 June 2019).

Street, Sarah. *British Cinema in Documents*. Taylor & Francis, London. 2000.

Street, Sarah. *British National Cinema* (2nd edn). Taylor & Francis, London. 2009.

Street, Sarah. *British National Cinema in Documents* (2nd edn). Taylor & Francis, London. 2016.

Sweeney, Gael. 'The Man in the Pink Shirt: Hugh Grant and the Dilemma of British Masculinity', in *Cineaction*, 2001, Issue 55.

Tasker, Yvonne. 'Fantasising Gender and Race: Women in Contemporary Action Cinema', in Linda Ruth Williams and Michael Hammond (eds) *Contemporary American Cinema*. Open University Press, Maidenhead. 2006. pp. 410–428.

Theakston, Kevin. 'David Cameron as Prime Minister', in Timothy Heppell and David Seawright (eds) *Cameron and the Conservatives*. Palgrave Macmillan, London. 2012.

Tirado Gilligan, Heather. 'It's the End of Men. Again'. *The Public Intellectual*, 27 June 2000. http://thepublicintellectual.org/2011/06/27/its-the-end-of-men-again/

Tolson, Andrew. *The Limits of Masculinity*. Tavistock Publications, London. 1977.

Turner, Alwyn. *A Classless Society: Britain in the 1990s*. Aurum Press, London. 2013.

Turner, Graeme. *British Cultural Studies* (3rd edn). Routledge, London. 2003.

Tyler, Imogen. *Revolting Subjects: Social Abjection and Resistance in Neoliberal Britain*. Zed Books, London. 2013.

Tyler, Imogen. 'Chav Mum, Chav Scum: Class Disgust in Contemporary Britain', in *Feminist Media Studies*, 2008, Vol. 8, No. 1, pp. 17–34.

Tyler, Imogen. 'Classificatory Struggles: Class, Culture and Inequality in Neoliberal Times', in *Sociological Review*, 2015, Vol. 63, No. 2, pp. 493–511.

UK Film Council. *Film Policy in the UK 2000–2010: An Overview*. https://www 2.bfi.org.uk/sites/bfi.org.uk/files/downloads/film-policy-in-the-uk-2000-2010 -an-overview-2015-07.pdf (accessed 1 June 2019).

Ventura, Patricia. *Living with American Neoliberalisms*. Palgrave Macmillan, London. 2017.

Walker, Alison et al. *Living in Britain: Results of the 2000/01 General Household Survey*. National Statistics Survey. HMSO, Norwich. 2001. https:// webarchive.nationalarchives.gov.uk/20100520011438/http://www.statistics. gov.uk/lib2001/index.html (accessed 1 June 2019).

Walker, Carol and Walker, Alan (eds). *Britain Divided: The Growth of Social Exclusion in the 1980s and 1990s*. Child Poverty Action Group, London. 1997.

Walker, Johnny. *Contemporary British Horror: Cinema, Industry, Genre, and Society*. Edinburgh University Press, Edinburgh. 2015.

Walker, Johnny. 'Nasty Visions: Violent Spectacle in Contemporary British Horror Cinema', in *Horror Studies*, 2011, Vol. 2, No. 1, pp. 115–130.

Walker, Johnny. 'A Wilderness of Horrors: British Horror Cinema of the New Millennium', in *Journal of British Cinema and Television*, 2012, Vol. 9, No. 3, pp. 436–456.

Wash, Fintan. *Male Trouble: Masculinity and the Performance of Crisis*. Palgrave Macmillan, London. 2010.

Watson, Gary. *The Cinema of Mike Leigh: A Sense of the Real*. Wallflower Press, London. 2004.

Weight, Richard, *Patriots: National Identity in Britain: 1940–2000*. Pan Macmillan, London. 2013.

Westlund, Andrea. 'Pre-Modern and Post-Modern Power: Foucault and the Case of Domestic Violence', in *Signs: Journal of Women in Culture and Society*, 1999, Vo. 24, No. 4, pp. 1045–1066.

Whelehan, Imelda. *Overloaded: Popular Culture and the Future of Feminism*. The Women's Press, London. 2000.

Whelehan, Imelda. 'Not to Be Looked At: Older Women in Recent British Cinema', in Melanie Williams and Melanie Bell (eds) *British Women's Cinema*. Routledge, London. 2010. pp. 170–183.

White, Michael and Wintour, Patrick. 'Blair Calls for World Fight Against Terror'. *The Guardian*, 12 September 2001. https://www.theguardian.com/ politics/2001/sep/12/uk.september11 (accessed 4 August 2019).

Whitehead, Stephen. *Men and Masculinities: Key Themes and Directions*. Polity Press, London. 2002.

Williams, Melanie. *Female Stars of British Cinema: The Woman Question*. Edinburgh University Press, Edinburgh. 2017.

Williams, Richard. 'Cinema Doesn't Get Much More Real than This'. *The Guardian*, 10 October 1997.

Williams, Richard. 'The Football Factory: Irresponsible, Ill-timed and risible'.

The Guardian, 12 May 2004. https://www.theguardian.com/football/2004/may/12/sport.comment (accessed 1 June 2019).

Wood, Jason. *Last Words: Considering Contemporary Cinema*. Columbia University Press, New York. 2014.

Young, Lola. *Fear of the Dark: Race, Gender and Sexuality in the Cinema*. Routledge, London. 1995.

Index

EU Authorised Representative:

Easy Access System Europe Mustamäe tee 50, 10621 Tallinn, Estonia

gpsr.requests@easproject.com

Printed and bound by CPI Group (UK) Ltd, Croydon, CR0 4YY

03/06/2025

01891023-0001